THE COMPANION GUIDE TO

South Wales

THE COMPANION GUIDES

GENERAL EDITOR: VINCENT CRONIN

*It is the aim of these Guides to provide a Companion,
in the person of the author, who knows intimately
the places and people of whom he writes, and is able to
communicate this knowledge and affection to his readers.
It is hoped that the text and pictures will aid them
in their preparations and in their travels, and will
help them to remember on their return.*

THE GREEK ISLANDS · SOUTHERN GREECE
PARIS · THE SOUTH OF FRANCE · BURGUNDY
ROME · VENICE · LONDON
FLORENCE · JUGOSLAVIA
THE WEST HIGHLANDS OF SCOTLAND · UMBRIA
SOUTHERN ITALY · TUSCANY · EAST ANGLIA
THE SOUTH OF SPAIN · MADRID AND CENTRAL SPAIN
IRELAND · KENT AND SUSSEX
DEVON AND CORNWALL · NORTH WALES
NORTHUMBRIA

In Preparation
MAINLAND GREECE · TURKEY
SOUTH-WEST FRANCE · THE ILE DE FRANCE
EDINBURGH AND THE BORDER COUNTRY
THE WELSH MARCHES · NORMANDY

THE COMPANION GUIDE TO
South Wales

❧

PETER HOWELL
AND ELISABETH BEAZLEY

COLLINS
ST JAMES'S PLACE, LONDON
1977

William Collins Sons & Co Ltd
London · Glasgow · Sydney · Auckland
Toronto · Johannesburg

First published 1977
© Peter Howell and Elisabeth Beazley 1977
Hardback ISBN 0 00 216772 7
Limpback ISBN 0 00 216774 3

Set in Monotype Times
Made and Printed in Great Britain by
William Collins Sons & Co Ltd Glasgow

Contents

❧

Illustrations

❦

Maps and Plans

Acknowledgements

❧

Accuracy is the goal of any guide-book writer. The mistakes which survive in this one are of course our own. There would have been many more had it not been for numerous friends who have helped us in all manner of ways.

First there are those who actually read through the whole of the galley proofs: Professor Ieuan Gwynedd Jones, Mr D. Morgan Rees and Dr A. J. Taylor. Others scrutinised parts of the proofs: Mr Alban Caroe, Mr Richard Haslam, Mr Douglas B. Hague, Mr Vernon Hughes, Mr K. E. Kissack, Mr Peter Smith and Mr Gwyn Thomas. We are indeed grateful to them not only for their corrections but their invaluable suggestions.

We should also like to thank most warmly Mr Lyn Allen, Mrs E. N. Bayly, Mr J. Barton, Mr H. M. Colvin, the Reverend Barry Davies, Lord and Lady Dynevor, the Reverend Wyn Evans, Mr John Hilling, Mr Paul Joyce, the Reverend Canon D. Parry-Jones, Mr Andrew Saint, Mr Christopher Taylor and Mrs Francis Webb. Mr H. Llewellyn Hughes kindly provided the engraving of the Llangwn screen. The Librarian of the National Library of Wales, Mrs Logan Dahne and Miss Vanya Howell of St Davids Cathedral Library and Mrs I. M. Rees of the St Davids Branch of the Dyfed County Library must be thanked for their unfailing assistance.

Mrs E. M. Corfield deserves special thanks for her invaluable help on numerous field trips. Mrs Paul Carlisle and Mr Paddy Dickinson also added greatly to such expeditions.

Mrs John Cory, Mrs Barry Davies, Mr Vernon Hughes, Mrs Richard Lechmere-Oertel and Mrs Penry Williams must be thanked for their most generous hospitality in providing us with bases far from home and reviving our sometimes flagging spirits after long days of exploration.

The maps were again most expertly made by Mr John Flower, who must also be thanked for his most useful corrections to the text. Numerous people valiantly battled with the typescript. Our warm thanks to them all but particularly to Miss Betty Stephenson, to Mrs Sandra Millikin, who expertly undertook the unrewarding task of cutting the first draft, and to Miss Jane Gordon-Cumming, who again made the index.

Introduction

*

This book was written before the new counties were formed and it will be some time before new maps are in general use, so both new and old county names have been included. The old came about as a result of either Edward I's Statute of Rhuddlan (1284) or of Henry VIII's Act of Union of 1536. The names of the new counties are mostly taken from ancient Welsh kingdoms – Gwynedd, Powys, Gwent, and Dyfed. The name Clwyd is taken from the river of that name. Glamorgan has now been split into three parts. Spelling of place names follows that given in the *Gazetteer of Welsh Place Names* (University of Wales Press) with a few exceptions where another name seems to be in much more common use. Spelling of names is in English, following the custom of this series (e.g. as Joan of Arc is not Jeanne d'Arc nor is Owen Glendower Owain Glyn Dŵr). We have generally worked N–S and E–W but have followed no fixed rules except to make it as easy as possible to follow the Guide.

Unless a house is specifically stated to be open to the public, it is to be assumed that it is not. Since opening times tend to change from year to year, it seemed best only to give rough indications. For precise details, see the annual *Historic Houses, Castles and Gardens*. Houses open on application have generally received grants from the Historic Buildings Council on condition that they are opened. Application usually has to be in writing. For details see *Historic Houses*. Monuments in the care of the Department of the Environment (DoE) are mostly open standard hours (roughly 9.30, Sundays 2.00, – dusk). Some are always open.

Some places described are on private property, so permission should be asked in order to visit them. Some (including parish churches) are not named even on the Ordnance Survey maps. Where we foresee difficulties the O.S. grid reference is given (e.g. 275/321): this system of reference is described on the O.S. maps.

Wales has been divided into two volumes, North and South, and to make the two approximately equal we have had to split

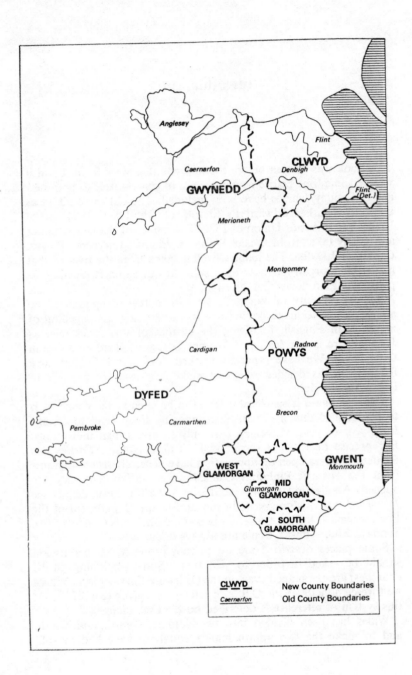

<u>**CLWYD**</u>	New County Boundaries
Caernarfon	Old County Boundaries

Powys, putting Breconshire into the South, where it seems naturally to belong. The inevitable result is that *South Wales* has to cover an area with a much denser pattern of settlement than *North Wales*. This explains why this book is so much more concisely written, and has to omit so much more, than the first.

North and South Wales are separated by the mid-Wales mountains, cut diagonally by river valleys. Roads are therefore indirect and there is little communication between the two. There is thus a marked difference in the Welsh spoken, but there is an even stronger topographical difference between East and West Wales. Perhaps the only parts of Wales which have a marked physical likeness are the extreme west: Anglesey, Lleyn and Pembrokeshire (akin to Cornwall and Brittany); and the eastern marches which in some ways resemble their English neighbours.

Probably the truest difference in character is between inner Wales, the North and West, and outer Wales, the East and South – that part which has constantly tempted invaders to settle.

South Wales means, to many, mining valleys: each separate community socially separate within each valley as beads on a string, and each valley separated from the next by empty hill. To others it means rich farmland – Monmouthshire, the Vale of Glamorgan, Gower . . . Throughout Wales there are strong links between the parts colonized by the Normans, both culturally and topographically. The Normans chose good land easily accessible by sea. South Pembrokeshire, for instance, has much in common with Gower, East Breconshire and with other parts of the Marches. Cardiff, like all capital cities, is a place apart.

Much of mid-Wales consists of high sheep walks – lovely rolling grassy hills with big blocks of forestry. If you look closely more small conifers are to be seen poking up through hundreds of acres of 'empty hill'. Clearly the character of the country will soon change dramatically. In 1831 the Reverend John Parker wrote:

> 'If they [conifers] were common in Wales, the country would not be worth looking at. These lower mountains cannot overcome such blemishes. We deal here in fantastic beauty, more than desolation and grandeur.'

What would he say now? The Forestry Commission is doing a great deal to absorb tourism but it must be remembered that one of the things that lifts the heart of those who live in Wales and tourists alike is the great spaces of the open hills.

There is much concern about the depopulation of mid-Wales.

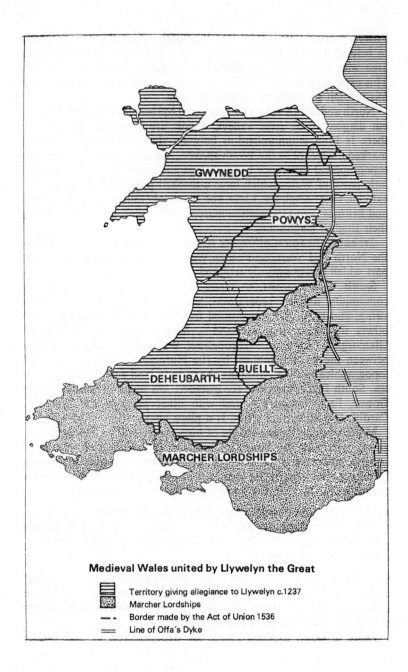

GWYNEDD

POWYS

BUELLT

DEHEUBARTH

MARCHER LORDSHIPS

Medieval Wales united by Llywelyn the Great

Territory giving allegiance to Llywelyn c.1237

Marcher Lordships

Border made by the Act of Union 1536

Line of Offa's Dyke

This seems in many ways an unrealistic worry. Empty farms are a sad sight but it is easy to forget that before the land hunger of the early nineteenth century few people were attempting to scrape a living on these inhospitable heights, except by sheep rearing based on a lower farm. The *hafod* was a summer dwelling and the *tyddyn* (small-holding) up here sprang up literally overnight and provided a very hard life. It is inconsistent to promote farm amalgamation and regret depopulation simultaneously. Although a landscape farmed by thrifty peasants is the ideal to look at, it is not necessarily the best to live in if you are one of the peasants. The thought of a bustling, thriving country community with corn being milled, saddlers making saddles, sycamore and alder being harvested for clog making, oak bark being garnered for tanners, each farm reliant on its neighbours for harvest and sheep shearing, chapels and churches brimming with singing festivals, is a wonderful nostalgic dream. The internal combustion engine coupled with the 'rising standard of living' has hit Wales, as everywhere else, and transformed it more dramatically than anything since the Neolithic and early Bronze-Age settlers brought with them knowledge of farming and so of settled life.

Wales has most of the rural problems of the rest of Western Europe with the added complication that these seem inevitably to become inextricably mixed with that of the survival of language. The problem of second homes (illegal in Switzerland except to foreigners) is but one, and it is a serious problem: no one wants to live in a ghost village. Yet it is also true that many outlying cottages would now be derelict if they were not used for holidays. It is a second-best solution but often the only one. This is as true of Provence as it is of Wales.

There is a real fear that the language will die. Indeed it could. In 1974, only 25 per cent of the people of Wales spoke it. Welsh, having been influenced by Latin which was used by the Celtic church and to some extent for administration, settled in its present form in the sixteenth century. Welsh poetry, with its intricate structure and fine use of language, has long been treasured by Welshmen.

Sadly, language has been a bone of contention from the time of Henry VII although at the Reformation Welsh became the official language of the church (Bishop Morgan's Welsh translation of the Bible appeared twenty years before the Authorized version). Even so, once Latin had ceased to have international use, it was essential to have English to get on. Universities were in England

and the law was administered in English. Parents as well as schools encouraged its use. There is now a movement to keep jobs for Welsh speakers and interesting experiments in bi-lingual education are under way. The tragedy is that while foreign settlers, whether English, Polish or Italian, are usually happy enough for their children to be taught Welsh, the English-speaking Welsh are becoming increasingly antagonistic to the pressures of the more extreme language protagonists. If there is one thing in which no one, even a Welshman, will succeed, it is in bossing the Welsh about. If they do not physically retreat into the hills, as they did in the Middle Ages, they will quietly go their own way, not telling anyone which way this is.

One minor but important cause of the diminishing use of Welsh is the Welsh love of conversation and speculation: it would be unendurably frustrating to converse with a learner in Welsh in preference to a common language. Death and the Hereafter, as much as rugby football and the price of potatoes, are subjects to discuss over a cup of tea or a pint of beer. Philosophy, genealogy and litigation are traditional hobbies all involving imagination and the use of words. 'Never believe anything you hear and only half of what you say' was the unexpected advice given recently by a postman who was delivering letters to a remote farm in the Cambrian hills; salutary to guide-book writers.

Those who do not know Wales yet should be prepared for a genuine welcome. The Welsh have a great capacity for enjoying life (although remnants of the austerity of the religious revivals linger in some places). And they have excellent manners, with none of that crushing disregard for the feelings of others in the interests of accuracy prevalent in some races. It is traditionally rude to disappoint people, so do not frame your questions in a way that makes them difficult to answer. Exhausted walkers, for instance, wanting to know the distance to the next village, have been known to receive an encouraging reply despite the actual mileage in question. John Cowper Powys wrote of his fellow countrymen 'The Welsh are such born "introverts" that it is second nature with them to treat people exactly as people like best to be treated.'

Any guide-book writer is confronted by two main tasks – exploring the country, and reading up its topography and history. In Wales both present special problems. Communications are often difficult, and the weather can be bad; cars may overheat on rough mountain roads and steep hills, and thick mist and rain may obscure the view. The problem of research is chiefly that so much has been written, and still is written. Interest in local history in Wales is enormous and scholarly. Booksellers find that second-hand Welsh topography sells like hot cakes, despite the fact that copies of old books have usually been used to destruction (unlike, we are told, those on Scottish topography). The industry which goes into contributions to the excellent national and county journals and the innumerable histories of counties, towns, villages, industries, churches and chapels is vast. Inevitably time, and our woeful ignorance of the Welsh language, have prevented us from making as much use of these riches as we should have liked. Another source inadequately tapped has been the local expert. Time and time again, one is told 'You should see Mr Dai Jones, the council houses.' And, sure enough, Mr Jones turns out to be another invaluable source. Inevitably a vast amount of fascinating material has had to be omitted for lack of space.

Lastly, perhaps, we should explain ourselves and how we have written the book. We divided the country geographically and contributed enthusiastically to each other's sections. The reader may however become aware that, although many of these enthusiasms are shared equally, others belong more to one writer than the other.

CHAPTER ONE

Breconshire (Powys)

Breconshire (Brycheiniog) takes its name from the mid-fifth-century St Brychan, grandson of an Irish prince, and of Marchell, daughter of Tewdrig, king of Garthmadryn (see *North Wales*, p. 280). When Brychan succeeded to the kingdom it was renamed Brycheiniog. According to tradition, he had eleven sons and twenty-five daughters. Many of them became saints.

Breconshire is a land of reds and greens – the reds of the earth, the sandstone and the mountains, and the greens of the grass, the fertile crops and the hedgerow trees.

HAY TO BRECON

Entering Breconshire from the direction of Hereford, on the A438, you follow the Wye valley as it narrows between the Radnorshire hills to the north, and the Black Mountains to the south. The boundary lies along the Dulas Brook, just outside Hay. **Hay-on-Wye** (Y Gelli) is an admirable little town – a paradise for the connoisseur of townscape. Parallel with the river runs Broad Street, with attractive stone, stucco and painted brick houses, pollarded limes, the plain stone, pilastered Congregational Church, pubs, and a café whose sign is a cycle wheel with propellers attached, inscribed 'Rest for the tyred'. At right angles to Broad Street is Bridge Street, with terraces, leading to the bridge, rebuilt boringly in concrete in 1958. West of Broad Street is a network of narrow climbing streets with every view closed by some good building. Serrated iron kerbs, and nice small iron name-plates. In the little market-place (The Pavement) stands a clock-tower of 1881, and near it are the handsome Town Hall and Market of 1833. Near by is 'Robert Williams and Sons, Implement Makers and Agents, 1886', with splendid coloured tiles of farm animals, and capitals with monkeys, heads, etc.

The town is dominated by the **Castle**. There are scanty remains of the Norman castle, important in the wars between Welsh and English and finally destroyed by Owen Glendower. The **seventeenth-century**

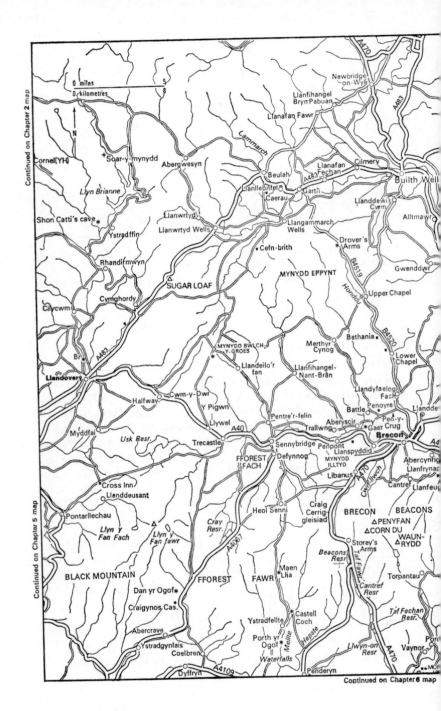

Continued on Chapter 2 map

Continued on Chapter 5 map

Continued on Chapter 6 map

0 miles 5
0 kilometres 8

N

Cornel (YH)
Soar-y-mynydd
Abergwesyn
Llyn Brianne
Shon Catti's cave
Ystradffin
Rhandirmwyn
Cilycwm
Cymghordy
Br
Llandovery
Myddfai
Halfway
Cwm-y-Dwr
Y Pigwn
Llywel
Trecastle
Cross Inn
Llanddeusant
Pontarllechau
Llyn y Fan Fach
Llyn y Fan fawr
BLACK MOUNTAIN
Dan yr Ogof
Craigynos Cas.
Abercrave
Ystradgynlais
Coelbren
Dyffryn

Newbridge-on-Wye
Llanfihangel Bryn Pabuan
Llanafan Fawr
Cammarch
Beulah
Llanafan Fechan
Cilmery
Builth Well
Llanlleonfel
Caerau
Garth
Llanddewi'r Cwm
Llangammarch Wells
Alltmawr
Drover's Arms
Llanwrtyd
Llanwrtyd Wells
Cefn-brith
MYNYDD EPPYNT
Gwenddwr
SUGAR LOAF
Upper Chapel
Honddu
MYNYDD BWLCH-Y-GROES
Merthyr Cynog
Bethania
Lower Chapel
Llandeilo'r fan
Llanfihangel-Nant-Brân
Llandyfaelog Fach
Battle
Penoyre
Llandde
Pentre'r-felin
A40
Aberyscir
Pen-y-Gaer Crug
Brecon
Trallwng
Sennybridge
Penpont
Llanspyddid
Abercynrig
Llanfrynac
Defynnog
MYNYDD ILLTYD
FFOREST FACH
Libanus
Cwm-llwch
Cantref
Llanfeu
Usk Resr.
Trecastle
Craig Cerrig gleisiad
Heol Senni
BRECON BEACONS
PENYFAN
CORN DU
WAUN-RYDD
Cray Resr.
Storey's Arms
Beacons Resr.
FFOREST FAWR
Maen Llia
Cantref Resr.
Torpantau
Taf Fawr
Taf Fechan Resr.
Ystradfellte
Castell Coch
Melitte
Hepste
Porth yr Ogof
Waterfalls
Penderyn
Llwyn-on Resr.
Vaynor
A4109
A470

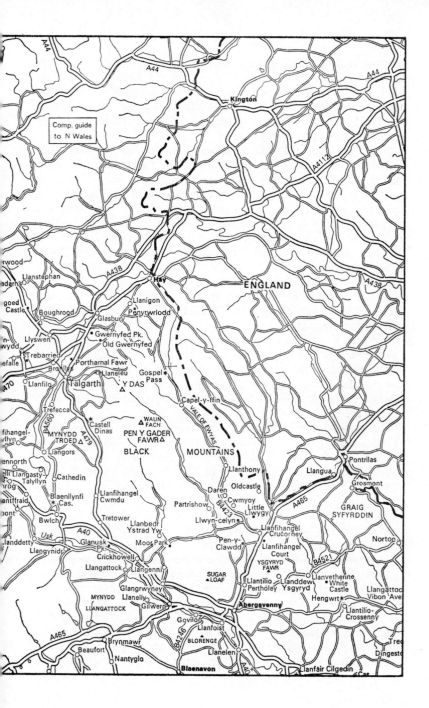

mansion that replaced it is the headquarters of the business which
has given Hay an unexpected recent reputation – Richard Booth, 'the
world's largest second-hand and antiquarian bookseller', 'more books
per head of population for sale in this town than any other town in
the world'. The business has spread to take over the cinema, the fire
station, a pub, and several houses.

Near the Castle is **Trinity Methodist Church**, with Sunday school
and chapel balancing an Italianate tower. The **Parish Church** is easily
missed, but not much is lost by missing it. The tower is medieval,
but the rest was rebuilt by Edward Haycock Sr. in 1833–4, in lancet
style. East of the churchyard, a path runs down (passing under the
old railway) to the lovely **River Bailey Walk**, along the Wye. Further
west it comes out into the open, with views back of castle and church.
The **Hay Railway**, first proposed in 1810, was opened in 1816–18.
It was intended chiefly to carry coal and general goods from the
canal at Brecon to Talgarth, Hay and Eardisley in Herefordshire
(where it linked with the slightly later Kington Railway). Virtually
the same line was used later in the century for the Hereford, Hay
and Brecon Railway.

The road from Hay over to the Vale of Ewyas, by way of **Gospel
Pass** (Bwlch yr Efengyl) is now made up, although in high summer
it is so crowded with cars as to be almost impassable. It climbs up
above Dulas Brook, then cuts diagonally across the side of Hay Bluff,
reaching 1778 feet. The views across the Wye valley and the hills
beyond are unbeatable.

The main road from Hay to Brecon follows the Wye. At **Glasbury**
(Y Clas-ar-Wy) there is another modern bridge, a handsome brick
chapel, and, further on, the church – remarkably far from the
Radnorshire village. It was rebuilt in 1837 by Lewis Vulliamy, in an
elephantine Romanesque manner – grey stone, with a big tower.
Just beyond Three Cocks is **Gwernyfed Park,** a house of 1877–80
by William Eden Nesfield, now a school. The lodge on the main
road echoes the house – Tudor, of stone, with some half-timbering
and tile-hanging, and brick chimneys.

There is more of interest along the minor road which runs parallel
to the A438 a mile or so south-west. **Llanigon** is an attractive village.
Llanthomas, where Kilvert's beloved Daisy Thomas lived (the
account of his hopeless passion for her is one of the most moving
parts of the Diary), has been demolished. The church is a strange
affair, with a wide-eaved roof and a remarkable fourteenth-century
south porch, huge just like a barn: the upper part, with stone
louvres, houses the bells. The nave retains its plaster ceiling, and

pews with doors, and a pretty Gothic barrel organ. In the parish there are many interesting houses, one of the finest being **Penyrwrlodd** (not open), half a mile south-east of the church. Two wings stand at right angles, one dated 1650, the other, proudly surveying the valley, early Georgian.

On the same minor road, a mile south-east of Three Cocks, is **Old Gwernyfed**, a many-gabled stone house, built *c.* 1610 by Sir David Williams, court physician and lawyer. A bad fire in the eighteenth century left the west wing a shell and damaged the great hall (half the plaster ceiling is now panelled). Gate piers (by Nesfield), surmounted by vigorous lions, guard the very attractive view across two courtyards to the present entrance with its thirteenth-century doorway (possibly brought from Brecon Priory). Charles I stayed here on 6 August 1645 after the Battle of Naseby, and the present owners also take in guests.

Further on, near the junction of the minor road and A4078, is **Great Porthamal** – just visible (right) from the road. A proud, tall, gatehouse of *c.* 1500 stands in front of an ordinary-looking farmhouse, which is, however, basically of the same date, and retains its medieval porch and magnificent timber roof.

Although the approach to **Talgarth** is unpromising, the town is friendly, with a good central market-place, dominated by a plain Town Hall (1877), and the splendid great thirteenth- or fourteenth-century tower, right by the bridge. The tower – very much like a Pele tower, and unusual for Wales – has a shop built into it, which sells everything from shovels to bread. Heaven forfend that the DoE should come and tear it out – already an unduly arty bank has been attached to it. The stream runs over rocky shelves. Across the bridge, among narrow and crooked streets, are an archaic Post Office and a wonderfully old-fashioned chemist's. Up above the village stands the **Church of St Gwendoline** (a daughter of Brychan), with a fine upright tower, and wide nave and aisle – clumsily restored in 1873. The church is mainly interesting for its monuments. The most famous is the big black slab to Howell Harris of Trefecca – 'Here where his Body lies, He was convinced of Sin, Had his Pardon Sealed . . .' This refers to his tremendous experience in the church, in 1735, when the Vicar urged the congregation to attend communion on Easter Sunday – 'I felt suddenly my heart melting within me, like wax before the fire, with love to God my Saviour.' But, when Harris took up preaching, the Vicar strongly opposed him.

Two miles east of Talgarth is **Llaneleu** (or **Llanelieu**), in a remote fold of the hills. The little church sits in a huge churchyard; small,

simple, and atmospheric, with a rood-screen. Key at the farm with
the sign 'Beware of Trains'. Below is the **Court**, said to have been a
cell of Llanthony Priory.

Up above Llaneleu rises **Y Dâs**, the north-westernmost spur of the
Black Mountains. South of Talgarth, the main road to Crickhowell
(A479) goes by way of an idyllic pass between Mynydd Troed
(1997 feet) and the main mass of the Black Mountains. The north
entrance to the pass is guarded by **Castell Dinas** (three miles from
Talgarth), on a steep hill, with tremendous views. There is a fine
Iron Age fort, with, in one corner, much ruined remnants of a
Norman castle – at 1476 feet the highest castle in Wales or England.
The earlier ramparts are more impressive. From here an excellent
walk on the **Black Mountains** can start, following up the ridge (Y
Grib) from Castell Dinas, its red-earthed sides cheerily clothed, in
early summer, with white hawthorn blossom. The top by contrast
is bleak and boggy, but the views compensate – covering the Black
Mountains themselves, the Wye and Usk valleys, and beyond. The
highest point is **Waun Fach** (2660 feet) – marked by a lump of
whitened concrete in the centre of a black bog – but the views are
better from **Pen y Gader Fawr** (2624 feet). The return can be made
via the sheltered Rhian-goll valley.

The A479 runs north from Talgarth to join the A438 at Bronllys.
By the confluence of the Dulas and the Llynfi stands **Bronllys Castle**.
DoE, and very tidy. All that survives is a tall round tower, on a steep
mound, built by Walter de Clifford in the mid thirteenth century.
The church at Bronllys has a curious detached tower, rough and
plain. In 1902 the Cambrian Archaeological Association decided
scornfully that it was 'the erection of a 19th century humorist', but
this seems inconceivable. Just east of the village is the attractively,
if extravagantly laid out **Hospital**, formerly a Sanatorium, founded as
part of the Welsh memorial to Edward VII, and begun in 1913. The
original buildings, in yellow roughcast, are pleasing, especially the
simple Chapel, added after 1920. The architects were Edwin T. Hall
and Stanley Hall.

Trefecca, on the B4560, from Talgarth to Llangors, will always be
associated with the name of Howell Harris (1714–73), the youngest,
and most famous, of three remarkable brothers, sons of a joiner
from Carmarthenshire who had settled here. After his 'conversion'
in Talgarth Church in 1735, Howell became a leader of the Methodist
Revival in Wales. Eventually he returned to his birthplace at Trefecca
to found his famous kibbutz. Influenced by the example of the
Moravians, the members of 'The Family', as it was called, lived a

strict communal life, working their 700 acres, and worshipping three times a day. At one time they numbered about one hundred and twenty. Harris was a practical agriculturalist: a founder of the Breconshire Agricultural Society, he was responsible for introducing the turnip into Wales (an important step, as it enabled farmers to feed stock throughout the winter). His 'Family' also processed wool and flax, made clogs and shoes, and did building, tailoring, and bookbinding. A printing press was set up in 1756. Ultimately the various Methodist factions were reconciled, and Harris is remembered as a great preacher and organizer, the founder of the Welsh Calvinistic Methodists (now called the Presbyterian Church of Wales). The principal building of his community, erected in 1752–9, was celebrated for its architectural eccentricity – at odds with its serious purpose. Malkin (1804) was amazed – 'Here a Gothic arch! There a Corinthian capital! Towers, battlements and bastions! Peacocks cut in box, and lions hacked in holly!' Alas, it has since been much altered and tamed, but a few pretty Gothic windows survive, and some plaster ceilings, as well as the gilded weathervane in the form of a trumpeting angel. It later became a training college for ministers, and is now a 'Non-Sectarian Residential Centre'. Near it stands a Gothic chapel with a spire, of 1873, in the vestry of which there is a fascinating museum. In 1768 the extraordinary Selina, Countess of Huntingdon, attracted by Harris's fame, founded a training college in Trefecca, at the house now called **College Farm**. A fine house of 1576, with a good porch, it too was Gothicized, in the manner of Harris's college. A little further south is Trefecca Fawr (open on written application), a plain late-seventeenth-century house, with interesting plaster ceilings.

West of Trefecca is hilly country with many good old houses. On the side of the hill above the Dulas valley is **Llanfilo**, whose church has been most fortunate over the last century. In 1881 the excellent tower and shingled spire were added. Then in 1913 restoration was begun by W. D. Caröe, only completed in 1951. The inside is whitewashed: the chancel retains its plaster ceiling of 1709. The splendid rood-screen was superbly restored, with new figures by Nathaniel Hitch. Many old pews remain, and the eighteenth-century pulpit. Caröe put in some new windows, basing their design on one in the chancel (? seventeenth century). The atmosphere is unusually light and bright. There are many good monuments, including two early Brutes (in black wooden frames), and several by a local man, D. Hughes of Felinfach.

North of A438 the country is hillier and less hospitable. **Tre-**

barried, on the A4073, three-quarters of a mile north of the A438, a good mid-seventeenth-century house, has a fine, slightly later, stable-court. The hamlet of **Llandefalle**, up the first turning left beyond Trebarried, already feels remote, and its grand Perpendicular church comes as a surprise. There is a simple rood-screen, and an exotic fretwork Victorian altar in the aisle.

It is worth driving over by **Felin-Newydd** (half a mile beyond Trebarried on the A4073), up the little road that crosses Llandefalle Hill, crossing moorland, mostly over 1000 feet, with glorious views of the Black Mountains and Brecon Beacons.

One and a half miles north of Brecon (between A438 and B4520) is **Llanddew**, quiet now, but once important for its palace, an occasional residence of the Bishops of St Davids. Of this all that remains (opposite the church) are an arch and a few fragments, together with 'Bishop Gower's Well AD 1340'. Here Giraldus Cambrensis lived as Archdeacon of Brecon, and in 1188 Archbishop Baldwin spent a night as his guest. The church stands on a fine site with great views to the west. It is a remarkably uniform cruciform building, with lancets all round (much renewed, however). The central tower and pyramidal spire were rebuilt in 1620. The interior is disappointing.

BRECON (ABERHONDDU)

Brecon is a busy, friendly, compact town, well sited where the Honddu joins the Usk. The centre is The Bulwark, a wide street, with handsome Georgian houses along one side, and shops the other, and an 1852 statue of Wellington by John Evan Thomas. Thomas (1809–73) was a native of Brecon, became a pupil of Chantrey, and acquired fame in London. The Bulwark is dominated by St Mary's Church. Apart from its great tower, it is rather a dismal building (restored by T. H. Wyatt) in spite of its Caröe fittings. Near it is the plain Guildhall (1888), a poor substitute for John Abel's Town Hall of 1624. Wyatt was also architect of the accomplished Grecian Shire Hall (1842) which faces grandly down The Watton – the main road to the east, lined with attractive houses. The Shire Hall now houses the excellent Brecknock Museum. South of The Watton is the head of the Brecon and Abergavenny Canal, near 'Captains' Walk', which runs from County Hall to the river beside the best remaining stretch of the town wall (the 'Captains' were Napoleonic prisoners).

Off High Street Superior is the Market, by T. H. Wyatt – market day is Friday. Along Castle Street, over the Honddu, are the remains of the castle, twelfth–thirteenth century, and now partly incorporated into the Castle Hotel. The fine motte and remains of the shell-keep are in the Bishop's garden on the other side of the road.

The **Cathedral** occupies a leafy site up Priory Hill. Not particularly striking outside, it commands affection rather than admiration. It became cathedral of the new Diocese of Swansea and Brecon only in 1923. Its size is due to its having been the church of the Benedictine Priory founded by Bernard Newmarch, Norman lord of Brecon, who also built the castle. The Priory was bought in 1542 by the Price family, one of whom founded Jesus College at Oxford in 1571. The church has been fortunate in its restorers – first Sir Gilbert Scott (1862–75), and then W. D. Caröe (1914–31). It is a big solid building with a squat central tower. In the celebrated view from the south-east, it is worth noting that the chapel projecting from the transept was rebuilt, from ruin, by Caröe, and the gabled organ chamber above is entirely his – an effective addition. The interior is perhaps too tidy, and over-deVictorianized. The finest part is the Early English chancel, with vaulting by Scott, and a huge sculptured reredos by Caröe. Note also the vigorously carved Norman font; the stone cresset (a multiple lamp); and the monument to Bishop Bevan, by W. Goscombe John. After the church became a cathedral, various surrounding buildings were ingeniously converted by Caröe to form Chapter House, Canonry etc.

Beyond the Cathedral are The Groves, wooded walks, where once stood a spa building. Until recently, the Cathedral was right on the edge of the town, but unfortunately the fields beyond are now being covered with speculative housing.

At the bottom of Ship Street is the fine bridge over the Usk, built in 1563, and widened in 1794 by Thomas Edwards, son of the famous William Edwards (of Pontypridd bridge). Across it is **Christ College**. Originally a Dominican Friary, founded *c*. 1250, it was refounded by Henry VIII as a college, again refounded in 1853, and is now one of the best-known public schools in Wales – rival to Llandovery College (p. 150). Its elegant chapel was the chancel of the Dominican church, restored by J. P. Seddon, who, with his partner Prichard, also built extensive new buildings in 1858–70 – fine examples of High Victorian scholastic design. The Chapel has typical Seddon wood-work, and remarkable glass in the five-light east window, also designed by him, and made in 1865 by Clayton and Bell – a Crucifixion, not in the usual naturalistic setting, but surrounded by patterned quarries, very light and bright. Caröe panelling covers the original tiled reredos, but the lively floor tiles remain visible, with flying fishes, whelks, and so on. In the antechapel are two grand monuments, one to Bishop Lucy of St Davids, d. 1677; and one to Rev. Richard Lucy and his wife, with a statue of their son Gam, d. 1697 aged 22 (by William Stanton).

B4520 BRECON TO BUILTH

North of Brecon, the road follows the wooded Honddu valley between bare hills. The church of **Llandyfaelog Fach** is prettily situated among yews, by a stone bridge over the river. It was much rebuilt in 1856–7 by W. G. and E. Habershon, under the direction of the Rector, G. C. F. Harries. It has a richly Victorian interior. Under the tower arch is the 'Briamail Flou' stone, said to date from the tenth century: about seven feet high, it is carved with the figure of an armed man and much Celtic interlace.

Three miles further on, beyond **Lower Chapel** (Llanfihangel Fechan) the road passes **Castle Madoc**, a very large, very plain house, cut off from the road by a huge swelling hedge. Just over a mile beyond is the handsome Bethania Chapel (1842/1877). The next village is **Upper Chapel**, with a tiny Gothic church of c. 1850 and a pink-washed pub. From here a road runs back south-west to Merthyr Cynog (p. 35). Half a mile beyond Upper Chapel, the B4519 goes off left (see p. 32), while the B4520 climbs up the bare moorland to a height of 1370 feet, and then goes down through the wooded Nant Gwyn and the little village of **Llanddewi'r Cwm** to Builth.

THE RIGHT BANK OF THE WYE: BUILTH WELLS TO LLYSWEN

Builth Wells is a compact town almost entirely on the south bank of the Wye. Seen from above it is dominated by the river (several others converge on the Wye here too). Its spa, which was beyond the golf-course, is no more, but Builth is an important market town (Mondays). The fine bridge, a stone six-arched structure (1799, 1879 and 1925) is best seen through the kissing gate on the Radnorshire bank.

The Norman **Castle,** now green and hawthorny earthworks at the east end of Builth, is a good viewpoint. Not a stone remains standing of the masonry castle built upon them by James of St George from 1278. The large stone **Market Hall** with its red hipped roof near the bridge (by Weyman, 1875) is now a cinema but the market still carries on in the undercroft with its stone arched stalls at each end and the river rushing at your feet. Three terracotta heads adorn the facade: Shakespeare, Beethoven – and who is the other? The stumpy medieval tower of the **Parish Church** survives. The rest is by John Norton, 1875.

The busy A470 follows the right bank of the river down the lovely Wye valley (see also *North Wales*, p. 335 for the road down the Radnorshire bank). **Alltmawr** church is a tiny medieval building with a later apse, perched high above the road with a big yew almost in the garden of Chapel House (take the lane before the big white house). It has a very touching 1936 low relief bronze to Lord Trevethin (who lost his life while fishing aged 92) and his wife. The Wye is a rewarding but dangerous salmon river; it is only too easy to step off an underwater ledge while wading. The sought-after beats rarely change hands; their price is based on the number of fish that might be expected to be killed in a season – in 1973, about £1000 a salmon.

Deep lanes lead up to small farms on the slopes of the wild Eppynt (see p. 32). That from Erwood leads to the snug hamlet of **Crickadarn**. The simple church (restored *c.* 1910 by Clough Williams-Ellis) has a good tower with a beacon turret, worth climbing. A 1666 communion table and several good memorials survive.

From Crickadarn go on up to Gwenddwr to find **Beili-heulog** (047/435), a couple of miles up the farm road to Nantyroffeiriad. It must be the most remote of remote Breconshire chapels and is worth seeking out for its site and simplicity. The only decorations are its memorial tablets. Look out for the corrugated-iron shed on the left and then walk through the fields. The chapel lies below beside the stream, a domestic little building of nineteenth-century character sheltered in a fold with oak, alder and gorse.

Returning to the Wye valley, the Scithwen Brook joins the river just below the suspension bridge at Llanstephan. One and a half miles downstream **Llangoed Castle**, a grand seventeenth-century-style mansion largely rebuilt by Clough Williams-Ellis in 1912, may be seen below the main road. He regards it as one of his best works.

One and a half miles due south of the Castle, up a winding lane, **Brechfa Pool**, beloved by Kilvert, is in open upland with wide views. The main road looks across the river to Boughrood spire (*North Wales*, p. 336). **Llyswen** is a suburbanized village, whose church was rebuilt by Charles Buckeridge in 1862–3. From here the A479 continues to meet the A438 near Bronllys (p. 26).

EPPYNT AND THE IRFON VALLEY

From **Upper Chapel** (p. 30) the B4519 climbs on to the bare moorland of **Mynydd Eppynt**, famous for its ponies. 29,000 acres of it are still occupied by the Army, as an artillery range; hence the sentry boxes, red litter bins, injunctions not to enter when the red flag is flying, and innumerable other notices – 'Night Movement Range', 'Sheep must be cleared from target area before firing commences', and, most sinister of all, 'Do not touch anything. It may explode and kill you' (even a sheep?). The road reaches a height of 1442 feet at Drovers' Arms, with glorious views, but if you hope for refreshment you will be disappointed. The few gaunt ruins bear a notice – 'Building Unsafe – Keep Out'. Beyond, there are views of the lovely Irfon valley as the road goes down the side of Cwm Graig ddu, which has striking limestone outcrops. It meets the A483 at **Garth**.

To explore the western part of Eppynt straightaway, go from Garth direct to Llangammarch Wells (p. 33). Otherwise take the A483 eastwards, enjoying the view of the steep side of Eppynt across the Irfon. It passes the neat little church of **Llanafan Fechan**, also by Buckeridge (1866). Just over three miles from Garth, outside **Cilmery**, a great rough stone stands right of the road in a rather municipal setting. It marks the place where Llywelyn the Last died, on 11 December 1282, killed by a man who did not realize who he was. He had only eighteen men with him when English troops came upon him.

Just south of Cilmery, between railway and river, is **Glan Irfon**. It was to a 'tiny cottage' here that the amazing Lady Hester Stanhope (1776–1839) retired in 1808, to get over her grief at the deaths of her uncle (the younger Pitt) and her brother. She came for 'the waters and the air', and occupied herself with dairying, and queening it over local society. However, this quiet life could hardly satisfy such a flamboyant woman for long, and in 1810 she left Britain for good, ending up as virtual ruler of a wild part of Lebanon (for the most evocative account of her, see Kinglake's *Eöthen*). The Irfon meets the Wye just north of Builth (see *North Wales*, p. 328).

From Builth, follow the A470 north, through Radnorshire, to **Newbridge-on-Wye** (p. 30), and take the B4358 back over the river into Breconshire. Two miles further, on a hilltop in rich wooded country, is another little Buckeridge church (1868), **Llanfihangel Brynpabuan**. A mile further on, across the Chwefri valley is the grand-looking, but dull church of **Llanafan Fawr**. After five miles more, the road meets the A483 at **Beulah**, an ordinary little place. Its church is a mile north-west, up the Cnyffiad valley. Called Eglwys Oen Duw (Church of the Lamb of God), it is a strikingly elaborate building of 1867 by John Norton, with a tall, Germanic *flèche*. The interior has polychrome brick tiles, and mosaic. Lavish fittings include good Clayton and Bell glass in the grouped lancets, and brass sconces in the form of waterlilies, complete with frogs. The church was built by the Thomas family of **Llwyn Madoc**, a big spreading house, further up the beautiful valley, which then becomes rockier and more wooded, as the road climbs over moorland to Abergwesyn (p. 34).

Back on the A483, half a mile south of Beulah, a Roman road runs due south. On the left of it, a quarter of a mile down, a farmhouse, **Caerau**, occupies the site of a sizeable Roman fort. As at Tomen-y-mur (*North Wales*, p. 238), the commanding site was used in medieval times for a motte. The A483 crosses the Cammarch, and winds round a hill, up on the east side of which stands the little church of **Llanlleonfel**. Kilvert describes a bazaar held in 1873 to raise funds for its rebuilding. It was so ruinous and little-used that a man coming to marry his second wife here found a lace handkerchief left behind by his first wife, at her wedding some years before, still hanging on the altar rails. It was nicely rebuilt in 1874 by R. J. Withers. Four identical eighteenth-century tablets commemorate members of the great Gwynne family, who lived at Garth, the big house which stands on the opposite side of the river Dulas above terraces whose walls are curved like fortifications.

Just before the main road crosses the river, a road goes south-west, to **Llangammarch Wells**, a funny little place, situated where the Cammarch joins the Irfon. The village is chopped in two by the embanked railway. The church, built in 1913–16 by W. D. Caröe, has a grand tower and a light and lofty interior. On the other side of the railway, and across the bridge, neat terraced houses flank the east–west road (the village is not even on a B road) below the wooded slopes of Eppynt. The 'wells' were at the Lake Hotel, a mile east. The water contains barium ('recommended in scrofulous cases').

Two roads, one on either side of the Irfon, lead from Llangammarch to **Llanwrtyd Wells**, back on the A483. The focus of this large village, spread out in its wide, open valley, is the river-bridge: with its substantial Victorian terraced houses, and the informal 'square' on the east, it has a decent townish air. Now that no one comes to take the waters, Llanwrtyd has found a new prosperity as a centre for pony-trekking. There is also the Cambrian Woollen Factory, just outside

s.w.

c

the village on the Builth road (A483): it was established in 1919 to employ disabled ex-servicemen.

For the wells, follow the road up the Irfon valley (from the square). A quarter of a mile up is the Dolcoed Hotel: walk past in front of it and up a conifer avenue. Three decrepit buildings stand in the field. Built *c*. 1920, one housed lavatories, another a refreshment room, while the third contained the well – the strongest sulphur spring in Wales. Behind a counter is a circular structure, in which the water rises – an airtight marble mosaic pedestal going down to bedrock. A mirror above enabled clients to watch its sinister bluish-white bubblings. The sulphurous smell mingles with that of the droppings of the ponies which wander in and out. The spring, known to country people as *Y Ffynnon Ddrewllyd* (the stinking well), was 'discovered' by Theophilus Jones, author of the excellent *History of the County of Brecknock* (1805–9). It cured him of his 'radicated scurvy'.

Three-quarters of a mile beyond Dolcoed, the road crosses the river, and here, beautifully situated overlooking the steep valley, is the old **Church** of Llanwrtyd, restored by Buckeridge in 1862. Beyond, the road winds for three miles along the lovely valley to **Abergwesyn**. Alas, the valley has suffered recent afforestation of the most insensitive kind, with sharp edges running straight up the hill. By the new bridge are, on the west, the ruins of the tiny old church, and, on the east, the white and red Moriah chapel (1828/1867). By the crossroads, in the hamlet of whitewashed cottages, all that survives of the 1870 church (demolished 1964) is a tiled floor. The drovers' road from Abergwesyn over to Tregaron is popular in summer (see p. 73). The first few miles, up the wild, rocky Irfon valley, are much the most beautiful. The road then climbs steeply through forestry before coming down into the Tywi valley, where it enters Cardiganshire.

Returning via Llanwrtyd to Llangammarch, from a mile out along the road which follows the south bank of the Irfon from Llangammarch, a quiet country road climbs south up the foothills of Eppynt, with views over the broad valley. After a mile, a track with a surface of rough bare rock leads to **Cefn Brith** (916/453), the birth-place of the Reformation martyr, John Penry (1563–93). It is a classic example of a longhouse, quite unspoilt. Penry advocated the preaching of the gospel in Welsh, but his courage and integrity led to his tragic death – ironically at the hands of those who had but recently achieved the preaching of the gospel in English. Only half a mile south is the old home of two other celebrated men – Thomas and James Howell. Thomas Howell (1588–1646) became bishop of

Bristol. His younger brother James (1594?–1666) was a Royalist
agent, who spent eight years in the Fleet prison, but in 1661 was made
Historiographer Royal. Friend of Ben Jonson and Lord Herbert of
Chirbury, his best-known work was his *Epistolae Ho-Elianae*, or
Familiar Epistles.

Beyond Cefn, the road winds through conifer woods. After three
and a half miles, a road climbs southwards up on to Eppynt. From
the summit of **Mynydd Bwlch-y-Groes** (1449 feet) there are tremendous views over the Brecon Beacons, Fforest Fawr, and the
Vans. Truckloads of troops rumble to and fro, and soldiers suddenly
pop up out of the heather. The road across the top goes down to the
A40 at Llywel (see p. 49). Half a mile back from here, towards the
north, a road runs south-east down into the beautiful Eithrin valley.
The church of **Llandeilo'r fan**, rebuilt in 1873, retains its medieval
roof and screen.

Two miles down the valley is Pentre'r felin: the road south over
the hill brings you past the army camp and over an elegant stone
bridge into **Sennybridge** (p. 47), on the A40. Alternatively, from
half a mile up from Pentre'r felin a road climbs over the hills to the
next valley eastwards, Nant Bran, which is straighter and more open.
Llanfihangel Nant Bran has a church rebuilt in 1882, except for its
stout tower, by J. L. Pearson.

THE NORTH SIDE OF THE USK – BRECON TO TRALLWNG

A mile north-west of Brecon, reached by the B4520, is **Pen-y-Crug**,
1088 feet. Best climbed from the north, it has a well-preserved fort
on top, giving marvellous views. Near by is **Penoyre**, a grandiose
Italianate house of 1846–8, designed by the versatile Anthony Salvin
for Col. John Lloyd Vaughan Watkins, and now a Golf and Country
Club. The approach is magnificent: a formal avenue of Irish yews
is aligned on the great belvedere tower. Behind this is the main block,
an elaborate palazzo, with a loggia round the ground floor. To the
west there is a long conservatory wing. The house is built of superb
masonry, the carved detailing excellent. Inside there is an enormous
top-lit staircase hall, with pretty decoration. Col. Watkins spent so
much money on house and estate that he could not afford to live in
it. Kilvert, who visited it in 1870, did not like it – 'a pretentious
house', but with 'only 25 bedrooms'.

Just west of Penoyre is **Battle**, named after the Sussex abbey, of
which Brecon Priory was a daughter-house. From here a road follows
the delightful Yscir valley. Near the top is **Merthyr Cynog**, with good

views from the hilly site of its large church. Well restored in 1861 by Buckeridge, it has a huge old tower, and a tough fourteenth-century screen. Beyond is the moorland of Eppynt (p. 32).

A mile south-west of Battle, where the Yscir joins the Usk, stands the hamlet of **Aberyscir**, with a pretty church of 1861, by Buckeridge, next to a farmyard. On the other side of the Yscir, on a raised plateau, is **Y Gaer**, reached via Pontaryscir, past a weirdly-shaped farmhouse of *c*. 1900. This Roman fort (possibly Cicutio) was the largest of its kind in Wales. Founded *c*. AD 75, it was manned by auxiliaries. *C*. AD 140 it was reconstructed: the ramparts were faced with stone, and the gates and main buildings rebuilt in masonry. It was excavated by Mortimer Wheeler in 1924–5, and the remains of the west, south and east gateways, and part of the wall and rampart, left exposed (DoE). Grazed by cows and sheep, it is a lovely spot, overlooking Usk and Yscir. Further along, on this side of the Usk, is **Trallwng,** with another church excellently rebuilt by Buckeridge, in 1860. From here it is six miles back to Brecon.

ABERGAVENNY TO BRECON

There are two possible routes – along A40, north of the Usk, or along B4209, A4077 and B4558, following the canal along the south side of the Usk. The second is much quieter and more pleasant, but the northern route will be considered first.

ABERGAVENNY TO BRECON, NORTH OF THE USK (A40)

Beyond Abergavenny the valley narrows between the Sugar Loaf and Blorenge. From Glangrwyney a small side road goes north up the wooded Grwyne valley to **Llangenny**, a tidy village, with a double-naved church by the river (restored by Buckeridge in 1863). A mile further on, near the junction of the Grwyne Fechan and Grwyne Fawr, is **Moor Park** (open on application), a most weird house built *c*. 1760: it has a quatrefoil-shaped plan, with the spiral staircase in a central hall, and four apsed rooms on each floor. The roofs are conical. It is said that the builder declared 'that if a similar building could be pointed out within the kingdom, he would immediately destroy this'. Half a mile north, on the Grwyne Fechan, is **Llanbedr Ystrad Yw,** a pleasant, well-kept village. It was the home of the Brutes, some of whom were still working as stonemasons here until quite recently. They were the best-known of the many makers of the excellent carved memorial tablets found in so many churches in

Breconshire, Monmouthshire and Herefordshire. Mostly of slate, sometimes of stone, they are distinguished by elegant lettering and charmingly unsophisticated decoration. Many of them are coloured. These colours – said to have been made from local vegetable dyes and lichens according to a recipe written in the family Bible (now, alas, lost) – are still amazingly fresh, and something of a puzzle, since it is held that no known vegetable or lichen dye can retain its colour for 200 years. At any rate, the Brutes were not the only ones in the know, for tablets by other makers have also retained their colouring. The most common signatures are Thos. or T. Brute (fl. 1721–82); Aaron or A. Brute (fl. 1754–83); J. Brute (fl. 1773–1840); Pr. (=Peter) T. Brute (fl. 1734–68); Pr. J. P. Brute (fl. 1752).

In Llanbedr **Church** there is a nice stone tablet to Thomas, two-year-old son of Thomas Brute, Mason, who died in 1724. Outside are two tablets by J. Brute. Brutes also worked as masons on the sensitive restoration of the church carried out by J. L. Pearson in 1896–7. The double-naved church is built of local red sandstone, and has a warm atmosphere. Pearson's fittings, in wood and stone, are simple and appropriate.

From the junction near Moor Park, a road runs east up the Grwyne Fawr valley and then turns north, where a narrow promontory of high ground, the southern end crowned by a fort, separates its valley from the Vale of Ewyas. Taking one of several steep and narrow lanes, one climbs through idyllic scenery to the lonely, but famous, church of **Partrishow**, or **Patrisio** (278/224), which combines perfection of site with architecture of exceptional interest and appeal. The old name of the church is Merthyr Issui. Issui was a holy man, whose cell was probably near the holy well still visible in the cwm below the church. He was murdered by a traveller he had sheltered – hence Merthyr (= *martyrium*, place of martyrdom). The place became a centre of pilgrimage, and legend tells that in the eleventh century a rich continental pilgrim, cured of leprosy by the water of the well, left a hatful of gold to build the church.

Through the excellent stone lychgate (by Caröe), you see, along a grass pathway which is lined in spring with daffodils, first a stone shed, said to have been used for stabling the priest's pony and with a fireplace for him to dry his clothes, then the western chapel, attached to the church, but entered by a separate door, and the church itself. The church and famous rood-screen were well restored in 1908 by W. D. Caröe. The two stone altars in front of the screen are a remarkable survival. On the west wall is painted a comic skeleton with a spade (a *Memento Mori*). The monuments include several Brutes. The huge font bears a Latin inscription meaning 'Menhir made me in the time of Genillin.' Genillin, or Cynhillin, only son of Rhys Goch, was Prince of Powys and Lord of Ystrad Yw shortly before the Norman Conquest. The western chapel may be on the site of the earliest church.

Crickhowell (Crucywel) takes its name from the Crug (hill-fort) above Llanbedr, on a conveniently-shaped outlier of Pen Cerrig Calch. It is a pleasant little town – quiet, except that its High Street is also the A40. At right angles to this is Bridge Street, which widens near the junction to form the market-place. In it stands a granite fountain of 1874, near the soberly Italianate Town Hall of 1833–4, an unusually successful job for T. H. Wyatt. Further down the street are some good houses, especially the pink-washed Dragon Guest House, with Venetian window. In Tower Street there is a small medieval tower, much rebuilt. This is a fragment of the Norman castle, destroyed in 1403 by Glendower. Its great motte can be seen further down Bridge Street, and a large round tower is best seen from the A40.

The **Parish Church** is down a lane west of Bridge Street, looking out over the Usk valley. It has a fine shingled broach spire (1861, said to be by Pearson), and red-tiled roof. At the bottom of Bridge Street is the splendid thirteen-arched stone bridge, widened in 1810. Across it is Llangattock (see p. 42).

On the main road west of the town is **Porth Mawr**, a fine big fifteenth-century gateway, which once led to the Herbert mansion, but now leads to a yellow-washed villa with a pretty iron verandah.

Further out is **Gwernvale**, a Regency house, once the home of the military engineer Sir George Everest (1790–1866), after whom the mountain was named. Here Frederick Rolfe (Baron Corvo) spent what were probably the happiest months of his life, on and off between 1906 and 1908, as guest of the Pirie-Gordons. On the other side of the river stood **Glanusk Park**, now demolished. It was built in 1826 by Robert Lugar for Joseph Bailey, the ironmaster, nephew of Richard Crawshay (see p. 259).

Near Glanusk the A479 to Talgarth leaves the A40. A mile up it is **Tretower**. **Tretower Court** is a remarkable survival – an exceptionally well preserved house, built round a courtyard, dating largely from the fourteenth and fifteenth centuries, with additions *c*. 1630. It was given to the Ministry of Works in 1930: at first they treated it gently and the timber restoration is particularly satisfactory. The oriel window, rebuilt in 1962, is thoroughly unpleasant, as indeed it may have been when first built. It is in Quarella stone (a greyish-white sandstone from near Bridgend), unsympathetic to the rest of the building; fragments of the original are incorporated in the new work. The balcony leading to the upper rooms is a very attractive feature. The Court belonged from the fifteenth century to the eighteenth (when it became a farm) to the Vaughans. The father of Henry Vaughan the Silurist (see below) was a younger son of the family. Beyond it is the **Castle**: the tall circular tower (thirteenth century) rises from a cramped site within the remains of the twelfth-century keep. The Bailey is still a farmyard: a notice reads 'Private – Beware of Bull – Survivers Prosecuted.' Opposite the Court, a fine stone barn has been restored by the DoE. Happily it still houses stock and hay.

Near the Court is the simple but elegant church, of pink and grey stone, built in 1877 by Sir Joseph Bailey (later first Lord Glanusk), to designs by J. L. Pearson, who also designed the church hall (1887–8) with its nice projecting bow.

Beyond Tretower, where the Rhian-goll valley narrows, is **Llanfihangel Cwmdu**, a peaceful village but too full of coaches and caravans. On the river are old mills. The church stands on a hillock. There is a stout tower of local type, and the rest – rebuilt in 1831–3, and again in 1907 (Hunt and F. Baldwin) – is odd but effective. It has a pretty Gothic organ and Royal Arms carved in marble. Beyond the village the road climbs through the pass (see p. 26).

Beyond Glanusk, the A40 skirts wooded Myarth, heads for Buckland Hill, but turns north and climbs steeply up to **Bwlch** ('pass'). Just north of Bwlch, at the head of the Llynfi valley, are the scanty remains of the medieval **Blaenllynfi Castle**, hidden among trees.

Two miles further on, the church of **Llansantffraid** stands above the road. This is the burial place of Henry Vaughan. He was born in 1621 at Newtown, a farmhouse which still stands, though rebuilt, beside the road a mile further on. He spent most of his life there, practising medicine and writing poetry, until his death in 1695. He called himself *Siluris* after the Silures who occupied South-East Wales, and offered strong resistance to the Romans. His rough tombstone, much repaired, stands right at the top of the churchyard. It bears his arms, and the inscription '*Quod in sepulchrum voluit: Servus inutilis: peccator maximus hic iaceo* † *Gloria miserere*'. ('[This is the inscription] which he wanted for his tomb: A useless servant, a great sinner, I lie here † Glory, have mercy'.) So the hope he expressed in his *To the River Isca* is fulfilled:

When I am layd to rest hard by thy streams,
And my sun sets, where first it sprang in beams,
I'le leave behind me such a large, kind light
As shall redeem thee from oblivious night.

The present church is a lavish sandstone effort by S. W. Williams (1885). There is an 1896 memorial to Vaughan, and an excellent collection of grand marble monuments, with pediments, putti and the lot, including Games Jones d. 1681 (the epitaph, beginning 'Stay Passenger, and know who lyes beneath this Stone, One who was no mans Foe, no not his owne, Who liv'd as ADAM did before he fell . . . ', may be by Vaughan).

A short distance north of Llansantffraid is **Llangors Lake (Llyn Syfaddan)**, the second largest natural lake in Wales (the largest is Llyn Tegid). It drains, not into the Usk, but into the Wye, at Glasbury. The setting, in a shallow basin with hills all round, is superb. The lake was once a paradise for ornithologists, fishermen, and rowing and sailing enthusiasts. Now its peace is shattered by speedboats. The southern approach to the lake runs past the marvellous group of church and school at **Llangasty Talyllyn**. Both were built by Robert Raikes of **Treberfedd**, the house which stands above , looking northward over the lake, and it is due to the Raikes family that this side of the lake is still unspoilt. Robert Raikes, a rich, Tractarian Yorkshireman, bought the Treberfedd estate in 1848 with the deliberate intention of introducing Tractarian ideals into a part of Wales where churchmanship was at a low ebb. The church was almost wholly rebuilt, and the school built, in 1848–50, to the designs of John Loughborough Pearson, later to become one of the greatest church architects of the century (his masterpiece is Truro Cathedral). The church, now most sympathetically restored, is notable for its simplicity and its characteristic High Church adornment, stencilled texts and all. Mrs Raikes trained a surpliced choir: there were daily services, and Welsh ones too on Sundays. The house too was completely rebuilt by Pearson, in 1848–52, and is most attractive, irregular and picturesque, its pink and grey stone beautifully weathered. It retains much of its original furniture and decoration. The Raikes family had to leave it in 1873, but returned in 1895 and have remained ever since.

The northern approach to the lake is via **Llangors** village (two miles on from Cathedin). Near it is a Dark Age crannog (artificial island) in the lake: a dug-out canoe found here is in Brecon museum. This may be the origin of 'the legend of the countrey people' which

Aubrey discussed with 'My Cosen Hen: Vaughan' in 1656, that there 'was heretofore a Towne drowned by an Earth-quake'. This side of the lake is spoilt by caravans and commercialization – even the crannog is threatened. Llangors was probably the lake which Vaughan had in mind in 'The Showre' –

> 'Twas so, I saw thy birth: That drowsie Lake
> From her faint bosome breath'd thee, the disease
> Of her sick waters, and Infectious Ease.
> > But now at Even
> > Too grosse for heaven,
> Thou fall'st in teares, and weep'st for thy mistake . . .

A mile south-west of Llanfihangel Talyllyn, on the road to Pennorth, is the old **Talyllyn Station**, at the entrance to a tunnel 674 yards long, built in 1812–16 for the Hay Railway (see p. 24), and rebuilt in 1863. It is now eerily dripping and booming.

Returning to the A40, two miles beyond Llansantffraid is **Scethrog**, with several largish houses, the most interesting being the Tower, between road and river, a tower-house unusual for Wales (thirteenth or fourteenth century, altered in the sixteenth century). From here it is four miles to Brecon (p. 28).

ABERGAVENNY TO BRECON, SOUTH OF THE USK

Three roads (B4269, A4077, B4558) run close to the Brecon and Abergavenny Canal, built in 1799–1812 to connect Brecon with the Monmouthshire Canal (near Pontypool – see p. 215), and so with Newport. Its 33 miles (only six locks) are popular with pleasure-boats. Boats can be hired at Goytre, Gilwern and Llanfoist. The Canal is the only one controlled by the British Waterways Board which is within a National Park. Restoration has been carried out since 1968 by the two County Councils. It is an exceptionally beautiful waterway, and flows almost the whole way through unspoilt country.

A good medieval bridge links Abergavenny with **Llanfoist**, beneath the steep wooded slope of Blorenge. A mile beyond, the B4246 climbs steeply over the side of the mountain south to Blaenavon. The whole district is pockmarked by remains of the iron industry (see p. 217). A tramroad ran down from the forge at Garnddyrys, up on the hill, to the canal at Llanfoist. (These names will be familiar to readers of Alexander Cordell's *Rape of the Fair Country*.) Beyond, on the B4269, is **Govilon**. Right by the canal, near a bridge, is

Llanwenarth Chapel, erected 1695, rebuilt 1870 – a famous centre of the Baptist cause.

The road crosses from Monmouthshire to Breconshire at Gilwern. Here the canal crosses the valley by means of a great embankment, while the Heads of the Valleys Road goes off up the wooded **Clydach Valley**, once a beauty spot famous for its waterfalls and limestone caves. According to the County Guide, 'records tell us that here Shakespeare conceived *A Midsummer Night's Dream*'. It is difficult to agree with the Guide's equally optimistic assertion that 'the new road has enhanced the rugged grandeur of the Valley'. Its sides have been blasted away for the monster highway. Up on the hill west of Gilwern is **Llanelly**, whose churchyard contains tomb slabs supported on iron columns.

Llangattock village (three miles up the A4077 from Gilwern) is opposite Crickhowell. It lies below the steep limestone cliffs of Mynydd Llangattock, once busily quarried, and connected by tramroad with the Nantyglo ironworks. Now part of the cliffs forms the Craig y Ciliau Nature Reserve. There are numerous caves. A narrow street leads to the church, much rebuilt in the nineteenth century. It is most remarkable for its memorial tablets, including probably the finest works of the Brutes. That to Mary Moses, d. 1777, by A. Brute, has an exceptionally pretty rococo surround, as has the unsigned one to Mary Herbert, d. 1782. One by J. Brute is to Ann Lewis, d. 1773 – 'being a Midwife, she was an Instrument in the Hand of providence, to bring to this World 716 Children'.

Beyond the village, the B4558 follows an exceptionally beautiful section of canal for several miles to **Llangynidr**, a spread-out village. St Cynidr was a son of Gwynllyw (see Newport, p. 204). There is a fine bridge of six stone arches over the Usk (*c.* 1600). Further on, the canal climbs up several locks. Two miles beyond Llangynidr, **Llanddetty Church** is beautifully situated between the road and the red-banked, placid river. During the Commonwealth the simple church was used as a farm building by the Puritan Col. Jenkin Jones, who took the title of incumbent. It is said that he was supervising the milking of his ewes in it when news came of the landing of Charles II. He mounted his horse, fired his pistol at the church door, shouting 'Ah, thou old whore of Babylon, thou'll have it all thy own way now', and rode off, never to be seen again in the parish. The bullet hole is still visible. Beyond the church, by the road, is **Llanddetty Hall**, large and gaunt, which was Col. Jones's house. Half a mile further on the canal passes through a tunnel a quarter of a mile long.

At **Talybont** a bridge of the former Brecon and Merthyr railway crosses the road. Across a neat white tip-up bridge over the canal, a road goes south-west up the Caerfanell valley, now filled by a reservoir supplying Newport. Beyond the reservoir, the road climbs up through trees with, away to the right, a view of the delightful waterfall at Blaen-y-glyn. At the top the road reaches 1400 feet. From here an excellent walk can be made over the eastern end of the **Brecon Beacons**. Start up Nant Bwrefwr, passing a waterfall in a hollow. The path climbs up Craig y Fan ddu. Then cross the shallow peat hags on top to Craig Cwareli. From here go eastwards along the path which follows the edge of the sheer drop, with marvellous views over the red and green scarp and the Usk valley. From the summit of **Waun-rydd** (2504 feet), there is a fine view eastwards towards Crickhowell. Return by Craig Fan-Las to the original path.

The pass which the road crosses was also the route of the Brecon and Merthyr railway: it crossed the summit in a half-mile tunnel. At the western end stood **Torpantau** station (1300 feet). The road goes on down past the Taf Fechan reservoir to Merthyr Tydfil.

Beyond Talybont, the B4558 and the canal continue side by side. **Pencelli Castle**, beside the road, looks best from the west: the farmhouse stands outside the medieval castle, with its now flattened mound. A quarter of a mile further on, a side road goes off by a farmyard with a black Van Gogh bridge and follows a quiet valley up to **Llanfeugan** (not named on the O.S. map). Beautifully sited among huge yews, at the confluence of two streams, the church has a good tower, seventeenth-century stalls, and remains of a medieval rood-screen.

The minor road which follows the canal leads to **Llanfrynach**, a neat village on the river Menascin. Its church stands in a big open churchyard, sadly tidied. The tower is old; the rest was rebuilt in 1856 by a builder, W. Jones, without the services of an architect. The result is not too bad, with rich fittings and memorials to de Wintons of Maesderwen. A brass in the chancel to Henry Powys de Winton proudly proclaims 'A member of Corpus Christi College, Oxford: Second Class in Honour School of Modern History June 1900'. Two years later he died, a soldier in India – 'Until the Reveille'. Maesderwen (half a mile west) is a delightful Regency villa, with bows at the sides. A nice local story tells that the village stocks were first used to punish the carpenter, who had spent the fee for his labours on getting drunk.

The B4558 joins the A40 by way of Abercynrig bridge, beside which the canal crosses the Usk by means of a venerable-looking stone aqueduct. Half a mile west is **Abercynrig**, an attractive old house (open on written appointment). It belonged originally to the Awbrey family, the most famous of whom was Dr William Awbrey, a great sixteenth-century lawyer and great-grandfather to John Aubrey. The present house, basically sixteenth century, was re-modelled c. 1700.

From Abercynrig the foothills of the **Brecon Beacons** and their quiet wooded valleys can be explored. By the river Cynrig stands the church of **Cantref**, with a solid old tower, the rest admirably rebuilt in 1867 by Buckeridge. A mile further up the river is a bridge, from which starts one of the best routes up the Beacons. A much used path goes up the Bryn-teg ridge on to Cribin: then there is a splendid ridge-walk round to the summit, **Penyfan** (2906 feet), and the oddly flat second peak Corn Du. The huge views are spoilt only by the over-numerous reservoirs. The Beacons (Bannau Brycheiniog) are formed of Old Red Sandstone. As a result, where the rock outcrops it does so in low crumbly cliffs, and tends to form steeply inclined slopes rather than rocky precipices. Towards the north these are, never-theless, very impressive, and the combination of red and green makes for glorious colour effects. The going is easy, with no really steep or rocky climbs. It is possible to return to the starting-place down the ridge of Cefn Cwm Llwch and Allt Du, or else to follow the ridge west of Corn Du, past the monument which commemorates little Tommy Jones, whose body was found here on 2 September 1900. He was the five-year-old son of a Rhondda miner, and came with his father to visit his grandparents, who lived at Cwm-llwch farm-house. On the evening of their arrival the boy got lost, and, after a search of 29 days which created a national sensation, was found here, at a height of 2250 feet. No one had imagined that the boy could possibly have wandered so far up the mountain. From here you can descend by a path which comes down close to the tiny **Llyn-cwm-llwch**, nestling below the cliffs in a textbook example of a volcanic cirque, and then follow the beautiful Cwm Llwch, with its waterfalls.

SOUTH-WEST OF BRECON

The A470, from Brecon to Merthyr, follows the pleasant Tarell valley up to the pass over the Beacons. Five miles out of Brecon is **Libanus**. From here the road up to **Mynydd Illtud** has been improved to allow access to the **Mountain Centre**. Opened in 1966, this was built by the Brecon Beacons National Park authorities. It is situated on the edge of a wide moorland common, at a height of 1100 feet.

Designed to provide information, a rendezvous, refreshment, and instruction, the Centre has proved enormously popular (200,000 visitors in 1971).

Near the Centre, at 974/263, is **Bedd Illtud**, a couple of rough stones and a bracken-filled dip supposed to mark the burial place of the great fifth-century Saint Illtud, founder of the famous monastery at Llanilltud Fawr (Llantwit Major). Half a mile west of the Centre is the church of **Llanilltud**. Its very large graveyard, surrounded by firs, is circular (always a sign of great antiquity). It marks Illtud's *llan* or enclosure. There are only a few tombs: the rest is bare. The little church, rebuilt in 1858, is utterly derelict, with DANGER notices; it retains its original interior arrangement, dominated by pulpit and reading desk.

A mile west of the church is **Castell Blaencamlais**, possibly built by Llywelyn the Last, with a large regular mound, surmounted by the stump of a solid stone tower.

Beyond Libanus the A470, as it climbs, is flanked on the right by the impressive cliffs of Craig Cerrig-gleisiad, a Nature Reserve with arctic flora. On the pass is the former inn of Storey Arms, now a Youth Hostel (1440 feet). From the southern end of the forestry plantation starts the easiest, but least interesting, route up the Beacons. Over the other side there are a series of reservoirs on the Taf Fawr – first Beacons, then Cantref, then Llwyn-on. They have jolly castellated water towers.

Just beyond the first reservoir, the A4059 (to Aberdare) strikes south-west over bleak moorland. Only a few miles bring you into an entirely different type of country, for this is a carboniferous lime-stone district, the hills dramatically outcropping with rock (similar, in places, to Eglwyseg Rocks near Llangollen). Seen from the air, the ground appears pock-marked with swallow holes, caused by solution of limestone, sinking streams, or the collapse of Basal Grit. There are more of them to the square mile in this area than anywhere else in Britain. There are also innumerable caves (a paradise for potholers), and the combination of millstone grit, sandstone, and shales produces many fine waterfalls. A road leads northward from the A4059 (six miles from the A470) to the place where the Afon Llia and Afon Dringarth join to form the Mellte. At the confluence (three miles from the A4059) is Castell Coch: on its wooded mound, much overgrown, heaps of red stones mark the lines of the walls. From here a mountain road crosses the bare grassy uplands of Fforest Fawr (the southern parts now, tragically, planted with conifers) to the Senni valley (see p. 47). At the top it passes Maen Llia, a huge

flat standing stone, about ten feet high, like an upright flounder.
South of Castell Coch is **Ystradfellte**, a tiny village, blocked in
summer by lost tourists. The medieval church has a tall tower and a
good chancel roof.

From here the Mellte flows underground, below a bed which is
usually dry. About three-quarters of a mile down, after reappearing,
it flows through a short gorge, and then disappears into **Porth Yr
Ogof**, perhaps the most remarkable natural feature of the district.
The cavern is 1400 feet long. The northern mouth is situated below
a steep cliff: a much used path comes down from a new car park. The
wide slot can easily be entered but only experienced cavers are
advised to try going right through. Others walk along the top, by
the old river bed. At the far end the river emerges into a deep pool
surrounded by smooth-worn rocks. A rough and muddy path continues for half a mile to an iron bridge: crossing here, and following
the west bank of the river you get the best views of the famous waterfalls – **Sgwd Clun-gwyn, Sgwd Clun-gwyn Isaf,** and **Sgwd y Pannwr**.
Each is different: at the top one the water falls across a great flat
shelf, while the lowest one is a torrential spout into a pool. The cliffs
are steep and wooded. An afternoon visit is best for the sun.

Anyone wishing to visit the **Hepste Valley,** with its famous fall,
must go back up to the iron bridge to cross the Mellte. It can also
be approached from Penderyn (four miles south-east of Ystradfellte).
The Hepste valley is very different from the Mellte, narrower and
steeper, and less thickly wooded – its sides covered with scrub oak –
but it is equally beautiful, and much less frequented. A good quarry
track leads to it from Penderyn village (at 944/089). The fall (not
marked on the 1-inch map) is called **Sgwd yr Eira**: the water pours
over a ledge, the underside of which has been washed away, so that
a path goes behind it (in fact the path crosses the valley by this
means). Nineteenth-century engravings show shepherds driving their
flocks round it.

WEST OF BRECON

The A40 follows the Usk valley. The first village is **Llanspyddid**
(Llansbyddyd). The church is plain and much renewed, but has a
good timbered porch.

Two miles further on is **Aberbran Fawr**, a sixteenth-century house,
near a fine bridge built in 1791 by James Parry (of Llanigon). One
mile beyond is **Penpont**, between road and river, the seat of the
Williams family, which claims descent from the same line as Ann

Boleyn. Built *c*. 1666, it was handsomely refronted in 1813, with a Doric loggia along the ground floor. From the wooded park came the oak beams which support Big Ben. By the road is the church of Betws Penpont, completely rebuilt in 1865 by Sir Gilbert Scott in crude Early English. Half a mile from Penpont is **Abercamlais**; a tall and plain early-eighteenth-century house, home of another branch of the Williams family. In the grounds there is a stone dovecote, square below, octagonal above, built *c*. 1720: it stands on a bridge over a stream, and formerly contained men's privies.

Three miles beyond Abercamlais is **Sennybridge**, a big village with a weekly fatstock market and an Army camp. It grew up after the Neath–Brecon railway was built in 1872, taking over the former importance of Defynnog, a mile south. By the Senni (up a lane beyond the chapel west of the village) are remains of a fourteenth-century castle, hidden by a bungalow. Here the Constable of Fforest Fawr imprisoned offenders against the forest laws. There are two World War II gun emplacements built into the ruins – a nice contrast. **Defynnog**, said once to have had seventeen cobblers, is now a quiet place, with a line of stone Gothic cottages. The church has a fine tall tower, with a Latin inscription built into the west side (below the stringcourse). The peculiar font is a great rarity, as it has on it the only Runic inscription found in Wales.

Due south runs the **Senni Valley**, remote and fertile, whose neat farms are strongholds of Welsh culture. Southwards the road goes up over **Fforest Fawr** to Ystradfellte (see p. 45). The Great Forest of Brecknock was a royal hunting ground. Only the valleys were wooded: much of its 40,000 acres was open grazing, and until its enclosure in 1815–19 was common land.

At Sennybridge the A4067 (to Swansea) leaves the A40. It runs up Cwm Treweren, with the hill of Fforest Fach on the west, past Cray Reservoir, to a height of 1212 feet. One and a half miles beyond the summit a road (to Trecastle) goes off northwards following the Tawe. Two miles up it is a stone circle. This is one of the best starting places for the walk up the **Carmarthen Fan** (Bannau Sir Gaer). Confusingly, it is also known as the Black Mountain – and the highest point is in Breconshire (Bannau Brycheiniog).

Follow the stream up to **Llyn y Fan Fawr**, close beneath the cliffs. There are no fish in the lake: an anonymous writer, *c*. 1695, points out that, although Llyn y Fan Fach is full of fish, 'Llyn-y-fan-hir hathe no fish attalle in't nither will any fish being put into it live, but as soon as they have tasted of this water turne up there Silver Bellies and dey'. A path leads up the red sandstone cliff at the south end of the lake. Near the highest point (2632 feet), an Iron Age hut (no roof) has been constructed recently for shelter: there is none other for miles. From there it is an easy walk round the scarp by Fan Foel to the other summit (2460 feet), overlooking Llyn y Fan Fach, beyond which you can walk down the shoulder to Llanddeusant (see p. 151). The return can be made by way of the impressively long escarpment Fan Hir. Paths down are marked by cairns.

The A4067, over the summit, enters the limestone district. A short distance west of the road are the famous **Dan Yr Ogof Caves**. Though commercialized, they are still worth a visit. There are two separate systems (two separate guided tours, two separate fees). The main system was discovered in 1912: the many stalactite and stalagmite formations have been given the usual facetious names. The guide-book tells of 'a White Parrot, the result of ages of effort by the greatest sculptor of all time – Nature'. A Group of Nuns stand close to a Broody Hen. The other system was discovered in 1953: its chief sight is the enormous Cathedral Cave, 160 feet long and 70 feet high.

A little beyond Dan yr Ogof, the ungainly stone bulk of **Craigynos Castle** stands beside the road. (It is now a Geriatric Hospital: the theatre and grounds can be visited on application.) The remarkably severe centre block, with four pyramidal roofs, rises abruptly from the edge of the steep drop down to the Tawe. Designed by T. H. Wyatt, it was built in 1842 for Rhys Davies Powell. In 1886 it was bought by Adelina Patti. 'Madame Patti', as she was known, may seem a rather misty figure now, but Verdi thought her the finest soprano of her time. She was born in Madrid in 1843, of Italian parents, and had a resplendent career, lasting 56 years. Her third and last marriage was to Baron Rolf Cederstrom in 1899, when she was 56 and he was 30. She died here in 1919. She made extensive additions to the house, including a clock tower, and a winter garden. Her architects were Bucknall and Jennings of Swansea, and their work is without merit, except for the delightful interior of the theatre (but that may be due to the decorators, the well-known London firm of Jackson and Sons). It was built in 1891. Fluted pillars stand round the walls, and there is lots of pretty plaster decoration, in pink, yellow and gold, incorporating names of composers, which are themselves period pieces (e.g. Flotow, Ambroise Thomas). By an ingenious arrangement the floor can be raised on jacks from its sloping position to a level one. The splendid backdrop survives, showing Patti in the role of Semiramide, driving a chariot. An opera is put on in the theatre each year by local amateurs. The winter

The hill-church of Llanfilo, in Breconshire: the lych-gate dates from c. 1700, and the tower and spire from 1881.

The proud gatehouse of c. 1500 at Great Porthamal, near Talgarth.

Sgwd Clun-gwyn Isaf, one of the three famous waterfalls on the Mellte near Ystradfellte.

garden is now the Patti Pavilion in Swansea (see p. 297). The grounds
are superb, if a trifle municipal, falling steeply to the river.

Beyond Craigynos, the A4067 follows the Tawe to the mining
village of **Abercrave**. From here the minor roads climb south up the
hillside to Coelbren (see p. 291). Further down the valley is the substantial industrial town of **Ystradgynlais**. Just after the main road
crosses the river, over on the opposite bank, a tall chimney-stack
(1872) and two big yellow brick walls pierced with rows of arches
survive from the once-celebrated Ynyscedwyn Ironworks. In 1823
the works were taken over by George Crane of Bromsgrove, who
made an important breakthrough by discovering how to smelt iron
using semi-anthracite coal as fuel. The Glamorgan boundary is a
mile further on, where the river Twrch comes south and joins the
Tawe (see p. 292).

Back on the A40, beyond Sennybridge the road follows the Usk
as far as **Trecastle**, a main-road village. The big tree-covered mound,
on the right as you go down the hill, is a castle motte. Here the A40
leaves the river. The parish church of Trecastle is at **Llywel**, a mile
further along the road. Excellently restored by Sir Gilbert Scott in
1869, it contains a cast of a tall stone, now in the British Museum,
with odd, crude figures, interlace, and inscriptions in Latin and
Ogam.

Beyond Llywel the road winds through the narrow wooded pass
of Cwm-y-Dwr, entering Carmarthenshire at **Halfway** (half-way between Trecastle and Llandovery). Two miles further on, the obelisk
(in a lay-by on the left) known as the Coachman's Cautionary, and
erected in 1841, should remind motorists too of the hazards of
drunken driving. This has been the main road only since an Act of
1787: the old road, originally Roman, went over the top of Mynydd
Bach Trecastell, to the south. On it, at **Y Pigwn** (three and a half
miles north-west of Trecastle – at 828/312) are two big Roman
marching-camps, one superimposed on the other, probably dating
from the first century AD. This is a good viewpoint, right on the
Breconshire/Carmarthenshire border. From Trecastle a popular
minor road cuts west across the north-east slopes of the Vans to
Pontarllechau (see p. 151). For the first couple of miles it follows the
Usk, which, three miles west of Trecastle, is dammed to form the
huge and ugly Usk Reservoir (1955), surrounded by forestry. The
source of the river is three miles south of the reservoir, on the slopes
of Fan Foel. Further on, the road is unfenced where it crosses the
open moorland, with fine views of the great escarpment.

CHAPTER TWO

Cardiganshire (Dyfed)

❧

For many people the mid-West of the Principality, that is to say, Cardiganshire, is the most Welsh of all. There are lovely hills but no spectacular mountains to attract huge numbers. The coastline, except around Aberystwyth, was never as easily accessible to large centres of population and Aberystwyth has retained its own special character and not allowed tourism to take over. Its early expansion as a seaside holiday town was balanced by the growth of the university which has made it a stronghold of Welsh culture. Cardiganshire claims a higher percentage of school leavers who continue their education at university or in some form of training establishment than any other county in Britain. Teachers are a major export.

Rural depopulation is a grave problem, particularly now that so many smallholdings are being swallowed into larger units. Small rural factories are one of the best answers and more are needed, but they can only provide work for a small percentage of those with higher education.

MACHYNLLETH TO ABERYSTWYTH – A487

Coming from Machynlleth, the A487 enters Cardiganshire two miles beyond Derwen-las (see *North Wales*, p. 300), just after crossing the river Llyfnant. The road follows the edge of the estuarial marshes, running at the foot of wooded hills. From the hills, several lovely valleys run down, most of them followed by roads or tracks, and lined with woods. Near the county boundary, right out on an island in the estuary marshes, is Dovey Junction Station, where the Pwllheli and Aberystwyth lines part company.

Two miles beyond is a village, strung out along the road, called **Furnace** on the signs, but strictly called **Eglwysfach**, or **Ysgubor-y-coed**. The unassuming 'little church' stands in a verdant churchyard by the road. Built in 1833 (chancel added 1913) it has a severe black and white interior, the nave floor made of slate slabs. The poet R. S. Thomas was vicar here from 1954 until 1967. The explanation of the other two names is provided by the towering great stone building, with battered walls, standing by the bridge over the Einion. Known locally as *y 'sgubor* (the barn), it was formerly the 'Dovey Furnace'. The site (and water-power) were used in the seventeenth century for refining silver. The present building was erected *c.* 1755 as a blast furnace for making iron, and operated as such until about 1814. The ore was brought by sea from North Lancashire and Cumberland. Within the building, the furnace survives almost intact, and you can stand inside and look up at the hole through which it was charged – which improbably takes the form of a red brick Gothic arch. The bellows providing the blast were worked by water-power, but the present iron wheel (31 feet in diameter) dates from a much later use as a saw-mill. The river above the picturesque waterfall beyond the furnace can be seen to have been tapped to supply the water. The old charcoal barn survives on the hillside above. The furnace has been given into the guardianship of the DoE by the Royal Society for the Protection of Birds, and is being restored.

Two miles further on, a road forks back left up the hill, and, after following a stream, contours along the slope. It crosses the pretty Clettwr valley. Half a mile beyond, a track goes off left. Near the junction is a biggish mound with some stones on it – **Bedd Taliesin**, or Taliesin's grave. This is not the Taliesin of history (the sixth-century poet), but the Taliesin of legend (the *Hanes Taliesin* which Lady Charlotte Guest included in her translation of the *Mabinogion* – see also Peacock's *Misfortunes of Elphin*), the Gwion Bach who was swallowed by the angry witch Ceridwen and was reborn as a baby with a beautiful forehead (*iesin ei dalcen*), who knew everything about the past, present, and future. The road leads eventually down to Tal-y-bont (below). Back on the main road the bypassed hamlet of **Tre'r-ddôl** contains two Methodist chapels, a new one with a spire, and a plain old one of 1845, which now houses a small museum. Humphrey Rowland Jones (1832–95), a local man who caught the revivalist spirit in Wisconsin, returned here to start the Welsh Revival of 1858–60.

At Tre'r-ddôl, the B4353 goes off to Borth (p. 55). The next village on the A487 is called **Taliesin**, in honour of the bard. Next comes **Tal-y-bont**, where side by side stand a nice pair of rival chapels – Bethel (Gothic) and Tabernacl (classical). Down the hill at the crossroads are rival pubs, the Black and White Lions, and also the Lerry (Leri) Woollen Mill. From here a minor road climbs gradually up the long, wide **Cwm Ceulan**. The road climbs round the top: a track goes off to lonely ruins of lead-mines – engine-houses,

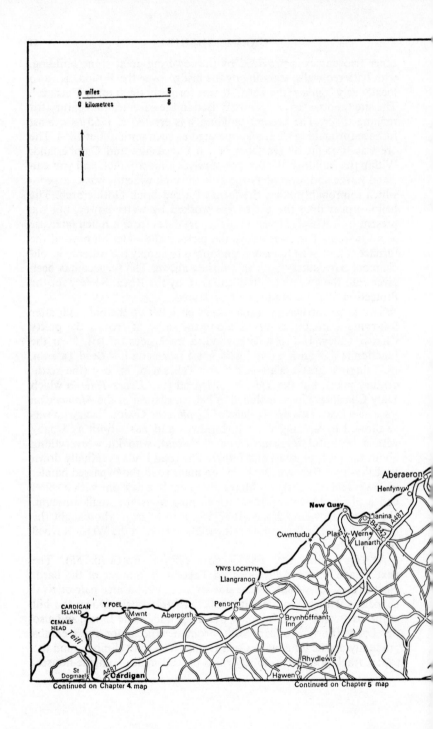

0 miles 5
0 kilometres 8

N

Aberaeron

Henfynyw

New Quay

Llanina

A487

Cwmtudu

Plas-y-Werne

Llanarth

B4342

YNYS LOCHTYN

Llangranog

Penbryn

CARDIGAN
ISLAND

Y FOEL

Mwnt

Aberporth

Brynhoffnant
Inn

CEMAES
HEAD

Teifi

Rhydlewis

St
Dogmaels

A487

Cardigan

Hawen

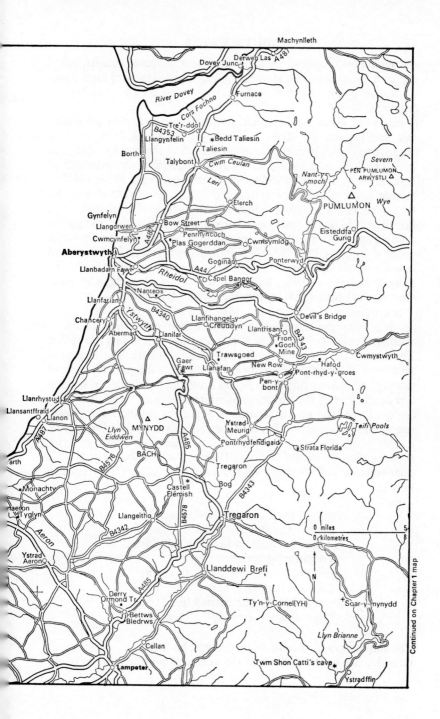

Derwen Las A 487

Dovey Junc

River Dovey

Furnace

Cors Fochno

Tre'r-ddol

B4353

Llangynfelin

Bedd Taliesin

Taliesin

Borth

Talybont

Cwm Ceulan

Leri

Elerch

Nant-y-moch

PEN PUMLUMON ARWYSTLI △

Severn

PUMLUMON

Wye

Gynfelyn

Bow Street

Llangorwen

Penrhyncoch

Cwmcynfelyn

Plas Gogerddan

Cwmsymlog

Eisteddfa Gurig

Aberystwyth

Goginan

Ponterwyd

Llanbadarn Fawr

Rheidol

A44

Capel Bangor

Nanteos

Llanfarian

Ystwyth

B4340

Chancery

Llanfihangel-y-Creuddyn

Devil's Bridge

B4343

Abermad

Llanilar

Llantrisan

Fron Goch Mine

Gaer Fawr

Trawsgoed

New Row

Hafod

Cwmystwyth

Llanafan

Pont-rhyd-y-groes

Pen-y-bont

Llanrhystud

Llansantffraid

Llanon

Llyn Eiddwen

MYNYDD △

A485

Ystrad Meurig

Teifi Pools

arth

BACH

B4576

Pontrhydfendigaid

Strata Florida

Monachty

Tregaron Bog

B4343

Tyglyn

Aeron

Castell Flemish

Llangeitho

B4578

Tregaron

0 miles 5

0 kilometres 8

N

Ystrad Aeron

Llanddewi Brefi

Derry Ormond Tr

A485

Ty'n-y-Cornel(YH)

Soar-y-mynydd

Bettws Bledrws

B4342

Llyn Brianne

Cellan

Lampeter

Twm Shon Catti's cave

Ystradffin

Continued on Chapter 1 map

reservoir ponds, and enormously deep and dangerous shafts, echo-
ing with the sinister sounds of dripping water. The road goes down
to Nant-y-moch reservoir, and to Ponterwyd on the A44 (see p.
56).

From the Cwm Ceulan road, another road branches off south-
east and follows the idyllic Leri valley southwards. It comes as a
surprise to find a striking Victorian church at the hamlet of **Elerch**.
It was built in 1868 by the Rev. Lewis Gilbertson, vice-principal of
Jesus College, Oxford, who had spent his youth here. From 1841–52
he was Vicar of Llangorwen (see p. 55), and, as at that church, he
employed as his architect William Butterfield. Although not large,
the church is tough and ingeniously articulated, with a pyramidal
tower over the choir. It has a severe interior, and an excellent east
window by A. Gibbs. Worship is still ultra-Tractarian: men and
women sit on opposite sides (as they used to at Butterfield's All
Saints', Margaret Street, London), and Gregorian chant is used.
Opposite is a little school, probably also by Butterfield.

It is possible to return to the A487 by a direct road to Bow Street
(p. 55). From the crossroads two and a half miles from Elerch, a
road goes south to **Penrhyncoch**, a spread-out village in a flat valley.
The neat little church is by R. J. Withers (1880). The lectern is
amazing – a brightly-coloured eagle crushing a dragon, all made of
pottery. Numerous tablets to Pryses have the peculiarity of bearing
a reproduction of the signature of whichever member of the family
erected them. The east window is to Pryse Pryse Pryse. The Pryses,
one of the principal families of mid-Wales, lived at **Plas Gogerddan**,
a mile west. This unattractive rendered house is now the Plant
Breeding Station of University College of Wales, Aberystwyth. It is
celebrated in the stirring ballad *I blas Gogerddan* ('This Garden
now'):

> 'Without thy Sire hast thou return'd?'
>   In grief the Princess cried!
> 'Go back! – or from my sight be spurn'd –
>   To battle by his side.
> I gave thee birth; but struck to earth,
>   I'd sooner see thee lie,
> Or on thy bier come carried here,
>   Than thus a craven fly!'

The son does as he is told, and is brought back dead, to his mother's
remorse, but to the acclaim of the ancestral portraits. Some of the

portraits formerly at Gogerddan were (wrongly) attributed to Van
Dyck, since Van Dyck's widow, Mary Ruthven, married Sir Richard
Pryse. The present structure incorporates medieval fabric (a fine
carved bressummer has gone to St Fagan's), and an eighteenth-
century staircase.

From Penrhyncoch, a road follows the Silo valley up to the evocative mining village of **Cwmsymlog**. A tall and excellently-built (but
crumbling) stone chimney rises from a desolation of waste. The mines
date back to the sixteenth century, and for many years were the most
famous in Cardiganshire, especially after a great vein of silver was
discovered. In 1617 they were taken over by Sir Hugh Myddelton (see
North Wales, p. 193), who made £2000 a month from them. North
Cardiganshire was the most important lead-mining area in Wales,
from Roman times until 1939. The industry declined from the 1870s
owing to the working out of the best veins and foreign competition.
The need for charcoal for smelting helped bring about the deforesta-
tion of the hills, until in the eighteenth century coal began to be used:
it was then cheaper to send the ore to Neath, Swansea, Bristol or
Flintshire to be smelted. Another by-product of mining was that
Cornish miners coming to work here brought with them the Wesleyan
form of Methodism, otherwise much less popular in Wales than
Calvinistic Methodism.

From Bow Street the A4159 cuts across southwards to the A44,
while the A487 climbs round on to the hills above Aberystwyth (p.
58). Just before the long descent into the town, the B4572 goes off
northwards. After a mile it goes down very steeply, with a hairpin
bend, past the grounds of **Cwmcynfelyn**. This eighteenth-century
house (now flats, with stables by C. R. Cockerell) was the birthplace
of the Rev. Isaac Williams (1802–65), the Tractarian poet and
theologian, friend of Keble and Newman. His family gave the land
for the church at **Llangorwen**, which stands by the road down in the
valley. Built in 1841, it was designed by H. J. Underwood of Oxford,
in the same simple lancet style which he had used for the church he
built for Newman at Littlemore outside Oxford. The wooden eagle
lectern was given by Keble, and the remarkable bronze chandeliers
are said to have been given by Newman. The porch and bell-turret
were added in 1848, during the incumbency of Lewis Gilbertson
(see p. 54), by William Butterfield, and are very characteristic.

Beyond Llangorwen the road climbs again over low hills for three
miles, until a steep hill, with great views over the Dyfi estuary, leads
down into the not very inspiring resort of **Borth**. Houses, chapels,
and hotels are strung out along the landward side of the road, facing

the sea over a dyke. The biggest hotel (built, like the one at Aberystwyth, by Thomas Savin) was taken over in 1876 by Uppingham School, which fled here after a typhoid epidemic caused by bad drains had killed several boys, and stayed for over a year. The road runs parallel with the sea right up to Ynyslas, on the Dyfi estuary, but is boring since the breakwater cuts off the view of the sea. Low tides here reveal ancient tree stumps, evidence of flooding dated to Neolithic times. They support the legend of the submerged land of Cantref y Gwaelod. (Sarn Gynfelyn, a natural stone dyke running out into the sea three miles south of Borth, was once thought – like Sarn Badrig (see *North Wales*, p. 247) – to have been one of the embankments which protected the Cantref). To the right, across the railway and the canalized river Leri, is the vast expanse of **Cors Fochno**, a bog of great botanical interest.

At the corner the road turns east, and it is a relief to come upon old farms on bits of higher ground, and then the hamlet of **Llangynfelyn**, with its tiny Victorian church. Another mile brings you to the A487 at Tre'r-ddôl (p. 51).

EISTEDDFA GURIG TO ABERYSTWYTH – A44

Eisteddfa Gurig (see *North Wales*, p. 306) is the starting-point for the shortest route up **Pumlumon**, by way of a mine track which starts right of the road just over the county border. But this is a very dull way of getting there. For a much better route, keep on the A44 as it goes down the Castell valley, past yet more mines, as far as the workaday village of Ponterwyd. Turn right here up the newly-made-up 'Mountain Road', with frequent cattle-grids, which keeps above the Rheidol valley. Much of the valley has been flooded to form Dinas Reservoir, part of the extensive and complicated Rheidol hydro-electric scheme. Three miles from the village, the road bears left and crosses the hideous concrete dam of the huge Nant-y-moch Reservoir, part of the same scheme. It then follows the edge of the reservoir (very nasty in a dry summer, for those who do not like mud), and goes up through forestry over to Cwm Ceulan and so down to Talybont (see p. 51). For Pumlumon, however, bear right before the dam and follow the road as far as it has a decent surface. From there it is not much more than a mile straight up to the summit, 2470 feet, but for a more interesting walk keep on up the Hengwm valley, and then approach the top by way of the impressively rocky Cwm Gwarin.

The chief attraction of Pumlumon is not the immediate surroundings, as on the mountains of Snowdonia, but the immense panorama of the whole of Wales. Even on a comparatively dull day it is possible to see the whole of Cardigan Bay, Snowdonia, Presely, the Brecon Beacons, and many more peaks. To vary the return, follow the grassy summit-ridge round to Pen Pumlumon Arwystli (2427 feet), one and a half miles east. The stream in the valley below is the source of the Wye. One and a half miles north bring you to the great watershed, a maze of peat-hags, in the middle of which a pool of water is labelled, with a neat green notice, SOURCE OF RIVER SEVERN. The river soon disappears into the immense Hafren Forest.

From Ponterwyd, the A4120 goes south to Devil's Bridge (p. 61). The A44 climbs past **Llywernog**, where an old mine has been turned into an open-air museum, with waterwheels and other interesting remains, and then winds down through **Goginan**, once surrounded by lead-mines. Two miles further is **Capel Bangor**, with a tall, plain early-nineteenth-century church. From here a road leads south-east down into the Rheidol valley. Three miles up is the dam which turns a long stretch of the river into a reservoir.

Back on the A44, from Capel Bangor it is only three miles to **Llanbadarn Fawr**, now a suburb of Aberystwyth, but historically and religiously of far greater significance than the town. It retains the air of a village round the crossroads, but the size and grandeur of the church, set in a large churchyard on the side of the valley, go beyond what one would expect in a village. A *clas* was founded here by St Padarn in the sixth century. The site, near the sea, but tucked away out of sight from it, is similar to the sites of the cathedrals at Bangor (*North Wales*, p. 138) and St Davids (p. 102). The monastery was a famous centre of scholarship. The Normans made it a cell of the Benedictine abbey of Gloucester, but in the twelfth century the Benedictines were expelled and the Celtic community moved back. In 1188 Giraldus Cambrensis claimed that the lay abbot was 'grown old in iniquity'. By the mid thirteenth century the *clas* had disappeared.

The present church was built in about 1200. Big, solid, and severe, it is cruciform, with a low tower and spire at the crossing. The thick walls are pierced with lancets, except at the east end, where three large windows were inserted in the fifteenth century. By the mid nineteenth century the church was in a bad way. Butterfield was asked to restore it, but resigned in 1862 after a dispute. J. P. Seddon was then appointed, and work began in 1868. He did an excellent job, leaving the severity of the structure unimpaired, but adding the handsome boarded chancel roof, and good fittings, including the tiled floor, and marble reredos. The glass is by Belham. Seddon's design for the east window was improved by F. J. Shields, the cranky religious painter. It was hardly surprising that Seddon did not go to William Morris's firm for his glass, as he had done at Llandaff (see p. 247): not only did he no longer think Morris's glass suitable, on the grounds that it was too assertive, but Morris had – without telling Seddon – written to the Vicar of Llanbadarn advising him not to let any architect 'restore' the church. The chancel contains several good monuments. One by Robert Wynne of Ruthin commemorates Sir Thomas Powell; another is to Cornelius le Brun of Cologne; while a third records the marriage of Sir Thomas's son William to le Brun's daughter Avarina. She inherited Nanteos through her mother, which is how it came to the Powells (see p. 64). Le Brun was a Huguenot engineer, who probably came to the district in connection with mining. There are other monuments to Powells of Nanteos, while those to Pryses of Gogerddan (p. 54) include one by Flaxman.

Also in the chancel, near the Powells who gave him so much trouble in his lifetime, lies Lewis Morris (1701–65), beneath a slab set up in 1884. He was the eldest of the famous Morris brothers, from Anglesey (see *North Wales* p. 205), and is best remembered as a poet and scholar. But he came to Cardiganshire as deputy steward of Crown manors, responsible for the Crown's silver-mining rights, which meant that he was in constant conflict both with the local landowners and with his employers. Another famous resident of the parish was the fourteenth-century poet Dafydd ap Gwilym (see p. 72), and one of his poems records his frustrated attempts to catch the eyes of the girls in Llanbadarn Church on Sundays. Two Celtic crosses, once in the churchyard, now stand in the south transept.

ABERYSTWYTH

Aberystwyth would more appropriately be called 'Aberrheidol', as it is really on the mouth of that river that the town is built. However, since the Ystwyth has been diverted (in order to scour out the harbour) right up the west side of Pendinas to reach the sea at virtually the same point as the Rheidol, there is less need to quibble. The historical origin of the name is that the original Norman castle was near the old mouth of the Ystwyth (south of Pendinas).

Familiarly known as 'Aber', this friendly town succeeds in blending its varied functions as shopping centre, seaside resort, and university town with unselfconscious lack of fuss. The **Castle** is both historically and scenically a good place to start looking at it. It was begun in 1277 by Edmund of Lancaster, brother of Edward I. The plan consisted of two concentric lozenges, with two double-towered gateways on the east. Also in 1277 Edward founded the chartered borough. The town was walled (like Conwy and Caernarfon),and the streets follow the medieval lay-out. Under Charles I a mint was set up in the castle.

In the eighteenth century the town developed as the port for the lead-mines inland, with quays along the mouth of the river. Towards the end of the century its second role as a seaside resort was heralded in 1788 when Sir Uvedale Price, author of the famous 'Essay on the Picturesque', and a friend of Thomas Johnes of Hafod (see p. 62) commissioned John Nash to build a house on the seafront near the castle. It was Nash's first complete house. Called Castle House, it was roughly triangular with three octagonal machicolated towers.

When Thomas Savin (with David Davies) built the railway from Shrewsbury in 1864, part of his project involved building luxury hotels at Aberystwyth, Borth and Aberdovey, the idea being to offer 'package tours'. The Aberystwyth hotel was begun in 1864. It incorporated Castle House as its nucleus, and the house survived until 1895. The hotel, still unfinished, opened in 1865, but next year Savin went bankrupt. The building, on which he had spent £80,000, was put up for sale. This was a golden opportunity for the committee which had been established to set up a University of Wales, and they bought it for £10,000. Savin's architect, J. P. Seddon, was asked to complete the building. As it stands now, the **College** is amazing enough, but it was much more so in its original form. The vast Gothic pile, with its romantic silhouette, could have been dreamt up by Ludwig II. The dull four-storey block south of the rounded section was designed by C. J. Ferguson (of Carlisle) to replace the Nash house. The south wing, with its conical turret, was rebuilt in about 1890 to replace a more fanciful wing with an upper storey in half-timber. The mosaic on the end, showing the marvels of modern science (including a steam engine) being shown to an astonished Archimedes, was presented by Seddon. The north part was rebuilt after a fire in 1885.

The story of the foundation of the University of Wales is in itself not without romance. The idea goes back to Owen Glendower, who envisaged two Welsh universities, one in the north and one in the south. By the mid nineteenth century there was a widespread desire for a national, non-sectarian university, and funds were collected from all over the country, poor as well as rich contributing. At least 100,000 people gave sums of less than half a crown. The College opened in 1872.

From the College Victorian terraces stretch right round the curving shingle beach to the foot of Constitution Hill. The **Pier** (now truncated) dates from 1864, like Savin's hotel. Further on is **Victoria Terrace**. The two Gothic houses at the south end were built by Seddon in 1870, but their splendid brick polychromy has been painted over. At the far end, a cliff railway was built in 1896 up **Constitution Hill**, which is messy as a result of sporadic quarrying.

St Michael's Church, just behind University College, is a large, dull building of 1889–1907 by Nicholson and Son. Only the chancel survives of the church it replaced, a humble job of 1833 by E. Haycock. The church stands in a broad square formed by the College on the west, and the L-shaped **Laura Place**, two terraces of delightfully varied houses, dating from c. 1800. On the east side stand the handsome former Assembly Rooms, built in 1820 by G. S. Repton (son of Humphry). They now house the Students' Union. Laura Place is typical of the wealth of eighteenth- and nineteenth-century domestic architecture which makes Aberystwyth such an attractive town. Within a basic uniformity of scale, and the remarkably rigid grid lay-out of most of the streets, an infinite variety of detail can be found, in elegant doorcases, bracketed cornices, projecting bows, and so on, making the exploration of the town a continual pleasure. The only other individual building to which attention needs to be drawn is **St Mary's Welsh Church**, tucked away among humbler terraces in the southern part of the town. It was built by William Butterfield in 1863–6. The interior is especially characteristic.

The **University** buildings up on Penglais are mostly by Sir Percy Thomas (from 1935 onwards) and his firm. Among them is an institution, not part of the university, but of wider significance – the **National Library of Wales**. Founded in 1907, it occupies a building designed by S. K. Greenslade, and built in stages since 1911. The handsome brick part at the back is by Charles Holden. The collections of printed books (it is a copyright library), of manuscripts (including, above all, the famous Hengwrt-Peniarth collection – see *North Wales*, pp. 242 and 261), and of prints, drawings and maps, are magnificent.

Aberystwyth Station, as well as being the terminus of the line from Shrewsbury, is also the starting-place for the **Vale of Rheidol**

Railway, the only narrow-gauge line on British Rail, the only one still using steam, and one of the very few not in the red. It was opened in 1902, on a two-foot gauge, chiefly to bring lead ore down from the mines round the terminus at Devil's Bridge. The railway is much the best way of seeing the lovely Rheidol valley.

Immediately south of the town is the shapely hill **Pendinas**, crowned by an Iron Age hill-fort and the crude pillar erected to honour the Duke of Wellington. Aberystwyth is fortunate to have a hill at each end of the town, preventing sprawl along the coast.

ABERYSTWYTH TO DEVIL'S BRIDGE AND BACK

The A4120 follows the south side of the Rheidol valley. From the bend about eight miles from the town, a spectacular 'hanging tributary', **Nant Bwa Drain**, can be seen on the opposite side of the valley. It falls over 600 feet in less than half a mile. From here it is less than three miles to **Devil's Bridge** (Pontarfynach), where the road crosses the Mynach by a bridge beneath which two earlier ones still stand, one above the other. The middle one is eighteenth century, and the lowest medieval. The name is explained by a legend (found all over Europe). An old woman's cow had strayed across the ravine, and she could not get it back. A monk appeared, and offered to build a bridge if she promised to give him the first living creature that crossed it. This she did, the bridge was built, and he beckoned to her to cross. However, the crafty old girl had spotted his cloven hoof, so she called her black dog, and threw a crust across. He ran after it, and she told the devil he could keep the dog.

The reason for the place's popularity is not the bridge, however, but the magnificent waterfalls by which the river goes down to join the Rheidol in its wooded ravine. The upper part of the Rheidol was originally the top of the river Teifi, but it was 'captured' first by the Ystwyth, and then by the lower Rheidol. One of the finest examples of 'river-capture' in Britain, it explains the depth of the Rheidol valley and also the sharp bend to the west at this point. The falls are reached through a turnstile, and well-built paths, steps and bridges lead visitors down to the bottom and back up the other side. However touristy, they are well worth seeing. Wordsworth saw them after rain in 1824, and was inspired to write a visionary sonnet. It is equally worthwhile paying yet again at the turnstile on the opposite side of the road, to see the great rock gorge through which the river boils and swirls, gouging out huge potholes, before it starts to fall. Near by stands the **Hafod Arms Hotel**, built by the Duke of Newcastle *c.* 1830, exceptionally attractive, with huge eaves.

The hill road south from Devil's Bridge to Cwmystwyth (B4574) is spanned by an unexpected arch erected to celebrate George III's jubilee. This is an appropriate outrider to the famous **Hafod** estate. Here Thomas Johnes made his seemingly doomed attempt to create a paradise. He inherited the property in 1783 and for the next thirty years poured his whole fortune, heart and energy into it, transforming this bleak unknown spot into a mecca for painters and poets, agriculturalists, and scholars of European repute. Five thousand acres were farmed by the latest improved methods; six million trees were planted; pleasure grounds with spectacular waterfalls and grottoes were devised. Nothing is left of the Gothic house designed by Thomas Baldwin of Bath. The original house (1786) and the octagonal library added by John Nash (1794) were destroyed by fire in 1807, and although they were quickly rebuilt the heart was soon to be knocked out of Thomas Johnes by the death of his only child Mariamne in 1811. After his own death (1816) the property was bought by the Duke of Newcastle (see p. 110), and later by Sir Henry de Hoghton. In 1846–51 he employed Antony Salvin to build an extensive wing with a tower (Italianate in style). In 1946, after war neglect, Hafod was bought by a merchant who clear-felled the timber and stripped the roof of lead. The house was demolished in 1962, having become famous through *Peacocks in Paradise* (Elisabeth Inglis-Jones). The Forestry Commission has now planted the valley and the site of the house is a caravan park. The cascade on the stream opposite is unimpressive except after rain. More exciting is the 'Robber's Cave', with a waterfall in it, high above the river further north-east. Johnes made use of old lead levels and miners' skills in creating such waterworks. An obelisk designed by W. F. Pocock (1803) commemorating the young Duke of Bedford, 'Friend of Agriculture', who was also a friend of Johnes, stands on a rocky crag to the north of the house. Behind it was Mariamne's garden, now a jungle. The dangerous ruin to the south of the terrace near the river was a big ice-house. In 1803 James Wyatt designed **Eglwys Newydd**. It was gutted by fire in 1932 and Chantrey's famous monument to Mariamne was irreparably damaged.

A mile east of Eglwys Newydd is the mining village of **Cwmystwyth**, beyond which the valley narrows. Another mile brings you into a fascinating nightmare scene, where lead-mining has irreparably changed the valley. The north side has been eaten away, there is hardly room for the road between the dead spoil-heaps, and vast corrugated iron sheds clank and creak in the wind. These sheds housed the concentrating mill, built in 1898 and worked by water turbines. The mine was worked from Roman times until 1916. At its peak in the seventeenth and eighteenth centuries it produced a sizeable proportion of the nation's silver and lead ore. The use of water in the separation and dressing of the ore has caused the river to be without any life whatsoever for two miles down, and its eery clearness is notable the whole way to the sea. There are very few fish. After another mile the valley opens out and welcome trees group round the handsome **Bridge** built by Thomas Johnes in 1783. Like the house, it was designed by Thomas Baldwin. Further on, the road climbs up on to bare hills, and over into Radnorshire (see *North Wales*, p. 311).

The return to Aberystwyth may be made by two different routes. For the first, take the B4343, below Hafod, but instead of crossing the bridge into the village of Pontrhydygroes, keep straight on. A mile up, New Row is a nice terrace of miners' cottages. Three-quarters of a mile beyond, turn right up the hill, and in a few hundred yards one of the most impressive surviving lead-mining complexes in Cardiganshire opens up – the **Fron-goch Mine**. Discovered in 1798, it produced some 1200 tons of ore a year in the mid nineteenth century. Small-scale drilling operations were recently conducted, but the buildings are all ruinous. Around the vast bare site stand the well-built stone engine house, dressing house, waterwheel house, magazines etc. A tramway ran under the road and down the hillside, to the dressing floors (impressive remains).

Half a mile north of the mine is the reservoir from which its power came, Llyn Fron-goch. On a hillock half a mile east of the grassy dam is the simple little church of **Llantrisant**, commanding huge views. Keep going north-west on the road which bends westwards and then goes gently down the side of a wide valley to the charming little village of **Llanfihangel-y-Creuddyn**, cosily set at the valley-bottom, and dominated by the very grand central tower of its thirteenth-century church. Well restored by Withers in 1871, it has an absolutely plain, whitewashed interior. The only elaborate object is the oak reredos, carved in high relief by a Belgian, Jules Bernaerts, in 1919. It represents the Last Supper: the display of emotions by the apostles recalls a Bateman cartoon. In the churchyard is the tomb of Richard Morgan who died in 1743 aged nine, with the epitaph:

> With tears, O Lord, I come to thee to beg,
>   And to Intreat,
> Even as ye Child that hath done ill
>   and Feareth to be Beat.

The road west from Llanfihangel leads on to the B4340, which goes back towards Aberystwyth. After a mile or two, the view opens out over a broad valley on the right, beautifully landscaped as a park, and over on the far side, sheltered by the hills on the north, is a handsome Georgian house – **Nanteos** (the valley of the nightingale). Open daily from June to September, it is reached by a road which forks back from the B4340 a mile before it reaches the A487. The estate came into the Powell family when William Powell married Avarina le Brun (see p. 58), and remained in it until 1952. The most interesting member of the family was George Powell (1842–82). As a boy he was so mild-natured that his father ordered him to go out and shoot the first thing he saw. He shot his father's prize bullock. He published poetry, and translations of Icelandic legends, which were admired by William Morris, and became a close friend of Swinburne, whose tastes he shared. His father died at last in 1878, but Powell presumably did not fulfil the hopes expressed by Swinburne in 1875, that he would 'celebrate his accession by such orgies as shall make Nant Eos a worthy rival in reputation to the Château de Lacoste – seat of the noble house of Sade'. Powell also knew Rossetti, Simeon Solomon, Beardsley, Longfellow, and Wagner – who stayed at Nanteos.

In 1967 the house was bought by Geoffrey and Rose Bliss, since when they have worked to restore the fabric and to furnish the rooms appropriately. They have succeeded remarkably in creating atmosphere. Architecturally, the house is fascinating, but puzzling. The foundation stone was laid in 1739, and the lead rainwater heads are dated 1757. Externally, its plainness is set off by the urns on the roof-line, and the handsome centrepiece, probably an addition of 1838–9, with three roundheaded windows over the ground-floor portico. Inside, it is hard to tell what is genuinely eighteenth century and what is a clever and successful nineteenth-century attempt to match the earlier style. The astonishing Music Room must be largely early Victorian. The splendid stables, round the back of the house, are entered through a stately triumphal arch. They seem to have been designed, like the centrepiece of the house, by Edward Haycock. The famous Nanteos Cup is no longer here. This battered wooden object, legendarily identified with the Holy Grail, and said to have come here from Strata Florida (see p. 71), is claimed to have healing powers. It is in the possession of a member of the family, and access is still granted to the faithful. It is actually a fragment of a medieval mazer bowl.

For the second route back from Pontrhydygroes to Aberystwyth,

The north-facing cliffs of the Brecon Beacons, formed of Old Red Sandstone.

Rocky coastal scenery, typical of South-West Wales, at Lochtyn in Cardiganshire.

The romantic pile of University College of Wales at Aberystwyth,
seen from the rocky shore.

keep on the B4343, into the village, and take a minor road (right)
which follows the Ystwyth valley. Two miles downstream where the
valley opens, a little footbridge leads to a pair of white houses. This
is the place to look up into the elusive timber-clad valley, particularly
beautiful on a bright autumn morning. The Forestry Commission
has opened paths including one up to **Castell Grogwnion** which
crowns the opposite hillside.

The stone arched bridge at Pen-y-bont might be said to mark the
end of steep valleys and wild upland. The valley floor widens and
the cattle are fatter, and the minor road meets the B4340, coming up
from Ystrad Meurig (p. 70). The first turning right after the bridge
leads to **Llanafan**, where the small church, built in 1840 by one
Coultart, was extensively remodelled in 1862–7 by W. Butterfield.
It is the estate church for **Trawsgoed** (Crosswood), just off the B4340,
a mile north. Seat of the Vaughans (after 1776 Earls of Lisburne)
from the fourteenth century until 1947, it now belongs to the
Ministry of Agriculture. The original seventeenth-century house has
been much altered. It is chiefly notable for its library with elaborate
nineteenth-century painted decoration. The Ionic portico has oddly
sliced-off volutes. A vast French wing was added in 1891. The very
Victorian grounds are celebrated for their specimen conifers.

Gaer Fawr (648/718) one and a half miles west-south-west, crowns
a grassy hill-top surrounded by neat enclosed fields. This Iron Age
fort, which has never been excavated, is one of the biggest in mid-
Wales. It has a marvellous site and it is possible to get a really wide
view of this very elusive country, and of the coast right across
Cardigan Bay from Cardigan Island to Bardsey and the Lleyn
Peninsula. Cadair Idris is due north and the great mass of mid-
Wales mountains, whose heart is Pumlumon, to the north-east. The
middle and foreground is a patchwork of hard-earned fields covering
small grassy hills, and winding hidden valleys, and forestry. The
fort is easy to reach from the narrow road immediately to the south.
Park in the quarry and take the iron field-gate fifty yards east of it.
A sheep path leads up through the bracken.

The minor road here joins A485 (Aberystwyth–Tregaron–
Lampeter). Three miles north back in the Ystwyth valley, is **Llanilar**,
an attractive village with the Falcon Inn, school and cottages grouped
round a low church tower topped by an octagonal slated spire which
looks squarely west up the valley. Here the river has a wide gravelly
bed, too big except when in spate; the water is clear and relatively
lifeless as a result of the lead-mining higher up. **Abermad**, built in
1870–2 by J. P. Seddon, is large and elaborate. Rich stone-carving

outside, much-notched woodwork inside. A circular stained-glass window represents (appropriately) Ruskin's *Seven Lamps of Architecture*. The porte cochère has columns of Shap granite.

A487 SOUTH FROM ABERYSTWYTH–ABERAERON

A487, the main coast road south from Aberystwyth allows tantalizingly few glimpses of the sea. The big rounded hills, which cut off Cardigan Bay, drop to a narrow shelf of fields above a shingly shoreline. Only a few lanes give access to the farms and occasional caravan site. **Chancery** is an attractive group of estate almshouses which straddles the road a mile south of Llanfarian. Now macadam has encroached on their forecourts, submerging the circular patterns of the cobbles, and several of the houses are empty. There were seven in all, designed with projecting bays at the ends, Gothic windows and important chimney stacks. The big TV mast is Blaen-plwyf; so powerful is the transmission that a baked bean tin makes an adequate aerial for some of the houses hereabouts. **Llanrhystud Church** was rebuilt by R. K. Penson (1852). Here the Wyre and Carrog meet to join the sea, high land and cliff give way to coastal plain. The village has some nice simple houses, snugly compact, as has Llanon, two miles south. They are nineteenth century, Welsh Georgian, plain with generous proportions and often a round arch or a pediment over the central door. They can be found in several villages, both in detached and terraced form, and must surely be the work of the same builder, or derive from the same copy-book.

Llansantffraid adjoins Llanon. It is humbler than its main road neighbour and was the original fishing village at the mouth of the Peris. The church has a sturdy medieval tower and the purple, slate-hung south wall of the nave is unusually adorned with memorial tablets (outside). It has clear glass Gothic windows and early nineteenth-century box pews and fittings.

Aber-arth, a small village in a steep valley, was the harbour for this coast before the construction of Aberaeron. Its medieval church stands high on a windy hill above, braving all gales. It continued for many years as the parish church for Aberaeron whose enterprising founders are buried in the churchyard.

Aberaeron is one of the most pleasant, rational and cheerful-looking towns in Wales. Strongly Georgian in character, this small port was only a dream when its Harbour Act was passed in 1807, and the main square, optimistically attributed to John Nash, was not begun until the 1850s. Aberaeron's creators, local landowners, were middle-aged cousins. Lewis Gwynne of Monachty was a rich bachelor; his cousin, Susannah Maria Jones of Tyglyn, an heiress. To the distress of her relatives, Miss Jones chose to marry another cousin, a penniless, widowed Hampshire curate, with four children, named Alban Thomas, whom they described as 'an old mad clergyman [he was forty-five] . . . the Oddest in Nature'. Some years later, when Lewis Gwynne died, Alban and Susannah inherited his fortune (and took the name of Gwynne). They set to work immediately and soon quays and wharves were under construction at the mouth of the Aeron. A much needed harbour was formed and a thriving shipbuilding industry established; the new town naturally followed. Its character derives from straightforward handling; its successful design relies on the rhythm of repetitive elements and the consistency of proportion. This is varied by contrasting details such as quoins, architraves and robust moulded keystones. In recent years, civic pride, taking the form of an uninhibited use of paint, has highlit these details by contrasting them with the main wall. Houses are constantly repainted, often in startling colours with a refreshing lack of fuss. The quieter traditional colours are, surprisingly, the smartest.

Street names give a clue to their date and to the activities of the town: Waterloo and Regent Streets, Mason's Yard . . . (Drury Lane tantalizes). Across the river, Wellington Street led to Vulcan Place where the smiths had their workshops near the mouth of the harbour. Chalybeate Street and the little well-house, upstream from the bridge, are reminders of Aberaeron's later aspirations as a spa. Of the public buildings, the Harbour Master's House (now a hotel) on the quay was naturally one of the first. The handsome Town Hall with cupola and clock (now council offices) were also early in the town's history. Tabernacl and Peniel Chapels date from the 1830s. Previously services had been held in houses or warehouses. Revivalist meetings were sometimes conducted to vast crowds from the decks of ships in the harbour. The church, a dull building, is from 1875.

In 1833, Samuel Lewis described how 'a general post-office and excellent posting-house and hotel [The Feathers] have been established, the latter affording to families an equal degree of comfort and privacy to any in the principality'. The town thrived. In 1864 the tradesmen contracted with a Glasgow firm to build a steamer to their own specification. But this was the beginning of the end; steamships and the coming of the railway into mid-Wales were soon to take away the business of the small ports which had served the sailing coasters so well. The last ship was built in 1884 and the busy town gradually became a quiet backwater.

THE VALE OF AERON

Inland from Aberaeron, the silver Aeron, its plenteous vale, the
herds and flocks which grazed there and, above all, its 'beauties',
were the subject of an eighteenth-century ode. It ends

> Were I possess'd of regal state,
>   Presiding o'er a nation
> With crowding senates at my feet
>   In humble adoration,
> I'd envy, if envying might avail,
> The happy swains of Aeron's vale.

A482, the Aberaeron–Lampeter road, follows the south side of the
valley. **Llanaeron**, the charming pink-washed house set in parkland
three miles upstream, off the minor road beside the river, is very
probably by John Nash, who may have had a hand in the church
at the edge of the park (its present dome is 1960).

Tyglyn, home of the founders of Aberaeron, on the right bank, one
mile upstream near the new bridge, is a plain Welsh mansion-house
in the best tradition: a fanlight over the door and dentils along the
eaves are its only concessions to decoration. No one has worried
whether the chapel dedicated to St Alban, and added by his name-
sake in 1809, precisely balanced the other wing. He must also be
responsible for the timber grain store raised on staddle-stones
(unique here, though common in England). It is entered by a ladder
which folds back like a draw-bridge, also to prevent its use by rats
and mice. Tyglyn is at present famed for its herd of Welsh Blacks
(see p. 330). **Monachty** (the seat of Lewis Gwynne), one and a half
miles north, built on the site of a hospice of Strata Florida, smacks
of being architect-designed: stuccoed and pedimented.

Back on A482, just beyond Ystrad Aeron, B4342 forks left off
the main road and crosses to the north bank (A482 goes south to
Lampeter).

Llangeitho is a quiet village near the head of the vale, where the
river comes down from the hill country. It is hard now to imagine
the thousands who gathered here on a Communion Sunday during
the eighteenth century to receive the Sacrament from the curate,
Daniel Rowland, and to hear his sermons. It is said that Holy
Communion was not celebrated in the neighbouring churches for
nearly fifty years, so popular were his services.

Daniel Rowland (1713–90) was perhaps the greatest of many great
preachers of the evangelical revival that swept Wales in the eighteenth

century (see also Thomas Charles, p. 317). The reasons for this surge of religious fervour are complex. Undoubtedly the great Circulating School movement, started and organized by Griffith Jones (p. 162), laid a sure foundation. Pluralities, absenteeism, and the appointment of non-Welsh-speaking incumbents to the Anglican church created a vacuum which the influence of a minority of conscientious rectors could not fill. The people had a thirst to hear the word of God and it was spoken to them with extraordinary power and eloquence. The *hwyl*,[1] the spirit of what is spoken, or enthusiasm, which the preacher conveyed to the vast crowds who gathered to hear him, was of great importance. Rational people alive now admit to having been moved to tears by the very sound of Lloyd George's voice, without comprehending a word of the language in which he was speaking, so it is small wonder that the congregations who heard Daniel Rowland, Howell Harris and their fellow preachers were transported by their sermons (some to the point of hysteria).

William Williams, Pantycelyn (p. 150), was often at Llangeitho. In 1762 he published a new volume of hymns which caused yet another blaze of revivalist fervour, and Rowland's licence as an Anglican curate was withdrawn the following year. He was thus unable to use the parish church so a larger chapel called the New Church was built in 1764. It was replaced by the present building (1813–15) following the split between the Anglican and Methodist churches. In the 1764 chapel, for lack of space, the Communion Table was lowered on pulleys when required: a rare device which underlines the priorities in nonconformist planning where the pulpit is always the focal point.

Daniel Rowland was buried in the graveyard of the parish church of which he lived and died a member. His grave slab has been reset within the present building (early twentieth century). It is difficult to link the white marble statue outside the chapel (by Edward Griffith of Chester, 1883) with the fiery young preacher.

MYNYDD BACH

B4342 continues from Llangeitho to A485 and Tregaron, but to the north of the Vale of Aeron and inland from the main Aberystwyth–Aberaeron coast road is a lovely bit of lost country. Much of it is hard-earned farm land; small fields, stone walls and beech windbreaks at times forming lovely diminutive avenues; some is bleak

[1] Canon D. Parry-Jones points out that *hwyl* means literally the canvas of a ship. When the soul of a man has caught the *hwyl* he is in full sail.

moor; some is blanketed in forestry.

The core of this country is **Mynydd Bach** (highest point, 1183 feet). B4576 which twists its way north out of the Aeron valley, three and a half miles west of Llangeitho, leads into it. There is a fine feeling of isolation up here and grand distant views. The Enclosure Act of 1815 was not taken quietly by the independent inhabitants whose common rights on Mynydd Bach gave them much of their livelihood (grazing, fuel, and any game or rabbits). Fences erected by Augustus Brackenbury, the new owner, were quickly pulled down and the house he built was burnt. To the south of the summit is a small lake, Llyn Eiddwen. The ruin on the island is that of an unfinished nine-teenth-century house built by a Mr Tredwell who, tradition has it, was persuaded that there was rich lead to be mined. He intended to live there but exhausted his funds before completion. The house was to have a substantial tower.

TREGARON BOG AND YSBYTY YSTWYTH–TREGARON– LAMPETER

A ruler-straight stretch of the Roman road, Sarn Helen (here A485 and B4578) runs due south for nearly five miles, between Mynydd Bach and Tregaron Bog. Less than a mile east of A485's sharp turn towards Tregaron, road widening on your right brings you very close to **Castell Flemish**, a pre-Roman fort dating from about the second century BC. Its ramparts are roughly circular with about fifty feet between the main inner and outer secondary banks. The intervening space is thought to have been for the protection of cattle. A fine viewpoint. Tregaron (p. 72) is a couple of miles on.

Those wanting to explore **Tregaron Bog**, now a National Nature Reserve, should ask permission from the Nature Conservancy, but a lot can be seen from the road and there are rights of way. It is the greatest peat-bog in Wales, about three miles north to south and two across at its widest, a giant saucer, undrained except for the Teifi which flows through it. Shimmering cotton grass, brighter than a white frost, transforms it in the summer, but more often its sedge glows red, burning life into the grey-green country. The bog is alive with marsh birds and has long been famous for duck and snipe; kite and harriers may be seen hunting.

A minor road runs north from A485 opposite Castell Flemish through Swydd-ffynnon along the west side of the bog to **Ystrad Meurig**. The village once boasted a medieval castle. A remarkable school founded in the eighteenth century by Edward Richard, son of the village tailor, and an outstanding poet and scholar, long flourished here (it closed recently). It was held in the parish church, but Richard left it endowed as a grammar school. John Williams, the first Rector of Edinburgh Academy, who was described by Sir Walter Scott as the best schoolmaster in Europe, was a pupil. (He later set up his own school in Lampeter, to which Scott sent his son.)

The present building dates from the early nineteenth century. This is now the **College of St John**. A dozen or so boys who have missed the chance to do so at school, temporarily leave their jobs to work for their A levels while boarding in the village houses.

From Ystrad Meurig, two roads run up to the Ystwyth valley (p. 65). B4340 goes north-west to Aberystwyth and a much wilder unclassified road goes north-east to **Ysbyty Ystwyth**, which is on B4343 a mile south of Pontrhydygroes (page 63). It takes its name from another hospice of Strata Florida. The church (R. J. Withers, 1872), high above the village, is a good landmark. Much of the character of these villages derives from their plain traditional masonry which is now being eroded by builders' merchants' vernacular; large horizontal windows gape where the vertically-proportioned sash windows once hung.

The road south now skirts the wonderful empty uplands of mid-Wales which form a solid block to your left (east). **Ffair Rhos** commemorates in its name one of the oldest fairs in Wales. It is at the crossing of ancient trackways, that from mid-Wales joining the north–south route on which you are travelling. The track up to the Teifi Pools (which are part of an elderly reservoir scheme) to the east is now macadammed but not, fortunately, for the last empty miles over to the Claerwen Reservoir. This is one of the most desolate and boggy parts of Britain. There are miles of marvellous pale grass and heather, peaty pools, sheep and curlew. Easy to get lost.

Pontrhydfendigaid is a mile to the south where the Teifi flows out of the hills, immediately to lose itself in Tregaron Bog. The village has long been renowned for its annual eisteddfod which has been exceptionally richly endowed by Sir David James, the local lad who made good. (He has been described as 'owning Oxford Street including the cinemas, Studios One and Two'.) The exceptionally generous prize money encourages choirs to travel great distances to compete. It was also Sir David's wish that some of the contests should be in English, an idea then unique, in this heart of Welsh-speaking Wales. The James's grave is in Strata Florida churchyard.

Immediately south of Pontrhydfendigaid, another road leads into the hills, up the Teifi, to the ruins of the Cistercian Abbey of **Strata**

Florida (DoE). The meadows by the river still abound in flowers: lady's smock, purple orchid, buttercup and cow parsleys.

Strata Florida was originally a Norman foundation (Cistercian houses were usually of Welsh origin; Benedictine, Norman), but the existing structure was begun in 1184 by Rhys ap Gruffydd after he had defeated its Norman founder. It quickly became a great centre of culture and influence. Its sheep walks, often run with rich veins of lead, stretched over the whole of the inhospitable mid-Wales mountains and its hospices gave succour to countless travellers. Being only sixteen miles from Aberystwyth and the sea, communication with the world was relatively easy.

Not much architecture survives apart from the great Romanesque west door (portrayed by generations of tourists). The mouldings of the jambs and arch are continuous, uninterrupted by capitals – probably a unique design. The medieval tiles (under the modern roof) should not be missed. The presence of the eighteenth-century farm buildings gives a sort of latter-day continuity of Cistercian spirit: plain, serviceable and well-proportioned. The parish church is c. 1815; a single cell with pointed windows, and a 1724 pulpit.

Dafydd ap Gwilym, possibly the greatest of all Welsh poets (fl. 1340–70), is buried in the huge churchyard under the yew. He came of an influential Cardiganshire family. Full of simplicity, humour, and vigour, his poetry blends complex traditional techniques with the new manner of the troubadours, and a strongly individual clarity of observation. It is chiefly on the theme of love and of nature, with everything seen in relation to his own colourful personality.

Tregaron, the last village before the hills or the first town in the lowlands, depending on the direction from which you have come, has still a basic unfussed Welshness about it. Sheep are more important than pony-trekking for much of the year, although the Emporium has recently become a Craft Shop. The Square is dominated by the black and cream Talbot Hotel and the statue of Henry Richard (Albert Toft, 1893) who was born here in 1812. He was Liberal MP for Merthyr and a great worker for international peace ('the apostle of peace'). He was also alive to the importance of explaining Welsh problems in Westminster where he was known as 'the Member for Wales'.

The general impression of Tregaron is of a likeable grey village but there is a considerable variety of building. The church, in the middle, has a great sturdy Cardiganshire tower, fourteenth century; the rest was much restored in the late nineteenth century. The big Presbyterian chapel on the Lampeter road is boldly slate hung. The

National Westminster Bank, half-timbered with carefully made lead signs, should have been designed for Chester. Tregaron also has some very attractive corrugated iron cottages.

The Tregaron–Abergwesyn mountain road (see also p. 34) has been macadammed fairly recently, much to the regret of some people. It is very popular with picnickers on hot Sundays and slow, being single track for most of its thirteen hill miles, with 1 in 4 gradients occasionally. On a winter day, when not snow-bound, it is superb. It was once an important drovers' road: vast herds plodded slowly eastward, grazing as they went, their drovers often carrying money and messages for the gentry to their sons in London and England.

FROM TREGARON TO LAMPETER

Two roads lead south-west on either bank of the Teifi. That on the left bank (B4343), just below the hills, leads to **Llanddewi Brefi**. This is a big, surprisingly compact village with some attractive plain stone houses and pubs. The church stands on the traditional site of the Synod of Brefi where St David (p. 318) refuted the Pelagian heresy with such success. In order that he should be audible in the large crowd the ground rose beneath his feet and he thus stood out head and shoulders above them. It was on this occasion too that the dove, which is often depicted on the saint's shoulder, inspired him to greater truths. It was not long after this that a dove alighted on Mohammed's shoulder for a similar purpose; both legends seem to strengthen each other.

The continuing strength of the Celtic church here is confirmed by the existence, perhaps as late as 1287, of a form of *clas*, possibly the last one to survive. This was replaced by a Latin-style College of Canons. One of the famous manuscripts it produced (now in the Bodleian Library) was a translation into Welsh of Rhygyfarch's (Latin) life of St David.

Inside, St David's Church is huge, grand and simple. The big square tower (late twelfth century) rests on the vaulted crossing of the long nave (rebuilt 1874) and the nearly equally long chancel with transepts which collapsed around 200 years ago (when nonconformism was especially strong). Indeed it was here that Daniel Rowland, curate of Llangeitho, heard the great Griffith Jones (p. 162) preach and was converted to the ideas of evangelism. Form is everything inside the church; the Victorian lancet windows in the nave are mostly clear and, at the crossing, there are attractive pointed sash

windows, presumably put in when the transepts were swept away.
Walls are cream-washed, floors nice polished slate (with red Turkey
carpets), nave and chancel roofs unceiled wagons; pews simple
pine, early nineteenth century. Several important stones (seventh–
tenth century) have been placed in the church. An Ogam inscription (now under the tower) is a reminder of the close connections
with Irish Christianity. Another, now broken up and built into the
north-west corner of the nave (outside), was read in 1698 and contained the earliest known reference to David (seventh century).

A stream runs below the banked churchyard to the north and
beyond this are the grassy hills with sheep. On the other side, in
delightful contrast, is the snug village square; cream-washed two-
storey houses and the Foelallt Arms. The Roman station, *Bremia*,
was on the opposite bank of the Teifi. From here Sarn Helen runs
due north, for nine miles; to the south the next clear stretch begins
after the Llanfair Clydogau–Farmers road leaves the Teifi valley.

The country above Llanddewi Brefi is submerged under large areas
of forestry, but around the 1000-foot contour there is still stonewalled
country with oak, ash, rowan and beech giving shelter to the narrow
lanes. The Teifi twists and glints in the wide green valley below and
to the north is the brown expanse of the Bog.

B4343 follows the left bank of the river through **Cellan**, which
has an attractive, primitive church, down to Lampeter. You are in
green dairy country rolling down from the hills to the river. A485
runs parallel, down another valley, a couple of miles west. **Bettws
Bledrws Church** stands by the lodge of Derry Ormond (demolished
in the 1950s), the seat of the Inglis Jones family. It was rebuilt, with
the exception of the tower, in 1886 in memory of John Inglis Jones.
It is small, compact and strongly Victorian. An inscription tells how
the stone was hauled from Llanddewi Brefi by his tenants as a mark
of love and respect. There is a memorial of 1836 by Richard West-
macott junior to John Jones, builder of Derry Ormond, on the north
wall of the chancel. The curious font cover is made up from pieces
of wood which were once part of other churches; each is neatly
labelled in gleaming brass.

Derry Ormond Tower is a great landmark, for all the world like a
factory chimney. It was built in 1821–4, possibly by C. R. Cockerell
who was rebuilding the house and designing St David's College,
Lampeter, at that time. It tops a grassy hill overlooking the now
derelict park. A Gothic door led to an inside stair,which has been
blocked as part of recent consolidation work.

Lampeter (Llanbedr Pontsteffan) is an exceptionally serene looking

small town of white and soft-coloured stuccoed houses with grey
roofs set among gentle green hedged hills. Earlier topographers
found Lampeter commonplace. Cliffe, writing in 1848, found that
'it . . . contains not a single object of interest except St. David's
College'. They had some justification: the prosperity of the town
sprang from the college which was opened in 1827. So Lampeter
is now a very pleasant, unassuming Victorian town with Georgian
scale and rhythm, indeed a rarity. The only vernacular part, attractive to twentieth-century eyes but unnotable to the earlier topographers,
is the Common. Humble terraces of cottages, punctuated by two
chapels, enclose a large treed open space now, alas, a useful car
park. (It is behind the Black Lion.)

The importance of the locality goes back to pre-history and, of
the town, at least to medieval times when a castle guarded the river
crossing (the castle mound is in the college grounds). Lampeter
(Llanbedr) derives from the church of St Peter; Ponsteffan, in its
Welsh name, relates to an early bridge over the Teifi built by one
Stephen (last rebuilt in 1933).

St David's University College was the inspiration of Bishop
Burgess, bishop of St David's early in the nineteenth century. His
idea was to revitalize the Anglican church in Wales by providing a
college where future ordinands who could not afford Oxford or
Cambridge might have a sound university education.

In 1819 the owner of an estate near Lampeter (the already derelict
house of Peterwell) came to grief over a government loan. By way of
repayment he gave this property to J. S. Harford of Blaise Castle
and his brother. Harford chanced to meet Bishop Burgess in
Gloucester and was told of his plans. Harford visited his new
property, offered a site to the bishop, backed his offer by contributing £1000 to the building fund, and proposed that the then
little-known C. R. Cockerell should be architect. They all met in
Lampeter where 'Cockerell beautifully sketched the plan of the
College'. It is one of his first executed works, and is in the Tudor
style. It is planned round a quadrangle like an Oxford college,
the rooms arranged off staircases, with the modification that Welsh
box-beds were used so that students had bed-sitting-rooms as today
(box-beds might be reintroduced?). Corner fireplaces made these
snug. Two pumps in the quad provided water. The buildings were
rendered (a common practice). Cockerell's Tudor windows have
cast iron subframes as well as iron casements.

The pleasant library has recently been restored. It has a rare collection of early printed books and manuscripts given by that extra-

ordinary collector Sir Thomas Phillipps (d. 1872). He at one time considered housing his whole collection, the biggest in private hands, in Wales. The original chapel was remodelled by T. G. Jackson (c. 1878) and later by W. D. Caröe. The painted stalls come from New College, Oxford.

Considerable building activity has taken place recently, notably the new hall for the arts faculty (Alex Gordon and Partners, 1972). Lampeter is the second oldest university institution in Britain after the ancient universities, a forerunner of redbrick. It was the first whose degrees were recognized by Oxford (in 1880). When the federal University of Wales with its great nonconformist background received its charter in 1893, Lampeter remained outside, conferring its own degrees. St David's College only became a part of the University of Wales in 1971.

St David's College School on Station Terrace is very much part of the College group and it is to be hoped a new life will be found for it. The whole is most pleasantly set off by the stuccoed Victorian houses.

St Peter's Church by R. J. Withers, 1867, has a commanding tower, and a striking west window (1938) by Wilhelmina Geddes, an associate of Harry Clarke and Evie Hone.

Market day is Tuesday. Lampeter serves a very wide area. Surprisingly, Lewis reports in 1833 that the road south down to Llandovery was only then planned and that 'the inhabitants procure groceries and various other articles of domestic consumption' from Bristol; these came by sea to Aberaeron.

ABERAERON–CARDIGAN

A487 continues south, some miles in from the coast. The hamlet of **Henfynyw**, two miles from Aberaeron, is traditionally where St David went to school. **Llanarth**, the next village, spans a steep valley. The church (R. J. Withers) has a handsome fifteenth-century tower, and some more of those well-proportioned standard 'Georgian' houses survive (see p. 66). Cardiganshire is the home of the Welsh cob (p. 330) and the village is probably now best known for the **Llanarth Stud** at Blaenwern Farm. Buyers come to the October sale (where you are welcome) from far and wide.

From Llanarth B4342 leads to the coast past the pleasant **Plas-y-Wern** where Henry Tudor spent a night on his way to Bosworth. **Llanina**, where a pleasant house crumbles beside a little Victorian church on the edge of the sea ,once hammered with ship-building.

There is extensive caravan and chalet development above the cliffs between here and New Quay.

John Rennie had plans, which did not prosper, to make **New Quay** the terminal of the Union of England and Ireland Railway. It is a thoroughly likeable little resort where sailing has replaced the coastal shipping which was its life-blood. The list of harbour dues (still displayed) conjures up a picturesque trade (1 ton of ivory 2/6d; marble monument or grave slab 5/– . . .). The last ship was built in 1898 and the herring went before the war. Now there are eight fishing boats, after ground fish: skate, plaice, sole and whiting. Scallops and lobsters are big business. At £1 a pound (1973) lobsters are not eaten much locally. They go to France. The big sheds at the end of **Rock Terrace** cover the eerie lobster tanks where they are stored from a wide area; they are taken by lorry to Southend and on by air.

Rock Terrace has very pleasant stone and plastered houses, some colour-washed, most retaining their original windows. Names like Snowdon View suggest happy retirement and summer lodgers over a long period. From the old slate warehouses by the harbour (mostly converted) to the handsome Capel Annibynol (Congregational, 1860) at the top of the town, New Quay gives the impression of spick and span serenity. But it is the town that Dylan Thomas knew as a boy; New Quay, not Laugharne, is said to be the topographical background for *Under Milk Wood*.

Bird's Rock, one mile west, can be reached by the coast path (start at the end of Rock Terrace) or from inland (walk to the coastguard lookout). Not a place for sufferers from vertigo, it allows a fine view of sea-birds. The fulmars on the wing are particularly fascinating; so marvellous while airborne, so hopeless at landing, they circle in seemingly endless indecision. The nesting colonies are easiest seen from a boat.

High cliffs continue to the inhospitable but tourist-worn cove of **Cwmtudu** where a curious junk warehouse functions in what looks like a pair of semi-d's (1950s vintage). Deep wooded cwms run inland from here and Llangranog. Immediately north, a particularly spectacular stretch crowned by Pendinaslochdyn, an Iron Age fort and wonderful view point, and ending in the superb headland of **Ynys Lochtyn**, belongs to the National Trust, and is accessible.

At **Brynhoffnant Inn**, the hamlet on A487 at the turning down to Llangranog, a World War II concrete pillbox has been charmingly painted with mock windows to represent an old toll-house. Each small gun hole is camouflaged as a window-pane.

Traeth Penbryn is a lovely stretch of sand at low water but access for cars in the narrow wooded dingle is difficult. The tough little medieval bellcote church has great character and has been well restored. You enter through a seventeenth-century west porch. The nave has a slate slab floor, white walls leaning slightly out, dove-grey nineteenth-century pews, a very sturdy timber roof with cusped ties and posts and arched braces.

Half a mile south-west at 289/514, in the middle of a field, stands the **Corbalengi stone**. This is taken to be the grave of an Ordovician from North Wales and it is boldly carved in a civilized manner CORBALENGI IACIT ORDOVS; it is refreshing to come upon it unannounced. (The site was explored by a mid-Victorian clergyman from Essex who found an urn and some Roman coins.)

Aberporth, once busy with coasters, is an attractive stone village, now somewhat overwhelmed by its Ministry of Defence Establishment. Farmers from Llechryd on Teifiside used to hold an annual feast on the beach here between hay and corn harvests.

Cliffs continue west towards the Teifi. **Mwnt** (National Trust) is the most accessible place on this stretch of coast. The sandy west-facing bay has long been popular because it is possible to park near to the easy walk down. **Y foel**, the high northerly headland, is a grand viewpoint, particularly out of season when the short sward below is clear of cars, but even in August there are wide empty views, while the holiday-makers on the beach below make fascinating patterns picked out in brilliant colours like mesembrianthemum against the pale sand. This hillside was a meeting place for clergymen of Methodist leanings. Earlier, wild games had long been held here on *Sul coch y Mwnt*, the Bloody Sunday of Mwnt.

The little **Church of the Holy Cross** is sheltered under the headland. Limewashed, humble and tough, with square-headed windows, a low pointed doorway and sturdy collar-brace roof, it feels dateless. The steps led up to the fifteenth-century rood; bits of the screen itself with bold traces of paint survive. Evensong is held in the summer months and there is an annual open air service in August.

The limekiln above the bay is typical of dozens which still survive in remote creeks round the Welsh coast and a reminder of the immense importance of liming to the poor, often acid, land of the typical farm. Many date from after 1830 when, after years of parliamentary battle, the duties on coastal coal were lifted. This injustice, long abandoned in Scotland, persisted south of the border and was particularly hard on Welsh rural economy which relied to such a large extent on the services of coastal shipping. Coal and lime (unless there were handy quarries) were landed at small creeks, where there was a little sand on which to strand the vessel, and taken by cart to the nearest kiln, hence their siting close to the water. The materials were packed in layers through the hole in the top. After burning, the lime was taken out of the arched opening at the bottom. Many of the kilns are made of rough rubble and are round in plan so as to avoid the need for quoins. Lime was of course also used for building (and coal for fires) but its importance to the land became widely understood during the agricultural revolution.

Good coastline, inaccessible by road, runs on to the Teifi estuary, two miles west. For the motorist unclassified roads lead back to A487 or to Cardigan (p. 89).

INLAND, NORTH OF THE TEIFI

Inland to the south of the coast road, A487, and to the north of the Teifi valley is lovely, unspectacular hilly farm country. It is cut by steep valleys of tributary streams running down to the Teifi and others flowing more gently to the sea. It consists mostly of scattered farms and hamlets without many centres of population. Lots of minor roads run south from A487 into this country. From Brynhoffnant Inn, for instance, B4334 goes to **Rhydlewis**, one of the main villages. The post office and shop are attractive corrugated iron buildings whose gently curving verandahs give a slightly rakish mid-West or gold-rush air and are a perfect foil to the good stone cottages. In **Hawen**, immediately south, the white Congregational Chapel has handsome round-headed windows with brick arches painted grey, all set off by well-clipped juniper bushes, a good beech tree and the caretaker's spruce cottage. Inside, the galleries are supported on iron columns painted like red-black stone with leafy capitals in gold and black, and rosettes on the bases. Curlew Weavers, who recently took the mill on the Ceri (one and a half miles west) are, like other enterprising firms, making their goods known far beyond Wales. Stimulating discords are their forte.

In Cardiganshire, perhaps more than any other Welsh county, a good share of domestic architecture survives. This ranges from the vernacular stone farmhouse, basically of rubble and usually limewashed, to the small *plas* or mansion house, trim and Georgian (often an older house refronted) and a few grander Georgian houses. The Edwardians and Victorians have also left their mark, particularly in the Teifi valley; their addiction to conifers is as unexpected in that setting as their glazed red brick and plate glass, but this taste produced colours of a tonal value which is more akin to stone than those given by the recent pale 'reconstructed stone' and porridge-coloured rendering.

Humble cottages have disappeared, although overgrown ruins of these diminutive dwellings and their adjoining byre-cum-stable may be found. Most were thatched, as were bigger dwellings and even the occasional church, until slate took over in the nineteenth century. Some had distinctive wicker chimneys, though only a few survive. But there are still good cottages of the small house scale, trim with their Georgian windows and central door. The mid-Wales tradition of whitening the mortar of the joints persists in a few. But in many, new windows with horizontal emphasis, which lighten the parlour or kitchen while wrecking the elevation, reflect recent relative prosperity.

CHAPTER THREE

Teifiside to the Sea (Dyfed)
(including parts of Cardiganshire, Carmarthenshire and Pembrokeshire)

❧

From Lampeter the Teifi winds its leisurely way, thirty miles or so to the sea below Cardigan. It is surprising to find a valley in a remote part of the country so studded with gentlemen's mansion houses. The reason for this abundance is hard to fathom for there are many more houses than the country could possibly have supported. It may be that, with Cardigan so long established as a port, sea communication put Teifiside within easy reach of the rest of South Wales, Bristol and the West Country. Coal, iron, and fortunes made in the Indies, were the basis of the relatively modest prosperity of some of the pleasure-loving gentry who enjoyed this beautiful vale to the full. Many of their houses, though on older sites, were early-nineteenth-century rebuildings. H. M. Vaughan in his delightfully period piece, *South Wales Squires* (1926), says that his forebears rebuilt Plas Llangoedmor during the reign of William IV from a fortune made in Madras. Younger sons who had not inherited the family house might also build, plant their gardens with damask roses, apricot trees and peaches, and their woodlands with beech and lime. They spent their time sitting on the bench and in the saddle. It was probably with ample justification that a South Pembrokeshire squire (quoted by Vaughan) rather tartly remarked that there was an error in the Book of Genesis: 'The authentic text should have run "On the first day He created the Tivyside, and He saw that it was good" '. He was referring to the twenty-mile stretch below Llandysul where there were, in terms of social geography 'some forty or fifty country-houses, all of which were in close touch with one another. Their connecting links were the Tivyside Foxhounds and the Lawn-tennis Club at Newcastle Emlyn.'

The Foxhounds, besides being one of the oldest packs in Britain, was one of the most independent in spirit. They even hunted on the day of Queen Victoria's funeral. The Great War was to finish the way of life long enjoyed, but some of the houses have survived as

Continued on Chapter 2 map

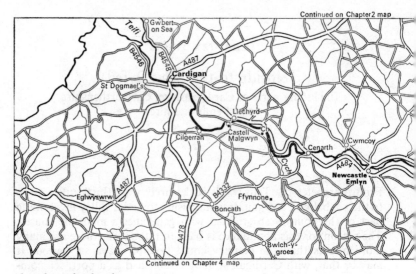

Continued on Chapter 4 map

hotels and schools.

Teifiside was also the subject of that masterpiece of accurate but poetic recording, *Welsh Country Upbringing*, which gives a very different side of the picture, that of the life in the first years of this century on one of the small farms in the valley. D. Parry-Jones lived at Llangeler, and his book, a classic of its kind, gives a close-up with eyes in sharp focus. The endurance, tolerance and resilience that combined to make possible not only a livelihood but an enjoyable life come across in the descriptions of farming and funerals, of getting stock to market, of Sunday-school outings and sermons where the Anglican parson, under the influence of the *hwyl*, might outshine the neighbouring non-conformist minister. Here is the firsthand authenticity which can only be conveyed by someone who remembers cutting the meadows at two in the morning before the dew was on the grass and the forgotten sound of the sharpening of many scythes.

The Teifi valley is closed in by low hilly country cut up into little grassy fields, and divided by the deep valleys of tiny streams. To the south these rise to a desolate block of plateau land, some moor, some forestry. To the north the hilly farmland continues up to the Vale of Aeron (p. 68).

The main Lampeter–Newcastle Emlyn road, A475, runs through highish country a few miles to the north of the Teifi. A485, and then B4336, follow the valley to its south. To explore Teifiside properly you will find yourself on the very attractive minor roads between.

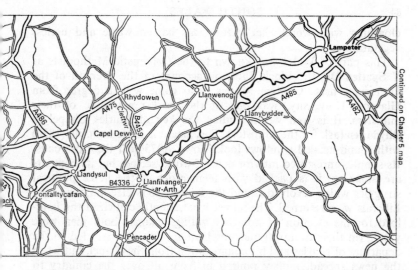

Continued on Chapter 5 map

Llanybydder is the first place of standing below Lampeter (reached direct from Lampeter by A485). Its famous horse sales take place on the last Thursday of each month when bidding officially starts at 11 a.m. Ponies take up the bulk of the business and an average of 400 are sold. Llanybydder was originally a famous sale for pit ponies and now the trekking business combined with the general popularity of children's riding ponies has once more made it busy. The village also has eight autumn sheep sales when about 40,000 change hands, fortnightly marts (Mondays), and special sales of store cattle.

Llanwenog, back across the bridge and just south of the main Lampeter–Newcastle Emlyn road, has an unusual, basically thirteenth-century church, well signposted. The big, battered tower was perhaps built by Sir Rhys ap Thomas (p. 327), whose arms are above the west door, to commemorate the victory at Bosworth in 1485 (Meyrick). It is an exciting building: through the small door under the tower, down the broad flight of five steps and into the pleasantly proportioned nave, barrel-ceiled in the eighteenth century. In the small south chapel stands a huge vigorously-carved late-Norman font which would allow for a baby's total immersion. During the Great War the Evans family of Highmead (now a school) transformed the church, adding new benches and glass. Among the memorials is one to Anne Evans (d. 1807 aged 69), who provided relief for the poor of the parish by giving them employment in 'the cultivation of an extensive tract of Land/converting into tillage and cloathing with wood/what before was barren waste and useless vegetation . . .'.

This part of Wales was known to the Calvinistic Methodists as **Y Spotten Du**, the Black Spot, on account of the strength of the Unitarians here. Gwilym Marles, who came with a degree from Glasgow University, was one of the most remarkable of their ministers. It is well worth finding the key of Marles Chapel in **Rhydowen** (ask for the Minister). This pleasant stone building (1834) with round-headed windows looks down A475 near the crossroads. Its simple, unrestored interior is itself worth seeing, but its contents are amazing: it is packed with mementoes of the fierce political struggles which revolved round the famous 1868 election, when the Liberals were returned. The minister persistently criticized the landlord for his eviction of non-tory voting tenants; both men were young (in their twenties) and unrelenting. This criticism led to the departure of Marles and his congregation from the chapel, but when the news spread, money poured in from all over the country to build the far bigger new chapel; hence the survival of the original, 'unimproved'. Besides several hundred books and unexpected relics like a bust of Lenin brought from Moscow by an Aberystwyth minister, it contains Marles's extraordinary collection of press cuttings and, in English, posters advertising the farm sales in which the tenants tauntingly describe themselves as BAD FARMERS (the reason given for their eviction).

Above the road is remote windy country where minute lanes are protected by great laburnum hedges, called locally *meillionnen spaen* (Spanish clover) – astonishing miles of lemon yellow. Laburnum field-boundaries are widespread in parts of West Wales; no explanation has been discovered.

From Rhydowen, B4459 follows the Cletwr valley which runs secretively south to the Teifi through **Capel Dewi** where the large Wesleyan chapel (1891) replaces the earlier Capel Enock (1832). Graves in this burial ground are unusual: the outline of a coffin formed in slate on edge and the space inside decorated with pebbles. Whole families are thus commemorated with pathetically small 'coffins' for their infants.

Woollen mills were a great feature in the Teifi valley between 1860–1920 when it became the main weaving area of Wales. Weaving by water-power was first introduced about 1860 and by the turn of the century it was said that there was 'hardly a spot on any stream where it would be convenient to build another mill'. Flannel was the main product; it went to industrial South Wales where flannel shirts were worn to keep off the heat in the tin-plate works. The reasons for this sudden surge of industry are not clear. Newtown's industrial troubles (*North Wales*, p. 293) were one factor. The existing links between Teifiside and industrial South Wales were probably another. It was not uncommon for a son of a Teifiside farm to go and set up a small shop in a Monmouthshire valley to provide an outlet for farm produce. It was a small step from selling butter and bacon, to selling flannel. The coming of the railway was a deciding factor. The Great War gave a boost to the mills but the slump, and in particular the miners' strike and the depression, were the death knell. A new lease of life for some of the mills has been brought about by the present popularity of Welsh woollens.

In Capel Dewi the **Rock Mills** (1894) still spin and card by water power; like other mills Rock have a shop on the premises. Downstream, a little above the Cletwr's junction with the main river, a fish-hatchery, at times open to the public (often Sunday afternoons), has been established. The Teifi is one of the best sewin (sea-trout) rivers in Wales.

Llanfihangel-ar-Arth, a name tamed by English-speaking evacuee children of the Second World War to Laughing-angel-on-earth, is the parish of the Fasting Girl, Sarah Jacob, who is buried near her family on the far side of the churchyard. She died in December 1869, aged thirteen. It is said that she had not eaten for many months and it was rumoured that her parents, who farmed at Lletherneuadd-uchaf, were doing nicely from the curiosity she aroused. Trainloads of sightseers alighted at Pencader to be met by boys wearing signs TO THE FASTING GIRL. Her parents were tried and committed to Carmarthen gaol after her death, which had followed a strict watch on the household in which nurses sent from Guy's Hospital took part. A particularly sympathetic account of the tragedy is given in *My Own Folk* by D. Parry-Jones.

Pencader, two miles south on the Carmarthen road, is where the great Lord Rhys paid the traditional homage to Henry II. It was here that the old man, on being questioned by the king on the long-term prospects, gave his famous reply, which has been translated: 'This nation may suffer defeat and be weakened by your powers, but neither our nation nor its language can be totally destroyed by the wrath of man unless the wrath of God shall concur.' The quotation in Welsh is inscribed on a slab in the village. The castle motte survives. Pencader was the southern end of the grandiosely-named Manchester and Milford Railway, which ran for 41 miles between here and Aberystwyth. It was built in 1865–7: the idea was to link the manufacturing towns of Lancashire with Milford Haven.

A pastoral stretch of the Teifi between steep wooded banks winds down to Llandysul, once an important weaving centre and still a humming small town. The widely-known Gomer Press thrives here. A surprising number of small presses were set up in nineteenth-century Wales, chiefly to publish the independent newspapers and Welsh literature which resulted from the integration in Welsh life of the nonconformist movement, education and liberal politics.

St Tysul's Church, down by the river, is an ancient foundation; the saint is believed to have been a cousin of David. The present building dates from the thirteenth century, including the handsome tower to which additions were made up to the late fifteenth century. The roof was thatched until 1783. The plan, a nave with side aisles and chancel, is not so common in Wales. Stones of great antiquity have been brought into the church. The grand ancient altar stone incised with cross patterns, found locally, is now the altar stone in the Lady Chapel. Also in this chapel is a crucifixion with the Virgin Mary and St John (this was on the west face of the tower). The Velvor stone, built into the north wall, is part of a memorial slab.

12 January, New Year's Day of the *Calan Hen*, or old calendar, is celebrated here on the nearest Sunday to it by a Sunday School Festival (a singing contest and catechism) for the neighbourhood. It was introduced to replace the New Year football match – the goals were the church towers of Llandysul and Llanwenog, five miles apart. This had developed into a bloody inter-parish brawl (see Mwnt). Llandysul's other sporting activity, a summer evening affair, is quoits (made of iron). The game is played as far south as Abergorlech, which also boasts a crack team.

The Teifi is handsomely bridged at Pontalltycafan (386/393), a huge single span for the river and a small rabbit hole in its footings for the railway which served the woollen mills (1885). The lovely valleys winding south are also haunted with ruins of the industry. The Cambrian Mill (352/391) below Drefach is working: the Welsh Folk Museum plans an outpost here.

A484 runs close to the water in one or two beautifully wooded reaches between here and Newcastle Emlyn; a riverside path runs upstream from the bridge near Henllan. Off A475, there is access to its north bank in a small field opposite the castle, shortly before you reach the town. See below. Also on the north of the Teifi, Felingeri, a corn mill grinding by water-power, is open to visitors. Take B4333 towards Cardigan and turn right short of Cwmcoy. Flour is on sale

Newcastle Emlyn is a thoroughly likeable small town which serves
a big area. It is at its best on Fridays, bustling with the business of
the sheep and cattle market, when the bar of the Emlyn Arms belongs
to prosperous farmers. It has few architectural pretensions except
perhaps in Church Lane where an upstanding chapel faces an outsize
lion and unicorn which adorn the courtroom. This may be taken
over by woolly-clad babies since it also serves as a clinic. The 1840s
church (J. L. Collard; enlarged W. D. Caröe) is very much more
impressive inside than out, spacious and simple with good use of
slate (including local Cilgerran): slab floors, pillars supporting an
open roof, and a modern font.

The **Castle** is reached by a small turning off the main street. It has
a lovely site; not spectacular, being lowish, but in a huge loop of
the river. The new castle was built here in 1240 by a grandson of the
Lord Rhys who was granted it by the Norman earls of Pembroke.
Sir Rhys Thomas found the place so attractive that he rebuilt it in
early Tudor times as a country seat. Its ruins make a lovely picnic
place. The river is fascinating here. Remnants of a dam which was
constructed to divert water into the mill-leet which skirts the castle
mound survive, as does the much later salmon leap (1880). The shell
of the mill is by the new Roman Catholic church. In 1908 it was
converted into an electric power station by Mr J. R. Parkington who
supplied the town's electricity until 1923, when it was sold to the
West Cambrian Electrical Company and Mr Parkington went on to
power Fishguard.

The next bridge is three miles down at **Cenarth**, a fine double-
arched structure, by the famous falls and salmon leap (there were
traps here too). It has long been a tourist attraction and deservedly
so. The corn mill, upstream on the left bank, is working (usually
early in the week; flour can be bought at the post office which is
generally open). Cenarth is still a centre for coracle fishermen
(regatta in August), but their survival is precarious. The coracles, like
shallow baskets the shape of half walnut shells, are covered with
calico impregnated with pitch. Each fisherman makes his own; it
takes about a day. Coracles must work in twos, the net being stretched
between the craft. When the end of the beat is reached the fishermen
carry the coracles on their backs upstream. To come up behind
these huge wet black shells moving through the trees on the river
bank is a primeval experience of the first order.

The Cych, a marvellous stream, runs down its long narrow oak
valley from the south – rather melancholy now the woollen factories
have ceased production. Nash's **Ffynnone**, above its tributary the

Dulas, commands grand views south from whence you can enjoy it
from the Bwlch-y-groes road. It was built in the 1790s by John
Colby (who also planted the extensive woodlands) as a square house
with four pediments. The two short wings were added in the 1820s
'in the Greek style', and the house was ably enlarged and altered in
1902–7 by Inigo Thomas, who was certainly not lacking in confidence
and replaced most of Nash's detail. Ffynnone is a house of exceptional
charm. Nash's exciting sequence of spaces (his stair survives) was
continued by Thomas.

St David's, one and a half miles south of Llechryd, the cheerful
1898 church (Prothero and Phillott) with Byzantine-inspired font
and pulpit (from the private chapel at Pentre), is almost a memorial
to the Colbys. It was built to replace **Manordeifi Church** on the river
bank below. Manordeifi is remarkable for its charming nineteenth-
century fittings. The box pews have fireplaces, the windows have
chiefly Georgian glazing, and there is a monument to Captain
Charles Colby of the 98th Regiment and Ffynnone who died at
Rawalpindi after an altercation with a tiger (1852).

A curious 'canal' ran from a weir below the church to Sir Benjamin
Hammet's tinplate works, at **Castell Malgwyn, Llechryd**, one mile
downstream. It was a leet, to provide water-power. The bridge
over it, beside the gates of Castell Malgwyn Hotel, has cast iron
plaques, bearing the name, the date (1799), and a castle and crossed
cannon. Remains of the works can be seen near the river beyond the
interesting Jacobean stable courtyard (1848). There are also extensive
remains of a fish trap here, originally owned by the monks and then
the squire. It was destroyed by the Cenarth fishermen during the
Rebecca Riots. The Teifi is spanned at Llechryd by a low five-arched
buttressed bridge.

Cilgerran, a couple of miles downstream, holds a cheerful coracle
regatta in late August. **Cilgerran Castle** (National Trust in DoE
guardianship), although the village is built hard against it, is out of
sight. Cars should be parked in the village; walk down the short
lane on the right towards the bottom of the street. This fine ruin,
perched high above the steep wooded banks of the Teifi, was a high-
light of the picturesque tour, although a little too remote to be in
everyone's sketch-book. Turner, however, recorded it (1799), as
did many lesser tourists (mostly describing it as Kilkerran), who had
a much more exciting view than most do, arriving as they did by
boat from Cardigan. The trip has recently been revived (from St
Dogmael's) and runs at high spring tides only.

Cilgerran was probably first defended by the Normans around

1100 and it often changed hands. In 1223 it was recaptured by William Marshal, whose father was still building Pembroke. He was almost certainly responsible for most of what is now to be seen: the two big towers, the gatehouse and associated curtain walls. At Cilgerran the young William Marshal placed the towers in the angles of the curtain wall instead of building one free-standing keep within the inner bailey, as his father had done at Pembroke. This was a comparative innovation in castle building, which was to be carried to perfection when Edward I built Beaumaris, seventy years on.

The gate-posts at the modern entrance (which is on the line of the ditch of the outer ward) are the village war memorial. The quotation: 'Come from the four winds, O breath, and breathe upon these slain, that they may live' is a sharp reminder, too, of the castle's hey-day. The river-bank path is very attractive: downstream it is overgrown. Take the track to the right of the castle gate between the cottages and past the stonecrop-ornamented spoil from the slate quarries which, with the salmon and sewin fishing, were for long Cilgerran's *raison d'être*. George Owen described the King's Weir, which was below the Castle, as 'the greatest weare in all Wales . . . where there have been often times taken a hundred or a hundred and forty [fish] in some days'.

St Llawdog's Church is 1855 with a medieval tower. For a record of a remarkably eventful, useful but short life see the tablet to Griffith Griffith (d. 1822) inside near the door. A combine harvester and tractor are depicted in its stained glass (south aisle).

Cardigan, at the lowest crossing of the Teifi, owes its importance to the bridge and to the busy port. The handsome warehouses down by the long five-arched bridge are a reminder of that bustle to which silting as well as railways put an end. Shipping had declined by the 1830s, but Lewis refers to vast hosts of coracles on the river. The Norman **Castle** which guarded the crossing (now a leafy ruin) was a rebuilding by Gilbert Marshal (another son of the Earl of Pembroke); it was finally dismantled by Cromwell's troops. The first eisteddfod in Wales is believed to have been held here by the Lord Rhys in 1176 (but see *North Wales*, p. 45).

All this can be glimpsed on the way into Cardigan from the south. Abandon the car as soon as possible; there is a big car park behind the Guildhall in the High Street. Despite Cardigan's much longer history the High Street has a Victorian flavour and reflects the predictions of the reporter in the *Builder* (1856) that the town was 'fast emerging from its primitive state'. Gas was about to be introduced

and R. J. Withers appointed architect to the Corporation. A water
supply, in iron pipes, had been laid down in 1831.

Saturday is market day and it is well worth being there both to
shop and to see Withers' astonishing covered market under his
Guildhall (1858). Here he is at his most inventive and accomplished.
The two lower floors consist of an arcaded market supported on
stone columns with boldly detailed arches in cream stone and slate
with red header bricks, reminiscent of a Moorish mosque (Cordoba?);
recently restored by the local council.

The narrow **High Street** which runs into Pendre Street is slightly
curved and has a nice medley of buildings which include Tudor
terracotta work, the pink Tabernacle Chapel, the Black Lion Hotel,
Woolworths, and much plate glass below Georgian and Victorian
houses (an Art Nouveau shop front survives).

St Mary Street runs east towards the church off the High Street.
The old **Customs House**, a respectable pedimented building in
Cilgerran slate, is now offices. St Mary Street continues, past the
confident Angel Hotel (Victorian/Georgian facade with bold labels
over the windows and pillared porch) to **Finch's Square,** opposite
the church, where the little Lamb Inn in a row of much humbler
dwellings is in marked contrast both to the Angel and the pleasant
Georgian houses towards the Strand, probably built by retired sea
captains. **St Mary's Church** has a lovely site on the river bank.
Recently many of the graves have been swept to the side and stand
resignedly against the wall. Here, finely engraved on slate, is commemorated the humming life of the port: master mariners, customs
officers, publicans and merchants.

The church has a fourteenth-century chancel which was later embattled and pinnacled; a nave rebuilt 1702–3 with some simple
square-headed stone-mullioned windows; a boldly buttressed west
tower rebuilt having collapsed only two years after the rebuilding of
the nave; and a south porch of the early seventeenth century with an
ogee-arched doorway.

Restorers who include R. J. Withers and W. D. Caröe have dealt
kindly with the building. Inside it is grandly spacious and uncluttered.
The fine perpendicular east window has remnants of its medieval
glass at the very top (the rest is twentieth century). Some of the fine
carving with which the Tudors embellished the church survives: the
octagonal font; two stone corbels with grimacing faces, and an
ornate piscina (note the rose through which it drains) in the chancel.

The Priory, next to the church, was one of the oldest buildings in
the town. Cardigan was the shrine of Our Lady with the Taper

(compare with the devotion at Arras) and it was a great place of pilgrimage. After the Reformation the Benedictine priory became a private house; at one time 'the matchless Orinda' (Katherine Fowler, 1631–64), the young poet so named by her admirers who included John Evelyn, lived here after marriage to James Philipps, later High Sheriff. In the 1790s the house was remodelled for Thomas Johnes of Hafod (p. 62) by John Nash (who built Cardigan gaol, now demolished, at this time). It was later converted into the Cottage Hospital but the late eighteenth-century Gothic can be seen in the windows, the front door and the pretty stair with its inlaid handrail.

Bethania Chapel (1848) in William Street is a building of unusual pretensions in chapel architecture with its Doric portico and other neo-classic touches. Aberystwyth Road (A487) runs north out of Cardigan past bay windows and iron railings and the Victorian Gardens with their gay little baby bandstand, and the new Roman Catholic Church. B4548 leads north to Gwbert-on-Sea, which has a huge hotel, golf links and holiday bungalows.

Downstream from Cardigan bridge the river banks are secret from B4546, the road on the left bank which leads to **St Dogmael's**. Big trees make you forget the sea is close. But the houses have a seaside air about them; more retired captains have dropped anchor here. The **Abbey** (DoE), left before the bridge, was founded in 1115 on the site of a Celtic *clas* by twelve monks and a prior from Tiron in France, on invitation from the Norman Lord of Cemais. The first church and monastic buildings were laid out during the first half of the twelfth century, an amazing enterprise from such small beginnings. This had an aisled nave, apsidal east end and transept chapels, but was never finished. A hundred years later saw a great period of activity, a new presbytery with a crypt to the east, remodelling of the transepts and the building of the aisleless nave. In the early fourteenth century the west end of the nave was rebuilt, including the fine doorway with ball-flower ornament in the north wall. In the early sixteenth century the north transept was rebuilt with stone vaulting and big diagonal buttresses, probably as a chapel. The remaining corbels from which the vaulting sprang represent St Matthew (north-east), St Mark (north-west); the Archangel Michael (centre west); the eagle of St John (now displayed in the lean-to) fell here. The view from this chapel, up the valley, is of terraced cottages at different angles and levels with a bracken slope above. There are also lovely views from the green cloister down, across the ruins, to the river. Besides the late medieval tiles which survive under the crossing and the carvings stored for safe-keeping in the lean-to, various stones which have been housed in the parish church (A. Ashpitel, 1859), adjoining the site, are worth seeing.

The grassy bank in front of the Tivy Inn gives a closer view of the river. Here the fishermen meet and draw lots for the all important beats which for generations have regulated fishing on the Teifi. Downstream the estuary widens before narrowing again at the awkward entrance. Cardigan Island, uninhabited, off the opposite point, is grazed by a herd of Soay sheep, introduced by the West Wales Field Society.

On the Pembrokeshire side the road ends in a big caravan site near the ever-popular Poppit Sands visited by generations of Sunday School outings.[1]

[1] *Give me yesterday*, James Williams, the Gomer Press 1971, gives a delightful description of one such outing.

CHAPTER FOUR

Pembrokeshire (Dyfed)

❦

As Cornwall is to England so Pembrokeshire is to Wales. It lies in the far south-west with the sea on three sides and this remoteness, coupled with its strong links with Ireland, made it an enchanted country in the minds of the legend makers. Most of the stories in the *Mabinogion* took place here in Dyfed, or have some strong connection with it.

It is impossible to stand more than eight miles from salt water anywhere in Pembrokeshire, for the tide runs up Milford Haven and on far up the Cleddau estuaries. That unprovincial consciousness of the outside world which is often found among seafaring people may manifest itself in the name of a bungalow or small-holder's cottage: St Helena or Constantinople.

The gales in the west are tremendous, but the climate is such that optimists leave geraniums out all the year and pessimists say they will have to mow their lawns on Boxing Day. Trees near the coast are rare and even inland a salt-laden summer gale may scorch their leaves, bringing autumn overnight. Near the sea few farms are without their shelter belt of sycamore cut to a wedge shape by the prevailing wind. The north and south of the county are quite different. The name generally given to Pembrokeshire, 'Little England beyond Wales', applies to the southern part. The north is Welsh and always has been except for pockets of Scandinavian settlement like Goodwick next to Fishguard (port for the Irish boats), or small Norman outposts like Newport. The reason for this division probably dates from the Danish raids up Milford Haven. The dividing line between the Welsh and the English is roughly at the limit of Danish penetration. This linguistic divide is known as the Landsker. The Normans, after they had gained control of the Haven by building the mighty castle at Pembroke, eventually built a line of castles along the Welsh-Danish 'line'. The most conspicuous of these today is Roch, not far from the coastline of St Brides Bay. Camrose, Wiston, Llawhaden, Narberth and Amroth completed the chain to the south coast. Even so, the division might not have remained so

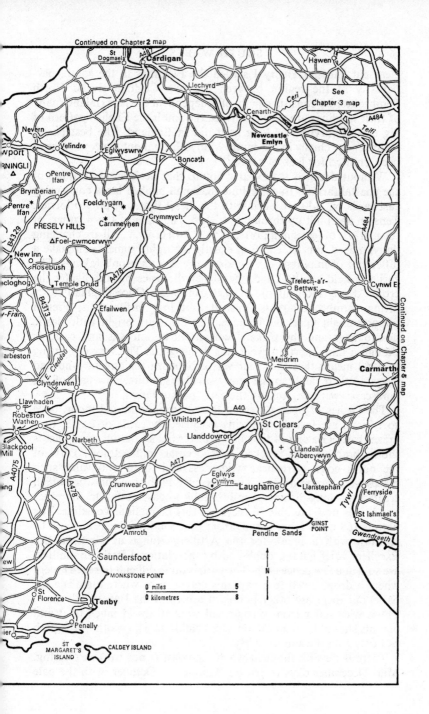

St Dogmael's   **Cardigan**   Hawen

Llechyrd

Ceri   See Chapter 3 map

Cenarth   A484

Teifi

Nevern   **Newcastle Emlyn**

wport   Velindre   Eglwyswrw   Boncath

RNINGLI   △

Pentre Ifan

Brynberian

Pentre * Ifan   Foeldrygarn *

PRESELY HILLS   * Carnmeynen   Crymmych

△Foel-cwmcerwyn   Cynwl E

Trelech-a'r-Bettws

New Inn

Rosebush   A478

cloghog   Temple Druid   A40
75

Fran   Efailwen

arbeston   Meidrim   **Carmarth**

E. Cleddau

Clynderwen

Llawhaden

Robeston Wathen   A40   Whitland   St Clears

Blackpool Mill   Narbeth   Llanddowror   Llandeilo Abercywyn

Crunwear   Eglwys Cymyn   **Laugharne**   Llanstephan   Ferryside

Amroth   Pendine Sands   GINST POINT   St Ishmael's

Gwendraeth

Saundersfoot   Tywi

MONKSTONE POINT

| 0 miles | | | | 5 |
| 0 kilometres | | | | 8 |

St Florence   **Tenby**   N

Penally

ier

ST MARGARET'S ISLAND   CALDEY ISLAND

Continued on Chapter 5 map

clear cut had not Henry I settled the Flemings in the south, particularly in the region between the two Cleddau rivers. North
Pembrokeshire consists chiefly of independent farmers (inland many
of their holdings are very small). In the south the English pattern of
big estates survived as long as it did in England. The best parish
churches are chiefly in the south. Many, throughout the county, have
been omitted for lack of space.

Without doubt it is the early potato that decides the fortunes of
the coastal farmer. In early June the small banked lanes converging
eastwards on A40 are filled with the diesel fumes of potato lorries.
Tension has built up throughout May. The state of the weather, of
the market, of foreign imports, of your own crop . . . All are changing
daily, indeed hourly. To lift at exactly the right moment can make a
difference of hundreds of pounds in the short season's takings. The
earlier a field can be lifted, the higher the price but the lighter the
crop. At any moment the market can crash. Once England starts
lifting, Pembrokeshire is finished, but long before this, French
imports might upset the balance. The fields are bright with plastic
potato bags and the pickers' cotton shirts, anoraks and cars, as
though a mini-sporting event was in progress. The very dry spring
of 1962 meant that that year was a bonanza for anyone who had
irrigated their land, so the many small reservoirs, now part of the
landscape, were dug out on the early-potato farms.

The flashes of open water on the common land and moor, once
so typical, are fast disappearing because few cattle or horses now
graze there. Grazing of the cliffs is also rare, so that in many places
thorn, bramble and bracken have become impenetrable. Parts of
the north coast were near wilderness and those who value such
places were incensed when it was recently cut by the bulldozer which
created the long-distance Pembrokeshire coast path. On the other
hand, it is now possible to reach all this marvellous coastline. The
path is 168 miles long. It runs from the mouth of the Teifi south to
Amroth with a break for the Artillery Range at Castlemartin.
Excellent brief guides, published by the National Park Committee,
are sold at a few pence each. The path is quite difficult to reach except
where it drops down to a bay (this may also be where there is a car
park) but there are other points of access as the leaflets will show.
Those who suffer from vertigo will want to avoid much of it and
parents should keep an eye on small children. The width of the path
can create an illusion of safety.

There is never a moment when the coast is not worth exploring.
Mild December days or tearing March . . . October, with the pale

A Cardiganshire cottage. The white-painted joints are a local tradition.

Mwnt Church, on the Cardiganshire coast.

Cilgerran Castle on the River Teifi. This painting, by J.M.W. Turner. hangs in Wordsworth House, Cockermouth.

The spectacularly-sited Carreg Cennen castle, south-east of Llandeilo.

grasses and fading heather seen through a filter of evening mist, is the best time to see young seals; it has a sun-soaked stillness that is almost melancholy, perhaps because there are no trees to burn fire into the landscape.

Towards the end of May and in the first half of June flowers carpet the cliffs in tens of thousands. Constant pruning by the south-westerlies makes those that survive exceptionally strong. Sea pink, often seen against the brilliant orange lichen, and white campion seem unaffected by the salt spray; bluebells thrive (notably on Skomer); honeysuckle sometimes makes a dense mat about a foot high on a little offshore island; the clear blue of vernal squill transforms the green turf. Yellow ladies fingers, moon daisies, primroses, oxlips, cowslips, early foxglove . . . and everywhere brilliant yellow gorse with its coconut smell. All this against the ever-changing sky and sea and the curious folds and contortions of the rocks.

The generally level plateau of Pembrokeshire farmland was once the sea bed, a great shelf of sedimentary rock through which the very hard pre-Cambrian thrust in some colossal eruption. Those ancient-looking hills along the north coast, Garn Fawr, Penberi, Carn Llidi and others are among the oldest rocks in the world and were once islands in this primeval sea.

The south coast is quite different. A sudden change from the sandstone to white limestone cliffs which drop from lawn-like cliff tops into an often Mediterranean sea and, beyond Tenby and Saundersfoot, sheltered woodland utterly foreign to the hard north.

THE TEIFI ESTUARY TO ST ANN'S HEAD

The coastal path cuts off Cemaes Head and runs south down a fine stretch of cliff to Newport Bay. The main road south (A487) drops into the sheltered wooded valley of the Nyfer after Eglwyswrw, once an important centre for drovers. In the hamlet of **Velindre** the stone building with two mullioned windows, hard by the road, was built as a school by George Owen, the seventeenth-century Lord Marcher and historian.

Nevern Church, half a mile north off A487, is sheltered in a snug valley beside its trout stream (the Nyfer). It was founded by St Brynach (p. 43) who lived a hermit's life on Carningli (p. 98) where, as might be expected from its name, angels saw to his needs. A fifteenth-century tower, battlemented and low, juts above the Irish yews (one bleeds), from the west end of what is now a basically fifteenth-century cruciform church which is one of R. J. Withers's best restorations (1863). Its interesting details include several memorial tablets and, in the south chapel, an Ogam stone (fifth century?) and a stone carved with a curious cross believed to be tenth century. Outside to the south is a great Celtic cross, probably *c.* 1000, one of the best in Wales, and up the sloping graveyard behind there are some finely cut slate tombs, with touching epitaphs.

Up the road at the hairpin bend, along a short path, is a Cross carved in the rough rock face: a station on the pilgrim's road to St Davids. Follow the road up a little further for **Nevern Castle** on the bluff above the church, now much overgrown. The Lord Rhys (p. 327) built a stone tower here when the Normans retired to Newport.

Pentre Ifan Burial Chamber (*c.* 2000 BC) is on the northern edge of the Preselis, two miles south of Nevern (099/370). Look out for the sign on A487 opposite the Nevern turning. This is one of the most spectacular cromlechs in Britain and has a splendid site with the sheltering hills behind, looking out over the Irish Sea, that wild highway which brought this civilization, with its knowledge of farming and thus the possibility of a relatively settled life, whence time to build and ponder. The giant capstone (approaching 17 × 10 feet) rests on three high pillars (one with pin-point support) in a roughly crescent-shaped forecourt. The fourth stone is a portal. The cromlech stands towards the end of a long barrow (*c.* 130 × 60 feet).

Two miles west of Pentre Ifan, crowning **Carningli**, are the extensive remains of a fortified Iron Age village whose walls surround the summit; hut circles and pounds abound. The easiest walk up is from the east (inland). Find your way by the small hilly lanes or turn left off A487 on entering Newport. But for a summer evening's picnic it would be hard to beat the mountain road to the west with its superb views over the vast sands of Newport Bay bounded by Dinas Head below you.

Newport, no longer a port, is an attractive, compact little town often gay with pennants across its narrow main street. It was founded by the Normans and its bounds are beaten annually by the Lady Marcher, the Mayor and the county's MP, mounted on ponies. It is dominated by the Norman castle (1191) whose gatehouse is now a private house (1859 restoration). The church, which was thoroughly restored twenty years later (John Middleton), still has its bold buttressed medieval tower with a fine weathercock. It is unusual in having twin-aisled transepts. **Addoldy y Bedyddwyr** (1789, 1817 and 1855), the Baptist chapel above the main street has very prettily glazed

Gothic windows. Within is a three-sided balcony supported on grey 'stone' painted columns with a recent pulpit and elders' pew. The modern baptismal pool is up Mill Lane above the mill.

Newport has pleasant small houses, the Castle Hotel, and one or two good shop fronts (notably the butcher, T. Glyn Davies and Son), spick and span with brown and black paint and buff which looks like gold. Newport bar was always dangerous to shipping and little remains of the quay at Parrog, once busy with the usual coastal trade. Surprisingly, a fine cromlech survives immediately behind the bungalows (opposite Cromlech House) at the east edge of the town off the road for Newport Sands. The road then crosses the Nyfer (reed-beds and heron). For the vast sands at the mouth of the river, keep left and aim towards the golf course.

Dinas, on the main road, has a particularly handsome chapel, Tabor. Dinas Island, the peninsula ending in Dinas Head, separates the two big bays of Newport and Fishguard: it has great cliffs and huge well-drained fields and is almost cut off by a deep valley from the mainland and its accessible bays, Pwllgwaelod (west) and Cwm-yr-eglwys (east) are very popular in summer. The remains of St Brynach's church stand by the shore at Cwm-yr-eglwys (most went in a great autumn gale in 1859). The turning from Dinas goes through Brynhenllan, a refreshingly unspoilt hamlet.

Good cliffs with a few small bays run west to **Fishguard** (Abergwaun), a most likeable small town. The lay-by (off the Cardigan road), at the top of the hill, just before you drop down into the lower town, is a good place to pause, particularly at dusk when you can see the lights of the Rosslare (Eire) boat moored on the far side of the bay against the quay at Goodwick. The late-eighteenth-century fort is five minutes' stroll along the cliff path from the lay-by. Immediately below is the old town and harbour at the mouth of the long, wooded Gwaun valley.

Richard Fenton, the barrister, who is best remembered for his early-nineteenth-century topographical books, lived at **Plas Gynmel**, a pleasant house of that date (now a guest-house) near the mouth of the valley, just upstream beyond the nice stone cottages. The well-lettered signboard in nonsensical Latin which has been fixed to the cottage near the gate presumably came from an inn; possibly found by Fenton on his travels. The lovely Gwaun valley is reached by B4313 from the middle of the town, and recommended out of season.

In the small Square in (upper) Fishguard the simple pedimented **Market Hall**, brought to life by sensitive painting in greys and whites in 1972, houses the National Park Information Centre and, on Thursdays, an excellent market. The produce stalls – farm butter, bacon, faggots, laver bread – are famous. In the entrance, Fishguard's seafaring life is enshrined in the records of lifeboat rescues: schooners, brigantines and smacks, and in the quayside portrait of the *Gwain Maid* of Fishguard, 119 tons, with Vesuvius in the background.

Opposite, the diminutive **Royal Oak Inn**, with its traditional grouted roof (see *North Wales*, p. 195), freshly-painted dormer windows and bold lettering, shows just how good khaki rendering can look. Here the treaty following the last invasion of Britain, 1797 (see below) was signed. **Hermon Baptist Chapel** (1776–1832) is the handsomest building in Fishguard. It stands opposite Bennett's Wine Store a few yards along High Street (A40) just where it is perfectly punctuated by bosky horsechestnut. The chapel has a grand portico of marbled columns and, inside, is well galleried and has a pretty pulpit.

Fishguard Festival is now an established musical event thanks largely to John Davies, the music master of the Comprehensive School who has recently created the Dyfed Choir (choirs are now less common in Wales).

Goodwick made a bid for the Atlantic trade at the beginning of the century, Fishguard Harbour station being opened in 1906 (a school holiday celebrated the arrival of the *Mauretania* in 1909). Unfortunately passengers had to come ashore by lighter and the new breakwater constructed in 1913 caused silting in the harbour, so Fishguard has had to content herself with the Irish traffic. Now a drive-on car ferry operates and Eire coinage is acceptable as far away as St Davids.

For grandeur, the north Pembrokeshire coast from Fishguard Bay, round mighty Strumble Head, and right on to the tip of St Davids Head would be hard to beat. Much of it can have changed little since the unfortunate Frenchmen under an American, Colonel Tate, landed at Carregwastad near **Llanwnda** (take the minor road north from Goodwick). Fenton, whose baby was with a wet nurse in a near-by cottage, described the event in some detail. Tuesday, 20 February 1797, was 'the finest day ever remembered at such a season . . . three large vessels were discovered standing in from the channel . . . which the inhabitants at first imagined to be Liverpool merchantmen becalmed'. Then, 'boats were seen putting off from their sides full of men, followed by others manned alike, in such rapid succession, as to leave no doubt of their being an enemy'. But, as Fenton realistically pointed out, '. . . fear, and love of the marvellous, magnified their hundreds into thousands'. Fortunately the invaders, who were convicts with no particular stomach for war, were soon enjoying generous supplies of wine which had recently been washed up from a wreck, so they were in no state to greet the arrival of the Pembrokeshire Militia.

Llanwnda is an attractive farm hamlet with a simple double bellcote church, rebuilt in 1881 (E. H. Lingen Barker); stones incised with ancient crosses are built into the outside wall of the chancel. The parish abounds in prehistoric remains.

Strumble Head Lighthouse was built in 1908 when harbour works were going on at Goodwick. High above you can see the vapour trails of trans-Atlantic aircraft which navigate on a transmitter here. It is reached by a footbridge, but the car park is a good viewpoint for the carbound as is that at **Garn Fawr**, the Iron Age fort which crowns the headland one and a half miles due south of the lighthouse. The fort has three widely spaced ramparts.

Grey Atlantic seals breed in the small shingly bays, mostly inaccessible, right down the coast. October is the best month for watching the calves and **Pwllderi**, just beyond the Youth Hostel on the west of Strumble below Garn Fawr, a good place. Wooded cwms run down to Aber Mawr and Aber Bach (good bays); a wool mill thrives at Tregwynt.

Mathry, a no-nonsense village, crowns the hill just off the Fishguard–St Davids road, surprisingly braving the gales instead of seeking shelter. Sloops traded from **Abercastle** just below to Bristol in Fenton's day. Of several cromlechs in this area that at **Longhouse Farm** (848/335) to the west of the bay is particularly good (c. 3000 BC), and **Castell Coch**, an Iron Age promontory fort, has a splendid site to the north-west of the farmhouse. **Croes-goch** on the main road has a striking Baptist chapel with an unusual plastered Gothicized front. John Knapp-Fisher, the landscape painter, has a gallery opposite.

Porth Gain is the only harbour on the whole of this inhospitable coast and it is as tiny as it is fascinating. The ruined stone buildings belonged to a brickworks which thrived at the turn of the century, and to the roadstone company whose giant hoppers survive to the left of the harbour. A tunnel runs through the cliff to the quarry behind and the lines of old railways can easily be followed to the quarries on the headland. Others connected the harbour with the slate quarry at Abereiddy (see p. 102). The first harbour was constructed in the 1860s; it was improved 1902–4 and a special fleet of

six 350-ton steamers was built but the last shipment of stone sailed
away in 1931. The Sloop Inn has old photographs of the harbour. A
very attractive row of cottages, traditionally painted with yellow
ochre in the limewash, are perhaps the only ones thus coloured in the
county.

The headland of Barry Island, a rich early potato farm, separates
Porth Gain from another fascinating abandoned settlement, **Abereiddy**. Here slate was quarried from the shaley rock (note the walls
built of it, with slates often laid vertically or herring bone). Eventually the quarry was opened to the sea making a deep harbour with an
awkward entrance. Traethllwyn, the sandy west-facing bay which
bites into the headland, is particularly good for bathing.

Between here and St Davids Head, two hills, Penberi and Carn
Llidi, give the coastline a monumental silhouette out of all proportion
to their height (under 600 feet). Ffos-y-mynach (the monk's ditch),
probably a boundary of the lordship of St Davids, cuts the headland just west of Penberi (see O.S. map).

ST DAVIDS

Kilvert (p. 322) arrived in St Davids in October 1871 (a good month
to choose). 'And so we came to the end of the world where the
Patron Saint of Wales sleeps by the Western sea', he wrote in his
diary, with all the satisfaction of one who has travelled as far as is
possible.

It was until recently a quiet grey village, but is now humming with
much new development. The heart has plenty of character but it is
strained by tourism in high season. The National Park Information
Office in the City Hall (High Street) has a lot of local material.

ST DAVIDS CATHEDRAL AND CLOSE

The best approach to the Cathedral (see plans pp. 104 and 108) is on
foot from the High Street. The sea and the rocky outcrops jutting
from the carefully farmed, gale-swept country are the backdrop;
plain houses and shops lining the street and the sloping Cross Square
(a triangle), whose medieval cross acts as an outrider proclaiming
what is to come, are your immediate surroundings. The big cathedral
tower hoves into view through the narrow gap in the buildings ahead,
its pinnacles, surprisingly, near eye-level. The small street through
the gap, the Pebbles, flanks the steep valley, in which the astonishing
Close (see plan, p. 104) is hidden. It leads straight to Porth-y-twr, the

landward gate for travellers arriving by road from the east. This is the only one of four to survive in the long medieval wall which protects the last rustic eighteenth-century-seeming cathedral close left in Britain. Black cattle and white geese graze the rough valley sides which drop steeply down to the stream in the bosky valley bottom. Big trees give it the special character of an oasis, in contrast to the windswept country above. The houses, mostly close to the sites of their medieval predecessors, are of varying dates and most certainly have very old foundations; most now are nineteenth century and have a very pleasant Georgian look (Kilvert found them disappointing 'plain rectangles'). Valerian grows in the walls which hide secret gardens.

William the Conqueror came to St Davids in 1081. There was no building here for which a Norman would spare a glance, but the importance and force of the ideas enshrined for over five hundred years at St Davids would not have escaped such an administrator. The Celtic church, both its Latin scholars and holy men, needed to be thoroughly Normanized and brought into the Province of Canterbury. This was not actually achieved until the death of Bishop Wilfred, in 1115, when the Celtic monks were summoned to London and forced to elect Bernard, Chancellor of Queen Matilda, as their bishop. The cathedral was then organized on the lines of an English cathedral of non-monastic foundation with canons and chapter, and rededicated to St Andrew and St David (1123). It was to continue under Canterbury until the disestablishment of the Church in Wales in 1921.

So strong was the Norman instinct for centralized authority that Giraldus Cambrensis, son of a Norman but with a Welsh mother, who passionately wanted to be bishop of St Davids, was never allowed the See. Successive English kings interposed between the Pope and Giraldus, who went twice to Rome to plead his cause.

Little is known of the life of St David (see p. 318) but certainly the idea of the saint had a powerful grip on men's minds. This great preacher and scholar is believed to have been born here and founded a monastery sometime in the mid-sixth century. According to his medieval chronicler, Rhygyfarch, David's birth had been foretold by an angel to St Patrick who had himself dearly wanted to found a monastery in this valley. The angel then showed Patrick all Ireland and he was told to preach there (on a clear evening the Wicklow Hills can be seen from the top of Carn Llidi).

The rule by which the monks lived was austere: worship, scholarship and farming left little time for sleep; only water was drunk. It

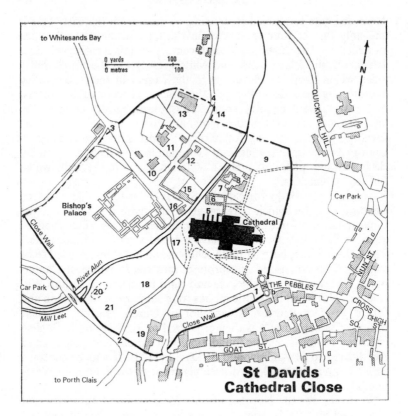

1. Porth-y-twr
   a. octagonal tower, former chancellery. Restored 1930 (W. D. Carōe) to original use as cathedral belfry. Practice night: Friday
   b. dungeon
2. Site of Porth Padrig
3. Site of Porth Gwyn
4. Site of Porth Boning
5. Site of cloister
6. St Mary's College Chapel c. 1365, now the Cathedral Hall. Restored 1965
7. Cloister Garden, 1972
8. Cloister Hall; garden over vaults; and yard

9. Site of Vicars Choral dwellings
10. Archdeaconry of St Davids
11. Brecon House (formerly for that Archdeacon)
12. The Treasurer's House
13. The Canonry (Chancellor's house)
14. Site of the Archdeaconry of Cardigan
15. Pen-y-ffoss (formerly for the Prebendary of St Nicholas and by 1570, Choristers' Lodge)
16. Domus Juxta Pontem (recently the Cathedral workshop)
17. Site of Nash's chapter house
18. Site of Archdeaconry of Carmarthen
19. The Deanery
20. Site of fish ponds
21. Site of Chanters' Orchard

produced an outpost of learning which was to endure; even the Vikings, whose raids became increasingly frequent in the tenth and eleventh centuries, did not manage to burn the library when they sacked the church yet again in 1088 shortly after William I's visit.

David is believed to have died on 1 March 589, and since late medieval times, when a bishop of St Davids became archbishop of Canterbury, this day has been kept as a major festival in that Province. Now 1 March is also Wales's national day: daffodils (introduced by Lloyd George) and leeks (dating from a battle in AD 640 when the Welsh thrust them in their caps for recognition) come to the fore. It is also a good time to be in St Davids, before the Easter rush. Rooks are beginning to build in the Close, their caws making a strange inland mixture with the cries of the gulls which perch ecumenically on the ridge of Ebenezer. If you can only be here in the tourist season, walk through the Close after dusk, preferably when a sea mist has drifted inland: the huge cathedral fills the valley, and as you walk down the flight of the Thirty-nine Steps to reach it, the building looms bigger and bigger like a great ship in a snug harbour. It is the parish church as well as the cathedral; those who like to sing should attend parish services.

To make the description of the **Cathedral** as plain as possible, the bare outlines of the development of the plan will be given chronologically (much of this can be appreciated from Porth-y-twr) and the more important detail then filled in.

Nothing is known of the Celtic monastic buildings: probably little survived the Viking raids.

1176–98	Bishop Peter de Leia built a large cruciform cathedral with a low tower, on the lines of the present building but ending at the east wall behind the high altar. The site is close to the river and the ground under it uncertain.
1220	The tower (9) crashed destroying most of the presbytery (11); the transitional Norman nave (3) survived.
13th C.	The tower was rebuilt on three great new (pointed) arches; the round west arch was optimistically retained. The wrecked presbytery was rebuilt (E.E.).
1248	An earthquake caused further damage.
c. 1275	The shrine of St David (12) was constructed in the chancel.
1296–1328	Bishop Martyn extended the building eastward. He constructed the Lady Chapel (19) and linking aisles and ante-chapel (18) leaving a courtyard (or lightwell) open to the sky behind east wall of sanctuary.

1328–47   Bishop Gower modernized the building; heightened the aisle walls; enlarged the windows; vaulted the Lady Chapel; added two storeys above St Thomas Becket's Chapel (7) for a chapter house and treasury; daringly added a second stage tower. He built the grand pulpitum (5), and the south porch (2) – a tree of Jesse decorates the south doorway. (See also the Bishop's Palace, p. 112.)

1348–49   The Black Death – a probable lull in building activity.

1365   St Mary's College (p. 104) was founded by Bishop Houghton and John of Gaunt for a Master and seven priest-fellows.

c. 1400   Buttresses constructed to prevent the nave capsizing.

c. 1500   Canons' stalls and bishops' throne. The presbytery was also re-roofed (note the line on the tower showing change of roof pitch – this meant raising the side walls).

1509–23   Bishop Vaughan formed Holy Trinity Chapel (15) by roofing the 'lightwell' with exquisite fan vaulting; lancets above the high altar were thus blocked; a large perpendicular window was constructed at a high level for light. The room above south porch (12) and a third stage to the tower were added.

c. 1540   Grand new nave ceiling constructed.

c. 1538   The Reformation. St Davids, being a non-monastic foundation suffered less than many cathedrals. 1549, chantries were abolished; their chapels became roofless. The holy relics disappeared. Henry VIII ordered Edmund Tudor's tomb (13) to be placed before the high altar.

17th C.   Interior lime-washed; the cathedral suffered from neglect as well as vandalism. Cromwellians stripped lead and broke glass.

1793   Restoration by John Nash who rebuilt the west end (it was demolished c. 1860, being both unstable and 'incorrect'). New chapter house (demolished 1829).

1846   William Butterfield put new tracery in the aisle windows and designed that in the north transept (6), based on one at Sleaford, Lincs, and put timber panelling above the pulpitum.

1860   Sir Gilbert Scott was called in. His thorough restoration began with the tower, now in a very dangerous state, and the reconstruction of its west arch. He redesigned the West end of the nave.

1906   J. Oldrid Scott revaulted the Lady Chapel (19). W. D.

Caröe continued the restoration of the Cathedral, followed by A. D. R. Caroe and Martin Caroe (son and grandson).

INSIDE THE CATHEDRAL

On entering the south door (2) you plunge into de Leia's late Norman (transitional) **Nave** of lilac-grey sandstone, which slopes up astonishingly steeply to the east. Huge round arches on outward-leaning clustered columns support another arcade, which is divided into a triforium with a simple pointed arcading and clerestory of single round-headed windows. Zigzag and other typical Norman carving decorates the arches, but the transitional carving appears in weird tubular stems, like seaweed. The nave is roofed by an extraordinarily sophisticated early-sixteenth-century ceiling of Irish oak. Great decorative pendants hang from the main intersections of the panelling; elaborately carved struts tie the pendants back to the roof beams giving the effect of criss-cross arcading. The light-hearted character of this rather arabesque design is in fine contrast to the austerity of the outside of the building.

The west end is Gilbert Scott's improvement on de Leia's, with remnants of Nash's circular window retained; it is said, to show how incorrect it was. Ahead, dividing the nave from the choir under the crossing, is Bishop Gower's unique fourteenth-century **Pulpitum** (5), really a small building in itself, being fifteen feet deep on plan. It is a most unusual design with niches arranged asymmetrically (now occupied by dull modern statuary). Gower's tomb is on the south side, and inside, to the left of the passage, above another tomb medieval paintings survive in the vaulting. The open rib vaulting over the passage is rare in Britain. Scott's survey of the screen is in the Cathedral Library. The rood is by W. D. Caröe and the organ (Willis, 1883) was re-cased by A. D. R. Caroe (1950).

The dramatic contrast between nave and **Choir** is heightened by the time it takes to walk through the narrow passage inside the deep screen and to climb the five steps within it. Behind you is the big nave, cool and open and slightly impersonal. In the choir there is a strong sense of being securely in the heart of the building. The emphasis is vertical; the space is enclosed by Gower's screen, the canons' stalls, the somewhat slap-happy parclose screen and, above, by the gaily painted timber vaulting, restored and copied by Scott from the medieval work. He raised it one storey thus allowing the light from Gower's tower windows to flood the choir. The colour of

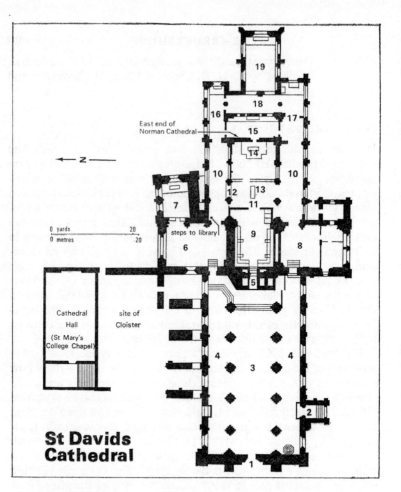

East end of
Norman Cathedral

← N →

0 yards 20
0 metres 20

steps to library

Cathedral
Hall
(St Mary's
College Chapel)

site of
Cloister

St Davids Cathedral

1. West front, Gilbert Scott, *c.* 1870.
2. South porch, Gower (1328–47).
   Room above, Vaughan (1509–23)
3. Nave, de Leia (1176–98)
   Nave ceiling, *c.* 1540
4. Aisles, de Leia (1176–98); roof raised
   and windows enlarged, Gower (1328–
   1347); windows restored, Butterfield,
   c. 1840
5. Pulpitum, Gower (1328–47)
6. North transept, de Leia (1176–98);
   timber vaulting, Scott; window,
   Butterfield, 1840
7. Chapel of St Thomas Becket
   (library over) vaulted by Gower
   (1328–47) who added upper rooms
8. South transept and vestries, de Leia
   and Scott.
9. Choir (under tower), thirteenth
   century, restored by Scott. Canons'

stalls and Bishop's Throne, *c.* 1500.
Ceiling, Scott
10. North and South choir aisles.
11. Presbytery, thirteenth century, re-
    stored by Scott. Reroofed *c.* 1500.
    Ceiling, Scott
12. Shrine of St David, *c.* 1275
13. Tomb of Edmund Tudor, + 1456;
    brasses 1873
14. High altar
15. Holy Trinity Chapel, Vaughan
    (1509–23)
16. St Nicholas's Chapel ⎤
17. St Edward's Chapel ⎟ Martyn
18. Ambulatory ⎟ (1296–1328)
19. Lady Chapel, vaulted ⎬ Restorations
    by Gower; revaulted ⎟ by Scott and
    by J. Oldrid Scott, *c.* ⎟ Caröe.
    1902 ⎦

the stone too is warm, after the mauves, purples and greys of the Cambrian sandstones.

The canons' stalls, with their spirited misericords, date from the fifteenth and early sixteenth century, as does the fantastic Bishop's Throne. The reigning Sovereign has been a canon of St Davids since the Reformation (origin unknown), whence the Royal Arms over one stall.

The **Presbytery** has simple Early English arcading and lancet windows. Those behind the high altar were blocked when Bishop Vaughan roofed in the lightwell behind them to form Holy Trinity Chapel. Their glowing mosaics (by Salviati and designed by J. H. Powell of Hardman's, Birmingham) date from Scott's restoration. Scott also removed Vaughan's perpendicular window above and substituted the lancets (their strident glass is Hardman's). He also restored the ceiling.

The display of the Saint's relics was one of the chief functions of the cathedral, and much of its prosperity depended on the many pilgrims, both royalty and commoners. Two pilgrimages to St Davids were the equivalent of one to Rome. The **Shrine** of St David was built on the north side of the presbytery (*c.* 1275) for the more appropriate display of the sacred relics. A reliquary was placed on top of the shrine (which also had some sort of wooden canopy) so that it could be seen by pilgrims processing round the cathedral under the cover of the presbytery aisle. Until then it had been placed either on or behind the high altar and was viewed by the vast numbers of ordinary mortals through the opening in the east wall or, on special occasions, the relics were shown from a platform outside. Neither arrangement can have been very satisfactory; queues indoors; wet and wind out. In the panels of the arcade were paintings of Saints David, Patrick and Denis. The ornamental recesses in the wall behind were for offerings.

The placing of the **Tomb of Edmund Tudor** (father of Henry VII and so of the dynasty) may reflect not only the change in religious priorities brought about by the Reformation but also the political uncertainties of the age as felt by Henry VIII. It was set here, before the high altar and in front of the shrine of the saint, by express order of the king when, following the dissolution, it was brought from the Grey Friars' church in Carmarthen. It is a fine altar tomb with brasses of *c.* 1873 (by Wallers), the originals having disappeared in Cromwell's time. Kilvert (p. 322) noted the dilapidated state of the tomb, 'the Dean and Chapter are hoping the Queen will restore it, so they have done nothing to it'. He poked his umbrella through 'a huge rent . . . and stirred the kingly dust. It felt much like common earth'.

The **High Altar** (Scott) has no reredos and stands clear of the wall; the plain masonry sets off the fine crucifix (T. G. Jackson, 1903) and candlesticks, and there is a sense of uncluttered grandeur. The floor is of medieval tiles. The medieval wooden sedilia have very successful embroidered panels (Gwendolen Caroe and Joan Taylor, 1965). The early-seventeenth-century tomb to Treasurer Lloyd on the north is one of the few of this date in the cathedral.

Holy Trinity Chapel lies immediately behind the presbytery. It is separated from the aisles by elegant sixteenth-century screening, and roofed by the fine fan vaulting which Bishop Vaughan substituted for the sky when he converted this dank patch of open ground (c. 1509–23). Its unusual plan, with the altar inevitably on the long wall, is particularly attractive. The altar, a masterly amalgam of medieval pieces by W. D. Caröe, has a moving fourteenth-century reredos. On either side, two modern statues stand in the sixteenth-century niches, one of Giraldus Cambrensis, unworn mitre at his feet. Behind, in the sanctuary, is the reliquary (W. D. Caröe) which now contains the holy relics. It stands in the opening through which pilgrims used to view the relics in the sanctuary before the c. 1275 shrine was constructed. It contains bones, discovered by Scott, plastered into the wall, when he opened the blocked opening. The arms on the bosses are of Henry VIII (supported by the dragon and greyhound) and the bishops of St Davids.

Two fine arches link the ante-chapel, which forms an ambulatory round the east end, with the **Lady Chapel**, which was revaulted by J. Oldrid Scott. W. D. Caröe was responsible for the monument of Bishop Owen, famed for his fight against disestablishment, under the fourteenth-century canopy.

St Edward's Chapel, in the south choir aisle contains a large monument to the benefactress, Lady Maidstone (d. 1923), by W. D. Caröe (she insisted on the use of alabaster, and, although unexpected, it has now become quite a period piece). Both choir aisles have effigies of medieval notables (labelled). It is possible that that of a priest in the south aisle is Giraldus Cambrensis but he died in Lincoln.

The **Transepts** have good timber vaulting by Scott. The south was once the parish church and is now partly screened off for vestries. The attractive icon of Elijah and the raven came from Talley Abbey (p. 148), by way of Dolaucothi House and Hafod (p. 62), and the Newcastle sale at Clumber Park (Notts.) where a member of the

Lloyd-Johnes family bought it back and gave it to the cathedral. The portable altar stone below with the five crosses is traditionally one presented to St David himself when he was in Jerusalem. An eleventh-century tombstone to two sons of Bishop Abraham is set in the east wall of the transept (within the vestry). The spectacular twentieth-century heraldic tiling recording the bishops (also in the vestry) is the work of a local family who lived in Warpool Court (now a hotel) where more can be seen (Aida Lansdowne Miller and Basil Miller Williams). In the **North Transept** is Butterfield's best window (p. 106); and the memorial (A. D. R. Caroe, 1956) to the great seventeenth-century composer, Thomas Tomkins, who was a native of St Davids, his father being cathedral organist. The **Cathedral Library**, above St Thomas Becket's chapel, is open to the public on certain days and is a very good place to browse.

That this cathedral survives is thanks to Gilbert Scott's engineering skill. He first got his foot in at St Davids because the **Tower** was about to collapse. 'I have never met a case so serious, and involving so great an amount of apparent and actual danger, as that of your Cathedral . . .' he wrote to Bishop Thirlwall (pointing out that he had already dealt with five other central towers). A wall had been built filling in the arch to relieve the piers at the west of the crossing long before. These were the piers which had been only partly re-newed after the 1220 collapse and they were on the verge of dis-integration, as was the tower wall above. A way had to be found entirely to rebuild them while supporting the tower. Scott gives a detailed account of how this was done (12,000 cubic feet of timber were used). Despite every precaution, the tunnels cut to take the supporting timbers nearly caused complete havoc. 'The middle mass [of the wall] began to pour out like an avalanche which was only stopped by the immediate insertion of sandbags and by subsequently running the wall from above with liquid cement . . .', Scott explained in his Report. Eventually the piers were rebuilt and much masonry besides.

Outside, the cathedral is grandly plain. Its architectural impact comes from its form and siting. The **West Front** has, during the last two centuries, been the subject of much feeling. Scott replaced Nash's west front, which consisted of one huge round-headed window (not a four-centred arch as shown in prints), with vaguely perpendicu-lar style tracery (four lights superimposed by eight with rose tracery at the top centre) using tracery from St Mary's College. The statue is of Bishop Thirlwall (p. 329), Scott's patron. It is a relief to leave Scott's fierce purple sandstone for the quieter north of the building where the quiet brown rubble masonry typical of much of the building again prevails.

Only traces are left of the cloister which once linked the cathedral to St Mary's College chapel – now the **Cathedral Hall**; it was converted in 1966 by A. D. R. Caroe. Behind it is a very attractive secluded small garden (Martin Caroe) wedged between the Hall, the stream and the upper storey garden over the fascinating vaults of **Cloister Hall** (8, p. 104), a charming house on the site of the College. For many years the Cathedral Builders lived here. Look through the high archway of the walled yard (like France) where a huge quantity of stone, quarried from the cliff at Caerbwdy in 1972, awaits future repair work. The better masonry in the cathedral is Cambrian sandstone from this cliff and Caerfai (p. 114), and oolitic limestone (yellowish). Both limestone and craftsmen came from across the Bristol Channel, using Porthclais (p. 114). West Country influence is strong.

The **Bishop's Palace** (DoE). This superb ruin conveys the immediate impression of having been built at one go; indeed it is usually referred to as Bishop Gower's work (1327–48). Such inaccuracy suggests what a great builder, showman and entertainer Gower must have been. He built only about half the Palace but he gave the whole his individual stamp by the simple stroke of crowning all the buildings, whether his own or his predecessors', with the fantastic arcaded parapet wall, unparalleled elsewhere except in his own work at Lamphey Palace (p. 133) and at Swansea Castle (p. 296).

The Palace is built round a great courtyard and its history is best followed on a plan (p. 113). Probably little existed before the end of the twelfth or the beginning of the thirteenth century; hospitality for Henry II's retinue is reported to have caused domestic strain among the canons. Looking from the gatehouse the earliest range is that on the right (north-west) – only the undercroft survives but it is grandly vaulted. Straight across from the gate is Gower's great hall; its marvellous porch faces you up the flight of steps with the lovely ogee arch over the door. Some idea of the scale of Gower's hospitality (or the strength of his urge to build) comes home when it is remembered that the bishop's great hall (to your left), already in existence, measured 62 × 23 feet; his new hall was to be 88 × 31 feet (excluding the extra room to the west). Compare this with the great hall at Penshurst built at about the same time, 64 × 39 feet.

Immediately following Gower's death, but almost certainly a part

St. Davids Cathedral, Pembrokeshire, lies in a deep valley, not far from the sea. (The hill in the middle of the picture is on Ramsey Island.)

Pentre Ifan burial chamber, near Nevern, is one of the finest in Wales.

The gun battery, Popton Point Fort, Milford Haven; now used by the British Petroleum Company to house pumping equipment.

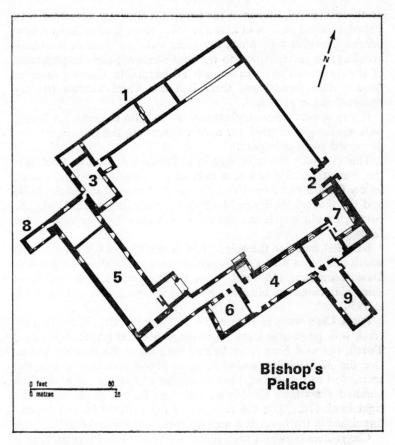

Bishop's Palace

0 feet 60
0 metres 20

1. ? 12th or 13th c.
2. Gatehouse, late 13th c.
3. Chapel, late 13th c.
4. Bishop's Hall and Solar, late 13th c.
5. Great Hall, 1327–47

6. Kitchen and passage, c. 1350
7. Bishop's chapel, c. 1350
8. Garde-robes, c. 1350
9. Addition by Bishop Vaughan?, c. 1500

of his plan, a new chapel, opening off the bishop's solar, was built immediately inside the gate, and a new kitchen, conveniently sited to serve both halls, was constructed at the end of the bishop's hall, with a passage linking it to both halls and a new porch to the bishop's hall. Around 1500, the wing off the bishop's solar was added, as was a porch to the earlier chapel.

The detail of the arcading can be particularly well seen on the north-west chapel. Elsewhere the parapet is elegantly decorated with a chequerboard pattern of lilac and white stone (and brilliant yellow lichen). The skill with which the gable walls are treated; the blank arcading; its juxtaposition to the rose windows; and the treatment of the corners of the arcading are all admirable. Carving includes good corbels (heads) and there is a fine wheel window (tracery restored) in the great hall.

If you should be so unfortunate as to miss the opening hours, walk up the grassy track for a view down into the generously proportioned green courtyard.

There is much else to be seen in and around St Davids. **Caerfai** is the nearest bathing beach, a mile to the south. To explore west, follow Goat Street from Cross Square past grand Tabernacle (1874) and the modest Wesleyan Methodist church (begun 1823). At the corner, an old warehouse has been imaginatively converted into a factory.

Bear left here for the ruins of **St Non's Chapel** (date unknown) which stand in a field a few hundred yards above the sea. Non was David's mother. Her well, in a twentieth-century enclosure, is shiny with coins and blue with hydrangea. The new chapel was built in 1934.

Porth Clais was the diminutive port for the city, a lovely little creek with good lime kilns. The 'quays' are new (1975). Long ago, Twrch, the wild boar from Ireland who killed the sons of Arthur (see the *Mabinogion*) landed here. St David was baptized in the spring lost in the undergrowth at the far end of the car park. Five hundred years later the Norman bishops built a castle above the right bank (745/253); the remains of the earthworks can be distinguished in the bracken a mile upstream, opposite the mill.

Clegyr-Boia crowns a rock beside the road to St Justinian's from Porth Clais. The Iron Age fort built on a Neolithic settlement was occupied by Boia in David's time. He first opposed and later supported the monastery.

At Rhosson farm, half a mile short of **Porth Stinian**, there is a huge round 'Flemish' chimney. Not many remain; there are others in the West Country across the Bristol Channel. No connection with the Flemings has been established. **St Justinian's Chapel**, an upstanding ruin rebuilt by Bishop Vaughan in the early sixteenth century, stands above the Lifeboat Station.

The roads in the peninsula which forms the hinterland to St Davids spread like the fingers of a hand from the city, so to explore St Davids Head you must return and take the road to Whitesands

Bay (popular bathing). The best place to get your bearings is from the summit of **Carn Llidi** (595 feet), and the best time of all a summer evening, a little before dusk. The lower slopes are a network of stone-banked fields, some enlarged where rock outcrops will allow, for early potatoes. Nowhere else in Britain is there evidence of longer continuous cultivation; crops here were ripened by the Iron Age sun. A track leads up to the Hydrophone foundations of World War I. Higher still every available inch between the rocks is brilliant with heather and gorse pruned very short by the gales. It is a rock-gardener's dream but quite unlike any rock garden.

Up here there is a sense of the remoteness of St Davids, of being far out on a spur in the westerly sea. At your feet lies **St Davids Head**, cut off by the fortification wall of its Iron Age settlement (six hut circles survive inside). Two Neolithic burial chambers lie between the summit and the head (one beside the path you have climbed).

Immediately to the south-west **Ramsey Island**, farmed by St Justinian, is separated by a roaring tide race from the mainland. It ceased to be farmed in 1968, so the dramatic contrast between the wild and the man-made landscape was vanishing, but is about to be reclaimed since Mr and Mrs Robin Pratt intend to farm the island and keep it as a bird sanctuary. Local boatmen take trips round the island – the best way of seeing the cliff-nesting birds and breeding seals. Boats go from Porth Stinian.

Beyond the island, a scatter of dangerous rocks called the **Bishops and Clerks** end with the South Bishop, easily identified by its light-house. **Grassholm** (RSPB), the lonely, distant hump, is now one of the world's largest gannetries whose population has been fast increasing ever since 1883 (1964 – 15,500 pairs; 1933 – 4000; 1905 – 300). Boats occasionally go out. The glow along the southern horizon beyond the huge sweep of St Bride's Bay is that of the oil refineries on Milford Haven.

ST BRIDES BAY–ST ANN'S HEAD

Solva, three miles from St Davids on the main Haverfordwest road, A487, is the best harbour before Milford Haven. Even so it is hard to imagine a shipload of emigrants embarking here for America in the last century. The fare was £3 10s. – single, of course. The attractive village runs up towards Middle Mill (tweeds and woollens) where there is a good Baptist chapel opposite the quarry. Both road and cliff come down to sea level at the great storm beach of **Newgale**; the huge wall of pebbles thrown up by the tide slides on to the road in wild weather. A487 here leaves the sea for Haverfordwest. New development breaks out sporadically and **Roch Castle** (now a private house), the first on the Landsker (p. 93), is the only landmark. To explore the coast keep down on the minor road. You can get down to the sea at Druidston. Broadhaven and Little Haven are popular holiday places.

There is a dramatic change from Cambrian sandstone to Old Red sandstone at the promontory fort near Mill Haven, half way along to **St Brides Haven**. Low red cliffs allow the path to be just above the sea and the coastline is much gentler. The medieval church near this little landing place was thoroughly restored in 1883. **Kensington**, the house in the trees (the first for many miles) was probably restored about the same time; it is now a hospital. (In London, the Kensington property takes Pembrokeshire names.)

Marloes has a sturdy little cruciform church with a barrel-vaulted chancel (like St Brides, restored by E. H. Lingen Barker). There are wonderful sands north and south (Musslewick and Marloes) with the headland thrusting out to Skomer dividing them. **Martins Haven** is the point of embarkation for Skomer: boats daily in the summer if it is possible to land; there is no quay. This small bay is a favourite also for skin-divers. The big wall across the headland cuts off the Kensington deer park, never much favoured by deer.

Skomer Island is particularly marvellous in early June, when, as a bonus to the nesting sea-birds, bluebells and red campion carpet the island. It is a National Nature Reserve run by the West Wales Naturalists' Trust.

Gateholm, at the end of Marloes Sands (accessible at low tide) had an Iron Age settlement and there is a promontory fort on Great Castle Head. They look out on to the red sandstone island of **Skokholm**, made famous by R. M. Lockley's writings in the 'thirties. In 1939 it became the first bird observatory in Britain. Stays of a week are possible here; no day trips. It is administered by the West Wales Naturalists' Trust and Dale Fort Field Centre.

A fair proportion of this fine coastline belongs to the National Trust who recently, thanks to Neptune, acquired that part lately occupied by the RN air direction centre at Kete. The lighthouse at St Ann's Head is at the entrance to Milford Haven (p. 125).

HAVERFORDWEST (Hwlffordd)

Haverfordwest, at the lowest bridge and on the highest navigable point of the Western Cleddau is in the heart of the old county. Its

stuccoed houses, which one fervently hopes will resist the rising tide
of supermarkets, were once the homes of prosperous citizens and
the town houses of Pembrokeshire families. Each year the second
week in November was dedicated to the Hunt subscribers, and a
week of balls, dinners, card parties and hunting meant that eighty
or ninety horses might then be seen exercising on St Thomas's Green.
In this 'little Bath', as it has been called, sedan chairs were still in
use in 1888.

The town is topped by the castle – a good place to start a tour on
foot. The County Museum and a National Park Information Centre
are in the 1820 gaol alongside. The original **Castle** was *c*. 1120 but
the surviving ruins of the inner ward date from the thirteenth century
and later. Except during the Civil War, when the castle changed
hands several times and was eventually slighted on Cromwell's
orders, it was never taken. Both Llywelyn the Great (in 1205 when
he burnt the town to the castle walls) and Owen Glendower (in 1405)
failed in the attempt. Henry Tudor, Earl of Richmond, who had just
landed near Dale, was here on 8 August 1485, on his way to Bosworth.

St Martin's Church, medieval with an attractive small spire on a
square tower, has a south chapel and porch added in the fourteenth
century. Tabernacle Chapel (1874) opposite and the Wesleyan Chapel,
a little further down, have interesting interiors. Barn Street has
pleasant late-Georgian-looking houses with iron balconies and the
survivors in City Road (to St Davids), which joins it here, step and
curve up the hill most attractively.

Turn back towards the middle of the town past the handsome
plastered front of the Mariners Hotel and the diminutive Gothic
Gloucester Arms. **St Mary's Church**, above you, has a very good
interior, graceful and light and very carefully detailed. In 1848, *The
Ecclesiologist* happily reported that it had been 'expensively restored
and refitted' several years before. Standing on the steps which run
right across the west end of the nave you are looking down into an
Early English church (*c*. 1240) enlarged and improved *c*. 1500: that
is to say built during the two periods of peace following Llywelyn
the Great's death and Henry VII's accession. It has a lovely Early
English arcade of clustered columns and capitals carved with medieval
vigour. The portraits on the chancel arch are of the Earl of Pembroke
and his wife Lady Joan de Clare. The east window has cinque-foil
lights in plate tracery above three lancet lights. In the late fifteenth
century, clerestories were added to the nave and chancel and the
carved and panelled oak roof was constructed (compare with the
much grander version at St Davids). It rests on nicely carved corbels

(hard to see against the light). The church has good memorials to the town's citizens, a boldly carved mayor's pew and bench, and an eighteenth-century organ (restored 1888). In the south-west corner of the nave is the effigy of a pilgrim (*c.* 1450) with scrip; the three scallop shells signify that he has been to the shrine of Santiago de Compostela.

From St Mary's cross the High Street, up Market Street (the market is architecturally dismal) and turn left into Goat Street: attractive, narrow and residential. There are pleasant houses and glimpses of apple trees over garden walls and of the surrounding country through the gaps. Foley House (John Nash, 1794), sensibly used by the Local Authority for meetings, has been insensitively restored.

At the bottom turn right into Hermon Hill from which a path leads to **St Thomas's Church** whose medieval tower is a good landmark. Back in Goat Street, a narrow road drops down into the steeply sloping High Street which has a pleasant, unprecious character, with St Mary's at the top and the small Castle Square at the bottom. The Shire Hall, pedimented, stuccoed, rather like a chapel, is here.

Quay Street leads off the square. It gives a faint reminder of Haverfordwest's importance as a port. Beyond the shops and depots, where nice facades still survive much camouflaged, there are good stone warehouses and the Bristol Trader pub. In the Middle Ages wool was one of the chief cargoes but smuggled wine was always of importance to the town. The new weir (near the small car park off Quay Street) is a good place to watch salmon and sewin leap.

Bridge Street, the other main shopping street, also leads out of Castle Square and you can make a complete circuit to the castle by taking it and bearing left (or, alternatively, by one of the steep paths off the High Street or the Square). Llywelyn's Churn Works in Old Perrot Road (alas! no longer making churns) is a building of real stature. Short of St Martin's is **Castle Terrace**, 1832, a bold pedimented facade designed as one; big scale and urban.

Rudbaxton, just off A40, in a green churchyard three miles north of Haverfordwest, must be one of the most enjoyable churches in Pembrokeshire. It was granted by Wizo the Fleming to the Knights of St John. The deep whitewashed porch leads into a thirteenth-century building, to which a south aisle was added, and linked to it by low arched arcading. Stand in the chancel and glance right for the most astonishing view of the seventeenth-century memorial to members of the Howard family. It takes up the whole east wall of the south aisle. They stand holding skulls, almost life size, and seem about to step out of their alcoves, like characters taking a curtain after an opera. Lovely soft colours, chiefly terracotta, black and off-white. There are interesting monuments to the Picton family of Poyston Hall (near by) including the general who fell at Waterloo, who is commemorated by the obelisk in Carmarthen.

THE CLEDDAUS

The Cleddau estuaries can be reasonably explored only by boat. These long arms of river, brimful of shining water at high tide, an ever-diminishing channel in the shining mud as it drops, are now barriers instead of passageways. It is a long time since a trader from Bristol arrived in Haverfordwest by water. Ruined quays and old ferries tell where life once hummed: ketches loaded with grain making their way up to Blackpool Mill or to the great tide-mill below Carew Castle; colliers puffing up to Hook or coasters collecting limestone at West Williamston; and all this criss-crossed by the urgent local life of rowing ferries and a boat to each household. But the rivers still shimmer with wading birds and are a refuge of countless wildfowl.

The right bank of the Western Cleddau can be reached at Little Milford and Hook Quay. Leave A4076, the Milford Haven road at Merlin's Bridge on the outskirts of Haverfordwest, and bear left on minor roads. You will find yourself amongst new housing, but the river itself and the views across are outstandingly beautiful. Hook was renowned for the excellence of its anthracite, and Llangwm, on its own creek below the junction of the two Cleddaus, for its cockles. Burton church tower is a good landmark; here the estuary turns west and you are only a couple of miles upstream from the new bridge across Milford Haven.

To return upstream, **Daucleddau**, the land between the two rivers, was granted to Wizo the Fleming by Henry I; it was probably politic to introduce new settlers into a land occupied by two uncertain elements, the powerful earls of Pembroke and the spirited Welsh.

To the south of A40, the parklands of Picton and Slebech run down to a lovely stretch of river. The unexpected steeple of **Slebech** church (J. H. Good, 1844), beside the main road acts as a marker to the road to Picton and one of the few places where you can reach the water. (On the opposite side of A40 is a perfect composition: a small white cottage with a diminutive Scots Pine seen against its gable end.)

Picton Castle was built in the late thirteenth century to replace an earlier motte which had almost certainly been constructed by Wizo to command the junction of the two Cleddaus. It was delightfully modernized in the eighteenth century and a castellated wing was added *c.* 1800. In the nineteenth century the main entrance, with its neo-Norman porch, was made at first floor level. It is not open, but can be seen by those visiting the **Graham Sutherland Gallery** which was opened in 1976 in a courtyard building. Here a permanent collection appropriately marks the painter's long connection with Pembrokeshire. Films on related subjects may also be seen. Part of the grounds is now open.

Slebech Park (not open) marches with Picton. The Church of the Knights of the Hospital of St John of Jerusalem, a Flemish foundation, is a rose-covered ruin in its grounds close to the river which here has biscuity reed beds. An annual service is held on St John the Baptist's day or the last Sunday in June. The present house, which is close to the church, dates from 1776. It is de-castellated, so shorn-looking, but has elegant rooms. J. Calvert, a Swansea architect, worked here at that time. Opposite, submerged in the woods, more ruins survive, known as the Sisters' House. This may have been a hospice for pilgrims on their way to St Davids.

For **Llawhaden Castle** (DoE) turn north off A40 half a mile west of Canaston Bridge and its junction with A4075. It stands high above the river at the end of a pleasant village street. The castle originally held a key position in the middle of the Landsker just below the Preseli hills but close to one of the highest navigable points of Milford Haven. It was built by the Norman bishops of St Davids to protect their rich possessions against the Welsh (and perhaps as a safeguard against the Lords Marcher), but as time went on the castle became more palatial and less defensive.

It was probably Bernard, the first Norman bishop, who built the ring motte, the moat of which survives. (Giraldus Cambrensis records that he was entertained at Llawhaden when his uncle was bishop in 1175.) That castle, razed by the Lord Rhys in 1193, was followed by an early-thirteenth-century structure, but the main ruins now standing date from the early fourteenth when the castle was turned into a great fortified bishop's palace. The splendid tower-flanked gatehouse was built last of all towards the end of the century. Straight ahead is the great hall flanked by the bishop's camera and kitchens. To your right are the chapel and guests' apartments. On the left were quarters for the garrison (next to the gate) and a large bakehouse. The constable had apartments in the top of the gatehouse.

Ruins of a late-thirteenth-century hospital survive at the other end of the village street. The parish church is beside the river, buried in trees far below. Its two towers are explained by a drawing inside.

THE EASTERN CLEDDAU, EAST BANK AND THE CAREW RIVER

Turn south on to A4075 at Canaston Bridge. A quarter of a mile on, a small road right leads to **Blackpool Mill** (1813) which stands by a fine round-arched estate bridge at the highest navigable point of the Eastern Cleddau. This good plain building, whose nineteenth-century machinery survives, can often be inspected since a tea-room has been opened here.

The river can be reached again beyond **Landshipping** (a fine romantic view of Picton Castle) and at Landshipping Quay, at **Lawrenny** at the mouth of the Creswell River (bustling with boats, chalets and caravans) and at West Williamston.

If time is short, miss all this and make directly from Canaston Bridge on A4075 for Carew (pronounced Cairey). Here, on the estuary of the Carew River, is a most exciting group of buildings. **Carew Castle** really now consists of two great houses, the one early and the other late Tudor, grouped round a courtyard of, and built into, a late-thirteenth-century castle. This most romantic building is best first seen from the dam below reflected in the huge tidal mill pool. Two massive round towers rise from their squared haunched-up bases with a forbidding curtain between them which runs back to the south-east tower.

Carew traditionally belonged to the princes of South Wales and is said to have been given as dowry for his fascinating daughter Nest (p. 324) by Rhys ap Twdwr to Gerald of Windsor. Their son took the name Carew.

The entrance path crosses what was the outer ward (between the castle and the road) to the outer gatehouse (*c*. 1500). An inner gate-house (pre-1320) leads into a splendid courtyard. From here it is easy to see the main building sequence. Ahead is the delightful two-storeyed porch to the great hall, built by Sir Rhys ap Thomas (see p. 327) who bought the castle from the Carews and thoroughly modernized it to suit the peaceful times heralded by Henry VII's succession. On St George's Day, 1507, he held a great tournament and entertained at Carew for five successive days all the nobility and gentry of Wales to the number of one thousand. A banner was hung across the gateway which tactfully depicted St George and St David in brotherly embrace.

The impressive but gloomy north wing (to the right), built by the flamboyant but quick-tempered Sir John Perrot, was never finished. Instead of entertaining Queen Elizabeth here, as he had hoped, Sir John was accused of treason and died in the Tower of London (1592). He was thought by many to be a natural son of Henry VIII; there was said to be a strong likeness.

The east wing, in which the gatehouse stands, was the least altered; it contains the smaller thirteenth-century hall, and the chapel which is built into the south-east tower.

The **French Mill** at Carew, on the end of the dam below the castle, is a double tide mill. The pleasant Georgian structure replaces a much earlier building. It has been restored (1972) and its fascinating machinery can be inspected.

Carew High Cross has a cramped site beside the main road near the entrance to the castle. Marvellously intricate interlacing patterns cover all four sides and the inscription, which refers to Maredudd ap Edwin, a king of Deheubarth (1033–5), is on the 'back'.

Carew itself is an attractive hamlet beside the bridge (on which markets were once held). A freestanding Flemish chimney survives in the garden of a house down the side road; it served the village bakehouse until 1927. **Carew Cheriton Church** tower can be seen a mile south. The church is part of another most attractive group of buildings – a medieval charnel house and chapel in the graveyard, the Old Rectory with its low square tower and a cedar tree, and some stone cottages. The church is mainly c. 1400 with Perp. and Dec. windows. It is quite grand: a cruciform plan with a deep chancel, two aisles, and a west tower which is barrel vaulted and has angle buttresses (rare in Pembrokeshire). Interesting tombs include an effigy which may represent Sir Nicholas Carew and there is a good seventeenth-century altar tomb to Sir John and Dame Elizabeth Carew. The fine sanctuary tiles, c. 1500, were originally in the castle. The church was restored by G. G. Scott in 1855.

You are now within easy distance of Tenby and the south coast (p. 133) or Pembroke (p. 128).

MILFORD HAVEN

Milford Haven, the long drowned river valley which divides Pembrokeshire even more dramatically than does the Landsker, is one of the world's finest natural harbours, and in the last decade it has become an international oil port.

The best way to explore it is by water,[1] and to let the tide carry

[1] Small steamers run from Hobbs' Point, Pembroke Dock.

you up into the remote creeks of the Cleddaus and other rivers which flow into it. Despite the huge tankers, there are still flourishing sailing clubs: the tankers must stick to the dredged channel so there is room for pleasure craft in the shallower water. Now much of the sloping pasture land which surrounds the Haven is smothered by refineries. From the water they can look dramatic, particularly at night, but the smell is often very nasty.

When the National Park was first designated, Milford Haven seemed a natural choice and it was not until the 1950s that the interests of the oil men became apparent. It was one of the few harbours that could take the big ships then envisaged. 75,000 tons (Esso's County class) were until recently thought to be huge but by 1971 the Haven was handling VLCCs (very large crude carriers: those who service them use mopeds to get about on deck) of up to 260,000 tons. The BP oil terminal, four refineries, and the Pembroke Power Station have come into being since the Milford Haven Conservancy Act was passed in 1958.

'All this may be indirectly ascribed to the fair face of Lady Hamilton', wrote Edward Laws, the Pembrokeshire historian, after viewing the tremendous mid-nineteenth-century fortifications on Milford Haven. Nelson considered it to be one of the world's finest harbours. Emma's connection with the Haven was first through Richard Greville, nephew of Sir William Hamilton. Sir William had inherited Pembrokeshire property in the vicinity of the present town of **Milford Haven** and had visited it with Greville under whose protection Emma was then living. Greville impressed upon his uncle the enormous capabilities of the Haven and it was agreed that he should become agent for the enterprise when Hamilton returned to the British Embassy in Naples. Buildings were laid out and docks planned but very soon Greville was being pressed for money by his creditors. Sir William, who had evidently been more impressed by Emma than his nephew, promised to act as security for the debts, provided (according to Laws) the reluctant Emma was sent out to Naples.

The Milford Haven Harbour Act had been passed in 1790 and soon some Quaker families immigrated from Nantucket, perhaps fifty people in all. Their **Meeting House**, a diminutive building with big friendly windows, was finished in 1811.

Shortage of money delayed general progress. However, in 1796 things looked much more hopeful when a site for shipbuilding was leased to the Navy Board and three ships laid down. About this time a dockyard constructor, Jean-Louis Barrallier, a native of Toulon who had left with the British Squadron when the town was evacuated, settled in Milford. He was responsible for its gridiron plan.

Money continued to be very short and the shipbuilder went bankrupt, but Greville was not to be daunted. It was at this point that
he persuaded the Hamilton household to celebrate the anniversary
of the Battle of the Nile by a visit to Milford Haven. Nelson laid the
foundation stone of the church, and made his famous speech extolling
the Haven at a dinner in the hotel (thereafter named after him) in
Hamilton Terrace. A year later Greville was writing 'I am satisfied
with the appearance of my Town. I am building a Church on the
East End and the Barracks will be to the West End by which extended
line of a mile gives to an Infant Colony the appearance of a Town
and the dockyard with 3 King's ships, the dock, etc., form a busy
scene'. Milford Haven still has an 'extended appearance', particularly
from the water. The long gleaming stucco **Hamilton Terrace**,
Milford's most desirable street, looks south across the Haven
sunning itself above the inland sea, now seething with gigantic
tankers.

St Katherine's Chapel (consecrated 1808, enlarged 1905), the
parish church, is rather papery Gothic revival, with a battlemented
tower and the air of being a stage set. Its unusual relics include the
truck of the mainmast of *L'Orient* (captured in the Battle of the
Nile) presented by Lady Hamilton, and a porphyry vase brought
from Egypt. This was intended as a font but the Bishop disapproved
of its pagan origin. They were to be a combined memorial to Nelson.

This flourish of prosperity was short-lived. In 1814, when the
lease for the shipyard was to be renewed, the Navy Board considered the terms to be extortionate and transferred to a site across
the water, thus giving birth to Pembroke Dock.

Hakin lies across the harbour bridge (1859) immediately west of
Milford. Originally a village, its new housing now covers an area
almost as big as the town. At Hubberston Point, there is an easily
accessible nineteenth-century fort with a huge dry moat (see below)
and the Milford Haven Conservancy Offices and jetty.

The **Hakin Observatory** (1811), behind the council estate on the
point, is Greville's most interesting building (to be restored). The
small observation dome (nineteen feet internal diameter) is daringly
designed; narrow slit openings continue up from the side walls
leaving only a narrow ring of masonry round the central 'eye' at the
top. Daniel Alexander (see *North Wales*, p. 214) may have had a
hand in the Observatory; he was concerned with dock improvement
at Milford. For permission to view, ask at the farm.

The mid-nineteenth-century **Fortifications** of the Haven are astonishingly grand. Surprisingly, nothing of note had been erected since the Normans secured control of the Haven by building their castle at Pembroke. (Two small forts were constructed to guard the entrance in 1580.) The first comprehensive nineteenth-century fortification scheme[1] was for the defence of the Admiralty Dockyard in Pembroke Dock. The general fear of France and the invention of the rifling of gun barrels led to the appointment of a committee to look into the defences of the Haven.

Two lines of defence were proposed behind the entrance fortifications to the Haven. The first would cross at Stack Rock (strengthened), and the second just west of Milford Haven, from a fort to be built at Hubberston (near the Conservancy Offices), via a floating battery, due south to Popton Point. This would prevent steamships from approaching within 7000 yards of the Dockyard. Each battery was also to be protected from landward attack. The following year, six land forts were also recommended but of these only one (Scoveston) was built. The fort at Tenby is also part of the main scheme. Although constantly modified, the plan was more or less completed by 1870, when it was already becoming outdated. However, the forts were garrisoned in both World Wars (chiefly with anti-aircraft batteries in the Second). Besides their architectural fascination, all now convey an impression of a dream quite out of scale with life. Some are very eerie indeed and those who explore should beware of unexpected holes and drops. Construction is of a high standard. Facing stone is chiefly grey limestone with some fine granite; most of the vaulting is in brickwork. The carving of the ashlar details is of extraordinary precision. In the more exciting and inaccessible, such as Stack Rock, even 1870 Paliser cannon remain, as do the tremendous iron doors and shutters.

MILFORD HAVEN: NORTH SHORELINE.
ST ANN'S HEAD–NEYLAND

From Dale (at the end of B4327) a minor road continues south to **St Ann's Head** on the tip of the Dale Peninsula which shelters the entrance to the Haven from westerly gales. The cliffs near the lighthouse (accessible by car) give a grandstand view of the giant tankers. It was at **Mill Bay**, immediately north, that Henry Tudor (pp. 329 and 131) landed on 7 August 1485; two weeks later, after the extra-

---

[1] For a detailed description, including armament, see the excellent National Park leaflet *The Fortification of Milford Haven and Pembroke* by N. J. Wheeler.

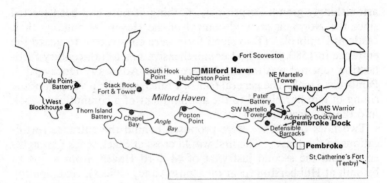

MILFORD HAVEN IN THE LATE 19TH CENTURY

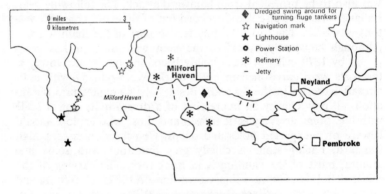

MILFORD HAVEN TODAY

ordinary march to Bosworth, he was King of England. **West Block-house Point Battery**, on the tip of the opposite arm of the bay, was built for a garrison of eighty men and had twelve guns in 1857. An open battery was added in 1900. With East Blockhouse across the Haven and Thorn Island (now a hotel), Dale Fort (a Field Studies Council Centre) and Stack Rock, it formed the outer defences of Milford Haven.

New navigation marks have been erected near West Blockhouse and on Great Castle Head to enable the colossal tankers to find the dredged channel. The new **Lighthouse** in the mouth of the Haven is a pre-fabricated steel tower secured by twenty-foot bolts to the sea-bed. Mid-December was (rightly) chosen as a likely time to produce a calm day for the tricky operation of lowering the tube from a helicopter on to its exact position.

Dale Roads, the sheltered anchorage just inside the Haven, is only separated by a narrow isthmus from the gale-swept bay of West Dale. **Dale** is the snug village tucked into the shelter; a few attractive houses and the Griffin overlook the Haven. The superior-looking 'council housing' is ex-naval quarters. Dale was a flourishing little port until the mid eighteenth century, when it all but died, but it rallied again in the mid nineteenth and is now a popular holiday and sailing centre.

A long bridge crosses the Gann estuary and its saltings. Just beyond a minor road (east) goes to **St Ishmael's.** The secret little church, medieval and Victorian, is hidden among trees in a deep valley running down to Monk Haven.

Sandy Haven is another quiet estuary, despite the close proximity of Esso. Amoco covers much of the country to the north of the town of Milford Haven (p. 123). Immediately east is Gulf. Here the village of Waterston just survives.

Scoveston Fort (1861–5) lies like a vast stranded whale a mile to the north-east in farmland. It is protected by a huge dry moat and inner bank (now buried in scrub) cut by heavily-guarded entrance tunnels. It is extraordinary to imagine regimental tea-parties, complete with the band playing on the lawn, within these defences in the 1920s.

Llanstadwell is the square-towered church (vigorously restored in 1876) with the lovely position on the edge of the Haven a mile to the west of **Neyland,** a pleasant, unpretentious town which came into being in 1856 as the Atlantic terminus of the Manchester railway. Long terraces of nineteenth-century cottages line the hillside, spick and span with unselfconscious paint basking in the sun. The name, Great Eastern Terrace, is the only reminder of more hopeful days.

MILFORD HAVEN: SOUTH SHORELINE. PEMBROKE DOCK TO WEST ANGLE BAY

The car ferry from Neyland to Hobbs' Point, Pembroke Dock, has been replaced by the new road bridge upstream. Steamer excursions, cheerful trips on a shiny day, run from Hobbs' Point. **HMS Warrior,** Britain's first iron-clad warship, now a hulk used as an oil jetty, lies under the steep wooded bank above the bridge. This mighty ship, which enthusiasts hope to save, is best seen from the water where the fine lines of her ramming prow and raking stern, with a gallery reminiscent of HMS *Victory*, can be best appreciated. *Warrior* was launched in 1861; her hull of four-inch iron plates and twelve-inch teak boarding is still watertight. She was designed with a retractable propeller so that she could use steam or sail, Permission to see her can be sought from the Dockyard.

The **Dockyard** (closed in 1920) which was transferred from Milford in 1816 is still surrounded by its grand wall. Near the main entrance, flanked by little lodges, are tall terraced houses of pleasant Georgian character. The old Dockyard buildings are attractively functional; a graving dock and an iron floating tidal gate of 1860 still survive; the huge hangars housed Sunderland flying boats in World War II. The gloomy-looking chapel, 1834, at the head of a long beech avenue has been enterprisingly converted into a motor-car museum. Its fascinating local records include old picture postcards and the lists of ships launched here; the wide variety includes three Royal Yachts – all *Victoria and Albert* – launched in 1834, 1855 and 1899.

Two small Martello towers (1849–57) survive. From the south-west tower there is a wide view down the Haven. Follow the road beyond the main dockyard gate, past the hospital. Across the Haven, almost opposite, is Gulf refinery (big tankers cannot berth here; oil is brought from Bantry Bay); Amoco is above Milford; Esso covers South Hook point just beyond the town. On the south shore, Texaco lies dead ahead. The 700-foot chimney of Pembroke Power Station (1969) – the biggest in Europe and maybe in the world – is immediately across Pembroke River. The possible effects of its pollution have been much argued.

The **Defensible Barracks** (1844–5) on the hill immediately above the Dockyard now house the Golf Club and Local Authority Depot (follow the road through the new bungalows). The Barracks are surrounded by a deep dry moat and huge wall, revetted on plan to allow no dead ground. Inside you find a pleasant 'Georgian' square.

The oil tanks below have a comfortable old-fashioned air. Like those above HMS *Warrior* they are connected by tunnels to the Dockyard. When bombed in the last war they burnt for three weeks, with 'a jet of oil 300 feet high'.

Pembroke Dock has numerous standard 'Georgian bungalows', presumably dating from the hey-day of the Dockyard. They are small dwellings with exceptionally large windows and wide, often round-headed doors – unusually attractive but fast disappearing.

Pembroke is one mile south on A4319. Its mighty castle (p. 129) is justly famous, but the remarkable survival of the early-fourteenth-century town walls[1] and of a town almost entirely confined within them, is surprisingly little known (perhaps because the three gates have gone). They defend the long narrow ridge which ends in the great rock on which the castle is built. This ridge separates two streams which join to form the Pembroke River. That on the north was dammed to form the tidal mill pool (longer even than the town) to work the mill which fed the garrison. A4319 crosses this dam as you approach the town.

Immediately after crossing, on your right, there is a handy parking place on the old quay (the main car park is near the castle). It is an excellent base for exploration of the town and is also a good spot to picnic. Sadly, the last mill on the dam was burnt down in 1955 (its position in the middle is marked and a short history given). Several pubs and an old warehouse are reminders that this was a port. The North Gate was behind the Royal George and a remnant of the adjoining wall survives behind the antique shop.

From the dam, follow the new esplanade beside the pool, immediately below the town wall. Alleys lead up to Main Street. Alternatively, continue along the whole length of the South Wall to Barnards Tower, which was presumably a refuge for those living in the east part of the town. **Main Street** runs the length of the ridge, not in a ruler-straight line but subtly faceted and, towards the east, briefly dividing to join again. The buildings are not individually remarkable, but collectively they make a good street and their survival is important. Mostly of Georgian flavour, many are nineteenth-century presumably with medieval foundations. There are bigger houses in East End Square. Small side alleys dive off, but the ridge is only one street wide so the houses are full of sun and view. The Lion Hotel forms the biggest group of buildings. Its human-faced lion looks across to the good square tower of **St Mary's**, the parish church, a two-aisled building, thoroughly Victorianized. The lovely fragment of the Adames 'tomb' appears to be a panel from some late-Decorated structure with a 1607 inscription on the back.

It is not easy to imagine the country and Haven pre-1840. For over six hundred years **Pembroke Castle** had dominated the scene. In 1093, Arnulph of Montgomery came by sea to subdue both the Welsh and the Vikings, and chose this site for his 'slender fortress of stakes and turf'. It was also to provide a base for Irish expeditions. The present castle (1189–1245) is largely the creation of another marcher lord, William Marshal, and his five sons. It is perched on a great knob of limestone jutting out into Pembroke River with steep

[1] *A Walk round the Walls of Pembroke* by Ken Cooper is an excellent short guide.

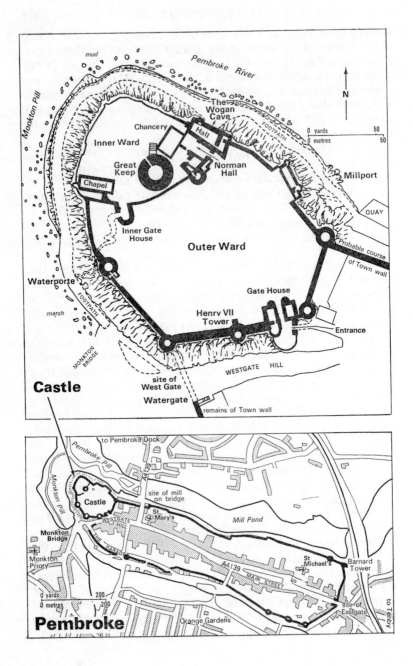

Castle

Pembroke

cliffs on three sides.

The huge drum of the Norman keep, one of the mightiest in Europe, towers above the outer curtain to which the post-Edward I town walls were linked. The main approach is still up Westgate Hill under the Bygate Tower (rebuilt in 1934), up the steep slope under the Barbican Tower, through the Barbican Gate (rebuilt 1888) and sharp right under the three portcullises of the Gate House and into the broad green outer ward. In 1880 J. R. Cobb (see p. 197) took a lease of the castle and began his most enjoyable excavations and reconstruction with the vaulting of the gatehouse. The castle is still privately owned but recently the DoE has worked on the Great Keep.

The curtain is protected by towers on the vulnerable town side. The first (working clockwise) is the traditional birthplace of Henry Tudor (see p. 329). Henry was brought up here under the protection of his uncle Jasper, Earl of Pembroke, until he was fourteen. Then, when siege was laid to the castle, Jasper escaped with the boy to Brittany (via Tenby) where he lived in exile until his landing near the mouth of the Haven (p. 125). The room in which he is believed to have been born was described by Leland (1538); the chimneypiece, which had already been put there before Leland's visit 'with the arms and badges of King Henry VII', was restored in 1929.

Before the building of the outer ward the only entrance to the castle was up a steep path on the south-west (about on the line of the later water porte) and on through what became the inner gatehouse (quite ruined) to the south-west of the **Great Keep**. This is of stupendous size and simplicity: over one hundred feet high with an internal diameter at the base of 24 feet and walls over nineteen feet thick. It is roofed by a stone dome. Also within the inner ward are the remains of the Norman hall and the later northern hall, the great hall of the castle. Below is the huge **Wogan**, a cave; it is reached by a stair cut into the rock and built out as a turret. The only other entrance to the castle is the small mill porte to the northeast which led down to the quay.

Pembroke was a very important Marcher Lordship (see p. 323). Among its earls was Richard Strongbow 'conqueror of Ireland' and during the centuries that followed it passed through several powerful families until, during the Wars of the Roses, Henry VI granted Pembroke to his half-brother Jasper.

During the Civil War Pembroke was first a stronghold for Parliament but, when John Poyer later declared for the king, Cromwell personally directed the siege which lasted for 48 days.

In all this history the best remembered event is probably the abduction of Nest, the Helen of Wales, whose attractions had already disturbed so many hearts, both Norman and Welsh (see p. 324). Owen, son of Cadwgan, who had seen Nest at a feast at Cilgerran Castle, saw fit to set fire to Pembroke Castle in order to carry her off to Powys (an event particularly suited to *son et lumière* productions). Afterwards he was constrained by the king to restore her to Gerald of Windsor.

From the castle a path follows the river bank and back to the quay.

A good distant view of **Monkton Priory Church** can be enjoyed from the Parade, a raised walk south of the West Gate. The church lies immediately across the inlet to the south-west of the castle. It was a Benedictine foundation built within a defence work which pre-dates that on which the castle is sited. The big tunnel-like vaulted nave is entered under the Norman arch of the south door but much of what is now seen of this ancient church dates from recent restoration. The north chapel will be of particular interest to Freemasons. **Monkton Old Hall**, the medieval house below the church, was leased to and thoroughly restored by Mr J. R. Cobb who did so much work on the castle in the 1880s.

A good view of the south wall of the town can be had from the road below. An attractive eighteenth-century gazebo has been built into one of the towers. There is a fine distinction of town and country since the valley has never been built up. South again is **Orange Gardens**, a gridiron layout of attractive single-storey (mostly) town cottages built in terraces, similar to those in Pembroke Dock (p. 128).

A4139 goes east to Lamphey; if continuing west along the Haven take B4320.

The low red sandstone cliffs which form the south bank of the Haven are eaten out by the wide shallow bite of Angle Bay. The fort on **Popton Point**, ingeniously re-used by BP to house administration and pumps for its pipe terminal, dates from 1859 with an open battery of 1900. **Rhoscrowther**, the substantial medieval church near the entrance, was restored by W. D. Caröe in 1910.

Angle village is hidden in a sharp east–west downfold which meets the sea again a mile away at West Angle Bay, an attractive small bathing beach with an old kiln. There is a little vaulted first-floor chapel behind the church (restored by R. K. Penson); a ruined keep and a small domed dovecot of uncertain date; and the battlemented Globe Hotel. Due north, on the cliff at Chapel Bay, the battery of the 1870 fort was remodelled in 1900. An MoD wireless station occupies the point above the defences at the mouth of the Haven.

Lamphey Palace (DoE) two miles east of Pembroke, had already been chosen as a country retreat by the Welsh bishops of St Davids before the Normans established themselves in that See, but here the Norman bishops were to find they could live the life of country gentlemen in country very much more like that to which they were accustomed. It seems particularly appropriate in this context that a vineyard has recently been planted on the south-facing slope above the palace.

The earliest surviving building is the early-thirteenth-century hall in the centre of the south range, to which a larger room (the camera) for the bishop's own use was added; the projection at the back was for the bishop's bedroom and garderobe. Bishop Gower (1328–47) added the new hall as well as the attractive little **Gatehouse** (now free-standing). Its roof gives an impression of how his other buildings (including the Bishop's Palace in St Davids) looked unruined. The arcaded parapet, which is the hallmark of all Gower's work, is much simpler here (no chequerboard pattern or colonnade). The **Chapel** immediately north of the hall is almost certainly by Bishop Vaughan (1509–23). The same oolitic limestone is used and building details are similar to those in his Holy Trinity Chapel, St Davids Cathedral.

The attractive plain building immediately to the north (for storage?) was not built until the late sixteenth century when the palace (which, like St Davids, had already suffered from lead stripping) had been granted to Richard Devereux. His sons, including Queen Elizabeth's favourite Robert (Earl of Essex), lived here as children. The circular chimneys were put into the great hall at this time.

THE SOUTH PEMBROKESHIRE COAST

The first stretch of cliffs along the south coast, starting at West Angle Bay, are old red sandstone, and to see them you must walk. This is the only remote stretch of a remarkably fine coastline.

B4320 runs west along the middle of the peninsula. B4319 turns south above the gleaming two miles of Freshwater West (dangerous bathing). Looking out over open miles of sea towards Cornwall with the sun high above, sky and water shimmer as one, and the inscription on the wayside war memorial 'Let light perpetual shine upon them' seems uniquely appropriate.

Castlemartin Artillery Range limits access to approximately eight miles of coast from Freshwater Bay to St Govan's Head, but when firing is not in progress the easterly part from Flimston is usually open. While lamenting the continued use of this outstanding stretch of coast as a tank range, one also feels gratitude that it was thus saved in the immediate post-war period from the pressure of caravans and holiday development, when it could all too easily have been inundated. Bilingual signs are an unexpected result of the military presence. Not, in Little England, in Wesh and English, but in German and English for the convenience of the Panzers who train here.

Castlemartin Church lies snug in a wooded hollow to the north of the village with a splendid many-trunked sycamore in the graveyard. Not important architecturally, but the tower and high porch make a particularly satisfactory composition from the lychgate. It is virtually a twin-naved church, plastered internally except for the Early English limestone arcade which is cut by the chancel arch. A curious ruin survives, just above the church, known as the 'Old Rectory'. It has a strange arcade of round-headed arches and, in the room to the north, a capital with crudely carved faces.

Eastwards from Castlemartin three brave church towers stand on the high open land: Warren (a spire has been added), St Twynnell's and St Petrox. Towers in South Pembrokeshire (as against the north of the county where they are rare) were useful as beacons and watch-towers as well as belfries. Typically, they are tall and slender, and battlemented with a corbel table, and with a stair turret climbing higher than the main tower. Many medieval towers survived nine-teenth-century rebuildings and make a powerful contribution in this open landscape.

Access to the coast when the range is open is opposite the turning to Warren. **Flimston Chapel**, which you will pass, lies alone beside a deserted farm in the range. This vaulted chapel had become a barn until it was thoroughly restored in 1903 and again following the war so that it has almost become a military memorial.

This part of the south coast comes as a complete surprise. The cliff tops are level lawns of fine turf which end without warning, sliced off like cheese vertically into the sea. Wave action is creating fantastic shapes in the carboniferous limestone; arches, stacks, weird blowholes and caves. The booming shingle can be heard working far below. The Elegug stacks and cliffs are patronized by innumerable nesting sea-birds – an amazing sight. There is a superb walk from Flimston to St Govan's Head (and on to Bosherston Pools) past eerie abandoned tanks on cliffs carpeted with flowers

(lime-likers). **St Govan's Chapel** is more quickly reached from
Bosherston (right off B4319). This diminutive building, fifteenth
century, wedged into a cleft in the rock above a holy well, is a
primitive vaulted cell with a mud floor, next to a smaller rock-cut
chamber. Fenton describes how 'crippled patients bathe their limbs
many of whom come from the remotest parts of the Principality to
seek relief here and leave their crutches behind, a votive offering on
the altar'. Huntsman's Leap, a dramatic unleapable cleft in the cliff,
is half a mile west.

One of the newest acquisitions of the National Trust (1976) is the
magnificent stretch of coastline and part of its intermediate hinterland which belonged to the Cawdor family, whose house, Stackpole
Court (eighteenth century with big nineteenth-century additions),
was demolished in the 1960s. **Bosherston Pools** formed part of the
enchanting landscape designed for its Park. Leave the car either at
Bosherston church or the car park for Broadhaven. The pools are a
series of long finger-like lagoons, formed by damming in the eighteenth century, and now renowned for their water lilies. They are cut
off from the sea by a high bank of shingle at Broadhaven (bathing
beach). First there is a deep oak and ash woodland; then after a limestone bluff the country is more open and the inland trees give way to
sea-stunted sycamore; then open dunes and finally the cliffs and open
sea. All this variety within a mile. Back at Bosherston, the cottage
with tables in the garden serves good old-fashioned teas with boiled
eggs.

Stackpole Elidôr, or Cheriton, Church, is tucked in near the head
of one of the little valleys which lead down to the pools. Its monuments are well worth seeing and are described inside the church in
the comprehensive notes.

Stackpole Quay, by a derelict farm, is in good condition but little
used. Lovely woodland runs down almost to the sea and there is a
car park among the ash trees for Barafundle Bay and blowhole-
riddled Stackpole Head. The cliff scenery changes again near the
Quay: old red sandstone to Old Castle Head, five miles across the
Bay, and then limestone again (except for blown sand in the Ritec
estuary) to Tenby.

Freshwater East has holiday shackery which the National Park
tries to tidy.

Manorbier was 'the pleasantest spot in Wales' according to
Giraldus Cambrensis (p. 320), but he admits to being biased, having
been born in the castle and spent his boyhood here. It stands above
a sandy bay and Giraldus could watch 'all the ships from Great

Britain' bound for Ireland as they sailed below. He describes with pride the orchards, vineyards and woods as well as the castle, but this was largely rebuilt around 1300 after his death. The inner ward is on the end of a spur, protected by a curtain wall and moat. Opposite the gatehouse a range of living quarters is built against the curtain. The chapel, in the south corner, was converted to a living room in the sixteenth century when the fine window and fireplace were put in. The history of the castle is sketchy and seems refreshingly peaceful. It changed hands during the civil war. There are now two unassuming houses in the inner ward which has an attractive, not overkempt garden.

The **Parish Church** across the valley is that to which Giraldus, aged seven, asked to be taken when the Welsh raided Tenby. Inside, its strong sculptural form still gives a powerful sense of security. Steps lead down into it through a vaulted porch (note the medieval painting) as into a crypt. The huge walls of the Norman nave have been carved out (or so it seems) to form arcades to the fourteenth-century aisles. The uninhibited intersections of the transept vaults cut the main vault of the nave at different levels. The sculptural character of the church must have been even stronger before the 1865 restoration (F. Wehnert) when a much larger arch was cut in the chancel wall. Then the old rood-screen and the Royal Arms were removed, and the perpendicular east window changed for the present three-light window. The tower has an unusual position in the angle between the chancel (rebuilt in the thirteenth century) and north transept. It was originally reached only by a ladder.

Many people know Manorbier through their military training. The permanent army camp gives a Salisbury Plain touch to this part of Pembrokeshire.

Penally, separated from the sea by broad burrows, was the site of an important *clas*. Two Celtic crosses have been placed in the church (enthusiasts should take a torch). The old Ridgeway route Penally–Lamphey, now a modern road, gives great views north and south. **St Florence**, off to its north, is a snug village with Flemish chimneys and a good church.

Caldey Island (Norse: cold island), only three-quarters of a mile from the mainland at Giltar Point (cattle were swum over here), is reached from Tenby. Boats take day-visitors in the summer (not on Sundays): a beautiful place to spend a fine day. The silent order of Trappist Cistercians, whose community numbers forty, came here from Belgium when they bought the island in 1928. Besides working a thriving mixed stock and arable farm, the Community exports the now famous herbs and scent made from the island flowers.

The Celtic monastery on Caldey was particularly renowned. Ynys Bŷr, its pre-Norse name, commemorates the first abbot, who was succeeded by Samson (a friend of David), who eventually went to Brittany where he founded the monastery at Dol. Samson is buried at Dol, and is now the patron saint of Brittany. After Normanization a Benedictine priory flourished on Caldey. Its remnants, humble and primitive, but a fascinating survival, are grouped round a small courtyard: a Prior's Tower and a church with a stumpy little spire.

Most of the present monastery, a vast pile in white stucco with a red Roman tile roof, is a highly original design by J. Coates Carter. It dates from 1910–12, and was built for a young Englishman, Abbot Aelred Carlyle, for whom the island was bought in 1906 for his community of Anglican Benedictines. He later became a Roman Catholic.

St Margaret's Island (West Wales Naturalists' Trust) was originally connected by a causeway to the north-west tip of Caldey (do not be tempted to try the crossing at low tide). In the nineteenth century, limestone was quarried and there were houses. Now there are sea-birds, but no puffins on account of the rats.

Tenby is the Brighton of West Wales. Stucco gleams on her tall seaside terraces: Regency in effect if not in date. The town had been renowned for sea bathing for nearly half a century when John Nash started work on the Royal Pavilion at Brighton for the Prince Regent. A tablet in the parish church (north-west corner) commemorates

PEGGY DAVIES
Bathing woman 42 years
to the Ladies who visited TENBY
Her good humour
respectful attention and
Gratitude
made her employers – Friends
On 29 of Sept 1809
In the Water
She was seized with Apoplexy
and expired Aged 82.

The town is peculiarly well-sited for a seaside resort, on a peninsula which divides the coastline into north and south bays; one of these is likely to be sheltered. Had Nash not left West Wales to return to

London in 1796 he would surely have been in his element working
here. The first 'seaside building' in Tenby was probably the conversion in 1781 of St Julian's Chapel, formerly on the end of the pier,
into a public bath-house by John Jones, Bachelor of Physic, Haverfordwest. In 1805 a grand new **Public Bath-house** was built at the
expense of Sir William Paxton. He employed S. P. Cockerell who had
recently designed his house in Carmarthenshire (Middleton Hall) and
was to be responsible for the folly there known as Paxton's Tower
(see p. 158). Paxton, who had made a princely fortune in India, set up
as a banker in London and decided to stand for parliament. Tenby
owes a lot to his energy and imagination. The Baths, no sooner built
than burnt down, he promptly rebuilt. They are below the castle,
handy for both shores, and now survive as flats. Paxton bought other
property in Tenby and was responsible for improvements to the
streets and, most important of all, to the water supply. He established
a theatre, which failed, and died much lamented in 1824.

Tenby had been an important port in the Middle Ages but began
to decline after the Tudor period. The harbour was lively with
fishing trawlers throughout the nineteenth century and good warehouses survive.

The **Town Walls** were begun before the end of the thirteenth
century. They were strengthened from time to time, particularly in
1457 by Jasper, Earl of Pembroke, and again in 1588, a reflection
of Tenby's Elizabethan importance. However, once they were no
longer necessary for defence the Corporation shilly-shallied about
their conservation. The battle for their preservation went on throughout the nineteenth century. A notice near the Five Arches (the big
rounded barbican of the West Gate) states how 'Arches and walls
were preserved to the Town by an injunction of the Court of Chancery obtained 23 June 1873 by the late George Chater FRCS'; today's
conservationists had their forerunners. The Arches here are constantly under threat as traffic increases. The other three gates were
demolished in the eighteenth century.

The **Castle** has a fine position on the headland. The present ruin
(from the thirteenth century) is traditionally on the site of the 'fine
fortress above the ninth wave' described in an early Welsh poem
(before AD 875) – the name, Tenby, derives from the Welsh Dinbych-
y-pysgod (small fort of the fishes). The castle changed hands often
between the Welsh themselves and the Earls of Pembroke. By the
end of the fourteenth century it was reported to be dilapidated.
Town and castle were garrisoned again in the Civil War, and were
besieged by both sides. Eventually it was taken by Cromwell in 1648.

On the summit is the statue of Albert the Good (John Evan Thomas, 1865). Before leaving Castle Hill be sure to see the small **Tenby Museum**, in a plastered house which is adapted from the domestic remains of the castle.

St Catherine's Fort, an outlier of the mid-nineteenth-century Milford Haven scheme, was built 1868–75 for a garrison of about sixty and an armament of six guns (cost £16,260). It is now a zoo.

The **Tudor Merchant's House** (National Trust), *c.* 1500, above the harbour gives some idea of how the more prosperous Tenby citizen lived. Adjoining buildings are partly of the same age and were once connected with it.

St Mary's Church proudly reflects the town's tremendous prosperity at that period. It is a splendid and almost complete fifteenth-century rebuilding of the thirteenth-century church, demonstrating close architectural links with the West of England, only a few hours' sail to the south in a fair wind. The barrel-roofed nave is separated by arcades of five deeply-moulded arches from the north (mid fifteenth century) and south (later) aisles. The south aisle absorbed various earlier parts of building; its open roof and west window are also late fifteenth century (glass by Kempe). The 1634 pulpit was recently restored. The east end is a complete surprise, but its drama is undermined by the absence of a chancel screen. About 1470 the chancel was lengthened and a flight of steps constructed across it up to the sanctuary. The walls were also raised and the wagon roof put in.

St Mary's has a fair share of the good tombs which might be expected in a rich town church, particularly in the two chapels. In the south that to the benefactor, William Risam, a tradesman who died in 1633, is especially enjoyable (see also p. 137).

The tall thirteenth-century tower is in the angle between the chancel and nave, as at Manorbier, but this time to the south. There was a chapel on the first floor. The tower is topped by an octagonal spire, almost as high again. The big south porch is *c.* 1500, as is the ogee-arched west door (protected by a large porch until 1831) and the wall opposite (part of a building known as 'the college'). The inscription states 'Blessed be God in his gifts'.

Tenby is a town to enjoy as a whole rather than piece by piece; and even in August it can be a thoroughly enjoyable small resort.

Monkstone Point (great views) separates Tenby Roads from Saundersfoot Bay. The cliffs are heavily wooded in the shelter of the headland. **Saundersfoot**, which now has an entirely holiday and sailing air, was a busy anthracite port (last shipload 1930) and it also had an early iron-works. The harbour was built in 1833 and in 1866 the railway arrived. Hean Castle (1876 and 1926), the big private house above the bay, was probably designed by the house architect of Hamptons, its builders.

The bay sweeps round to **Amroth**: luxuriant woodland in steep secretive dingles hides holiday bungalows. This is the end of the Pembrokeshire coast path. Inland this small stretch of country, so intensively used at its edges, can be surprisingly and refreshingly remote. It is hilly, folded farmland with little churches down farm tracks and farmers talking in their South Pembrokeshire way, more West Country than Welsh. **Crunwear** (187/108), three miles north-west of Amroth, up a track off A477, is most solitary. The main road goes on east to St Clears (p. 161).

A478 links South Pembrokeshire with A40. **Narberth** is a couple of miles short of the trunk road. It was here that Pwyll, Prince of Dyfed, first saw the beautiful Rhiannon riding on her great white horse. His palace here, which seems to have been particularly favoured as a hunting lodge, is mentioned in several of the tales from the *Mabinogion*. Its cattle fairs were once widely popular, English graziers and drovers regularly attending, and pretty souvenir plates, the sort with roses and a lazy edge, saying *A Present from Narberth*, were sold in the town.

A478 is the main road north to Cardigan (p. 89) but B4313 leads up into the Preselis. If heading back to Haverfordwest, B4314 joins A40 at Robeston Wathen. Its church tower is a grand landmark as you approach on the main road from the east: battlemented and corbelled with a shallow turret, it gives a foretaste of South Pembrokeshire towers.

THE PRESELY HILLS (MYNYDD PRESELY)

The Presely Hills, traditionally open sheep-walk, are smooth, beautiful and unspectacular. Presely Top, Foelcwmcerwyn, is only 1760 feet. Their character derives from great empty stretches of heather and mountain grass, bilberries and occasional outcropping rock, and plenty of sky. This makes forestry a particularly dangerous threat in visual terms; its results can be seen around Rosebush.

Presely is an elusive range of hills to explore. The northerly part is cut off by the Gwaun valley, and its two great man-made features, Pentre Ifan and Carningli (described p. 98) are more often approached from the north coast road. Two roads, B4313 Narberth–Fishguard and B4329 Haverfordwest–Cardigan, bisect the range diagonally, crossing at New Inn. The main mass of mountain lies to the east of this crossroads.

The best way to get into the hills on foot is to take the Bronze Age track (*c.* 1500 BC) which was part of the route from Salisbury Plain to Ireland. It is marked on the O.S. maps, and can be picked up above Crymmych or at the westerly end on either of the roads north of New Inn. This will be a ten -to twelve-mile walk but it can also be done in parts; no climbing but some wet going is likely. It is very easy to get lost in a mist even with a map and compass. Near the east end of the track there is a good hill-fort at **Foeldrygarn** (157/337) where 27 hut circles were discovered in 1899. A mile further on is **Carnmenyn**, subject of archaeological debate. It is once again accepted that the blue stones at Stonehenge were brought from here, the nearest known source of spotted dolerite. An astonishing feat. Even if scholars' ingenious theories of transference of sanctity should go with the wind, Presely itself seems to have had great religious significance to the Bronze Age people. Numerous standing stones, stone circles and cromlechs suggest this. Many are marked on the O.S. maps. The Pembrokeshire Coast National Park has published a handy leaflet, *The Presely Hills*, which gives precise directions.

It is worth keeping an eye on the local paper for the lamb sales, notably at Brynberian, and sheep dog trials. Sheep have increased greatly in number in the last few years, probably as a result of the government subsidies. Welsh mountain sheep are quite able to weather a winter on the hill but now there are too many for the grass available and they are sent down to Castlemartin.

At the end of the last century **Rosebush** (one mile east of New Inn) made a brave bid to be known as a resort. The slate quarries here were already connected by rail with the GWR at Clynderwen and the row of quarrymen's cottages had been built. The Prescelly Hotel, the Wild West corrugated iron building now painted a sad grey, was erected and tourists were further encouraged by the digging out of two lakes (one had an island complete with pagoda reached by an oriental bridge). But the quarries did not prosper and the Rosebush water failed to contain the medicinal properties necessary to a spa.

Maenclochog, on B4313, two and a half miles south-west of New Inn, is the chief village. It is a substantial place of considerable character (stone cottages and chapels) on the southern slope of Presely. An astonishing number of signposts in Pembrokeshire point to it. The very pleasant-looking house, which you see from the road a mile to the east, is **Temple Druid** by John Nash, *c.* 1794 (not open).

Crymmych, on the east edge of the hills, is another place of strong individuality with the feel of a small frontier town: the railway has left it but the main Cardigan–Tenby road A478 dashes through. Preseli school is the fierce-looking brick and glass building of the Brutalist period in the 1950s, an all-Welsh-speaking comprehensive. A minor road with magnificent views runs north-west from the middle of Crymmych. Bear left, skirting the hills to join B4239 at Crosswell.

The first Rebecca Riot (see p. 326) took place at **Efailwen** (on A478 seven miles south of Crymmych). In May 1839 the Whitland Turnpike Trust put up a gate here. On the night of 13 May it was wrecked; its successor went on 6 June and a third in July. The attackers, who were disguised in women's clothes with blackened faces, took their name either from the biblical text '. . . let thy [Rebecca's] seed possess the gate of those that hate them'[1] or, some say, because their leader, Thomas Rees, who was a very large man, got his dress from a local giantess known as Great Rebecca.

South of Presely, and east of B4329, the **Llys-y-fran Reservoir** (1972) must be the only one in Wales to be almost universally approved. Above the dam the view is of a pleasantly meandering lake with wooded banks and branching inlets running up into farmland. A launching ramp for dinghies has been provided, and it is stocked with brown trout. Do not be put off by the entrance sign. Llys-y-fran is at 040/245, 3 miles north of Clarbeston Road railway junction, home of the factory where the delicious Arbeston butter is blended; New Zealand in origin but more Welsh in taste and texture than much pure Welsh farm butter – salty and yellow.

[1] Genesis xxiv: 60.

CHAPTER FIVE

Carmarthenshire (Dyfed)

❧

Carmarthenshire claims the largest milk-collecting centre in Europe (at Whitland). This may surprise those who think of the county in terms of heavy industry, seaside holidays, or near wilderness. Stands bearing an impressive number of churns appear in quite unexpected places, much of the dairy country being hilly upland.

THE UPPER TYWI

Before the construction of the **Llyn Brianne**, 1971–2, the little known upper Tywi valley and those of the tributary streams which join it were among the most remote and beautiful places in Britain. The small, steep-sided valleys, and the sun filtering oak and hazel woodland dropping down to their flickering streams, were a secret paradise that could only survive if never exposed to the onslaught of car-borne tourism. Much is now submerged by the new reservoir (for Swansea) and opened up by scenic drives. Their popularity inevitably means that other valleys are within orbit of the motor car and of those wanting to stretch their legs between drives. The reservoir's indented wooded shoreline makes it one of the most attractive in Britain. If wilderness was in good supply, such taming might be regarded as gain: sadly, it is not.

Llyn Brianne is usually reached from the south but far more attractive approaches are now possible from the Tregaron–Abergwesyn mountain road. Eight miles west of Tregaron, a newly-made-up road south leads to **Soar-y-mynydd,** now on the edge of a big block of forest, but once at the heart of a great sheep-walk. Until recently this was the most isolated of all the Calvinistic Methodist chapels in Wales, and was the focal point for farms for miles around, its congregation coming on foot or mountain pony on the small green tracks which converged here. The poignancy of these empty farmsteads makes it easy to forget the drudgery and loneliness of much of the life they sheltered. Inside the chapel a feeling of time-less remoteness lingers: pine pews, pulpit on the long wall, and that

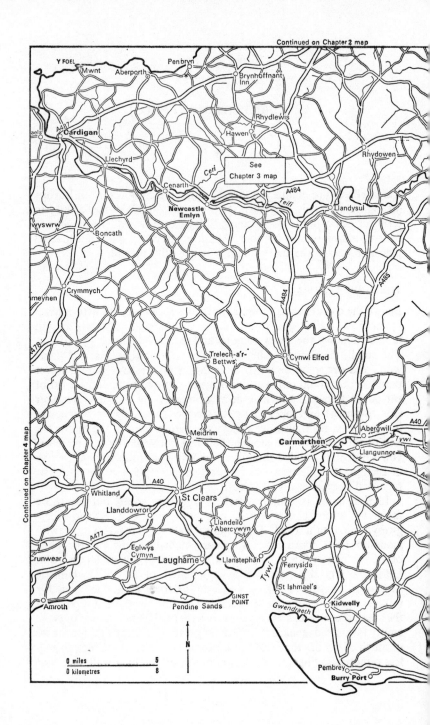

Continued on Chapter 4 map

Y FOEL

Mwnt

Penbryn

Aberporth

Brynhoffnant Inn

Rhydlewis

Hawen

aels

A487

Cardigan

Llechyrd

Ceri

See Chapter 3 map

Rhydowen

A484

Teifi

Cenarth

Newcastle Emlyn

Llandysul

wyswrw

Boncath

A485

meynen

Crymmych

A478

A484

Trelech-a'r-Bettws

Cynwl Elfed

Meidrim

Abergwili

A40

Carmarthen

Tywi

Llangunnor

A4

A40

Whitland

St Clears

Llanddowror

Llandeilo Abercywyn

Eglwys Cymyn

Laugharne

Llanstephan

Tywi

Ferryside

Crunwear

St Ishmael's

A477

Amroth

Pendine Sands

GINST POINT

Gwendraeth

Kidwelly

Pembrey

Burry Port

0 miles — 5
0 kilometres — 8

N

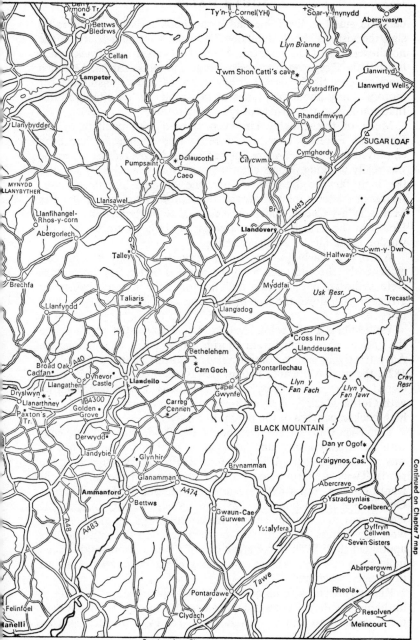

Continued on Chapter 7 map

dampish smell in the Bible and hymn books. Hundreds (literally)
sign the visitors' book annually. The road continues south to the
north-west tip of the reservoir where it is joined by a track which
has left the Tregaron-Abergwesyn road five miles further east at a
junction dauntingly signed 'Llandovery 17 miles, unsuitable for
motors'. Only about two miles of this road are 'unsuitable': after
that you are on the tarmac of the scenic route.

Much of this country has been planted with conifers by the
Economic Forestry Group. A forester told us that he had been
employed for fourteen years but had never discovered for whom he
was really working. Horse chestnut surprisingly survive by some of
the high farmsteads; occasionally one of park-like proportions
thrives in sheltered folds above the thousand-foot contour. Two miles
west is **Ty'n-y-Cornel**, which once claimed to be the remotest Youth
Hostel in the British Isles. It is accessible only by tracks, and the
warden is the farmer at Blaendoethie.

When you reach the dam (huge car park), it may be only too
evident why the approach from the north is better. The harsh concrete spillway, out of scale and far too pale in tone, makes an
arrogant gash down the face of the dam, itself made of huge lumps
of rock.

Ystrad-ffin is a mile below the dam. **Capel Ystrad-ffin** stands beside
the ancient road from Strata Florida (to which it once belonged).
An attractively simple, barrel-ceiled Anglican chapel replaced, in
1821, the medieval Capel Paulin. It was restored later in the nineteenth century and is lit by a fine oil lamp. Square-headed windows
with Gothic glazing, eighteenth-century communion rails and good
high-backed benches in the porch all survive.

Twm Sion Catti's Cave, high above the Tywi, near its confluence
with the equally lovely (and less spoilt) Doethie, can be reached by
way of the Dinas Nature Trail, on the RSPB Reserve (signed on the
road). Twm, a sharp-witted trickster and thief of the early seventeenth century, and a natural son of the famous Sir John Wynn of
Gwydir (see *North Wales*, p. 123) and Catherine Jones (whence his
name), was not without charm. He courted, and by unfair means
won, the heiress of Ystradffin; he then gave up thieving and was
appointed sheriff. This country is one of the last strongholds of the
indigenous oak (sessile) and so of many of the creatures that thrive
in its open woodland.

Rhandirmwyn, with its abandoned lead-mine, is the first village
in the main valley. Across the river a road leads up the Melyn over
the watershed to join the lovely Cothi (p. 147), or keep left for

Cilycwm (Llanfihangel-yng-Nghilycwm) on the Gwenlas. It has cobbled gutters and an attractive medieval church with remarkable eighteenth-century (and perhaps earlier) wall paintings. Capel y Groes (1859), down the alley opposite the church, is a charming small building, pink and Gothic and made slightly Swiss by its roof and wavy barge board.

Dolauhirion Bridge (1773) crosses the Tywi half a mile above Llandovery, just off the Cilycwm road. This single splendid arch, spanning 84 feet, is perhaps William Edwards's most graceful design (see also p. 254).

A483 – THE SUGAR LOAF TO LLANDOVERY

A483 from Llanwrtyd Wells swings down round the **Sugar Loaf** just after it has crossed into Carmarthenshire. This is a favourite viewpoint and a short sharp walk for those who want to scale the hill. The Central Wales Railway crosses the stone Cynghordy Viaduct three miles south. Those planning walks will find this enjoyable line particularly useful. The road is now following the valley of the Bran. Beside the river, about a mile below the hamlet of **Cynghordy**, stand the gaunt remains of Glanbran, built by Roderick Gwynne in 1777. The house was nicely described by Mr Thomas, gamekeeper, in his history of the property (typed 1931): 'The ancient palace makes a perfect and splendid ruin although slightly out of repair.'

THE COTHI, AND COUNTRY TO THE NORTH OF THE TYWI AND A40

The gentle but beautiful country to the north of the Tywi and A40 is relatively empty and travelling west there are few direct roads. The Cothi rises high up in a bog on the Cardiganshire borders and follows its beautiful valley (sessile oak) to be joined by the Twrch at **Pumsaint** on A482, the road south-east from Lampeter to A40. This likeable unglamorous stone village is the social centre of a big area; the dances held in the corrugated iron institute are famed for miles around and fishermen have long patronized the Dolaucothi Hotel. Two Roman forts were discovered under Pumsaint in 1972 (by Mr John Little). Their function was to provide the technological expertise and security to mine gold at **Dolaucothi** (National Trust), one mile east, and to turn it into bullion for export to the imperial mints. The method of mining at Dolaucothi ties up with descriptions left by Pliny of mining in Spain (which previously no one had been

able fully to understand). A detachment of mining engineers was
working as early as AD 74 on the site. The gold-bearing quartz was
found in the long spur between the Cothi and the Annell; initially
two channels 7–14 miles long (visible in places), were brought along
the flanks of the spur to feed tanks from which water was released
to rush down the hillside causing exposure of the quartz by erosion.
Later, shafts were dug. All this, and the walks leading to it, are
described in the lean-to in the main opencast (665/405).

Pumsaint takes its name from a stone (probably a crude form of
quern) in which five saints left footprints. It is near the road beyond
the opening of the main quarry opposite the lodge of Dolaucothi
House (demolished). Good stretches of the Roman road, Sarn Helen
(p. 70), can also be picked out (north and south of Farmers).

Caeo church (one mile east) has a grand tower which juts proudly
from the heart of this friendly stone village. Important cattle fairs
were held here until 1918; a local landowner used to interpret to
the English buyers.

Llansawel, a grey and white stone village proudly topped by
Shiloh, its 1868 chapel, is about five miles west by minor roads; it
is a useful junction of several others. To the south, B4337, the
Llandeilo road, runs below much quarried Pen y Ddinas. The oak-
lined road to the right, half a mile south, was presumably a result of
estate planting. From it there are fine views down the two lakes to
Talley Abbey (Talyllychau), enclosed by farmed hills. It was founded
towards the end of the twelfth century by the Lord Rhys (see p. 327)
for the Premonstratensians whose motto was 'Devotion. Learning.
Service'. Not much survives and it is mostly very plain – even crude
– late twelfth century. Go when the evening light on the hills can be
seen through the two great pointed arches of the crossing, and the
distant bleating of sheep is the only interruption.

The **Parish Church**, immediately next door, has an unusual 1773
plan with two doors in a plain west end and, therefore, two side aisles
and no central aisle. This plan, together with a boarded barrel ceiling,
simple box pews, flagged floor, and loudly ticking clock, makes a
nice contrast to the usual, and is more akin to a nonconformist chapel.

For **Taliaris** turn right off B4302, four miles south. Its most
civilized elevation can be admired from the B road near Maerdy
church but the house is open on written application. It was ingeniously refronted in 1791 to give the impression of a large square
block, but this is a facing to an already altered Jacobean house.
Good panelling and the staircase survive.

You can now make your way by hilly roads north to the Cothi

valley or, from Llansawel, follow B4310 west through Abergorlech to Brechfa, a no-nonsense village to the south of the big block of Brechfa Forest which clothes the southern side of the high uplands which separate this region from Teifiside (p. 82). The rector of the primitive little **Llanfihangel Rhos y Corn** (549/347) has only fifteen parishioners but God alone knows how many conifers in his parish. The road eventually climbs over Mynydd Llanybydder, and on to Llanybydder on the Teifi. The church is twin-naved – almost certainly a *c.* 1500 addition to a thirteenth-century church – and pink-washed within with a slab floor; oil lamps have been converted to electricity and sunflowers in Gothic panels decorate the pulpit. Mauve sweet rocket and columbine grow around the graveyard.

From Brechfa B4310 goes south to A40 as do deep lost roads which cling close to the Cothi. **Llanfynydd**, snug in a deep valley, is a compact village with two pubs and a good little church with a low tower in the hills to the east. But from Brechfa an attractive minor road runs west and locally useful lanes continue west in an unhurried way and cross the little river Gwili which eventually joins the Tywi near Carmarthen (see Abergwili). Some are marvellously lined by beech trees, others, particularly on the higher land, by laburnum (see also p. 84). This wandering route will be cut by two main roads running north from Carmarthen, A485 and A484.

Cynwyl Elfed is at the junction of A484 and B4333, a fine road over the hills to Newcastle Emlyn. It is a friendly-looking painted village crowned by Bethel Baptist Chapel, a modest building dating from 1792.

In the high, still empty country of the watershed which is the barrier to Teifiside, ruler-like minor roads cut the uplands. These date from nineteenth-century enclosures when a great land-hunger led many cottagers to run up *tai-unnos* (one-night houses) and farm these unproductive uplands. To the south of this bleaker country, green farmland cut by steep dingles continues.

From Cynwyl Elfed minor roads ramble westward to **Trelech a'r Betws** where the chief building is **Rock Chapel** (1791 and 1827); a plain stone building with the unusual feature of outside steps leading to the galleries. Its plain box pews are bright with golden yellow paint.

Meidrim, five miles south, at a road junction and river crossing, is a prosperous hillside village serving rich agricultural country. Small roads continue west and eventually cross A478 (from Cardigan) to climb into the Preselis (p. 142).

THE VALE OF TYWI, LLANDOVERY–LLANDEILO AND
COUNTRY TO THE SOUTH

Llandovery (Llanymddyfri) comes into its own on market day (Friday)
when sheep, store cattle, farmers and dealers throng the market and
spill into the surrounding streets. This small no-frills town, where the
hills meet the lush Tywi valley, was once a great gathering place for
drovers. At the centre are the early-nineteenth-century Market Hall,
Soanian, with an octagonal cupola, and the taller but duller Town
Hall (early Victorian), the Black Ox and the numerous other pubs.
The medieval Castle makes a good view-point above the market.

The Romans had a camp here and **Llanfair-ar-y-Bryn Church** (off
the Builth Wells road) is built on the site of a Roman fort. It is like
a great tithe barn with a sturdy thirteenth-century tower. Parapets
and gargoyles were added (*c.* 1500) but, despite this and its size, the
whole gives a sense of humility, with its rough plastered walls; nave
partly open and partly barrel-ceiled and a clear west window letting
in a flood of light (restored W. D. Caröe 1913). William Williams,
Pantycelyn (1717–91), perhaps the greatest of many Welsh hymn
writers (the one best-known in English is *Guide me, O thou Great
Jehovah*) is buried here under a simple slab and commemorated
by the pink granite obelisk to the south of the church. (Pantycelyn
Farm is three miles east.) Vicar Prichard (also of Llandovery) who
wrote *Canwyll y Cymru* (*The Welshman's Candle*), early-seventeenth-
century moral verses which became so popular as to be household
sayings, is commemorated with Williams in Kempe's east window.

St Michael's College was founded in 1848 to teach Welsh, and is
the only public school where Welsh is taught and used. The original
buildings, by Fuller and Gingell, are dullish Gothic, but the 1971
conversion of a stone building into the music school is sturdily done.
The first headmaster was John Williams (see p. 71).

Myddfai, a snug stone village, lies four miles south of Llandovery
over steepish farmland. It has long been famed for its medieval
Physicians and their descendants; the British Museum holds an
early manuscript of their cures. In the thirteenth century, Rhiwallon
and his three sons practised here under the patronage of Prince Rhys
Grug[1] (Rhys the Hoarse: could they not cure him?). The very likeable
church is in the middle of Myddfai; a barrel-vaulted thirteenth-
century building to which a south aisle was added, *c.* 1500, by a
pointed arcade on octagonal columns, which gives the whole building
a great sense of width and light. A simple chancel arch leads to the

[1] His probable tomb is in St Davids Cathedral.

lower barrel-ceiled chancel. Bold eighteenth-century lettering of the prayer of consecration, a richly painted Gwynne hatchment, and memorials to an eighteenth-century surgeon and his son in the porch are among its attractive details.

Beyond the village, narrow lanes climb little valleys up to Cross Inn. Here you can strike east over moorland towards the Usk Reservoir (p. 49) and on to Trecastle, or keep going past Llanddeusant church for **Llyn y Fan Fach**. Once you are past the dam and the NO BATHING notice there is nothing to break the magic. The lake lies in an amphitheatre right under the beetling crags of the Carmarthen Vans. Dead calm is suddenly disturbed by whirlwinds. It is easy to understand how the herdsboy saw the beautiful Lady of the Lake, courted and won this enchanted maiden. Eventually he was to lose her and all his flocks in these black waters, on account of an unfair spell cast upon their marriage, by which, if he struck her three times, she would vanish. This he did, gently and under strong provocation, but the spell worked. They had, however, by this time raised three remarkable sons who were to become the Physicians of Myddfai.

From the lake the climb up to the Carmarthenshire Fan is steep (but see also p. 47).

The choice is whether to return to the Vale of Tywi, which is joined at **Llangadog**, a proper valley village; to go over the hills to Carreg Cennen (p. 152); or to make first for the astonishing Iron Age fort of **Carn Goch** (690/244) in the hills on the way to Llandeilo. Turn left off A4069 for Bethlehem (lovely views and a great place for posting Christmas cards), and follow the lanes round the west of the hill above the village and up the farm road towards Crûg-las. Suddenly the massive fortification wall will appear across the skyline on your left. This is one of the biggest camps in Wales and it would be hard to imagine a more dramatic site. A smaller fort lies immediately to the west.

Llandeilo, four miles downstream, is the market town in the heart of the lovely Vale of Tywi, a place of great charm with unassuming stuccoed houses joined in terraces (often differing from their neighbours).

The Dynevor clumps, two magnificent groups of beech planted by Capability Brown in the park of Dynevor Castle (p. 156), crown Llandeilo. The bridge over the Tywi is the other really grand thing about this little town. Approach it if you can via this bridge (i.e. from the south, not A40). The town stands out on a bluff and Dynevor Castle dominates the crag to the west.

The **Bridge**, designed by Edward Haycock in 1848, is best admired from the short lane immediately downstream on the right bank. The close-up view of this huge single arch is stunning. A small plaque on the parapet of the bridge itself shows an engraving of the 1771 seven-arched structure which it replaced; a very nice idea. The houses stepping up the hill into Llandeilo were related to the level of the old road and bridge. The road then cuts the steeply sloping well-treed churchyard walled in by stuccoed houses and shops. (The church was rebuilt by G. G. Scott, 1848–51.)

Quay Street and the remains of the Abbey wall are reminders of Llandeilo's past. More stucco, with occasional grand injections of glazed red and yellow brick (as in Ammanford) by Lord Dynevor's agent in the late nineteenth century, leads to A40. The plain stone Provision Market faces the suitably Gothic school building (alas, empty) at the top of the town. At the lower end, just off A40, the Railway Station survives – very useful but, alas, disintegrating.

Carreg Cennen, four miles south-east of Llandeilo is another castle not to be missed (DoE). Turn left off A483 and then right on the minor road for Trapp in Ffairfach just south of Llandeilo. Carreg Cennen farm is the last outpost of the valley. The approach is fairly gradual but to the south the rock plunges 300 feet to the river; beyond lie miles of open hill. The original castle was built by the Lord Rhys in the twelfth century, but the building here is late thirteenth–early fourteenth century. The path leads up through the wall of the outer ward, up the long ramped approach through the barbican and the gatehouse (protected on its way by six pits) to the square inner ward. This is flanked by a great hall and solar to the east, with a projecting chapel tower (all at upper floor level). A long tunnel leads to the cave in the heart of the rock where water drips into a small natural basin.

Llandybie is due south of Llandeilo on the Ammanford road (A483). **Derwydd**, to the north of the village (private, but occasionally open to antiquarian parties) was a mansion of Sir Rhys ap Thomas. Despite its Victorian appearance it is at heart a Tudor and Jacobean rebuilding of an earlier house from which that gentleman and the Earl of Richmond traditionally set forth for Bosworth. It still belongs to descendants of its builders, the Stepney Gulstons, and has some grand plastered ceilings, carved chimneypieces and the superb fifteenth-century Rhys bed, huge and richly carved like a latterday Bayeux tapestry.

Back on the main road the famous **Lime Kilns**, for which the designs, by R. K. Penson, were exhibited at the Royal Academy in

1858, can be seen to the right half a mile on. The facade of one of the kilns is dramatically decorated with pointed arcading and a corbelled cornice. Even more dramatic (and thoroughly dangerous and private) is the view into the top of the Welsh kiln ('the highest in the land') above Pentre Gwenlais. It smoulders fearsomely from its depths; every leaf in the valley below seems to have been decorated for Christmas.

Llandybie is a likeable village and described itself in its first-class 1972 guide-book as 'a most convenient centre for tourists and shoppers alike'. Part of this claim is based on its spick and span, freshly painted railway station (1855), five trains each way on week-days, on the useful and beautiful Central Wales line – Swansea to Shrewsbury. The church has several spirited baroque monuments, recently surprisingly repainted in predominantly pastel hues (by Edward Wilkin). Back on the main road are two American-looking clap-board houses. They were built in 1897 by the Davies family, carpenters who returned to Llandybie after spending eighteen years in USA.

Glynhir, one and a half miles east of Llandybie, now a sad farm with fine outbuildings and an octagonal Tudor dovecot (ruined), has long been famous for its oft depicted picturesque waterfall (642/151) on the Loughor, its gorge here darkened by dense jungle. Two miles upstream (668/180) on the west flank of the Black Mountains the Loughor emerges from a miniature cliff below which a lovely pool overhung by ash becomes an instant river. Nasty fencing encloses the site which is only a ten-minute stroll from the mountain road to Capel Gwynfe. Leave the car about two hundred yards beyond the crossing of the Nant Gwythwch. There are spectacular views of Carreg Cennen.

Only a couple of miles below bosky Glynhir, is **Ammanford**. It did not exist a hundred years ago but the gleaming chips of anthracite in the backgarden coal-bunkers explain its surge to life. Private coal-workings still exist; some, for instance, off the road over the grassy tops to Pontardawe (the grand views here include Gower and silhouettes of pithead machinery). This road leaves Ammanford through Betws, the original village.

Glanamman, another busy valley town, is four miles east of Ammanford up the Amman, just below the Black Mountains. The A474 follows the river and railway in the valley bottom in the usual pattern. The hill roads abound in the sharp contrast typical of such regions: mine, chapel, and long lines of terrace-housing, suddenly terminating in open hill. Close-up views and vast views. The chapels continue to produce bards. **Brynamman,** for instance, provided both the crowned and the chaired bards in the 1972 National Eisteddfod.

LLANELLI AND THE COAST WEST TO CARMARTHEN

Llanelli faces Gower across the Loughor estuary. Its rugby football team, the famous Scarlets (whose home ground, Stradey Park, is off A484 to the west of the town) celebrated its centenary in 1972 with seven choirs and 46 chapels. Rugby is *the* game in South Wales, but not in the football-playing north where the influence of Liverpool and Manchester was strong. It was introduced about a hundred years ago and caught on quickly in the mining communities, possibly because mining children were already accustomed to playing with an inflated pig's bladder, the shape of a rugby ball. The great hymn-singing tradition sprang from their chapels; most clubs have their office hymn, Llanelli's being Sospan Fach.

Little survives of the steel and tinplate works that once made Llanelli so prosperous. The docks are largely silted up or filled. Friendly houses with defiant paint survive between the water and the railway and the great landmark is Zammit's chimney, until recently the highest in Wales but now partly demolished. There are few buildings of note but miles of pleasant-looking plastered terraces, painted every shade of pearl, rather like a pigeon's breast.

The middle of the town is undergoing drastic redevelopment so a guided tour becomes nonsensical. The ponderous Town Hall (1895) faces this area. There is a nice bandstand in the garden behind. Opposite, the new Magistrates' Court (J. Morgan Harries, 1970) is attractively set among trees, human in scale and well detailed, particularly inside. **Llanelli House,** now the District Valuation Office, was built to be the town house of the Stepney family in the early eighteenth century but, after the death of Sir John Stepney, 1722, was deserted by its owners, the ground floor becoming shops.

Llanelli's churches are all locked and only those with particular interests are advised to search for the keys. **St Thomas's Church** (opposite Llanelli House) was thoroughly restored by G. F. Bodley in 1907. A couple of hundred yards north, off Hall Street, **All Saints,** Goring Road, big and solemn, is by G. E. Street, lengthened and added to in 1887 by his son A. E. Street. **St Albans,** at the top of the hill on the east side of the town by the technical college, is by Colonel Bruce Vaughan (1912–15). The big Baptist Chapel, **Zion,** at the foot of the hill, had as its pastor the great revivalist preacher, Jubilee Young. There is another church by Street at **Dafen,** a mile east of the town – a fine building of 1873–4, with a circular turret sprouting out of the aisle roof, and an excellent series of windows by Clayton and Bell. Taking A476, Felin Foel Road, north out of Llanelli, **Parc Howard** is on your left. The house, now a museum, has a good collection of Llanelli pottery (it closes at 4.30 p.m.).

Felinfoel, a mile north, has a church of 1857 by R. K. Penson, with a slate-hung spire of remarkable shape (rather Germanic), and a big Victorian brewery producing Cwrw Felinfoel (Felinfoel ale). The coastal land west of Llanelli can best be seen from the railway. This cuts the docks at Burry Port; industry here is dominated by the enormous Carmarthen Bay Power Station. Vast dunes, large parts planted with Pembrey Forest, divide the railway and road from the sea. All very flat.

Pembrey (Penbre) is the old village to the west of Burry Port. The parish church is worth seeing (key in vicarage up road to east, across whizzing A484). Late thirteenth century, enlarged (tower, aisle and north chapel) in the fourteenth. The handsome south door is dated 1717; nave and chancel roofs are sixteenth century; so is the unusual window in the south of nave with carvings of Lancaster arms and emblems of the Passion.

Kidwelly (Cydweli), at the mouth of the Gwendraeth, is renowned for its castle, church and early tinplate works (dismantled 1946). The castle (DoE) site appears above housing from the west but is well silhouetted from the main road north. It is a fine concentric castle, entirely rebuilt in the late thirteenth and early fourteenth century. The original Norman castle was one of those built to secure road communication with England in a position where it could be supplied by sea. The outer ward is Ꝺ shaped on plan; its grand gatehouse and outer curtain are fourteenth century. The inner ward with its four corner turrets is *c*. 1275; hall and solar are ranged along the river-side from which the chapel juts dramatically. Few traces of the town wall survive except in the fourteenth-century gatehouse between the Castle and the bridge.

The **Church** tower, topped by its steeple (unusual in these parts), can be seen across the river to the east, where the town has now grown up. It was a Benedictine Priory, affiliated to Sherborne (as was the church at Pembrey). The present building followed that of the new castle. It has a broad, aisleless nave (once considerably longer) with a barrel roof (now unceiled), short transepts and a big chancel. It is light and spacious and all dates from the early fourteenth century, or so G. G. Scott pronounced, after some hesitation, in 1854 when he was called in to advise on restoration. The fourteenth-

century alabaster figure of the Virgin, since 1963 above the altar, is
the church's chief treasure. The organ is mid eighteenth century.

The derelict red-brick **Tinplate Works** (upstream from the castle)
date from an 1801 rebuilding of the 1719 works (second oldest in
Britain).

The main road runs up the Gwendraeth, and then due north to
Carmarthen. The railway clings to the estuaries; lovely views, particularly at low tide and when the sun lights Llanstephan castle.

A minor road follows the estuary round the hem of the hill. **St
Ishmael's Church** (363/084), five miles on, has a fine site built into
the hillside overlooking the confluence of Tywi and Taf with
Laugharne in the distance and Llanstephan just upstream across the
water. The church is tough and primitive without; late thirteenth
century with added north aisle; the door is under the low saddleback
tower with its 1725 sundial (a taller battlemented one went in a
storm). The thorough-going Victorianization inside (1860, by R. K.
Penson) comes as a shock but there is a beautifully-carved memorial
to Catherine Mansell (1631) with an admonitory epitaph. Oil
standard lamps have survived.

The road follows the river only as far as Ferryside where it turns
inland to join A484 to Carmarthen. However, travellers by rail can
enjoy a grandstand view of the tidal Tywi winding its way through
the saltings right up to the county town.

THE VALE OF TYWI, LLANDEILO–CARMARTHEN

The Tywi follows its delightfully indecisive course west from Llandeilo. A40 runs down the north side of the Vale and B4300 follows
the opposite bank. They are linked by bridges every three or four
miles and readers may well prefer to zigzag as they explore. For
clarity each bank is taken separately here, but some of the best views
are from the bridges.

Following A40, the entrance to **Dynevor** (Dinefwr), one of the
most romantic of all Welsh castles, is on your left just at the edge of
the town. It stands on the far side of the park on its oak-clad outcrop above the winding Tywi whose silver course through the water-
meadows marks the boundary between the estates of Dynevor and
Golden Grove (p. 158), each new meander adding or taking acres
of lush grazing from either property. It is an idyllic setting for an
almost impregnable site. The heart of the present castle is the twelfth-
century keep, the curtain having been rebuilt, perhaps by Sir Rhys
ap Thomas during the peace that followed Henry VII's accession.

In the frequent disputes within this powerful family ownership of Dynevor was always the most sought prize; the authority of leadership seemed to go with it.

In the seventeenth century a new house was built about half a mile to the north and the old castle seems to have become a kind of summer plaisance. Wild strawberries abound here and within living memory the ivy-clad walls of the curtain were regularly clipped. The castle may be taken into guardianship by the DoE – inevitably it must pose a difficult problem, the claims of conservation of character and of masonry being in total opposition.

In 1856, the house was refaced by R. K. Penson. His turrets and pinnacles have gone, leaving a rather forbidding exterior, but fine seventeenth-century plaster ceilings and a staircase survive. The famous Dynevor cattle, great white beasts not unlike the Chillingham breed, graze the deer park.

Three miles on, at Broad Oak, turn left for **Llangathen Church**, medieval with a south aisle added around 1500. It is particularly worth seeing for its Tudor communion table and very up-to-date Rudd tomb (1616): grand and classical under a big pedimented canopy. The faces of the kneeling boys are movingly portrayed; the daughters are stern and elderly.

Cadfan, a striking sixteenth- and early-seventeenth-century farmhouse, to which a later dwelling has been added, is across A40 to the north (578/232). Private, but easily seen from the road. Three big octagonal chimneys and a stone slab roof crown the simple building whose main rooms are on the first floor.

West again, **Dryslwyn Castle** crowns a rocky outcrop in the middle of the Vale. It was held during the thirteenth century by a Welsh family, deadly enemies of Dynevor. It is now very romantic, overgrown and ruined. Behind, you see the strange silhouette of Paxton's Tower (p. 158).

As you approach **Abergwili**, the Vale is dominated by Merlin's Hill, named after the Carmarthen lad who became a wizard. It is topped by an Iron Age fort. Abergwili is the centuries old site of the palace of the bishops of St Davids. The old palace (largely rebuilt in 1903 after a fire) is to be the Carmarthen county museum. Its first-floor chapel is the only room of interest. **St David's Church** (C. C. Nelson, 1843; altered in 1889 by E. Christian) is rather papery. The very wide chancel is said to derive from Bishop Thirlwall's reluctance to travel to St Davids for ordinations. Note the vigorous Griffith Phillips memorials. Their house, **Cwmgwili** (not open) is seen from the Newcastle Emlyn road, a very attractive eighteenth-century adaptation of a much earlier house, charmingly panelled.

For the other side of the Vale of Tywi leave Llandeilo on A476, the Llanelli road, and bear right about three-quarters of a mile on. There are grand views of Dynevor Castle across the river. Turn left at the crossroads for **Golden Grove** (Gelli Aur), the rival estate to Dynevor, which was the seat of the Earls of Cawdor. The present house, now a farm institute, is by Sir Jeffry Wyatville (1826–37). Tudor, with stepped gables and a gabled tower, it looks oddly like a small house that has been blown up beyond its proper proportions. There is a delightful little Tudor estate village. The school, inscribed 'Honour the King', is by Wyatville's partner Henry Ashton (1848).

Three miles on **Paxton's Tower** (National Trust) above Llan-arthney is one of the best viewpoints for the Tywi valley, particularly on a bright morning when the water meadows are submerged in white mist and Dryslwyn, Grongar Hill and Dynevor stand out like islands lit by the early sun. It was designed by S. P. Cockerell for Sir William Paxton (see p. 138) in memory of Lord Nelson. *Grongar Hill* is the subject of John Dyer's nature poem of 1726 (for Dyer see *North Wales* p. 295).

The **Capel Dewi Water Treatment Works**, 1970 (Consultant architect, J. A. Strubbe), four miles west again, provide a cheering surprise. This building is well sited and enclosed by agricultural fencing instead of municipal railings. Inside: a spacious, galleried barn with a scarlet overhead crane and brilliant blue and orange pumps.

Llangunnor, despite expensive urbanization of this lovely hill-top churchyard, is still worth a visit. The lane up leaves B4300 just short of Tygwyn, the farm where Mary Scurlock, Sir Richard Steele's wife, lived before her marriage. She is buried in Westminster Abbey next to Dryden. His memorial, carved in slate 'Chief Author of the Immortal Essays/named Tatlers, Guardians and Spectators . . .' is inside the church. The nave and south aisle are unusually linked by four Tuscan pillars carrying a beam; there is a fine Commandment board and a boldly lettered wood memorial board with a pedimented top of the late eighteenth century. This is the best place from which to enjoy the site of the bishop's palace, Abergwili (p. 157). B4300 soon joins A48 from Neath on its way into Carmarthen.

CARMARTHEN–WHITLAND ON A40, AND THE COUNTRY TO ITS SOUTH

Carmarthen, the capital of Dyfed, is at the time of writing a shambles. The heart is being torn out of it and much needed by-pass roads are exposing unloved no-man's land. It is not a good time to view what was a very important medieval town and an eighteenth–nineteenth-century county centre of standing.

Tywi salmon and sewin are famous, and some are still netted here from coracles (see p. 87) by the Elias family. Their craft may be seen lying on the waste land beside Spring Gardens, a short row of villas above the bypass near the Bailey bridge. They fish below the railway bridge and it is said that their activities make considerable difference to the rods further up and on the Cothi, hence the stringent licensing of coracles.

The name Carmarthen (in Welsh Caer Fyrddin) comes from the Roman name *Moridunum*. In the *Mabinogion* it was one of the strongholds built for Elen (*North Wales* p. 141), though the etymology given there (from *myrdd*, myriad) is as mythical as the one deriving it from Myrddin (Merlin). The Roman site of Moridunum was beside the Tywi at the east end of the town. Excavations in the late 60s have identified a civil town (Priory Street area) and the site of an amphitheatre as well as the military fort already discovered.

Approaching from the east, A40 skirts **St Peter's Church** (large car park immediately north), a medieval building, double-naved with a square tower, dominated by Victorian restoration, but worth seeing for its contents. These include the restored tomb of Sir Rhys ap Thomas. This fine sixteenth-century tomb, brought here from the Franciscan Friary, is now heavily protected by Victorian railings. There is a brass to Steele, 'the first chief promoter of the Periodical Press of England', who spent the end of his life in the house which is now the Ivy Bush Hotel. A delightful memorial to virtuous Anne, the Lady Vaughan (1672), is on the south chancel wall and there are others of interest. The organ was built for George III who did not like it.

Carmarthen's claim to architectural fame rests on John Nash's sojourn here *c.* 1785 but everything of note which he did has gone. His gaol, on the site of the Norman castle, has been demolished for huge county offices in French Renaissance style (Percy Thomas & Partners), and the parish church ceiling, like his work at St Davids, was pulled down in the middle of the nineteenth century.

Houses near the church and in Spillman Street give some idea of Carmarthen's past prosperity. King Street leads into Nott Square. Here demolition has recently revealed a late medieval gateway of the Castle. The statue of General Nott (1851), hero of the Afghan wars, is by Edward Davis who also did Bishop Thirlwall (p. 329) for Westminster Abbey. His father was a Carmarthen man.

The **Guildhall** (1770), surmounted by a later clock in a gabled dormer, is quite handsome and the market buildings are (or were?) well worth seeing. The provision market is Wednesday and Saturday but as this book is being prepared the delightful little standard timber market shops are disappearing. The pleasant iron-colonnaded timber buildings whose faded paint declared CLOG MARKET, BOOTS AND SHOES and so on in good nineteenth-century lettering seem doomed. The Italianate market clock-tower (F. E. H. Fowler, 1843) survives.

The town **Museum** in Quay Street has Roman material from local sites and you can see Nash's extraordinarily elaborate designs for the **Picton Memorial** to the west of the town. It was taken down (presumably collapsing) and was replaced by the present modest pylon by F. E. H. Fowler (1846). General Picton, who lived at Colby Lodge, commanded the 50th Division and fell at Waterloo. Above is Trinity College, now the well-known Teachers Training College, founded in 1848. (Original building by Henry Clutton.)

Immediately west of Carmarthen the country south of A40 is bounded by two big estuaries of the Tywi and the Taf. For **Llanstephan**, at the mouth of the Tywi, take B4312. This attractive fishing village turned seaside holiday is topped by the medieval castle. It has an upstanding thirteenth-century gatehouse and the inner bailey protected by its ruined curtain is not overkempt. There are marvellous views, distant to Worm's Head on the tip of Gower, and across the everchanging tidal estuary to the sampler-like terraces of Ferryside. Plas (not open), the big Georgian house below the castle, has a grand stable block (1780).

The **Parish Church**, with its thirteenth-century battlemented tower, is sturdy, simple and cruciform plus a north chapel. It has good monuments, including a particularly delightful verse to the Reverend William Lloyd ('In doeing good who was imploy'd'). He died in 1706 and is commemorated on a flat slab between the chancel and north chapel.

Medieval pilgrims used the route across the peninsula, the estuaries being much ferried until the motor car took over. The ruined pilgrims' church and hospice still stand in the farmyard at **Llandeilo Abercywyn** (310/131) a few fields from the Taf. The great Thomas Charles of Bala (1755–1814 – see *North Wales*, p. 224) preached his first sermon here.

The isolated ruin of **Llanfihangel Abercywyn** old church stands in its tree-sheltered enclosure surrounded by fields, above the marsh on the opposite side of the little Cywyn (at 304/134). To find it from A40:

one mile east of St Clears, take the turning south by the 1847 church
(1915 chancel by W. D. Caröe and Norman tub font in which Charles
was christened); continue two miles due south to Trefenty and ask
permission to park in the farmyard. Trefenty is a well-set-up farm
with an attractive house, unusually built in two parts, and a marvellous position looking down the estuary. Make for the estuary and
find a faint track in the field. You will see the church below. It has
no roof but the trees protect it; wrens nest in the thirteenth-century
nave and an owl roosts in the tower, which like the big chancel is
said to be *c.* 1500. There are very interesting graves outside to the
south, in a later setting. Primitive carvings on flat slabs and small
rounded headstones include strange figures, Maltese crosses, and a
cross or sword tapering to a fork. The RCAM Inventory dismisses
any connection with pilgrims and associates the graves with a
near-by motte-and-bailey castle.

St Clears tends to be a slow incident on A40 but the old part of
this small town is south, on the road to Laugharne. The **Town Hall**,
1848, is a plain classically-minded building, with doors now filling
the ground-floor arcade. Opposite, down a long path, is the battlemented thirteenth-century tower of the **Parish Church**. This was
originally a small Cluniac priory, ruled from France, so suppressed
by Henry V during his French wars. A striking Norman chancel
arch survives, with robustly carved capitals, rare out here in the
west, and there are delightfully-worded memorials.

A4066 follows the Taf with glimpses across to the pilgrims'
churches and so to **Laugharne**, mecca of mid-twentieth-century
pilgrims to Dylan Thomas's grave and the Boathouse, his house
perched above the idyllic estuary.

The **Church** is a little aloof from the town, above the road on the
left as you arrive (there is an immense car park for motor-borne
pilgrims). Dylan Thomas's grave is across the bridge; a white wooden
cross with Gothic lettering. The church is a rather grand building,
cruciform in plan, stepping up dramatically towards the chancel.
Now mainly fourteenth century, severely restored (R. K. Penson in
1856 and again in 1873). The scraped walls are thick in tablets as
befits the church of such a borough, but the effectiveness is somewhat
dimmed by the dark Victorian glass.

Laugharne, to all who know it through *Under Milk Wood* (where
it is called Llaregyb – try it back to front phonetically, pronouncing
y as in Welsh) is to be congratulated on the way it has eschewed
Thomasiana in the form of curios and tearooms. There is only one
'Under Milk Wood' restaurant. The main street is unusually attract-

ive with Georgian houses, some positively grand, quietly colour-
washed and grey, chestnut trees and a clock-towered town hall
(1746) with the clink attached. The charming Castle House, pink-
washed with Venetian window and Dutch gables, is just beyond.
All this suggests retired naval officers, whist, and dining-out and
seems remote from the fishermen's part of Laugharne below.

The **Castle** (DoE) was almost entirely rebuilt by Sir John Perrot
who was also busy at Carew (see p. 122). He transformed the late-
thirteenth-century fortification into a Tudor palace leaving only two
huge towers of the earlier castle.

Laugharne abounds in back lanes, some still cobbled, and has a
pleasant riverbank walk through the trees above the water. It
abounds also in literary associations: the author Charles Morgan
often stayed in Cliff Cottage which belongs to relatives of his wife,
the novelist Hilda Vaughan. Dylan Thomas retreated from the
Boathouse (the white house with the balcony) to write in the blue
wooden cabin.

Leaving Laugharne on A4066, the Pendine road, steeply rising
wooded cliff is separated from the sea by extensive marsh and
burrows. Much of this is now occupied by the MoD. Access to the
beach at **Ginst Point** is usually allowed after 16.00 hours and at
weekends (bear left as you enter the gate). Access for naturalists to
the Witchet Pool may be arranged by written application.

Pendine Sands, where Sir Malcolm Campbell in the famous Blue-
bird took the land speed record, are to the west. There is development towards Pendine in the narrow gap between road and marsh.

Eglwys Gymyn (232/107) lies beside the Pendine–Red Roses road.
This humble, vaulted building was simply restored in 1901–2 by
William Weir, under the direction of Philip Webb. A massive wall
in which a simple round arch has been cut separates nave and chancel.
Three different periods for the fresco work on the north wall are
recorded in the Inventory (figures, red lettering of early Tudor
character and, in black Elizabethan, the Commandments in Welsh
and English). Nice benefaction boards also survive.

This part of Wales produced yet another great religious leader. It
was at **Llanddowror,** three miles to the north-east, that Griffith Jones
(1683–1761), of Circulating Schools fame, was minister, and trained
teachers. His idea, brilliant in its simplicity, sprang from the realiz-
ation of the difficulty of instructing illiterate people in religious
matters. Schools open to all ages, lasting about three months, were
set up wherever there was a need, often using the village church and
providing evening classes for those who could not attend during the

day. These schools circulated for 24 years during which time over 150,000 people from the age of six upwards are claimed to have been taught to read. Jones married the sister of Sir John Philipps of Picton Castle (p. 119), who had granted him the Llanddowror living and was himself a prominent reformer.

It was in the parish of **Whitland** (back on A40) that Howell the Good (Hywel Dda), c. 900–50, one of the great law-givers of history, codified the laws of Wales (see p. 320). The site of his palace Ty Gwyn, on the banks of the Taf, is not known, and of the great Cistercian Abbey, Alba Domus, also beside the Taf, the ruins are scant, but both are remembered in the name of the village.

CHAPTER SIX

Monmouthshire (Gwent)

❧

Monmouthshire is a county which is too little appreciated. It has its famous tourist attractions, like Chepstow, the Wye valley, Raglan, and Llanthony, but the rest is not well known. The scenery is not spectacular, for the most part – rolling hills, quiet valleys, fields and hedgerows. But for peace and quiet it is hard to beat. And there are innumerable places of interest. The number of old churches is enough to reduce a guide-book writer to a state of indigestive despair. Many are now isolated from any settlement, often little-used or even abandoned, but they bear witness to the former prosperity and more intensive settlement of the district.

One matter which was fortunately settled some years ago once and for all was the question whether or not Monmouthshire was part of Wales. The only substantial reason for doubt was that it came under the English court system rather than the Welsh, but that was purely for administrative convenience.

Rural Monmouthshire is treated separately from the valleys west of the River Usk.

A465 – PONTRILAS TO ABERGAVENNY

The A465, from Hereford to Abergavenny, enters Monmouthshire just beyond Pontrilas, as it crosses the river Monnow near its confluence with the Dore, coming down from the Golden Valley. The countryside is gently hilly and richly pastoral. In the flat valley between road and river stands the little church of **Llangua**, with a timber belfry.

A mile south-east – accessible by a hill-road which, like so many in these parts, gives wonderful views – is **Grosmont**. This quiet little village has a small and venerable Town Hall which is surprisingly dated 1902, and boasts two great sights, the castle up above the main street, and the church down below. The **Castle**, overlooking the winding Monnow on the west, is one of the 'Three Castles', which form a triangle around the wooded hill Graig Syfyrddin: the others are Skenfrith and White Castle. All three are of Norman origin, and they remained in common ownership throughout the Middle Ages. Now all three are cared for by the DoE. The ruins of Grosmont stand proudly on a shapely motte, surrounded by a deep moat. Far the finest feature is a tall fourteenth-century chimney, of amazing delicacy.

The **Church** is of remarkable size and grandeur, bearing witness to the former importance of the place. Mostly Early English, it has an octagonal central tower and spire. The interior comes as a shock: the great aisled nave, although roofed, is unused, and has a roughly paved floor. The aisles have steeply-pitched roofs, and elegant arcades. In the nave are the 'Grosmont Hutch', a chest, and an extraordinarily large and crude effigy of a knight. The chancel and transepts are cut off from the nave by a great glazed screen, installed at the time of the excellent restoration carried out by J. P. Seddon from 1869 onwards. On the south side of the huge chancel is a row of seven beautiful arcaded lancets. The large vestry south of it is known as 'Queen Eleanor's Chapel'. There are rich Victorian fittings, and some of the large flat stone slabs with inscriptions cut in low relief which were so common in this part of the world in the seventeenth and early eighteenth centuries.

Beyond Llangua the A465 continues along the valley, with the Black Mountains on the right. Only the southern end of their eastern slopes is in Monmouthshire, but this includes the peaceful hillside hamlet of **Oldcastle**. The church, lushly overgrown, was re-built in 1864 by J. P. Seddon. In the west window is beautiful glass of 1864, designed by Seddon and made by Chance, showing angels with musical instruments.

A mile beyond the Oldcastle turning is **Llanfihangel Crucorney**. Llanfihangel Court, down a drive opposite the church, is a late-sixteenth-century house, altered in 1627, and restored after 1903 (open to the public). It was famous for its radiating avenues, one of Scots firs, and seven of Spanish chestnuts. The Skirrid Mountain Inn, which claims to have been in business since 1100, retains some medieval features. A mile south-west of the village is **Pen-y-Clawdd**, where near a castle mound stands the Court, a well-preserved sixteenth-century stone house to which a larger and grander wing was added in the early seventeenth century.

From Llanfihangel the B4423 goes north up the **Vale of Ewyas**. This is the narrow winding valley of the river Honddu, stretching up into the Black Mountains, which rise steeply on each side. Its beauty and peace have attracted recluses through the centuries, from

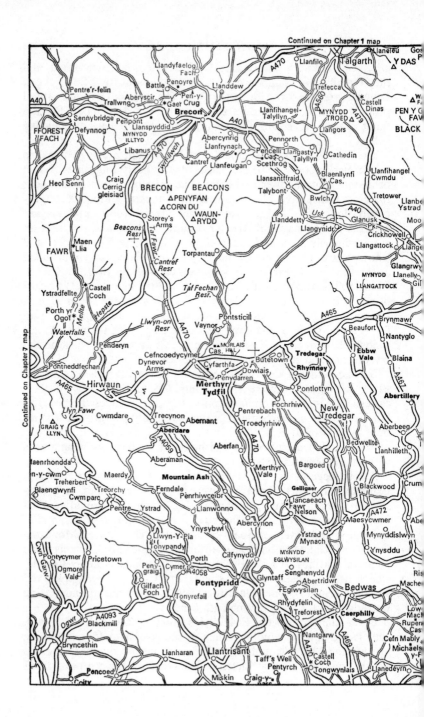

Continued on Chapter 7 map

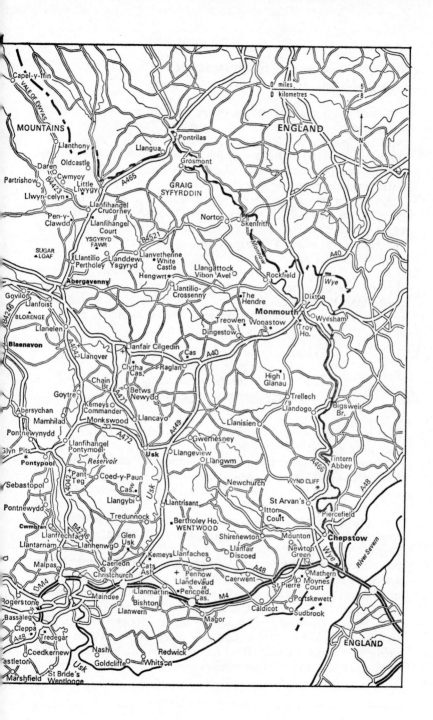

the Austin Canons in the twelfth century, up to its more remarkable recent residents – Walter Savage Landor, Father Ignatius, and Eric Gill.

A mile from Llanfihangel, a minor road goes westwards along Cwm Coedycerrig: this is one way of reaching **Partrishow** (see p. 37). Near the junction is Llwyn-celyn, basically sixteenth-century, with stone farm-buildings. Half a mile north-west is Little Llwygy, a rare survival of a one-room stone house (*c.* 1500), open to the roof, with a steeply sloping floor of natural rock.

A little further on, another by-road crosses the river and climbs along the east side of the vale to the village of **Cwmyoy**, perched on the slope. Its church is splendidly sited beneath round hillocks. It is memorable for being so utterly drunk: owing to movements of the rock, subsidence has occurred, so that the tower leans crazily and has to be supported on vast buttresses, while the chancel leans in the opposite direction. There are many good things in it: curious plaster panels in the porch, a thirteenth-century cross (found on a near-by farm), and many memorial tablets including some by Brutes. One in the chancel is inscribed:

> Thomas Price he takes his nap
> in our common mother lap
> waiting to heare the bridegroome say
> awake my dear and come away
>   1682

It seems an odd epitaph for a man. The road back to the B road goes through a gated farmyard.

Above Daren there are impressive sandstone crags. Two miles further on is **Llanthony,** one of the most ravishingly beautiful monastic sites in Britain (DoE). Founded in 1103 by Austin Canons, the great priory church was built between 1175 and 1230. Much of the nave walls and arcades, the crossing, and the great western towers survive. Built of warm red stone, the details are simple but elegant. The Welsh locals were not friendly: on one occasion the refectory was seized by a gang of riotous women. The monks soon fled and founded a daughter house, also called Llanthony Priory, at Gloucester, in 1136. The Gloucester house always prospered more than the Welsh one. The subsequent history of the ruins was unfortunate. The estate was bought from the Harley family in 1799 by Col. Mark Wood, MP, of Gatton, Surrey. He cared little for the medieval remains: the east front had fallen shortly before, and Colt Hoare saw the three central windows of the west front collapse in

1803. Wood built a house (for use as a shooting-box) into the ruins, part of it in the south-west tower, to which he added a roof and Gothic windows.

In 1808 Wood sold the estate to Walter Savage Landor, the poet, author of *Rose Aylmer* and many tedious tragedies. Despite the disapproval of his family he had conceived a romantic passion for the valley, and had grandiose ambitions for restoring the ruins, building himself a house, and improving the estate. Landor's attempts all met with deserved disaster. He took down stones and numbered them, intending to rebuild the nave, but got no further – so making matters worse. He collected carved stones together, but his dreadful tenants (English, not Welsh) used them for road-building. His house (of which he said 'never was anything half so ugly') was never finished, and he never lived in it. Known as 'The Sharple', its ruins stand on the hillside up behind the Priory. They are said to be haunted – a nice irony, since one of Landor's chief complaints against the Welsh was their superstition. In 1809 he wrote to Bishop Burgess of St Davids: '. . . if drunkenness, idleness, mischief and revenge are the principal characteristics of the savage state, what nation, I will not say in Europe, but in the world, is so singularly tattooed with them as the Welsh? . . . The wretched Welsh repeat their idle legends from first to second childhood, bring forward a thousand attestations to the existence of witches and fairies, boast of their illustrious ancestors and of the bards more illustrious who have recorded them, and convert the tomb of Taliesin into a gate-post.' In 1813, the year he left Llanthony for good, he wrote: 'I shall never cease to wish that Julius Caesar had utterly exterminated the whole race of Britons. I am convinced that they are as irreclaimable as Gypsies or Malays.' His intention was to remove Wood's house; but luckily it still survives, in use as an inn. The ruins are not fenced in, so that it is possible to visit them at any time: they are particularly lovely in the quiet of evening. South of the church, some of the monastic buildings survive. The former infirmary forms the parish church – rather gaunt, but with good memorials. A short distance north-west of the Priory, by the road, is the gatehouse, long used as a barn.

Three miles further up the valley (just over the Breconshire border) is **Capel-y-ffin** which takes its name ('boundary chapel') from the funny little church by the crossroads. Kilvert spoke of 'the old chapel short stout and boxy with its little bell turret (the whole building reminded one of an owl), the quiet peaceful chapel yard sheltered by seven great solemn yews'. It was built in 1821, and retains galleries, and paper glued on to the east window imitating stained glass. In the graveyard there is a headstone by Gill – 'Remember Charlie Stones – Carpenter – died 1935 – R.I.P.'

Kilvert walked here from Clyro, in April 1870, to visit the monastery whose foundations were just being dug, up the lane a quarter of a mile west of the chapel. Its founder, Joseph Leicester Lyne, better known as Father Ignatius, had hoped to buy the ruins of the Priory, but Landor's son refused to sell. So, in 1869, he bought 34 acres at Capel-y-ffin. Father Ignatius (1837–1908) was an astonishing character. He has been the subject of several biographies, of which the newest is *The Enthusiast*, by Arthur Calder-Marshall (1962); he also figures in several of Peter Anson's books, most recently *Building up the Waste Places* (1973). He felt himself called to revive Benedictine monasticism in the Church of England. His life was a tragi-comedy, in which his attempts to found a monastery culminated in his success (of a qualified sort) in this spot, which at that time was wild and remote, not even reached by a proper road. It is easy to make fun of him, what with his miracles and his visions, his spurious ordination, his child acolytes and his misfit monks. But it seems undeniable that he himself was completely genuine, and possessed real saintliness. Even Kilvert, passionately prejudiced against all forms of Puseyism, was sympathetic.

The monastery building was begun in 1870, and the church in 1872. Most of the monastery was built, around a cloistered garth. Only the choir of the church was ever put up, although, as a visitor wrote in 1878, 'a facsimile of old Llanthony is intended'. The architect was Charles Buckeridge (after whose untimely death in 1873 the work was continued by J. L. Pearson): he clearly took his style and details for the church from the medieval ruins. Unfortunately the vaulting eventually became unsafe and had to be taken down, and even the walls themselves suffered much decay, until, within the last few years, they have been secured by the 'Father Ignatius Memorial Trust'. Nevertheless, the ruins are very moving.

Father Ignatius himself lies in the centre of the choir, beneath a tiled tomb. It is hard now to imagine the marvellously exotic and melodramatic services that took place here, with the windows blacked out to enhance the effect of innumerable candles, the procession of monks, in gorgeous vestments, entering to the clash of cymbals, amid clouds of incense, while the solemn organ accompanied the sentimental singing.

The monastery itself is a rather ungainly heap of buildings, no doubt because of the numerous problems involved in its building. In 1924 it was bought by Eric Gill. He and his associates worked here, and some of their work can still be seen, including carvings by Gill and Laurie Cribb, and paintings by David Jones and others. The building still belongs to his family. The chapel, in an attic, can be visited, its atmosphere redolent of all Gill stood for, with nicely lettered inscriptions. Beside the lane up to the monastery there is a wooden cross in memory of Fr Ignatius: it is inscribed 'Burning Bush opposite'. This was the bush where the apparitions of Our Lady took place in 1880: a rhubarb leaf from it was supposed to have cured one of Fr Ignatius's nuns of a chronic disability. Beyond Capel-y-ffin the road climbs gently up through the wild head of the valley to Gospel Pass (Bwlch yr Efengyl), reaching a height of 1778 feet. From there it goes down to Hay, giving marvellous views over the Wye valley (see p. 24). The grassy hills make great trekking and walking country, where farmers still see to their sheep from small sturdy ponies.

Returning to Llanfihangel Crucorney, and continuing southwards on the A465, on the left is the remarkably steep and shapely **Ysgyryd Fawr** (or Skirrid) (1596 feet). This is no ordinary mountain. Legend tells that the great cleft on the west side of the summit ridge appeared when the veil of the Temple was rent at the Crucifixion. A chapel was built on the highest point, dedicated to St Michael. Faint traces of it survive: the trig. point stands within it. It was a place of pilgrimage. It is interesting testimony to the survival of the old Faith in these parts that a rescript of Pope Clement X dated 1676 survives, granting a plenary indulgence to those visiting the chapel on St Michael's feast. It was considered lucky to take away a piece of earth from the top. Evidence of present-day veneration is provided, not only by a large wooden cross, but by the graffito on the trig. point – instead of the usual SKINS, it says JESUS MY SAVIOUR. The mountain can be climbed either from the north (Llwynfranc) or south (by the Skirrid Farm track).

On the outskirts of Abergavenny, the church of **Llantilio Pertholey** (Llandeilo Bertholau) stands in a big churchyard between road and railway. It is an odd spreading building, with a dark cluttered atmosphere. The north chapel is divided from the aisle by huge octagonal timber piers. There are many good memorials, including some of the best early Brutes (e.g. John Powell, d. 1728, by Thos. Brute, with typical skinny trumpeting angels).

Abergavenny enjoys a marvellous situation, where the river Gafenni, flowing from the north, joins the Usk. It is surrounded by hills: to the north-east is Ysgyryd Fawr, to the east the wooded Ysgyryd Fach, to the south-west the great mass of Blorenge, and to the north-west the Sugar Loaf, an outlier of the Black Mountains. It is a position of strategic importance, for here the Usk valley forms the obvious route westwards between the masses of hills north and south: consequently the valley is followed by the A40, the A465 (Heads of the Valleys Road), and the Brecon Canal. The Romans had a fort here (Gobannium), and the castle was important in medieval times. And of course it has always been a busy market town. The narrow streets round the central crossroads contain many old houses, but little atmosphere. All is dominated by the great **Town Hall and Market**, of purple stone and green copper, with a tall clock-tower, built in 1871 by Wilson and Willcox, to replace the Market House of 1794–5 by John Nash. The houses along Market Street are arcaded.

In the main street the King's Head Hotel has a medieval archway, and the Angel Hotel a handsome early-nineteenth-century front. Up a lane beside it is the **Castle**. Not DoE, the unimpressive remains have been laid out as a very municipal park, with tennis and clock golf. But it is worth a visit for the views, and also for the interesting Museum, housed in an early-nineteenth-century castellated 'Keep', built on the Norman motte for use as a shooting box by the Nevills, who have owned the castle since 1507. In the twelfth century the castle belonged to William de Braose. The existing remains, including the two towers, are probably early fourteenth century.

St Mary's Priory Church is on the opposite side of the main street from the castle. The Benedictine Priory was founded c. 1100 by Hamelin de Ballon, the builder of the Norman castle. It was a daughter house of the monastery of St Vincent, near Le Mans, and remained French in character until the fourteenth century. It was burnt by Owen Glendower in 1403. At the Dissolution St Mary's became the parish church in place of St John's. The large cruciform building has been badly handled through the centuries, but it contains some fascinating treasures. These include the elaborately carved fifteenth–sixteenth-century choir stalls, and a rough oak figure ten feet long of the recumbent Jesse, probably from the reredos. Best of all is the famous series of monuments – although it is re-markable what a state of dirtiness and general mess they are in. Far the finest is the superb wooden effigy, in the nave, possibly repre-senting George de Cantilupe, 10th Lord of Abergavenny, who died in 1273 aged twenty. In the Herbert Chapel are the alabaster Hastings and Herbert tombs: the earliest, of c. 1450, is said to represent Sir William ap Thomas of Raglan, father of Sir William Herbert, 1st Earl of Pembroke, and his wife Gladys. It is in a sadly muddled

state. In the chapel north of the chancel stands the tomb of David
Lewis, first Principal of Jesus College, Oxford, d. 1584. It is signed:
IHON GILDON MADE THIS TOWME. John Gildon or Guldo was a
Hereford stone-carver, several of whose monuments are known, the
finest being at Bosbury in Herefordshire (1573).

In the northern part of the town is the Catholic **Church of Our
Lady and St Michael**, a lofty and well-detailed building in the
Decorated style, designed by Benjamin Bucknall (architect of that
extraordinary house Woodchester Park in Gloucestershire), and
built in 1858–60. The church possesses a remarkable collection of
pre-Reformation vestments.

The ascent of **Sugar Loaf** (Mynydd Pen-y-Fâl, 1955 feet) is easy
and enjoyable. A mile out of the town along the A40 turn right past
The Pentre and follow the lane up the hill: at the top there is a
National Trust car park. From here a path goes through the lovely
oak woods of Deri Fach and then climbs round the head of the cwm
to the summit. Although from a distance the mountain looks flat-
topped, there is in fact a rocky ridge.

For the routes westward from Abergavenny see pp. 36 and 41.

ABERGAVENNY TO SKENFRITH

Three miles out of Abergavenny on the B4521, beneath Ysgyryd
Fawr, is **Llanddewi Ysgyryd**. The church lies back from the road,
by the big house. Apart from the tower, it was excellently rebuilt in
1879 by John Prichard. The village is now celebrated far and wide
for the Walnut Tree Inn, on the main road – one of the Good Food
Guide's most highly recommended restaurants. The food is mostly
Italian. 'People think nothing,' says the Guide, 'of booking a month
in advance and driving 70 miles for dinner.' The village school, on a
bend on the main road, is a delightful Gothic effort in faded maroon
and yellow corrugated iron.

The next village is **Llanvetherine** (Llanwytherin). The church,
down a slope below the road, has a tower of the characteristic local
type, with the top stage boldly corbelled out. A mile beyond, a
turning leads south to **White Castle** (DoE), the best preserved and
most beautiful of the Three Castles. Mostly twelfth–thirteenth
centuries, it has an Inner Ward reached by a Gatehouse with two
stout round towers, a Hornwork, and an Outer Ward surrounded
by a wall with towers. The inner moats are filled with water, on which
ducks swim. The castle stands in quiet and rural isolation, with
splendid views all round. The thirteenth-century refortification was

perhaps carried out by Edmund of Lancaster *c.* 1270 as a defence against Llywelyn the Last.

After winding through wooded hills, and crossing the B4347 at Norton, the road comes down to **Skenfrith** (Ynysgynwraidd). This delightful village possesses the third of the Three Castles, guarding the bridge over the Monnow, and also a church of exceptional interest. The river does not actually mark the border here – the latter cuts off a big bend. The bridge was rebuilt in 1824. The castle is not as fine as Grosmont or White Castle. Rebuilt by Hubert de Burgh in the early thirteenth century, it consists of a roughly rectangular bailey surrounded by a curtain-wall with round towers, and a great round keep within it. The river flows close to the eastern side of the castle: it is made even more attractive by a weir and a mill-leet running right under the castle wall, to the big mill near the bridge.

The **Church** has a big square tower with a splendid two-tiered pyramidal belfry of timber, of Herefordshire type. The tower is propped up by a colossal buttress. In the north aisle is the elaborate tomb of John Morgan, Steward of the Duchy of Lancaster, and last Governor of the Three Castles, who died in 1557. Near the tomb is the Jacobean Morgan family pew. The church's most remarkable possession is a magnificent fifteenth-century cope, embroidered with figures of the Virgin, saints, and angels.

Four miles south, at **Rockfield**, there is another tower with timber belfry. The church, dedicated to St Cenedlon (= Kenelm), was rebuilt in 1859–60 by Prichard and Seddon, with elaborate stone-carving and wrought iron. Rockfield is very much an estate village: the stuccoed Rockfield House, with extensive Victorian grounds, belongs to the Rolls family. Their principal seat was formerly **The Hendre**, one and a half miles west along the B4233. This big house, brick and stone Tudor, in a large, well-kept park, was built in the early nineteenth century, much extended by T. H. Wyatt, and further enlarged by Sir Aston Webb. The most celebrated member of the family was the Hon. Charles Rolls, the co-founder of Rolls-Royce (see p. 177).

A mile north of The Hendre is **Llangattock Vibon Avel** (Llangatwg Feibion Afel). The church, now sadly derelict, is reached down a rough track left of the road, and is idyllically set in a pastoral valley. The church was rebuilt (quite well) in 1875 by T. H. Wyatt, except for the tall strong tower, which has a pyramidal tiled roof with odd horizontal openings below. In the porch beneath the tower there is a remarkable collection of carved headstones, mostly eighteenth–early nineteenth century. Above the sloping churchyard is Llangattock

Manor, another Rolls house, rebuilt by T. H. Wyatt. Charles Rolls is buried here.

The B4233 follows the river Trothy to **Llantilio Crossenny** (Llandeilo Gresynni). At the crossroads a turning signed 'Hostry Inn 1459' leads to the grand church, well sited by the wooded park of the demolished Court. It has a shingled broach spire at the crossing, a lofty nave, and large chancel, but the tower arch is so low that from the nave you can only just see the altar. The church was restored in 1857 by Prichard and Seddon. There are many good low-relief memorial slabs, and also a touching marble tablet by Flaxman showing Mary Ann Bosanquet (d. 1819), on her deathbed, with her little son, who died aged one, coming down rays to meet her.

Just by the crossroads, on the north, is **Hen Gwrt**, a surprising DoE site, consisting of absolutely nothing except a rectangular moat, filled with waterlilies, and crossed by a wooden bridge, set among neatly-mown meadows. It was the site of a palace of the Bishops of Llandaff, who held land here, and later of a manor house of the Herberts. From here it is seven miles to Abergavenny (p. 171).

MONMOUTH TO ABERGAVENNY – A40

The A40 enters Wales as it comes down a wooded hill into the Wye valley. At the bottom it passes the picturesque church of **Dixton**, white-rendered, except for the short and bulbous stone spire (thirteenth century). Long and narrow, its interior is also whitewashed. Thomas Bankes, vicar 1770–1805, never visited the parish until the year he died, but his Bible (kept in the church) shows how profitably he spent his time – in making such calculations as that 'there are 3,566,486 letters in the Bible'. The Wye flows alongside the church-yard, and disastrous floods often occur: brass plates high up on the chancel arch show the levels reached in 1929, 1947, and 1960.

Just beyond Dixton, the main road bypasses **Monmouth** by keeping close to the river, then crosses the Monnow and enters a short tunnel. This bypass has made Monmouth, one of the most enjoyable small towns in Wales, even more enjoyable. An exceptional number of good town-houses, many renovated in Georgian times, survive. There are plenty of pubs, and some tempting food-shops. The town is sited on a large peninsula formed by the confluence of the Monnow and the Wye. The old centre is a tightly-packed rectangle which preserves its medieval street-plan. From it the wide Monnow Street runs south-west to Monnow bridge. This is now the main street, but it lies outside the line of the medieval walls. These incorporated at

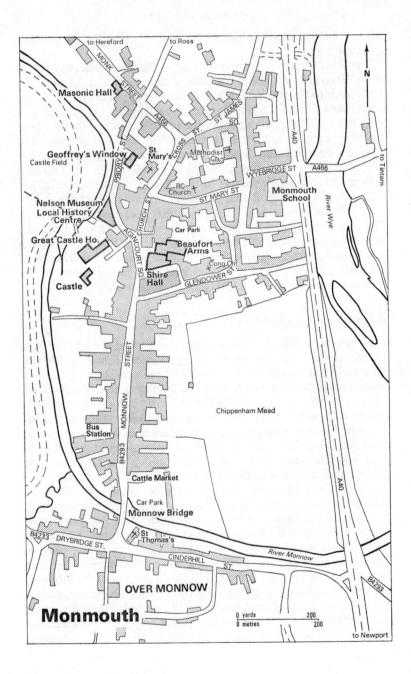

their west end the castle on its hillock, which falls steeply to the Monnow on the north and west.

The obvious place from which to start looking at the town is the market-place, grandly called **Agincourt Square**, just east of the Castle Hill. The explanation of the name is that Henry V was born in the Castle, in 1387, hence the statue of him in the niche on the handsome Shire Hall, built in 1724. The lower part of the Hall is open and market stalls are set up there. Additions were made at the back in 1829 by E. Haycock: these include a remarkable staircase, its upper flight boldly sailing above the lower one, towards a screen of Doric columns. It is lit by a glazed dome, with elegant Grecian decoration, like that at Clytha (p. 183). Shakespeare represents the archers at Agincourt as wearing leeks in their 'Monmouth caps', but this is said to be anachronistic, as it was only in the sixteenth century that the knitted caps for which the town became famous were first made. In front of the Shire Hall is a statue (by Goscombe John) of Charles Rolls, of The Hendre (p. 174). He was a pioneer aviator – hence the biplane – as well as being co-founder of Rolls-Royce. Next to the Shire Hall is the Beaufort Arms, with its name in splendid early-nineteenth-century lettering.

Castle Hill Road leads up from the Square. The **Castle**, still in military occupation, was built by the Normans. Not much is left – only ruins of the twelfth-century Great Tower (remodelled in the fourteenth century) and the thirteenth-century Great Hall, at right angles to each other. Great Castle House (DoE), an impressive stone mansion with mullioned windows, hipped roof, and pairs of pilasters supporting a decorative arch as centrepiece, was built in 1673 by the 3rd Marquess of Worcester (later 1st Duke of Beaufort). Inside are lavish plaster ceilings, on which foliage, flowers, and fruit are represented, sometimes in three-dimensional relief.

From Agincourt Square, Priory Street runs high above the Monnow valley. It was constructed in 1837, slaughterhouses having first been built along the river to support it and the new **Market Hall**, a severe Grecian composition by G. V. Maddox, a local man. After being burnt out, it has been restored as the Post Office and two museums. The Nelson Museum exhibits an enjoyable collection, made by Lady Llangattock (Charles Rolls's mother), of things connected with the admiral. He visited Monmouth briefly in 1802, with Sir William Hamilton and Emma, on their way to Pembrokeshire (p. 124). (Nelson had been asked to report on the state of the timber in the Forest of Dean.) The Local History Centre is a fascinating town museum, small but lively, the creation of Mr K. E. Kissack (to whom we are indebted for much of our information).

The name of the street refers to the Benedictine priory to which the **Church of St Mary**, founded *c*. 1080, was entrusted. Since the then Lord of Monmouth, Wihenoc, was a Breton, he gave it to the Breton abbey of St Florent de Saumur, and it remained theirs until 1399, when it became independent. Geoffrey of Monmouth (1090?–1155), author of the famous *Historia Regum Britanniae*, was probably one of Wihenoc's Breton followers. Almost nothing is left of the priory buildings. The fifteenth-century 'Geoffrey's Window' (in the school in Priory Street) clearly had nothing to do with him. The only surviving medieval part of the church is the lower part of the tower (fourteenth century), together with a Norman half-column. The upper part, and the slim and elegant spire, were added *c*. 1750 by Nathaniel Wilkinson of Worcester. The rest of the church was rebuilt in 1736–7 by Francis Smith of Warwick. In 1879 G. E. Street produced a scheme for another rebuilding, but lack of money meant that he had to be content with remodelling and extending Smith's work, in the Early English style (1880–2).

From the church a narrow lane leads back to Agincourt Square, and Monk Street (the Hereford road) runs north: in it are several fine detached houses, including St Bride's of *c*. 1700. Set back between the first two on the left is the **Masonic Hall**. It was built as the theatre in 1797, and altered for its present use by Maddox in 1837.

West of the church is St James's Square, actually a triangle, with a catalpa in the middle and good houses all round. Set back off the road is George Maddox's Ionic Methodist Chapel, of 1837. St James's Street leads south to the top of Wyebridge Street, which goes down to the old bridge over the Wye, ingeniously widened in 1879. Along the south side of the street are the large and grimly Gothic buildings of **Monmouth School**, founded in 1614 by William Jones, a haberdasher of London. These buildings, and those in Almshouse Street, were erected in 1865–78 by an architect called William Snooke.

Set back from Glendower Street is the grand Corinthian Congregational Chapel (1844, by Armstrong of Bristol), painted pale green. Monnow Street, a handsome shopping thoroughfare, leads down to the **Bridge** over the Monnow, the only bridge in Wales to retain its medieval defensive gate (comparable to that on the Puente San Martin at Toledo). Both have been altered and widened, but the gate, with its bold machicolations and its Chinaman's-hat roof (comparatively modern) is highly picturesque. Across the bridge is the suburb of **Overmonnow**, with the church of St Thomas Becket, elaborately Normanized by John Prichard in 1873, in harmony with the few twelfth-century fragments. The interior arrangement cannot be his, and is probably due to Arthur Wyatt (1830): pews, galleries, and stalls, all richly Norman, are arranged in a thoroughly un-ecclesiological manner. Funniest of all is the tiny stone font with its tall thin cover.

South of the Wye the suburb of **Wyesham** has a characteristic church of 1875 by J. P. Seddon. Above it is a hill called **The Kymin** (National Trust), the top of which (840 feet) can be reached by a road which goes right off the A4136 about three-quarters of a mile from the Wye Bridge. This steep and wooded hill was, in the late eighteenth century, the scene, every Tuesday in summer, of the meetings of the 'Kymin Club'. This association of local gentry met here for 'a cold collation, and a desert of fruits, with wine and other liquors to a certain limitation', and to enjoy the splendid views – even more extensive then when there were fewer trees. In 1794 they built themselves a Banqueting Pavilion, circular and embattled. It is now occupied as a cottage. Then in 1800 they erected a charming **Naval Temple**, to commemorate the recent British victories. It was dedicated to the Duchess of Beaufort, who was daughter of Admiral Boscawen. The little square building is decorated with medallions of the various commanders, with the dates of their victories on white, red and blue (for their respective flags). Originally there were also paintings of battles, and, to crown it all, a statue of Britannia. It was opened in 1801. Nelson breakfasted here in 1802. He was delighted with the Temple, calling it 'the only monument of its kind erected to the English navy in the whole range of the kingdom'. The verandah was added later in the century.

From Monmouth, the new A40 blasts its way through the hill and along the river Trothy. The old A40 winds around this hill. Just off it, beside the Trothy, is **Troy House**, a large and severe stone house, with a pedimented front. Dating from about 1675, it belonged to the Dukes of Beaufort.

More of interest is to be found along the minor road which runs parallel to the new A40 half a mile north. One and a half miles from the town, a track leads south to **Wonastow**, where church and Court enjoy great views. The Court is eighteenth century, stuccoed and derelict. The church was rebuilt in 1863. The stone porch, of 1909, is an exquisite Arts and Crafts piece, with striking carving. After another one and a half miles, a drive leads north to **Treowen**, a tall early-seventeenth-century house (open on written application). Its compact plan is unusual. Half is four storeys high, but the south side

was lowered in the eighteenth century. The gabled, two-storey porch
has columns, strapwork, and the Jones arms. Inside, there is a
splendid staircase of turned oak, and remains of fine plasterwork.
The Jones's left the house in the late seventeenth century and moved
to Llanarth (see p. 182). Just beyond is **Dingestow**, where the castle
mound and church stand by the river north of the village. The church,
rebuilt in 1846 by T. H. Wyatt, contains monuments to the Bosanquets
of Dingestow Court. This handsome Elizabethan-style house, given
its new front in 1845 by Lewis Vulliamy, and altered in 1859 by J. P.
Seddon, overlooks the valley from its park half a mile south-west of
the village.

Three miles from Dingestow along the A40 is **Raglan**. The road
runs between the village and the castle, magnificent even in ruins
(DoE). Situated at an important road junction, it was begun by the
Normans. However, the earliest existing building, the Great Tower,
was put up by Sir William ap Thomas, probably between 1432 and
his death in 1445. He was a strong Yorkist, and his son, Sir William
Herbert, was one of Edward IV's most powerful supporters, partly
through his huge wealth, acquired in trade, and partly through his
military activities, which included the taking of Harlech Castle, in
1468, with his brother Sir Richard Herbert (see *North Wales* p. 245).
For this he was made Earl of Pembroke. He built most of the rest of
the castle, but work came to a halt when he was beheaded in 1469.
Eventually its ownership passed to his granddaughter Elizabeth, who
had married Charles Somerset, Lord Chamberlain to Henry VII
and VIII, created Earl of Worcester in 1514. His grandson, William,
3rd Earl, remodelled the Hall, added the Long Gallery, and completed the rest of the castle, *c.* 1550–70. His son, though a Papist,
retained the queen's favour, and held state offices in her reign and
the next. He was the patron of Spenser and Byrd. He ornamented
Raglan both inside and out. The 5th Earl was a leading Royalist,
who entertained the king here and was created Marquis of Worcester.
However, after a great siege in 1646, he had to surrender the castle,
which was ruthlessly slighted. The 3rd Marquis, builder of Great
Castle House, Monmouth (see p. 177), was created 1st Duke of
Beaufort in 1683: he began to build Badminton, and Raglan was
abandoned. In the early nineteenth century, the ruins, by then
romantically overgrown, were laid out for the benefit of visitors by
the Duke's agent, Arthur Wyatt – complete with rustic bridges and
seats, and resident caretakers.

In spite of its complicated building history and irregular plan, the
castle must have been amazingly impressive, in its combination of

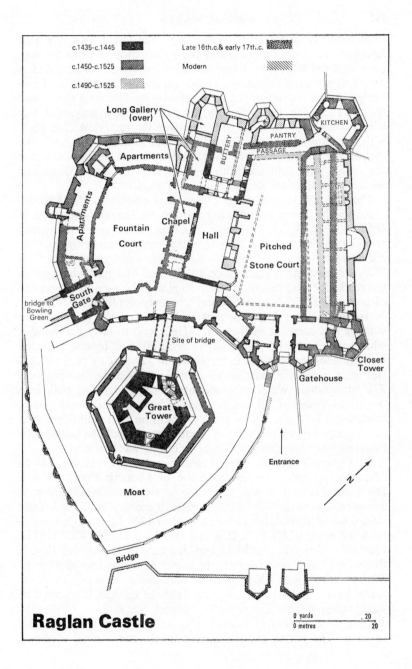

Raglan Castle

c.1435–c.1445
c.1450–c.1525
c.1490–c.1525
Late 16th c.& early 17th.c.
Modern

Long Gallery
(over)

Apartments

Apartments

KITCHEN

BUTTERY

PANTRY

PASSAGE

Chapel

Hall

Fountain

Court

Pitched

Stone Court

South
Gate

bridge to
Bowling
Green

Site of bridge

Great
Tower

Closet
Tower

Gatehouse

Entrance

N

Moat

Bridge

0 yards   20
0 metres   20

impregnability and domestic splendour. The Great Tower, a vast hexagon, was even higher. Attempts to demolish it from the top, after the Civil War, were abandoned, and two sides of it were undermined. It was surrounded by a moat, and reached by a double drawbridge. Along the top of the wing between the Fountain Court and the Hall ran the Long Gallery, terminating in a polygonal bay window at the north-west, which enjoyed the vast view. The Hall, with its tall oriel and porch, had a double hammerbeam roof, like that of Middle Temple Hall. The state apartments, facing south over the moat, were adorned with rich carving, of which fragments survive, and the parlour had a tall oriel window.

The **Church**, in the quiet village, was rebuilt in the fifteenth century. The tower is good, but the rest was savagely restored in 1868 by T. H. Wyatt. The Beaufort Chapel contains a few battered remains which are all that survive of the once splendid effigies of the 3rd and 4th Earls, and of the 4th Earl's wife – destroyed in the Civil War. An inscription commemorates the 2nd Marquis 'who gave to the world the first practical Steam Engine to be used in the service of man (1663)'. This is inaccurate. The sixty-eighth of his 'Century of Inventions', published in that year, sets out the principles on which a steam engine might work. (He is said to have got the idea while watching the lid of a saucepan being lifted off by steam, during his imprisonment, 1652–4, in the Tower of London – a proto-Watt.) But there is no evidence that he ever put the scheme into practice. The 'stupendous Water-commanding Engine', which he built into the Great Tower of the castle, seems to have been a sort of pump, worked not by steam but by gravity. Tradition even maintained that he had hoped that a model of his steam engine would be buried with him, but when his grave was opened nothing was found.

Two miles beyond Raglan, a road runs north from the A40 to Llanarth, past the Gothic gatehouse of **Llanarth Court**. Now a Benedictine school, it was the home of the Jones family (also of Treowen – see p. 179) from the fourteenth century until 1947. They were descended from the Herberts, and in 1848 John Arthur Jones took the name of Herbert. It is said that he asked the then Earl of Pembroke if he minded: he replied that he didn't, provided that, if there were more such requests, he might be allowed to change his own name to Jones. The house was remodelled, in heavy, rendered Ionic, by W. and E. Habershon, *c.* 1851. In the hall is a screen of 1627, brought from Treowen. The chapel was built *c.* 1780 – the Jones's were Papists. The park was improved in 1806 by John Loudon. The parish church, on the north, has a good medieval tower, and contains a monument (with delightful epitaph) to Elizabeth Jones, who died in 1787.

Further along the A40, a more remarkable monument to this same lady will be seen at the top of the wooded hill on the left as the road winds down towards the Usk valley. This is **Clytha Castle**, whose inscription records that it was 'erected in the year 1790 by William Jones of Clytha House . . . husband of Elizabeth . . . It was undertaken with the purpose of relieving a mind afflicted by the loss of a most excellent wife . . . to the memory of whose virtues this tablet is dedicated'. It is a charming Gothic folly: one square tower and one round tower are joined by a wall whose battlemented parapet describes symmetrical parabolas on either side of a tiny square turret. Loudon was not amused: in his *Treatise on Country Residences* (1806) he called it 'gaudy and affectedly common'. Now that the estate has been acquired by the National Trust, they have handed the castle over to the Landmark Trust, who have restored it for holiday occupation.

Clytha Park (open on written application) can easily be seen from the A40. The spiky ogival entrance arch was also built by William Jones, in 1790. The new house was begun in 1824, to designs by Edward Haycock, and is one of the most attractive Greek Revival houses in Britain, its severe grandeur tempered by its moderate scale and rich decoration, as well as by the warm-coloured stone. One mile south of the castle is the Iron Age fort of **Coed-y-bwynydd**, which also belongs to the Trust. It is covered in bluebells, below oak and ash woodland. A walk, with splendid views west, is planned to link the two.

A mile beyond Clytha, the A471 goes off south towards Usk. It crosses the Usk by means of a superb stone bridge (by John Upton, 1821). Just the other side, opposite the handsome Pant-y-Goitre, a road goes off left into a flat crook of land formed by a bend in the river. Here (at 356/087) stands the simple little church of **Llanfair Cilgedin**, largely rebuilt in 1876 by J. D. Sedding. There are good furnishings, including the alabaster and mosaic reredos, the wooden pulpit, the screen (partly medieval), and the curious medieval font-cover. But all these are outshone by the amazingly vigorous and colourful scheme of decoration which covers the entire wall-space. This was executed in sgraffito (cut-away plaster) in 1888 by Heywood Sumner, one of the leading designers of his time. It illustrates the Benedicite, and many of the scenes are entrancing – the sea-lions, the ploughed fields, children with hoops, the winged Winds, and so on. Existing memorial tablets are left *in situ*.

From the A471 junction, it is four miles along the A40 to Abergavenny (p. 171).

(p. 171)

ABERGAVENNY TO CHEPSTOW VIA USK

From the roundabout south-east of the town, the A465 (Heads of the Valleys road) goes off up the south side of the Usk valley, with the B4209 branching off at Llanfoist (see p. 41).

The A4042 goes due south towards Pontypool. It crosses the Usk at **Llanelen**, a rather suburbanized village. The three-arched bridge was built in 1821 by John Upton of Gloucester, who later settled in Russia, built fortifications at Sebastopol in the Crimean War, and was taken prisoner by the Allies. From here the road runs parallel to the Brecon and Abergavenny Canal (see p. 41), which contours along at the foot of the hills. A mile south of Llanelen, a tall castellated gatehouse stands left of the road. This once led to **Llanover Court**, and is presumably, like the now demolished house, by Thomas Hopper, and *c.* 1830. Augusta Waddington brought the Llanover estate to her husband, Benjamin Hall. He was an MP, and is best remembered for having been Commissioner of Works in 1855, when the clock on the Houses of Parliament was erected – the bell being called after him 'Big Ben'. He became Lord Llanover in 1859. He was a great figure in church reconstruction in the Llandaff diocese, and a leading advocate of the use of the Welsh language in ecclesiastical affairs in Wales. His wife (1802–96), although she spoke little Welsh, was passionately interested in everything to do with Welsh culture – music, folk-dancing, costume, cookery, manuscripts, poetry. She was equally passionate about temperance and protestantism.

The side road which goes left by the gatehouse leads past Cwrt Porth-hir, a sixteenth-century house (open on written application), and in a mile, after turning south along the river, reaches **Llanover Church**. It is nicely situated on the edge of the park. The river is crossed by a tiny fishermen's suspension bridge. The church is mostly Perpendicular, but the porch is dated 1750. In the churchyard stands the immense stone tomb of Lord Llanover, said to have been designed by himself.

Three-quarters of a mile beyond the gatehouse, the A4042 passes on the right the charming model village built *c.* 1925 by Alfred Powell, who was an associate of Ernest Gimson and the Barnsleys. A short avenue leads to a formal green, with the war memorial ahead – a slim monolith with an iron cross on top. Around the green are small stone cottages, roofed with stone slates, beautifully weathered. The drive on the opposite side of the main road leads to a red-brick Georgian house called Llanover. Just beyond, up a road left, is the pretty little Hanover Independent Chapel. Its name may be a corruption of Llanover.

A mile south of this turning, a road goes left to meet the A471 at **Chain Bridge**, rebuilt without chains, but with curved iron girders, in 1906. Half a mile south, just right of the road, is the sweet little hamlet of **Kemeys Commander**, with a minute fifteenth-century church, with old timber porch and screen. A mile east of Chain Bridge is **Betws Newydd**, a beautifully-situated village spoilt by California-type development. The humble little church, up a lane to the east from just south of the crossroads, contains a remarkable late-fifteenth-century rood-screen, richly carved, and reaching right up to the roof. Two miles south, back on the A471, at **Llancayo** a great ruined windmill, tall and conical, forms a conspicuous landmark. From Llancayo it is just over a mile to Usk.

Usk (Brynbuga) is a nice, unassuming little town. The A471 enters it past the Puginian Catholic church, built in 1847 by Charles Hansom, with a tower added in 1865. Above the church rises a hill, crowned by the ruined **Castle**. Still in private hands, and not regularly open, it is reached by a drive from Castle Parade. The keep was built in the twelfth century, and the curtain wall, with angle towers, was added by William Marshal (see p. 129) early in the next century. The gatehouse (still inhabited) was added in the fourteenth century. The centre of the town is **Twyn Square**, just north of the main crossroads. It has two neat pubs, a Congregational Chapel of 1862 and a lurid red clock-tower of 1887.

From the south end, Priory Street leads to the **Church**, built for a priory of Benedictine nuns *c*. 1135. The priory was founded by Richard de Clare, and was for 'virgins of noble birth'. The original church was cruciform, with an apsidal chancel, and central tower. The north aisle was added, for the use of the parish, in the thirteenth century. The chancel and transepts eventually disappeared, so that the sanctuary is now beneath the tower. The nave was lengthened westwards by T. H. Wyatt in 1844. The two delicate porches were added in the fifteenth century. A restored medieval screen (of Gloucestershire or Somerset type) runs across nave and aisle. Attached to it is a brass plate, bearing the epitaph of Adam of Usk (1352?–1430). It is said to be the oldest Welsh epitaph extant, and is in the *cywydd* metre. It celebrates his learning and fame as a lawyer. Adam was an ecclesiastical trouble-maker, who was involved in the

St Scholastica's Day Riots at Oxford, in the deposition of Richard II, and in a dispute over a prebend which led to a charge of highway robbery. He fled to Rome, and won the Pope's favour. But he died in obscurity, and even the Chronicle for which he is chiefly remembered had to be written up after his death.

The organ is a stunning object, and deserves a better position. It is one of the small number out of all the splendid fittings designed for Llandaff Cathedral at its restoration which survived the War (see p. 246). Built in 1862, by the firm of Gray and Davison, it was sold to Usk in 1899. The case was designed by Seddon: elaborately-painted pipes stand on a chunky wooden base. A row of vast trumpet pipes project *en chamade* (horizontally), their ends painted to represent dragons with gaping jaws. On the west wall is a curious epitaph to Watter Jones, d. 1646. In the churchyard near the west door is buried St David Lewis (Baker) S.J., born at Abergavenny in 1616 and executed at Usk in 1679 – the last Catholic priest to die for his faith. Near the path is buried Philip Mason, who 'died 1772 aged 51, weighing 554 pounds' (over 34 stone). In the north-west corner is the tomb of Sir Matthew Digby Wyatt, the architect and designer (1820–77). The polished granite tomb was designed by his brother, T. H. Wyatt.

South of the church is **The Priory**, reached through a Gothic gateway. It is partly medieval, partly sixteenth–seventeenth century, but was much rebuilt in the mid nineteenth century. Church Street leads to Maryport Street, running south. In it stands the **Sessions House**, looking as if it might be in Italy – a single-storey, round-arched building, with a cedar tree and balustrades in front. It was built in 1875 by T. H. Wyatt and D. Brandon. The impressively but-tressed Gaol, of 1840, is also by Wyatt.

Near here recent excavations have revealed parts of the important Roman fort of *Burrium*. Built in the time of Claudius, it is the earliest Roman fort to have been discovered in Wales. It was rebuilt in about AD 65 to cover 51 acres, presumably as the base for the final campaigns in Wales. About ten years later this larger fort was demolished and a smaller one built in one corner. This fort remained until the next century, but a flourishing industrial settlement con-tinued until the fourth century.

From near the Sessions House, Old Market runs south-west to the old market-place, formed by a widening of the street, and now a quiet backwater of stuccoed houses. In the middle stands the Town Hall, partly eighteenth century but given its present Italianate appearance in 1859. New Market Street leads north to the Bridge, rebuilt in 1836. The Usk is a famous fishing river, noted for its salmon, which, according to local legend, King Arthur caught and served up at the Round Table.

A mile east of Usk, reached by a lane running south from the new road, is **Llangeview**, whose tiny, unspoilt church is picturesquely set in a grassy churchyard, overlooking the monster Newport–Raglan highway. Its rood-loft survives, but has lost its screen and ornaments. The new road goes on up the Olway valley, while the B4235 goes south-east through the hills towards Chepstow. The first village is **Gwernesney**, whose little church has an old chancel screen, and another screen formerly round a chantry, but now round the font.

Two miles further on is **Llangwm**. Most of the village lies south of the road, but both its churches lie north of it. The nearer, half a mile from the crossroads, is St John's, Llangwm Isaf, quite small and simple, and rebuilt in 1858 by Prichard and Seddon. It has pretty oil lamps set on poles among the pews. Five hundred yards higher up the valley, beautifully situated, is St Jerome's, Llangwm Uchaf, a much bigger church, with a grand tower, unusually placed on the north side of the chancel. The foundation of St Jerome's dates back to about 700: there may have been a *clas*. There were already two churches here by 1128, but the reason for this is unknown. Their siting is more explicable, since the old road to Chepstow went up this way and along the ridge. The church's chief claim to fame is its magnificent late-fifteenth-century rood-screen and loft, the finest of the numerous screens which survive in the Usk area. Covered in elaborate carving, it was restored, with red, blue and green colouring, at the time of the church's restoration in 1870 by J. P. Seddon. Seddon designed the wooden lectern to go with it, the gorgeous tile pavement covering the chancel and tower floors, and the stained glass in the east window.

From Llangwm, the B road winds up the wooded Golden Hill, and then follows the valley to Chepstow, but, for a more exciting route, take the turning left, a quarter of a mile beyond the crossroads, which climbs up steeply below the double-ramparted camp Gaer Fawr. The road follows the ridge to **Newchurch**, giving tremendous views over the whole western part of the county, from the mountains north and west to the Bristol Channel on the south. The windswept church, rebuilt in 1864 by Seddon, is approached by a wide green path. From Newchurch, steep and narrow lanes lead two miles south-east to **Itton**. The main part of the village is at Itton Common. Half a mile beyond is the Village Hall, a simple L-shaped building by Guy Dawber (1913). Just beyond the Hall, a road leads right up to Itton

Court, a large, sprawling house, with a medieval gatehouse and big additions made in the eighteenth and nineteenth centuries. Beside the Court stands the church. It contains two elegant tablets to members of the Curre family (of the Court), one to E. M. Curre and his wife, by Guy Dawber (erected 1914), and one to Sir William Curre, d. 1930, who 'hunted his White Fox Hounds from 1896 until his death'. Although the Curres no longer live at Itton, the famous pack of hounds is still kept there. Beyond the church, the road leads back on to the B4235.

On the other side of this road, a mile south-west, is **Shirenewton**, a big village spreading around the hill-top on which stand the grand Perpendicular church, with a central tower, rebuilt in 1853 by John Norton, and the Hall, hidden among Victorian trees, which was extended in a romantic Tudor style *c.* 1910 (by Norman Evill). The Home Farm, a quarter of a mile south-west, has a huge pedimented archway with a cupola above. From Shirenewton it is three miles into Chepstow.

CHEPSTOW

The strategic importance of Chepstow's site is obvious: it occupies a stubby promontory, formed by a bend in the Wye, at the lowest point where the river could be crossed. Both the A48, from Gloucester to Cardiff, and the railway cross here. Recently added significance has been given by the opening of the Severn Bridge, which incorporates a shorter bridge over the Wye estuary and enters Wales less than two miles south of Chepstow. Immediately the M4 reaches Monmouthshire, an exit leads on to the A466 (to Monmouth), which fortunately bypasses the town.

The A48 curves down the hill on the Gloucestershire side and crosses the river over the charming iron bridge built in 1815–16 by John Rastrick, on the advice of John Rennie. The bridge provides a splendid view of the **Castle**, stretching out its enormous length above cliffs which drop sheer to the brown river. It is built on a long, narrow ridge, separated from the town on the south by a grassy dip ornamented with trees. The castle (DoE) was begun by William Fitz Osbern, Norman Earl of Hereford, *c.* 1070. He built the huge, solid Great Tower, at the narrowest and highest point on the ridge. In 1115, Henry I gave the castle, and much of the present counties of Monmouth and Gloucester, to Walter Fitz Richard, of the great Clare family, so creating the marcher lordship of Striguil, which survived until 1536. Walter's great-nephew was Richard de Clare, known as 'Strongbow', the conqueror of Leinster. In 1189 his daughter married William Marshal, and brought him Chepstow and Pembroke (see p. 129). He built the curtain wall between the Middle and Lower Baileys. He was one of the first in Britain to use round towers and true shooting slits.

William was succeeded by five sons in turn, who continued his work – remodelling the Great Tower, strengthening the Middle Bailey, rebuilding the Upper Bailey, on the W, and adding the Barbican, and adding on the east the Lower Bailey – the biggest of all – with its double-towered Great Gateway. All of this work was done *c*. 1225–45. The castle later came into the possession of Roger Bigod III, Earl of Norfolk: as well as rebuilding the church at Tintern Abbey, and building the town wall at Chepstow, he added to the castle (*c*. 1270–1300). His work included the west gatehouse, the domestic buildings on the north side of the Lower Bailey, and the immense round tower at the south-eastern angle (Marten's Tower). In 1468 Chepstow was acquired by William Herbert, Earl of Pembroke (see p. 180), and so came eventually, like Raglan, to the Somerset family, Earls of Worcester, and later Dukes of Beaufort. The castle was altered in the sixteenth century when larger windows and extra fireplaces were added. In the Civil War it was twice besieged, and suffered damage, but afterwards it was repaired for use by a garrison. During this time it was used as a prison, its most famous inmates being Bishop Jeremy Taylor and the regicide Henry Marten (see p. 190).

Apart from its great size and superb site the castle retains many architectural details which suggest its former splendour. The Great Tower (whose construction incorporates courses of Roman tile) has a Norman doorway with tympanum, while inside the remains of the windows and transverse arch put in by the Marshals are of great elaboration. Fragments of floriated carving survive in the chapel in Marten's Tower, and in Bigod's Hall, suggesting that his work too was of high quality. His range of domestic buildings was used as a dwelling in the nineteenth century, and is extremely picturesque, with its pretty leaded windows, brick patching, and general air of decay.

Opposite the castle, an old school houses the **Museum** of the Chepstow Society (only open in season), old-fashioned in its arrangement, but containing lots of fascinating material on, for example, the Wye Tour, the port of Chepstow, ship-building, the iron industry, and local printing. **Bridge Street**, running up to the centre of the town, is lined with the quiet eighteenth–nineteenth-century houses, mostly stuccoed, which make it such a good-looking place. The pedimented Hospital is rather grander. At the top are L-shaped Almshouses, founded in 1716 by Thomas Powis of Enfield, Vintner, a native of the town. **Beaufort Square** is the hub of the town. It is now spoilt by coarse intruders, the saddest of which is the egregious new Barclay's Bank, which replaced a tall and stately palazzo of 1849.

The **Parish Church** is down to the north-east of the Square. Vast and barn-like, it has suffered greatly through the centuries. It was the church of a Benedictine Priory. The west tower has a Norman doorway, but the top was altered in the eighteenth century. The nave, also Norman, has lost its aisles, and chancel and transepts were rebuilt in 1838–40 in a grim round-arched style, only to be again rebuilt (except the north transept) in 1890–1904 by J. P. Seddon and J. Coates Carter. In the south transept is the tomb of Thomas Shipman, d. 1620, garishly painted, especially the figures of Death and Time – down to the blue veins on their hands. The comic Gothic organ-case is of *c.* 1800. In a lean-to at the western end of the nave is the tomb of the 2nd Earl of Worcester and his wife, with reclining figures. This too has been luridly repainted. Under the tower is the tombstone of Henry Marten, a judge at the trial of Charles I, who died in the castle in 1680 (see above p. 189). He had a weird sense of humour. When Cromwell was about to sign the king's death-warrant, he inadvertently spattered some ink on Marten's face. Marten seized the pen and spattered Cromwell's face in return. His acrostic epitaph, written by himself, begins:

> Here, or elsewhere (all's one to you and me)
> Earth, fire or water gripes my ghostless dust . . .

In the nave stand the works of a clock made in the late eighteenth century by William Meredith of Chepstow.

North of the church **The Back** runs by the river, looking across to the tall grey wooded cliffs opposite, and giving good views of both the road bridge and the cumbersome railway bridge originally built in 1852 by I. K. Brunel. Brunel's structure consisted of iron tubes from which were hung the fixed suspension chains. It was similar to that used for his famous Saltash Bridge, but the tubes were not curved, but straight. The new bridge of 1962 is by a local firm which is the descendant of the firm which made the original ironwork. South of it is the charming little Italianate Station, with the all-round canopy characteristic of Brunel's original stations. It is now boarded up and unmanned.

South of Beaufort Square, High Street leads up to the **Town Gate**, the principal entrance through the so-called Port Wall built to enclose the town on the west and south (the river protecting it on the other two sides) in the late thirteenth century. The gate was rebuilt in 1524, to serve as a prison, and has been much restored. The wall, with its round towers, now runs from the castle as far as the railway line. The part between there and the river has disappeared. Steep Street climbs south from the gate. Off it a road runs east into the **Hardwick Estate**, a widely-known housing scheme built just before the First World War. Designed by W. Curtis Green, the houses were built of concrete blocks made with local stone aggregate.

CHEPSTOW TO MONMOUTH AND BACK – A466 AND B4293

At the roundabout north of Chepstow stands a handsome entrance lodge. It now serves as the entrance to Chepstow Race Course, which occupies most of the park of **Piercefield**. This once formed the high spot of a Wye Tour. The estate came into the possession, after the death of his father in 1743, of a remarkable man – Valentine Morris (1727–89). Although born in Antigua, the son of a plantation owner, he came of a family which claimed to have originated in this part of Monmouthshire. He was rich, extravagant, and generous. He laid out the park on thoroughly up-to-date lines, taking the fullest advantage of its exceptional site on a promontory formed by a sharp bend in the river (an 'incised meander'). The walks were diversified, not only with carefully contrived viewpoints, but with such fancies as the Chinese Seat, the Grotto, the Druids' Temple, and so on. The most original of them was the Giant's Cave, over the mouth of which was carved a giant holding a huge stone as if about to let it fall on the visitor. Lover's Leap was a drop of 180 feet. It was all freely open to tourists who flocked to see it. They included Thomas Gray, Sir Joseph Banks, Clive of India, John Wesley, Gilpin, and Coleridge. In 1771 Morris, already heavily in debt, stood for Parliament. He lost, and returned to the West Indies, in hopes of repairing his fortunes. He became Governor of St Vincent, but after many trials had to sell Piercefield in 1784. The buyer was George Smith, who commissioned John Soane to build a new house. However, Smith went bankrupt, and in 1794 the estate was sold to Col. Mark Wood (see p. 168). In 1797 he commissioned Joseph Bonomi to finish the house: he designed the saloon, with scagliola pilasters and marble-inlaid floor, and the staircase, and added a semicircular portico and pedimented pavilions. Wood, in his turn, sold Piercefield in 1802, and eventually in 1923 it was sold to the Race Club. The house fell into utter ruin. The main facade, however, survives almost intact. The park, although neglected, is beautifully wooded, and the site remains incomparable. Something should be done to rescue this enchanting place.

The B4293 leaves the A466 at **St Arvan's**, a neat village with a marvellous magnolia tree and an iron fountain with a pair of putti, made in Glasgow. Near the junction is the Village Hall, so similar to that at Itton (p. 187) that it must also be by Guy Dawber. The road descends steeply between Lover's Leap, on the right, and Wynd Cliff on the left. **Wynd Cliff** ceased to be part of the Pierce-field estate when this new road cut it off from the park, c. 1820. The woods became a nature reserve in 1959, and the Forestry Commission maintain the path up the cliff (as a Nature Trail). To reach it, carry straight on where the A466 turns sharp right, half a mile from St Arvan's. From the car park, the path climbs steadily, with woodland on the right and pasture on the left, to the viewpoint (the 'Eagle's Nest'), a balcony with a small grotto beneath. The limestone cliff drops 700 feet below. The view is all the more breathtaking for being so long concealed. In the foreground is the broad Lancaut promon-tory, encircled by the brown river, and beyond are the woods of Piercefield. In the distance are Chepstow and the Severn estuary. It is possible to go down the cliff by means of 365 steps, built in 1828 by Osmond Wyatt for the Duke of Beaufort. Beyond Wynd Cliff the A466 climbs over the shoulder of yet another big promontory (the course of the Wye here looks like a demented serpent), and then follows the valley round to Tintern (five miles from Chepstow).

Samuel Palmer visited **Tintern** in 1835, and wrote, 'Such an Abbey! the lightest Gothic trellised with ivy and rising from a wilderness of orchards – and set like a gem amongst the foldings of woody hills.' The ivy has gone, and the orchards have made way for a car park, but the magic is still strong (DoE). The remarkable state of preservation of the ruins actually displeased William Gilpin, the apostle of the picturesque: he criticized the 'gabel-ends that hurt the eye with their regularity and disgust it by the vulgarity of their shape. A mallet judiciously used (but who durst use it?) might be of service in fracturing some of them.'

The abbey was founded in 1131, by Walter Fitz Richard, Lord of Striguil (see p. 188), as a Cistercian house. This was only three years after the foundation of the first Cistercian house in England. It was almost entirely rebuilt during the thirteenth century, starting with the refectory c. 1220, and ending with the church, of which the high

Tintern Abbey: the ruined church of the Cistercian house founded in 1131.

Tredegar Park, outside Newport, is the finest late seventeenth century house in Wales (built 1664-74).

The Gilt Room is the most lavish at Tredegar Park: the painted panels may be French.

altar was first used in 1288. By then the monastery was under the patronage of Roger Bigod (see p. 189). The abbey, like all the Welsh Cistercian houses, was famous for its wool, which was exported to Flanders and even to Italy. A late-thirteenth-century Florentine treatise states that, although Margam (p. 284) exported a greater quantity, Tintern's was far the best quality in Wales. Little building was done subsequently. The plan follows the usual Cistercian lines, except that the monastic buildings are placed north of the church, to simplify drainage. The church is far the finest part. The view of wooded hillsides seen through windows which retain much of their tracery, and which are echoed by the great arches of crossing and arcades, is unforgettable. Parts of the wall which surrounded the conventual precinct survive on the west, and on the south, along the old road from Chepstow. Also on this road is a house which incorporates the gatehouse chapel, with a three-lancet window. North of the car park, by the Anchor Hotel, is a medieval gateway which leads to the slipway of the old ferry.

On the hillside up above the abbey is the **Parish Church** (St Mary's, Chapel Hill), mostly rebuilt in 1861–6 by Prichard and Seddon. It is well worth the climb, if only for the view, the ruins being seen in summertime across a foreground of the flaming fireweed which rampages in the churchyard, for the church is derelict.

Three miles up the narrow valley beyond Tintern is **Llandogo**. The church, dedicated to St Dochau (Odoceus) is of ancient foundation, but was rebuilt in 1860 by J. P. Seddon, in red and yellow stone, quite elaborate, with a pretty bellcote. The lofty chancel was decorated (by Seddon and Carter) in 1889. A mile further on, the A466 crosses the river into Gloucestershire by means of Bigsweir Bridge, very striking with its curved iron span. A minor road continues up the Welsh side, and then turns west to follow a lovely secret valley, where old houses and ruined mills stand by the wooded stream.

A quarter of a mile west of the point where this road comes out on to the B4293, hidden in the woods, is **High Glanau** (not open), the last Monmouthshire home of H. Avray Tipping (see p. 194). As an elderly bachelor, and in postwar conditions, he wanted something smaller and more manageable than Mounton. The site is marvellous, enjoying tremendous views westwards. The house, built in 1922–3 of local stone, is simple and unpretentious, but very attractive. The romantically natural gardens survive in remarkably good order. A mile south is **Trellech**. The village is dominated by its big, tall church, which has a fine octagonal spire. In the south aisle stands a stone sundial, which used to be outside in the village. It was erected by

Lady Magdalen Probert in 1689, as a kind of tourist's guide to the place. On three of the sides are crude representations of its three chief antiquities. A big lump is inscribed MAGNA MOLE – O QUOT HIC SEPULTI ('Great in its mound – how many are buried here!'). This refers to the Norman castle motte, south-west of the church. Called Tump Terrett, it was once thought to mark the burial place of Harold's troops, killed in battle. The second side shows three phallic stones marked 8, 10 and 14, with the inscription MAIOR SAXIS – HIC FUIT VICTOR HARALD ('Greater in its stones – here Harold was victorious'). These are the three red monoliths which stand beside the B4293 south-west of the village. The figures give their respective heights. Known locally as 'Harold's Stones', they are really prehistoric. They give the village its name. The third side shows a round hole, with flowers and cups, and is inscribed MAXIMA FONTE ('Greatest in its spring'). This ferruginous spring ('The Virtuous Well') is situated on the left of the minor road which runs south-east from the village.

Two miles south-west of Trellech is **Llanisien**, whose pretty little church of 1854, by Prichard and Seddon, is perched on the hillside. From here it is eight miles back to Chepstow (p. 188).

CHEPSTOW TO NEWPORT

Needless to say, the quickest route from Chepstow to Newport is by the M4, but little can be seen from the motorway. The route suggested here is anything but direct, but takes in most of what is worth seeing.

From the A48, a mile beyond the Chepstow roundabout, a road goes off left through the Victorian estate village of **Newton Green**. The estate is that of Wyelands, a pretty Regency house by Robert Lugar, set in a fine park. Beyond the motorway is **Mathern**. The church has a tall Perpendicular tower, unusually fine for the area: on it is a huge sundial.

In the churchyard stands a wellingtonia, said to have been planted by H. Avray Tipping. He bought **Mathern Palace**, next to the church, in 1894. Tipping (1855–1933) is best known for his articles on country houses and gardens in *Country Life*, republished in the nine volumes of *English Homes*. He was also a sensitive garden-designer, and used his considerable wealth to create three successive homes in Monmouthshire – Mathern, Mounton House (p. 195), and High Glanau, near Trellech (p. 193). Mathern Palace was the residence of the Bishops of Llandaff from the early fifteenth century until the early eighteenth century. After that it fell into decay, until Tipping lovingly restored it. He also laid out the delightful gardens, with terraces and topiary. The palace is now the guest-house of the British Steel Corporation. It is not open, but the L-shaped entrance front can be seen from the churchyard.

Only a quarter of a mile east of Mathern stands another interesting house, **Moynes Court** (close to the M4). It dates from 1609, and is of gabled Cotswold type. It is approached through a tall gatehouse, which is basically medieval, and is curious in having two turrets projecting from diagonally opposite corners. Half a mile south-west is yet another important house, **St Pierre**, but this one has to be reached by going back on to the A48, crossing the M4, and following the drive across the park, which is now a golf course. The much-rebuilt house is a country club. It too has a gatehouse, of three storeys, and dating from the sixteenth century. Just in front of it stands the little church, built *c*. 1100 by a knight from Caen (hence the French name). A Norman window survives, and there are two medieval tomb slabs. The wooden screen is partly of *c*. 1400. In 1415, Lewis Philip of St Pierre, governor of Calais, made a loan to Henry V, to help finance his French wars, and kept the Crown Jewels here as security until they were redeemed in 1437.

Opposite the Mathern turning, another road goes north off the A48 to **Mounton**. It enters a romantically narrow valley, with steep wooded sides. Here the little church (of 1881) stands: opposite it is a small graveyard, with some fine early-twentieth-century headstones. H. A. Tipping (p. 194) was so taken with the valley that in 1907 he bought land, just above the church, and laid out 'wild and water gardens'. There were some offensively ruinous old cottages near by, so he bought and sensitively restored them. Not far beyond the church, the valley widens out: here an old farm has a barn set on tall stone piers, and further up an enterprising householder has covered part of the wooded hillside with rockeries, gnomes, and miniature windmills (charming to us, but what would Tipping have thought?). Tipping also bought land on the plateau up above the east side of the valley, and began to build himself a large house. He felt Mathern was complete, and obviously wanted to try his hand at building from the ground up. His architect was the talented young Eric Francis (1887–1976), a former assistant to Guy Dawber and to Detmar Blow. Although Tipping liked to claim all the credit for both Mounton and High Glanau, and for other joint works (see p. 243), this was hardly just. **Mounton House** is a complete success. It is reached by a drive which leaves the A48 at the top of the hill in

Pwllmeyric. Now a County Council Special School, it is well looked after, although inevitably most of the gardens have run wild. The gardens were laid out before the house was begun. The generous and simple house (completed in 1912) is built of pinkish-grey local stone, with grey stone slates for the roof. The central part of the entrance front is of half-timber. Inside, some rooms have Jacobean-style panelling and plasterwork, but the dining-room is in late-eighteenth-century style, with a chimneypiece and doors brought from Brasted in Kent (by Robert Adam), and a marble floor.

Back on the A48, half a mile beyond the St Pierre drive, a road goes left towards the Severn. **Portskewett** (Porthiscoed) is said to have been the landing-place of St Tathan, who, like other bold Irish saints, went wherever his boat took him. From the partly Norman church a road crosses the railway to **Sudbrook**, a surprisingly and attractively industrial place, with a long street of terrace houses (some with defiantly varied roofing-materials). It is dominated by the bold brick bulk of the Severn Tunnel pumping station (1882). The tunnel goes under the river here, where formerly was the well-known New Passage ferry. The tunnel, four and a half miles long, was built in 1880–6 by Thomas Andrew Walker. The pumps keep it dry. The water which they pump out (20 million gallons a day) supplies the vast new paper mill near by. Behind the paper mill are the huge ramparts of an Iron Age fort, right on the edge of the estuary – in fact, the cliffs form one side of the fort. Within the ramparts is a football pitch. Near by are the overgrown ruins of a medieval church.

Beyond Portskewett, the road leads back on to the B4245, which soon enters **Caldicot**, a village which in recent years has undergone what the county guide calls 'a Cinderella transformation', its population having increased from 1700 to 7000. Unfortunately, a truer comparison would be with the Ugly Sisters. However, the church and castle remain unspoilt (turn right where the B road goes sharp left). The church is a fine medieval one, with a central tower and a rich south porch, and unusual window tracery. It was restored by Henry Woodyer in 1858, and most of his characteristic fittings survive. He also built the splendid vicarage (1862). The **Castle** belongs to Chepstow RDC, and is open from Easter to September. Well-preserved, and picturesquely situated among trees, it is surprisingly little-known. The earliest part is the circular keep (twelfth century). There was further building in the thirteenth century by the Bohuns, Earls of Hereford, and in the fourteenth century by the Duke of Gloucester, who put up the very grand gatehouse, with an upper hall.

Many of the architectural details are of exceptional refinement. On the outer doorway of the Woodstock Tower, on the north, is carved the name Thomas: this was Thomas of Woodstock, later Duke of Gloucester, whose uncle, Richard II, had him smothered in feather beds in 1396. The castle was bought in 1884 by Joseph Richard Cobb (1821–97), lawyer, promoter of the Brecon and Merthyr Railway, and antiquary. He carried out a sympathetic restoration (as at Manorbier, p. 136, and Pembroke, p. 131). His son, G. E. Wheatly Cobb, was keen on rescuing old sailing ships. In 1892 he bought the 80-gun *Foudroyant*, Nelson's 'darling child', but it was wrecked in 1897. The huge figurehead stands in the castle court.

The road beyond Caldicot church leads over the motorway, and approaches **Caerwent** from the south. The unsuspecting visitor might well be amazed that the village should be defended by a huge stone wall, 500 yards long on its southern side, still standing, in places, to a height of seventeen feet, and defended by a series of polygonal bastions. He might be even more amazed to learn that the wall was built in about AD 300, and the bastions added about forty years later. This was in fact the Roman town of *Venta Silurum*, 'the market town of the Silures'. The Silures were the Celtic inhabitants of the area. Their main local centre had been the hill-fort of Llanmelin, a mile north of Caerwent. They were finally subdued by Julius Frontinus, governor in AD 74 (see p. 208). It was Roman policy to move natives from their hill-tops to new towns down on the plains, and that is what happened here. The town, which covered 44 acres, was laid out on the usual rectangular plan. The present village occupies only part of its area.

Now that it has been bypassed, it is possible to explore it in peace. For the benefit of those who have not got the DoE guide-book, there is a plan set up by the churchyard wall. The finds from the various excavations are in Newport Museum. They include a fourth-century pewter bowl with a XP monogram on the base – the earliest surviving trace of Romano-British Christianity in Wales. The main east–west street represents the Roman street, but is a good deal narrower. The main junction (where the War Memorial stands) represents the centre: the forum stood immediately east of here, with the basilica behind it. Just east of the forum there was a temple. Across the main road from this was the main bath building (there were three others). North of the temple was a small amphitheatre. Nothing is now visible of these buildings: the only remains exposed within the walls are those of two houses in Pound Lane, which runs north about one hundred yards west of the War Memorial. The houses on the street had (as usual in Roman towns) shops along the front: a colonnade was added later. In the church porch two inscribed stones are kept. The larger and finer records the setting up of a statue to Tiberius Claudius Paulinus (who, after commanding the 2nd Legion, became proconsul of two of the provinces of Gaul) 'by decree of the tribal senate', by 'the commonwealth of the Silures'. It dates from shortly before 220. The second stone is a small altar to 'Mars Ocelus': Ocelus was a native god, identified with Mars.

The **Church** itself is large, with a tall thirteenth-century chancel, and a substantial tower. It was heavily restored in 1893–1901 by G. E. Halliday. The horrible south aisle was added later: built into its west wall are some big fragments of Roman carving. The wooden pulpit is dated 1632, and inscribed 'Woe unto me if I preach not the Gospel'. On one side is a representation of Llandaff Cathedral.

It is possible to walk almost the whole way round the walls (the exception being the section between the north and west gates): the DoE is still clearing and consolidating them. They were built to replace the earlier earth ramparts late in the third century AD. The addition of the bastions on the north and south sides was probably in response to the menace of sea-raiders. The south gate is well-preserved, having been blocked, probably at the time the bastions were built. In the south-east angle of the walls there is a small motte: the Normans clearly took advantage of the work of their predecessors. The north gate rather oddly survives, piled with old beer-crates, in the back yard of the North Gate Inn.

A mile beyond Caerwent is the crossroads of Five Lanes: from here it is a mile north to **Llanfair Discoed**. Up on the hill are the ruins of the thirteenth-century castle, thoroughly overgrown, and just below them is the church (rebuilt 1854 and 1883), tucked into the hillside. Inside the porch is a stone, inscribed:

> Who Ever hear on Sonday
> Will Practis Playing at Ball
> it May Be be Fore Monday
> The Devil Will have you All.

The road climbs round the side of the bare Gray Hill, and comes out (one and a half miles beyond Llanfair) above Wentwood Reservoir, which has a thin castellated straining tower. By the crossroads north of the reservoir, at **Foresters' Oaks**, there is a picnic site from which Countryside Trails go off through the conifers of Wentwood. It enjoys a great view over the Severn estuary. Wentwood (Coed Gwent) once rivalled the Forest of Dean: it was continuous with

Chepstow Park Wood, to the north-east, though now separated by a three-mile gap. It had a Ranger and Forest Courts, which used to meet at this place. The road down the other side of the reservoir leads to **Llanfaches**, now rather spoilt. The church, which has a saddleback tower, was restored in 1863 by Prichard and Seddon, and charmingly done up inside in 1908 in Arts and Crafts style, with whitewash, a carved screen and coloured glass. In the same year the same architect, A. Groves, built the delightful little Church Room. Llanfaches is chiefly famous because it was here that William Wroth founded the first 'gathered church' of nonconformists in Wales. Wroth (1576–1641) became Rector of Llanfaches in about 1615. Sometime about 1630, he became a zealous Puritan, and in 1638 he was forced to resign his living. In the next year Henry Jessey, a Puritan preacher, came from London to form Wroth's followers into a church in the 'New England Way'. They did not build a chapel. To quote Dr Thomas Richards, 'It is no wonder when one remembers Wroth's irreproachable character, his simple evangelical preaching, his unique position as the first minister of the first Independent church in Wales, that some of his contemporaries called him an "apostle" and looked upon Llanfaches as an Antioch amidst a gentile country.'

The road through Llanfaches leads back (one mile) to the A48. Up above the road is **Penhow**, a romantic place, its castle set on a steep grassy knob, dotted with projecting rocks, and the church even higher up. The part of the castle towards the road is a tall three-storey house, painted white, and dating from the early eighteenth century, but behind are medieval remains (open on written application). The chief of these is a rectangular towerhouse of about 1300, built by the St Maur (Seymour) family. The hall block dates from the fifteenth century, and contains two halls, one above the other, lit by traceried windows. The rather odd church has been much renewed, although part is twelfth century. The tower (rebuilt 1913) stands over the middle of the south aisle. The plaster barrel vaults survive.

Two miles beyond Penhow, another church also stands on a bump just south of the main road, at **Llandevaud**. Built in 1843, by E. Haycock, it has a west window by Morris and Co., to Mary Phelps (d. 1873). Half a mile further on, a road climbs steeply north up to Kemeys Graig, a long wooded ridge which runs south-west from Wentwood, above the Usk valley. Right on the top is Kemeys Folly, a castellated tower (inhabited), rebuilt in 1911–12, as an inscription records, in memory of two masters of foxhounds. On the end of the

ridge, at Coed-y-caerau, are two circular earthworks, and a small
Roman fort – possibly the predecessor of the legionary fortress of
Caerleon.

The road comes down at Cat's Ash, from where another road
goes north over the hill to the Usk valley. From it can be seen, over
the other side of the river, **Glen Usk**, a charming white house of
c. 1820: the picture gallery, on one side, has a Greek temple facade.
This side of the broad Usk valley has recently been blasted apart for
the Newport–Raglan road (A449). Just above the old road, a mile
from the junction where the Cat's Ash road joins it, is **Kemeys House**,
a seventeenth-century reconstruction of an earlier tower-and-hall
house (open on written application). One and a half miles north of
Kemeys House, a long and rough drive leads steeply up the hillside
to the ruins of **Bertholey House**. This elegant mansion, built in about
1830, was gutted by fire in 1905, and the centre part of its handsome
pilastered front, including the semicircular portico, has collapsed.
The service wing at the back is still inhabited. Beyond Bertholey, the
road goes on through Llantrisant to Usk (four miles).

Back on the A48, a few hundred yards east of Llandevaud church
a road runs south leading in a mile to another sad ruin, **Pencoed
Castle**. There was a castle here in Norman times, but the earliest
surviving feature is the thirteenth-century round tower, at the south-
west angle of the forecourt. In the fifteenth century the castle was
acquired by Sir Thomas Morgan (d. 1510), and he is said to have
built the present house. However, this seems too early for most of it,
and something nearer 1600 would surely be more likely. What seems
to have happened is that part of the castle enclosure was retained as
the forecourt to what is really a castellated house rather than a defensible castle. In front is a gatehouse, reached by a bridge over a dry
moat. The asymmetrical front has a three-storey porch, and big
mullioned windows. A restoration was begun in 1914, by G. H.
Kitchen, for Lord and Lady Rhondda, and continued by Eric Francis
in 1919–20, but it was never finished. The castle now belongs to a
farmer, and an immense pool of dung festers against the facade. A
mile west of Pencoed is **Llanmartin**. By the junction of the Pencoed
road and the B4245 stands the Rectory, of stone with brick decoration, a characteristically tough and quirky work of J. P. Seddon, who
rebuilt the church in 1858, except for the tower. It is well situated on a
hillock by old farm buildings. There is an elaborate, but mutilated,
tomb to Sir Thomas Morgan of Pencoed (see above).

From Llanmartin church, a minor road leads over the M4 to
Bishton (two miles), quite a pleasant village, but its Perpendicular

church with a fine tall tower (all much renewed in 1887), overlooks nothing now but the immense Spencer Works of the British Steel Corporation. No less than three miles long, this was opened in 1962, to have an output of two million tons a year. It is the most highly automated steelworks in Britain. **Llanwern** is a mile west of Bishton. Llanwern Park has been demolished: it was built *c.* 1725 by Francis Smith (of Warwick), for the Van family. Later it passed to the Salusburys of Denbighshire, and was the home from 1887 of David Alfred Thomas, Lord Rhondda (1856–1918). The fifteenth of the seventeen children of an Aberdare coal-owner, he became Liberal MP for Merthyr, and a coal-owner himself. Eventually he retired to Llanwern, and occupied himself with his famous herd of Hereford cattle. In 1917 he became Food Controller. One of his policies was the introduction of rationing. He is commemorated by a big cross in the churchyard. The church is not of usual local type: it has a buttressed tower, and nave and chancel in one. The nice Village Hall is by Oswald P. Milne.

Llanwern is only just outside Newport, but it would be a great mistake not to explore the **Moors**, the flat lands between the railway and the Severn. They have a distinct character. They are crossed by drainage ditches, known as 'reens', and lined with pollarded willows. The many farms look prosperous, and often have big eighteenth-century farmhouses. The roads tend to run straight, and then turn suddenly at a sharp angle. Return from Llanwern into Bishton, and then turn right, passing under the railway by means of an alarmingly low arch (a level crossing provides an alternative). Then turn left for **Magor**, a big village on the B4245. The church stands off the main road, by a little square in which stands the well-designed War Memorial, incorporating a memorial (with portrait plaque) to Lord Rhondda. The church is quite grand, with its central tower, and its two-storey vaulted porch (the elaborate doorway dates from John Norton's restoration in 1868). The long thirteenth-century chancel was built by the monks of Santa Maria di Gloria at Anagni (near Rome), to whom the church had been given in 1238. The capitals of the nave arcades take the form of angels with outstretched wings (restored).

From Magor a road runs south (two and a half miles) to **Redwick**, a spread-out village which feels very remote. It is only half a mile from the estuary, but one might never know. The big church is similar to Magor, with a richer crossing-tower, but a less elaborate two-storey porch. It too was restored by Norton (in 1876). Good medieval details include the beautiful Decorated east window, with flowing outline, the niche in the north aisle, and the carved supports for the former rood-screen, now supporting a nineteenth-century gallery. By the church gate is a curious half-built bus-shelter, with Gothic door-jambs and windows, made of moulded concrete, including the lower part of a big mullioned window in front. Inside is a huge stone cider-press, and a big mill-wheel. Built into the walls are other mill-wheels, boundary stones, and bits of inscribed tablets. In front is a footscraper, and an iron tethering-ring, and at the side are mounting steps. There cannot be many bus-shelters like this one, a villager's labour of love.

Whitson is only two miles west of Redwick, but to get from one to the other it is necessary to travel a good five miles. Whitson is a strung-out place. At the north end Whitson Court stands by the road, looking very pretty with its pale red brick. Designed by John Nash, *c.* 1795, it has a blank arcade along the ground floor, a cumbersome later porch, and balancing detached pavilions. There is also a little stuccoed Tudor lodge. The grounds now contain a zoo. The village cottages are nearly all set back from the road on the other side of drainage ditches, and are reached by little bridges. The church (restored in 1861 by Prichard and Seddon) is down a lane, exceptionally attractive; the funny little cone on top is known as 'the thimble'. The road through the village leads straight (one mile) to the estuary at **Goldcliff** – the only place along here where a proper road does lead to it. The name, according to Giraldus Cambrensis, derived from the golden colour of the cliffs when struck by the sun. This was probably due to mica in the grit or sandstone cliffs, now no longer visible because of the great sea-dyke built against them. This may possibly go back to Roman times, for an inscription was found near here (now in the National Museum), recording that 'a century of the 1st cohort built $33\frac{1}{2}$ paces'. The dyke inevitably spoils the shore, even though it does make a good promenade.

The 'lighthouse', on the point, is just a light on an iron pedestal. A notice forbids interference with the putchers. These are the salmon-nets, shaped like ice-cream cones, which are stacked in piles. Fishing was an important element in the economy of the Benedictine Priory, founded *c.* 1113 by the Norman Robert de Chandos, as a cell of the abbey of Bec. The monks had a difficult time with the locals. In about 1320 the prior was held captive for six weeks. In 1442 they drove out the monks and took the prior prisoner, and did the same again four years later. The monks were also troubled by robbers, by a prior with forged credentials, and by accusations of stealing from wrecks. Practically nothing survives of the monastic buildings: they have partly collapsed into the sea. Back in the village, the parish church is set back behind the pub. Mostly rebuilt in the 19th century, it has a plain tower with lancets, and a nice colour-scheme inside. Set two feet three inches up the north wall of the chancel is a small brass plate with the inscription:

1606
ON . THE . XX . DAY . OF . IANVARY . EVEN . AS
IT . CAME . TO . PAS . IT . PLEASED . GOD . THE
FLVD . DID . FLOW . TO . THE . EDGE . OF . THIS
SAME . BRAS
AND . IN . THIS . PARISH . THEARE . WAS . LOST
5000 . AND . OD . POWNDS
BESIDES . XXII . PEOPLE . WAS . IN . THIS . PARISH
DROWND

For another record of the same flood, see St Bride's Wentlooge (p. 230).

Two miles west of Goldcliff is Nash, sadly suburban (too close to Newport), but with a most remarkable church. It has a big stone spire (fifteenth century), attached to the north-east corner of the nave. The chancel was rebuilt by Prichard and Seddon in 1861. The south porch is eighteenth century, classical, with a grand pilastered doorway. The inner door is Gothic, as is the huge barn-like nave, which retains its box pews and three-decker pulpit. From Nash it is only two miles to the outskirts of Newport.

NEWPORT (CASNEWYDD-AR-WYSG)

Newport has not got much of a reputation as a tourist attraction. In some ways, its ill-repute is deserved: a great sprawling industrial town of about 120,000 people, it has most of the disadvantages of such a place, with few of the advantages that can accompany it. The chief historical monuments have been badly mauled, some of the most attractive old areas are being allowed to fall into decay, the best nineteenth-century buildings have in several cases fallen victims to fire or demolition, and there is little decent modern building. However, Newport does have sights worth seeing – the grandest late-seventeenth-century house in Wales, a medieval church of unusual plan, one of the only two surviving transporter bridges in the country, and a good museum. It is a friendly place, full of life, and not inclined to put on airs and graces.

The origin of the settlement goes back to the sixth century. The tradition is that Gwynllyw, the lord of Gwynllwg (Wentlooge – the coastal area between Newport and Cardiff) was the founder, in about 600, of the church up on the hill which is dedicated to him (in the corrupted form 'Woolos'). He married Gwladys, a daughter of Brychan Brycheiniog, and their son was the famous St Cadog. In the twelfth century the castle was founded, to command the crossing of the Usk, but the place grew slowly, and in 1801 the population was only 1087. In the nineteenth century, when Newport was the port for the iron produced at the heads of the Monmouthshire valleys, and the market town for the area, expansion was rapid. The most famous episode in its history occurred in 1839 – the tragic Chartist march on the town. John Frost, a prosperous draper and former mayor of Newport, had been chosen as local delegate to the Convention to be held in London, with a view to presenting the Charter to Parliament. In April 1839 occurred the trouble at Llanidloes (see *North Wales*, p. 302). In November a local Chartist, Henry Vincent, was imprisoned. This infuriated the Monmouthshire ironworkers and coalminers, who decided to hold a great demonstration at Newport on the night of 3–4 November. Three columns were to march on the town – from Blackwood (led by Frost), Ebbw Vale, and Pontypool. A storm threw out their plans, and by the time they arrived troops had been installed in the Westgate Hotel. A scuffle broke out, and the troops fired. About twenty men were killed. The mayor, Thomas Phillips, was wounded. He was later knighted, given the freedom of the City of London, and invited to dine with the queen. Frost and the other two leaders were condemned to be hanged and quartered, but the sentence was commuted to transportation for life. They were transported to Australia, but Frost was pardoned in 1854, and died near Bristol in 1877, at the age of 93.

More recently, Newport has become an important industrial town. A new shipbuilding yard has been built. The Docks, now that the export of coal is no longer their *raison d'être*, have been developed as one of the most highly mechanized ports in Europe, exporting steel, importing timber, and also operating container services. The town centre is being thoroughly redeveloped, with the ultimate aim of ensuring that 'all points will be within 150 yards of a car park'.

The best place from which to start exploring the town is the bridge over the Usk, built in 1927, to replace the one put up in 1800 by Thomas and David Edwards (sons of William Edwards). Beside it are the ruins of the **Castle**, looking best from the river side, although the river itself is hardly beautiful. (The Usk has a greater rise and fall of tide than any other river in Britain – hence the mud banks.) In the care of the DoE, they are open 'at discretion of local authority'. Only the east side of the court remains: the polygonal buttressed towers replaced earlier buildings in the fifteenth century. South of the bridge, the new Kingsway follows the river. Parallel to it is Dock Street, in which is the grandiose towered facade of the **Market** (1887–9, J. Linton and C. Kirby). Inside, the iron and glass hall has shops on two levels. The other side of the Market is on **High Street**. Here stands the half-timbered Murengers House, now a pub, dated 1530 but much restored. The junction of High Street with Stow Hill and Commercial Street is the heart of the town. Commercial Street is very much what its name implies. Near the junction is the Westgate Hotel, scene of the Chartist débâcle (see p. 204). It was nastily rebuilt in 1884 by E. A. Lansdowne. On the other side of the street is the best commercial building in Newport, now Burton's. This splendid Gothic effort has two tall pyramidal roofs, and lavish ironwork, which includes gorgeous barley-sugar downpipes. East of Commercial Street is Llanarth Street, in which is the **Museum and Art Gallery**. Contents include the finds from Caerwent (p. 197), and material relating to the Chartists.

At the bottom of Commercial Street is St Paul's Church, 1835, by T. H. Wyatt, so dreadful as to be quite entertaining. Next to the church is Palmyra Place, which leads up the hill to **Park Square**, part of an attractive early Victorian area which ought to be better maintained. Stuccoed Tudor villas, and a stone Grecian villa, face over a little park from which a bronze seated statue of Sir Charles Morgan, Bt, of Tredegar, overlooks the estuary. It is signed J. E. Thomas, 1848. Victoria Road leads out of the square. On the corner with Hill Street is the amazing **Congregational Chapel**, by A. O. Watkins, built in 1858–69. Its stone-fronted exterior is basically classical in style, but the lavish decorative carving is entirely original. From Victoria Road, Victoria Place, lined with handsome stuccoed terraces, with Ionic porches and iron balconies, leads to Stow Hill.

At the top of the hill, dominating the town, is **St Woolos' Cathedral**. It became a cathedral in 1921, when the new diocese of Monmouth was created out of the diocese of Llandaff. Although of considerable architectural interest, it is not a building of much character or charm. Harshly restored in 1853–4 by W. G. and E. Habershon, it was more sympathetically dealt with in 1913 by Sir Harold Brakspear. A large new chancel was built in 1960–4 by A. D. R. Caroe. The tall west tower was built c. 1500. Between it and the nave, which has wide aisles, comes the Lady Chapel, the same width as the nave, but without aisles. It was built in the thirteenth century, probably on the site of a pre-Norman church reserved for the parish, while the rest belonged to the *clas*. The windows and monuments have been mutilated. The nave dates from the twelfth century, built after the church was given to the Benedictines of Gloucester. The west doorway (from the Lady Chapel) dates from *c.* 1160, and has crudely carved capitals. The Norman nave arcades and clerestory are much the finest feature of the church.

Down the hill south of the cathedral, reaching to Cardiff Road, is **Bellevue Park**, laid out by the celebrated landscape gardener Thomas Mawson. He won the competition without anyone noticing that he had by mistake made a scheme for the wrong site.

The area north of the cathedral and west of Stow Hill consists of stuccoed two-storey terraces, enlivened by the occasional chapel. Near the bottom of Stow Hill is St Mary's RC Church, built in 1838–40 by J. J. Scoles. Bridge Street runs west from the bottom of Stow Hill: in it is St Luke's, an awful church (Habershon and Fawckner, 1904), worth a visit for its ornate reredos of 1922 by J. Coates Carter. On the other side of the railway is the **Civic Centre**, a vast symmetrical pile with a silly clock-tower. Begun in 1937, it was designed by T. Cecil Howitt. Up on the hill above, called **Gold Tops**, the big Perpendicular church of St Mark, with an elaborate tower of Somerset type, forms a striking landmark (1874, Habershon and Fawckner).

Below the main bridge, two other bridges cross the Usk. The first is George Street Bridge, an immense new suspension bridge, and the second, much further downstream, is the **Transporter Bridge**. (It can be reached by following Commercial Street and its continuation as far as possible: on the other side of the river it links up with the A455.) This splendid piece of engineering was built in 1906 by F. Arnodin (builder of the famous Marseilles transporter bridge) and R. H. Haynes. It runs between 5.30 a.m. and 11 p.m., carrying both people and cars (six at a time), free of charge. (But in high winds it may not be running.) The ride is enormous fun, and not to be missed. The tower can be climbed for 3p. The 'captain's bridge' has a small pointed hat, painted blue.

South-west of the town, within the borough boundary, is **Tredegar Park**, easily the finest late-seventeenth-century house in Wales. Cardiff Road (A48) runs round the park. The entrance to the house is from the road, about half a mile south of the M4 roundabout. The estate was sold to pay duties after the death of the 5th Baron in 1954, and now belongs to the Newport Corporation, who open it occasionally. For some time it has existed in a kind of limbo: vandals smash everything they can lay their hands on, while vast sums have been spent on the repair of the house by the Historic Buildings Council (so it is open on written application). Until 1954, the estate had never been bought or sold. The Morgans of Tredegar acquired it by marriage in the fourteenth century. They became one of the most powerful families in Monmouthshire. In 1645, after the Battle of Naseby, Charles I stayed here with Sir William Morgan. His grandson, another William (d. 1680), made an advantageous match with his cousin, Blanche Morgan, who possessed great estates in Breconshire. He succeeded his father in 1664, and it seems that it was then that he began the present house. The Morgans provided a whole succession of MPs for either Monmouthshire or Brecon, and of Lords Lieutenant, and also involved themselves in industrial developments, such as New Tredegar ironworks, Newport Docks, the Monmouthshire Canal, and the Sirhowy Tramroad. The most colourful nineteenth-century Morgan was Godfrey Charles, 2nd Baron and 1st Viscount (1831–1913), who took part in the Charge of the Light Brigade at Balaclava.

The oldest part of the house is the hall range on the south-west side, which dates from about 1500. The new house built in 1664–74 is tremendously grand. It consists of two great wings at right angles to one another, forming a square with the old hall and the later offices. The main front faces north-west. It is built of warm red brick, with Bath stone dressings. Of the eleven bays, the outer two at each end project. The windows are all mullioned: those on the ground floor have broken pediments over them, with elaborate cartouches, while the upper windows have swags below. The doorway is an astonishing Baroque composition, with barley-sugar columns supporting the two halves of the broken pediment, on each of which a figure reclines. Unfortunately the old roof of stone tiles, with pedimented dormers, has been replaced by slate. The forecourt is entered through three sets of splendid iron gates, made in 1714, probably by William Edney. On the north-east front there is a large nineteenth-century porch. The interior of the house is even richer than the exterior. All the main rooms are panelled from floor to ceiling, including even the bedrooms. Some of the sumptuous plaster ceilings gave way in about 1870, but some remain. The most lavishly decorated room is the Gilt Room, which has twisted columns above the chimneypiece, and painted panels (possibly French) incorporated in walls and ceiling, but far more distinguished is the splendidly carved Oak Room.

North-west of the house are the immense stables, of the same date. The great doorway is boldly carved with weapons and armour, and above is a white-painted pediment. In the gardens west of the house, a circular hedge surrounds the monument to Sir Briggs, the horse which carried the Hon. Godfrey Morgan at the battles of the Alma and Inkerman, as well as in the Charge of the Light Brigade, and which died at Tredegar in 1874 aged 28. North-east of the house is the long lake, backed by woods.

CAERLEON TO USK, PONTYPOOL, AND BACK

East of the Usk, Newport has little of interest, apart from two churches, and both of them were burnt out by an arsonist in 1949. The first is St John's, **Maindee**, just north of Chepstow Road (A48). It was designed in 1859 by Prichard and Seddon, and, if built with its intended spire, would have been one of their finest churches. The present tower top, of 1911, is feeble and discordant. One and a half miles north-east of St John's, up on the ridge just north of the motorway, is **Christchurch**, whose tower is a landmark. The church was restored after the fire by G. G. Pace.

The small park, west of the church, gives a splendid view over **Caerleon**, which is a mile north, on the north bank of the Usk (reached more directly from Newport by the B4596). The name represents 'castra legionum', the camp of the legions. This flat site between the river and the hills was chosen, in about AD 74 or 75, as the site of the permanent fortress of the Second Augustan Legion. Its Roman name was Isca Silurum – Isca being the Celtic name for the Usk. The walled area was about 540 yards by 450. The defences were rebuilt in stone before about 120, and most of the buildings were similarly rebuilt or completed by about 150. In the early third century, the garrison was reduced, and after about 260 the fortress began to decay, being almost deserted by the end of the fourth century. It appears that the civilian settlement which usually grew up outside Roman forts was comparatively insignificant here, probably because of the proximity of Caerwent. The church at Caerleon is said to have been founded by St Cadog (see p. 204) in the mid fifth century. Geoffrey of Monmouth maintained that St Dyfrig (Dubricius) was Archbishop of Caerleon at the time when Arthur had his court there. Dyfrig probably had no connection with the place at all, but the association with Arthur is widely attested in myth. According to the story *Gereint Son of Erbin* in the *Mabinogion*, he held court here because it was 'the most accessible place in his dominions, by sea and by land'. Tennyson stayed in Caerleon in 1856 to gain inspiration for the *Idylls of the King*. This was soon after

The Congregational Church, Victoria Road, Newport, designed by
A.O. Watkins, and built in 1858-69, from a painting by Evan Charlton.

The magnificent late 15th-century screen at Llangwm Uchaf Church is
the finest of the many in the Usk district (from a 19th century engraving).

Elliot Colliery, New Tredegar, closed in 1967, but the winding-house of 1891 is to be preserved.

Elliot Colliery and typical terraces of houses seen across the Rhymney Valley.

the scientific investigation of the Roman remains had begun. Caerleon figures, as 'Caermaen', in *The Hill of Dreams* (1907), by the too
little-known novelist Arthur Machen. It includes a romantic evocation of the town in its Roman heyday. Machen (1863–1947) was
born here, and he regarded it as a great blessing that in childhood
he had before him 'the vision of an enchanted life'. His grandfather
had been vicar of Caerleon, and his father, John Edward Jones, was
vicar of Llanddewi Fach. His father added his wife's name,
Machen, to his own, and the son later dropped the Jones. Other
novels and stories of his are set in South Wales or based on Welsh
legends.

Caerleon is an attractive little town, and its immediate surroundings have been preserved from development. But its outskirts are
dismally suburbanized, and almost all the surrounding hills are now
crowned with housing estates. On the south side of the river, in
'The Village' (Caerleon-ultra-pontem), is a nice little early-nineteenth-
century toll-house. The bridge was built in 1806 by David Edwards
(the stone dated 1800 comes from his bridge at Newport – see p.
204). The old bridge was further upstream – probably near the site
of the Roman bridge. By the old bridgehead stands a thirteenth-
century tower, now joined to the Hanbury Arms. This formed part
of the medieval castle (see p. 210). From here runs **High Street**. In it
the Priory and the Bull Inn stand opposite one another, both with
sixteenth-century windows. Beyond is a small square, on which are
the church, museum, and school. The pretty **School**, with round-
headed windows, was founded in 1724 with money left by Charles
Williams (1633–1720). He was born at Caerleon, but after killing a
cousin in a duel had to flee the country. He settled at Smyrna, and
made a fortune in trade. Eventually he returned to London. He also
left money for repairing the church, and for improving the local
roads.

The large **Church**, in a big churchyard, occupies part of the site of
the praetorium (headquarters) – probably no coincidence. It is
mostly Perpendicular, but a Norman arch survives in the north wall
of the tower. The church was largely rebuilt in 1867 by Seddon, but
most of his fittings disappeared in 1935, when the chancel was extended, and the Lady Chapel added, by W. D. Caröe.

The **Legionary Museum** is a handsome little building, in the style
of a Greek temple, with a portico in front. It was built in 1848–50,
and designed by H. F. Lockwood of Hull. The Greek temple design
suits the building's function excellently, since there are no side
windows, but only top-lighting (however unarchaeological that may

be). The well laid-out display includes a series of interesting in-scriptions, some also of great beauty, especially the great marble tablet dedicated to the emperor Trajan in AD 100 by the 2nd Legion. There are other remarkable objects such as a lead burial canister, with a pipe down which libations could be poured from above ground.

The main archaeological site is down Broadway, opposite the church. The famous **Amphitheatre**, once known as King Arthur's Round Table, was excavated in 1926–7 (now DoE). It was built at the end of the 1st century AD, and renovated c. 125–30. Wooden seats rested on an earth bank, supported inside and out by stone walls, the outer 32 feet high, and the inner twelve. Its seating capacity was about six thousand, so it would comfortably take the whole Legion. Four stones, still in position, record the building of various sections by their respective centuries or cohorts. In the middle of each of the sides was a 'box' for distinguished spectators.

The only other excavations which have been left open are those of the **Barracks** in the west corner of the fort, about three hundred yards north-west of the Amphitheatre (also DoE). Part of the ramparts, with three turrets, can be seen, also a series of ovens, with the cook-houses which superseded them, and a latrine building, which had wooden seats round three sides, set above a stone channel through which water flowed. The barrack buildings lay in facing pairs all along the north-west and south-east ends of the fort. The remains of the end one have been left exposed, while the sites of three others have been marked out at ground level. Each building housed a century, under a centurion, and was about two hundred and fifty by forty feet. The centurion occupied rooms at one end, while the men occupied twelve double cubicles, with a colonnade in front. The south-west section of the rampart, including the curved south corner, is clearly marked by the line of trees running from Broadway down past the Amphitheatre.

In the east corner of the town is **The Mynde** (in private gardens), a Norman motte: as at Caerwent (p. 198), the Normans used a Roman site. It was landscaped in the early nineteenth century. The huge stone walls around it are built largely of Roman masonry. The bailey walls ran along the Roman rampart and then cut down to the river (see p. 209). The great bath building, just outside the fortress, which was excavated by Lee in 1849, was just south-west of The Mynde.

From Caerleon, the former A449 (now declassified) runs up to Usk. A mile out of the town, a minor road goes off right to **Llan-**

henwg, on a fine site overlooking the Usk valley. The little church was restored in 1863 by Seddon, and has characteristic fittings. The road runs along the ridge, giving great views westwards. This was the route of the Roman road from Caerleon to Usk. At the bottom, turn right for **Tredunnock**, a pleasant village down near the Usk. The church was sensitively restored in 1910 (commemorated in an inscription cut by Eric Gill). It has tiny Norman windows in the chancel, an old roof, and a carved stone font of 1662. Above the font is set a fine inscription of the second century AD recording the burial of Julianus, a soldier of the 2nd Legion, by his wife Amanda. It was found in the churchyard. Below the village the road crosses the river at Newbridge-on-Usk by a bridge built in 1779, and joins the road along the other side of the river below Bertholey (p. 200). One and a half miles west of Tredunnock, a road goes off on the other side of the main road into the peaceful hilly country which lies between the Usk and Afon Lwyd valleys. About three miles on, a road goes off right, crosses the valley, and climbs to **Common Coed-y-Paun**. Here there is a church built by Sir Matthew Digby Wyatt in 1860 (he is buried at Usk – see p. 186). It is a simple Early English building, with a big west tower, effective from a distance, but extraordinarily old-fashioned for its date. West of the village, a road crosses the dam of the big Llandegfedd Reservoir. The road north leads down to Usk.

However, back on the Usk road, two miles beyond where we turned off, is **Llangybi**, with numerous old houses in the village, and a substantial Perpendicular church overlooking the wide, level valley. Half a mile beyond is the drive to **Llangibby Castle** (it retains the old spelling). On the opposite side of the main road is an avenue of Scots firs, known as 'Llangibby Walks', first planted in 1707. This was not long after the house was built. It was demolished in 1950, but the stables survive, with oval windows along the top. Up on the wooded hill-top beyond the stables are the ruins of the castle, also called Castell Tregrug (permission to visit should be sought from the owner, Major Addams-Williams, who lives in the village). It is one of the least-known castles in Wales, but one of the most remarkable. It is beautifully sited on a large plateau. The ground falls steeply on north and west, and there are woods all round, noisy with woodpigeons. The castle covers a huge area – in fact it is the biggest inner ward in England and Wales. The inside is now unfortunately planted with Christmas trees. Ruined walls and towers survive around the whole circumference. The great keep-gatehouse, at the south-west corner, had two big round towers. Only Beaumaris has a bigger gatehouse. At the north-west corner is a hexagonal tower with remains of vaulting. Some of the towers retain evidence of ingenious sanitary arrangements. At the south-east corner is another gatehouse. Strangely the castle has little recorded history. It is not even known who built it, but, as it must date from about 1300, being of the same type as Caerphilly, Harlech, and Beaumaris, but more complex, it has been attributed to Gilbert de Clare, last Earl of Gloucester (1307–14). It was certainly never finished – no trace has been found of any internal buildings. After the reign of Edward II, things were quieter, and the castle may have been thought superfluous. Within a century it had fallen into neglect.

Two miles beyond Llangybi, the A449 crosses the bridge into Usk (p. 185), but the A472 carries on west of the Usk, and then goes off westwards through **Monkswood** (two miles beyond Usk), once the site of a grange of Tintern. Two miles further on, the A472 meets the A4042, which comes down from Abergavenny through Llanover (p. 184). Just beyond the junction is **Mamhilad**, where the huge ICI Fibres factory (built 1946–8) indicates the nearness of industrial Pontypool. Both it and the recent Parke-Davis factory next to it were designed by the firm of Sir Percy Thomas and Partners, and they make an interesting contrast. A mile up the road which runs past the side of the ICI factory is Mamhilad church, restored in 1865 by Prichard. The splendid medieval rood-loft (closely related to the one at Betws Newydd – p. 185) now fronts the gallery, and there is medieval glass in the east window. Beyond Mamhilad, the A472 passes the strange little church of **Llanfihangel Pontymoel**, whitewashed, with spreading eaves and a peculiar bellcote.

From the roundabout just outside Pontypool, the A4042 goes down the east side of the Afon Lwyd valley, through industrial suburbia. A mile from the roundabout, a lane goes 600 yards east to **Pant-teg** church, remote and rural-feeling. This odd building was rebuilt, with a wide nave, in 1849, and then altered again in 1876 by Henry Woodyer. Three miles further down the main road, the B4236 goes off south-east back to Caerleon, passing (one mile) through **Llanfrechfa**. By a bend in the road stands the Vicarage, a splendidly colourful and elaborate affair of 1856 by Prichard and Seddon. The church is up a lane a quarter of a mile east of the road, in a peaceful setting. The tower and porch are old, but the rest was nobly rebuilt in 1873 by Charles Buckeridge (completed after his death by Pearson). From Llanfrechfa it is two miles to Caerleon (p. 208).

THE VALLEYS OF GWENT

The **Valleys** which make up the western part of the county of Gwent
are not essentially distinguishable from the valleys of Glamorgan.
They run in a south-easterly direction, parallel to the Usk valley,
but they come down from the foothills of the Brecon Beacons. From
east to west, they are the valleys of the Afon Lwyd, Ebbw Fach,
Ebbw Fawr, and Sirhowy. The Rhymney valley was half in Monmouthshire (the river formed the boundary with Glamorgan) until
1974, since when only a small part has been in Gwent.

Their character is, of course, strongly industrial, and the contrast
with the rural part of the county could hardly be greater. Although
in area only a quarter of the county, they house three-quarters of the
county's population. The chief industry was, from the sixteenth until
the mid nineteenth century, ironmaking. This was originally con-
centrated at the heads of the valleys, where wood, to produce the
charcoal needed for smelting, was plentiful, the iron ore was near the
surface, and there was abundant water to provide power. In the
nineteenth century, coal, mined at first chiefly to make coke as a
substitute for charcoal (less available as the woods were progressively
cut down), later became the staple of the economy, all the more so
towards the end of the century when the ironworks declined.
Transport costs naturally made it more economic to site new processing works near the sea. Now that coal-mining has declined, to
such an extent that a working colliery is a rare sight, efforts have
been made to attract a wide range of new industries.

Before ironmaking began on a big scale, the valleys were almost
uninhabited, and used mainly for sheep-farming. The old settlements
were not down in the valleys, but up on the hills, to which the old
roads and trackways kept. Hence the lonely old parish churches such
as Llanhilleth, Bedwellte, and Mynyddislwyn. The pubs next to or
near the churches have often survived, and have become favourite
resorts of the valley residents, who enjoy the walk up on a fine
summer's day.

To an outsider, the element of contrast can come as a tremendous
surprise – the contrast between Ebbw Vale itself and the bare mountain valley just below, the contrast between the long, tight-packed
terraces on the lower slopes, and the hills above whether piled high
with coal-tips, covered in recent conifer plantations, or left as bare
grass, the contrast between the towns and the open moorland hill-
tops just beyond the Heads of the Valleys road (a contrast emphas-
ized by the cattle-grids across the main roads on the top edges of

these towns, an attempt to cope with the recurrent problem of sheep who prefer urban life to the hills). For the people living in the towns, the possibility of escape up on to the open hills has always been a vital compensation for the hard and oppressive jobs by which they have supported themselves.

NEWPORT TO PONTYPOOL, VIA CWMBRAN

Half a mile beyond the M4, the A4042 passes the remarkable little church of **Malpas**. There was a Cluniac cell here, but the present church is entirely of 1849–50, and is – exceptionally for its architect, John Prichard – in the Romanesque style. Very elaborate, and built of red and yellow stone, it has a chancel arch ornamented with big dogtooth, and an amazing stone lectern covered in Romanesque carving. Some of the vigorous stained-glass windows commemorate Thomas Prothero (1780–1853), whose home was at Malpas Court, three-quarters of a mile north. He offered £500 towards the building of the church, on condition that it was built nearer his house. When the offer was rejected, he gave only £250 – a mean act not untypical of this pushful and unsavoury character, the arch-enemy of John Frost. He victimized the people of Newport, and in his capacities as agent to the Tredegar estates, town clerk, etc. managed to acquire a fortune, often by dubious methods. Some of this was spent on his house, built by T. H. Wyatt in 1838. It is now (ironically) a community centre.

Two miles beyond Malpas is **Llantarnam**. Near the road junction are the church and the pub. Over the door of the pub is a charming tablet, dated 1719 and inscribed '*Y Ty Gwyrdd*' (The Green House) showing two drinkers. Llantarnam Abbey is reached through a nice Jacobean-style lodge, with shaped gables and a little tower, a few hundred yards back on the A4042. The house (now a convent) was built by T. H. Wyatt in 1835 but incorporates fragments of the Cistercian monastery founded from Strata Florida in 1171, at the invitation of Hywel ap Iorwerth, lord of Caerleon.

The left fork at the junction (A4051) leads into **Cwmbran**, the only completely New Town in Wales. Begun in 1949, it now has a population of 44,000. The entire town is heated from a colossal boiler-house at the base of the 22-storey block of flats called The Tower, the highest building in Wales. New industry lines the valley, and the new County Hall has been built here. Although not exciting, the architecture and lay-out of the town are decent, and imagination has been shown, for example, in the way the canal, which runs along the west side of the valley, has been laid out with trees and walks. An unfortunate lack of imagination, however, was shown in building over the canal in such a way as to preclude navigation. In the upper part of the town, west of the canal, is the old village of **Pontnewydd**, which has a striking church (Holy Trinity) of 1857–60 by Prichard and Seddon. The wings Prichard and Seddon added to the near-by school have even more remarkable constructional polychromy than the church. For an amazing contrast with the new town, go on up the hill beyond Pontnewydd to **Upper Cwmbran**. The Square is right up on the mountainside, at 700 feet, with tremendous views. Unfortunately many of the houses round it have been demolished. A steep climb from the valley below leads up on to a moorland road which is an exciting way to approach Pontypool. It passes the Mountain Air Inn (at nearly one thousand feet), and then gives splendid views over Pontypool and the valleys.

From the main road from Cwmbran to Pontypool, a road branches left (two miles beyond Cwmbran) to Sebastopol, crossing the Monmouthshire and Brecon Canal by means of Crown Bridge. When this was recently rebuilt, the canal was reduced to a culvert, so that this now represents the lowest point to which the canal can be navigated. (It is hoped that the bridge will again be rebuilt to enable boats to go down to Cwmbran.) However, from here it is possible to navigate all the way to Brecon (35 miles). The **Monmouthshire Canal**, now disused except for this short stretch, was built in 1794–9 by Thomas Dadford Jr. The main line ran from Newport to Pontnewynydd, and a branch ran off from Crindau to Crumlin. The Brecon and Abergavenny Canal (see p. 41), also built by Dadford, leaves the Monmouthshire at Pontymoile Bridge, just south-east of the junction of the A4051 and A472.

Pontypool has been an important industrial centre since the sixteenth century, when ironmaking first began (a little later than in Glamorgan) on a considerable scale. The chief protagonist was Richard Hanbury, who came from Worcestershire. Another member of the family, Major John Hanbury (1664–1734), was the pioneer of the tinplating industry. The rolling mill was invented by his agent, Thomas Cooke (of Stourbridge). Another of his agents, Thomas Allgood, made experiments with lacquer, which were developed by his son Edward, who established the japanning works, for which the town became famous. Pontypool japanware – trays, tableware and so on – was at its best in the mid eighteenth century, when the foreman and chief painter was Benjamin Barker (father of Thomas Barker of Bath, the landscape painter). Another japanworks was set up by members of the Allgood clan at Usk, in 1761. In the nineteenth century, Pontypool industry – ironmaking, tinplate, and coal-mining – developed rapidly, and the population grew from 1500 in 1801 to 27,000 in 1891. The notorious 'Tommy Shops', run by the employers, where prices were high but employees could get goods on credit to be deducted from wages, survived here until 1877.

The town developed along the south side of the Afon Lwyd valley. Across the river is **Pontypool Park**, once the home of the Hanburys, but now municipal. At the east end of the park, beside the A472 (just north of the bridge), are a pair of lavish wrought-iron gates, said to have been given to Major John Hanbury by his friend Sarah, Duchess of Marlborough. (He was one of the executors of the Duke's will.) The piers on which they hang were made at Blaenavon in the early nineteenth century, and are a little absurd – trying to outdo the previous century. The house is up the other end of the park. It is said to have been built by Major Hanbury's father in 1659, and enlarged by him after 1701. It is now a school, and is hemmed in by new buildings. The original house, of six bays, with a hipped roof, is still visible, amid extensive later additions. On top of the hill is a large mound. Inside this is a grotto, which sounds wonderful from the description in Barbara Jones's *Follies and Grottoes*, but which is now unvisitable, having been entombed to protect it from vandals. Vaulted roof and walls were lavishly decorated with shells, ivy stems, stalactites, and so on, and the patterned floor was made of bones. The grotto was begun in 1830, and was said to have been decorated by a hermit who never left the place for seven years, finishing his task in 1844. When the Hanburys held luncheon parties in it, fresh moss was arranged in crevices of the walls.

In the main street, surprisingly unimpressive for a place of such size, stands **St James's Church**, built in 1820, enlarged 1854. Up Crane Street is the **English Baptist Chapel**, which has a grand Doric porch, with pediment and columns *in antis*. Built 1846–7, it was 'designed by Aaron Crossfield Esq., improved and perfected by Mr Langdon, architect'. The interior was originally lit only by the enormous coved roof-light, decorated with an anthemion frieze, following the erroneous theory that this was how Greek temples were lit (compare Caerleon Museum, p. 209). Much of the original decoration survives, as also does the magnificent mahogany reading-desk, with Doric columns.

From the High Street, a road goes down over the river, and then climbs up the opposite hillside. Up at **Penygarn** is the eighteenth-century Tabernacle Baptist Chapel, almost indistinguishable from a

two-storey house. Near it, a gate leads into the upper part of Pontypool Park, wooded grounds of such Victorian atmosphere that one
is not too surprised to come across the Rustic Cottage, built of huge
rough blocks of pebbly stone. It has half-hipped roofs with curly
bargeboards, and lattice windows. It must date from about 1850.
On the opposite side of the valley is the suburb of **Waunfelin**: the
church of St John the Divine is a characteristically original work of
J. Coates Carter (1912), in a plain but satisfying version of Perpendicular. Further north is **Pontnewynydd**, terminus of the Monmouthshire Canal, and home of Gwyneth Jones, the Bayreuth Brünnhilde.
St Luke's Church, beside the A4043 (one and a half miles from Pontypool centre), is tall and handsome, Early English in style, begun in
1873 by Charles Buckeridge, and completed (except for the tower,
which was never built) in 1879 by J. L. Pearson.

Beyond Pontypool is **Abersychan**, with nothing much to see except
the splendid stone railway viaduct at Talywaun, and the 'Big Arch'
(so called) three-quarters of a mile south, leading below the railway
(from the B4246) to the site of a demolished ironworks. Beyond
Abersychan, the road passes through moorland country before
reaching **Blaenavon**, which feels almost like a hill village, tidy but
windswept. It does in fact stand above the 1000 foot contour. Ironworks were founded here in 1789 by Thomas Hill, of Stafford, with
Thomas Hopkins and Benjamin Pratt. In 1877–8 experiments were
carried out by Percy Carlyle Gilchrist, the works chemist, which
assisted his cousin, Sidney Gilchrist Thomas, in perfecting a suitable
lining for the Bessemer steel converter when using phosphoric pig-
iron. The pleasant Gothic church was built in 1805, at the expense
of Thomas Hill and Samuel Hopkins. It has later galleries, on iron
columns, and even the font is of iron. The road beyond the church
leads up the hill past the huge and impressive remains of the ironworks – one of the finest industrial archaeological sites in South
Wales. It is now in the guardianship of the DoE. Of the five blast
furnaces, built up against the hillside, as was usual, so that they could
be charged from above, two are now being consolidated. There are
also remains of a water balance tower, and a number of cast houses.
Stack Square, with very small terrace houses round three sides, survives, but the great stack that stood in the centre has gone. The
works were connected by tramroad with the Monmouthshire Canal
terminus at Crumlin. From Blaenavon, the B4246 goes over the
side of Blorenge (1833 feet), enjoying marvellous views, and down to
Govilon, passing Garnddyrys, whose forge was associated with
Blaenavon ironworks (see p. 41). Cast iron was sent up there by

tramroad for finishing. The B4248 goes up over bleak moorland to
Brynmawr (five miles).

Brynmawr (actually in Breconshire) claims to be the highest town
of any size in South Britain, 'with the possible exception of Buxton'.
It stands between 1100 and 1300 feet above sea level, and certainly
feels a good deal more exposed than Buxton does. It is bypassed by
the Heads of the Valleys road (A465). St Mary's Church was built in
1895 (Nicholson and Hartree) to replace an earlier one which blew
down. It is dull, but contains two striking objects. One is the vast
and elaborate pulpit, supported on a short fat column from whose
capital fierce chained dogs glare out of luscious foliage. The other
is the excellent reredos, made for St Mary's, Richmond, Yorkshire,
and acquired by Brynmawr through an advert in the *Church Times*.
It was almost certainly designed by Sir Gilbert Scott. The Vicarage
was built in 1888 by J. D. Sedding, but has been considerably altered.

From Brynmawr, the A467 runs down the Ebbw Fach valley.
It passes the big Dunlop Semtex Rubber Factory, built in 1945–51
by the Architects' Co-Partnership. Renowned for its pioneering use
of shell concrete, this very interesting building has unfortunately
been messed up by subsequent extensions. The famous Ironworks at
Nantyglo ('coal valley') were bought in 1811 by Joseph Bailey, the
Yorkshire-born nephew of Richard Crawshay of Cyfarthfa (see p.
259), and Matthew Wayne, who dropped out in 1820 and was replaced by Joseph's younger brother, Crawshay Bailey. They were
among the most ruthless and successful ironmasters. By 1827 they
had seven blast furnaces going. They were so unpopular that they
built two large stone towers (still standing in ruins) up behind their
house, to which they could escape if necessary. Nantyglo was one of
the areas where the 'Scotch Cattle' – bands of men dressed in the
skins and horns of animals – terrorized blacklegs. Joseph Bailey
retired in 1830 to his estate, Glanusk Park (p. 38), leaving Crawshay
in charge. The ironworks were connected with the canal at Llanfoist
by a tramroad. Crawshay Bailey's memory lives on, perhaps surprisingly, in a folk-song which can even be found in the Labour
Party Song Book (as 'Cosher Bailey'). It is regularly sung at gather-
ings in South Wales, with innumerable different verses, many
rather risqué. One version begins:

> Crawshay Bailey had an engine
> And he found it wouldn't go,
> So he pulled it by a string
> All the way to Nantyglo.

Crawshay Bailey had an engine
She was puffin' and a steamin'
And according to her power
She could do four miles an hour.

When she came into the station
She was frighten all the nation,
She was wiggle, waggle, wiggle,
She was shiggle, shaggle, shiggle.

He was buy her second hand
He was paint her up so grand,
But the driver he did oil her
And she went and bust her boiler.

Crawshay Bailey's sister S'lina,
She was living in the Blaina,
She could knit or darn a stockin'
But her cookin' it was shockin' . . .

Blaina is the next town down the valley. Then, after an open stretch, comes **Abertillery**, where the Tyleri valley joins the Ebbw Fach. Famous formerly for coal mining and engineering, and still for rugby, it is a very up and down and winding place, its chief landmark a chapel with an absurdly thin tower. The valley turns sharply south-west at Six Bells (scene of a colliery disaster in 1961 in which 45 men died), joining Ebbw Vale at Aberbeeg. From the road junction, a minor road goes up left, and then shoots straight up the hill, amazingly steeply, to St Illtyd, the old church and settlement of **Llanhilleth**. Bleak and windswept (at 1150 feet), but with great views, it is almost deserted, and the church is walled up and abandoned. It has a saddleback tower, with primitive Norman windows. Next to it is a castle mound, inexplicably called Castell Taliorum.

Three miles down the winding valley is Crumlin (see p. 220). From here the A472 goes to Pontypool via Cwm Glyn, a surprising journey. At first it is a beautiful mountain pass, with bracken and trees, then suddenly a huge modern colliery appears on the right. Grubby saddle-tanks shunt coal-trucks. About four miles along the valley, near Old Furnace, are **Glyn Pits**. Just beyond an electricity substation (on the right), turn right along a narrow lane which crosses the railway by a bridge. (If coming from Pontypool, turn left just beyond the Furnace Garage.) A track leads up to this most impressive site, which it is hoped will be restored and looked after. The coal-pits are said to have been sunk in 1848, although the pumping engine house bears the date 1845, and the initials C.H.L. (Capel Hanbury Leigh, of the Hanbury family). There are two engine houses still standing, both well built of stone, and both retaining their engines, made at the Neath Abbey Works in 1845. The pumping engine house has a Cornish-type beam engine, the beam and the seventeen-foot wheel still *in situ*. The winding engine house is bigger, and has some Italianate trim. The engine is cased between four elegant fluted Doric columns, supporting a fine entablature. High up above are the winding wheels, each fifteen feet in diameter.

From Glyn Pits it is one mile into Pontypool.

EBBW VALE AND THE SIRHOWY VALLEY

The valley of the Ebbw is not something Wales can be proud of: the river is officially categorized as 'grossly polluted', and much of the valley is filled with dismal industrial development. A lot of it is, however, still surprisingly beautiful and there is a fair amount of architectural interest to be seen. In terms of human interest, the valley is full of fascination.

The A467 leaves Newport by Risca Road. Half a mile after crossing the M4, it passes close to the Crumlin branch of the Monmouthshire Canal (see p. 215). It is then joined by another road, which comes from Newport via Rogerstone, site of the biggest aluminium works in Britain (Alcan). **Risca** lies below **Twm Barlwm** (on the north), a hill with a striking silhouette. On top (1374 feet) is a motte, built within a hill-fort. A mile beyond Risca, the Sirhowy joins the Ebbw. At **Abercarn**, St Luke's Church is grandly set high up on the right of the valley. This most extraordinary church was built in 1924–6 by J. Coates Carter. It is constructed of greyish-brown stone, now tinged with green lichen, and concrete is also used quite extensively. The style is a drastically simplified Gothic. The tall tower has the top stage corbelled out, in local fashion. The doorway of the north porch is made of cyclopean blocks, and much of the interior is deliberately left rough. The nasty roofs are recent. Abercarn belonged in the nineteenth century to Sir Benjamin Hall (see p. 184), who is said to have designed the nearby Welsh church himself.

Two miles beyond Abercarn is **Crumlin**, once renowned for its enormous, but delicate, iron viaduct, built in 1853–7 to carry the Newport, Abergavenny and Hereford Railway across the valley.

Alas, it was demolished in 1965. From Crumlin, the A472 goes west to Pontypool (p. 215). Beyond Aberbeeg, where the Ebbw Fach comes down (p. 219), Ebbw Vale is remarkably countrified, with woods on either side. This lasts only a couple of miles, and then the first mine appears. From then on the valley is more and more built up, until the town of **Ebbw Vale** is reached. The ironworks were founded in 1789 by Jeremiah Homfray (of Penydarren – p. 257). The vast steelworks now spread all along the valley. It is the one great steelworks on an inland site which still operates (see p. 213), but ironmaking and steelmaking will soon end. Everything around it is covered with brown dust. The town's chief landmark is Christ Church, built in 1861 by John Norton. The fine spire was added in 1881 by Kempson and Fowler. From down in the valley, the church looks strikingly foreign. At the head of the valley is **Beaufort**. The iron-works there were bought by the Baileys in 1833, and like those at Nantyglo (p. 218) were connected with the canal at Llanfoist by tram-way.

From Beaufort, the A4047 climbs up over Waun-y-Pound towards Tredegar, and it is up here (at 152/106) that the memorial to Aneurin Bevan (who was MP for Ebbw Vale) was erected in 1972. It consists of four enormous monoliths, one in the centre, and three smaller ones representing Ebbw Vale, Tredegar, and Rhymney. He used to address crowds of his constituents up here. **Tredegar** is at the head of the Sirhowy valley. There were two great ironworks here, the Sirhowy works, begun in 1778, and later run for a time by Richard Fothergill, and the bigger Tredegar works, established in 1800 by Samuel Homfray (of Penydarren – p. 257), who had married the daughter of Sir Charles Morgan of Tredegar. The present town, spread out at the valley head, does not have much of visual interest to offer. Much the nicest thing is the very cocky and unsophisticated clock-tower, at the main crossroads. Remarkably tall, it is (appro-priately) made of iron, and painted pale blue. It was erected in 1858 and made by Charles Jordan, Iron Founder, Newport. Great schemes of land reclamation are going on around the town. Below Tredegar, the Sirhowy valley is rough, unspoilt, and very attractive. Several collieries are still in operation. Six miles below Tredegar, up on the hill-top west of the valley, is the church of **Bedwellte** – very lonely. It has a weird plan: the chancel is set midway on to the twin naves.

Further down the Sirhowy valley is **Blackwood**, now a featureless place, but once the scene of an interesting social experiment. J. H. Moggridge owned a house called Woodfield on the east side of the river. He felt a desire to improve the condition of the workers living in the area, and consulted Robert Owen. Moggridge's scheme involved letting plots of land (one-eighth of an acre) at moderate rent, on condition that the tenants built cottages, towards which they would receive loans. Begun in 1820, his village by 1829 contained 260 houses, with 1550 inhabitants. Trees were left standing wherever possible, and there was a village green of an acre, shaded by oaks and beeches. Moggridge built a market-house, also used for divine worship, and laid out a burial ground 'according to Mr Loudon's suggestion'. The tenants were encouraged to keep vegetable gardens on their plots. Most of them worked in the local collieries or farms. Two other villages were established at Ynysddu, three miles down the valley, and at Trelyn, in the Rhymney valley. Nothing is visible now of all this enterprise.

Just south of Blackwood, the A472 crosses the valley. One and a half miles south-east of the crossroads, on top of the hill, and reached by a maze of narrow lanes, is the old parish church of this whole area, at **Mynyddislwyn**. The church is basically medieval, but the outer walls were rebuilt in 1820 with splendid great Gothic windows, made of iron. Just south of the church is a big mound called Twyn Tudur, said to be the burial place of Roman soldiers killed by the Welsh (wishful thinking, no doubt). The road straight on down to Wattsville is only for the brave, as it is steep and rough. Most will prefer to go back and down to **Ynysddu**, birthplace of the poet Islwyn (William Thomas, 1832–78), who spent most of his life as a Methodist minister at Rhymney. Three miles further on, the Sirhowy joins the Ebbw just north of Risca (p. 220).

CHAPTER SEVEN

Glamorgan (Morgannwg)

❧

THE RHYMNEY VALLEY

The A468 from Newport (p. 203) crosses the Ebbw at Bassaleg. Three miles beyond is Lower Machen, where the Romans had a lead-mining settlement. A mile south is **Ruperra Castle**, a romantic house (private), proudly sited on the hillside. It was built in the early seventeenth century by Sir Thomas Morgan, who had become rich as steward to the Earl of Pembroke. It is square, and has a circular tower at each corner, with battlements all round. It was clearly not intended to be defensible, so the martial air must have been intended as an evocation of the Middle Ages, a characteristic of the period best exemplified at Bolsover (1612). Ruperra may have been inspired by Lulworth Castle in Dorset, built c. 1608. There is certainly one similarity between the two houses, and it is a sad one, even if it does increase the air of antiquity: both have been gutted by fire. The interior of Ruperra had been rebuilt in the 1780s.

Between Lower Machen and Machen the road now enters Mid-Glamorgan. (Until 1974, the river marked the county boundary.) Machen and Bedwas are colliery towns.

Beyond Bedwas, the road crosses the river and comes into **Caerphilly** (strictly Caerffili). It leads straight to the castle (DoE). It is no exaggeration to describe it as one of the most sensational in Britain. Its area, thirty acres, is second only to that of Windsor. It is an outstanding example of a concentric castle (the same type as, for example, Harlech and Beaumaris). Immediately north-west of the castle stood a Roman fort, occupied c. AD 75–150, and sited near the Cardiff–Gelligaer road (see p. 228). Within it, a Norman motte-and-bailey castle was built. However, for his new castle, begun in 1268, Earl Gilbert de Clare chose a site a little lower down, presumably so that he could use the water of the stream further south. De Clare, Lord of Glamorgan, who had seized the formerly Welsh lordship of Senghenydd (the area from Whitchurch to Merthyr Tydfil) in 1262, built the castle to counter the influence here of Llywelyn the Last, following his recognition by the Crown as Prince

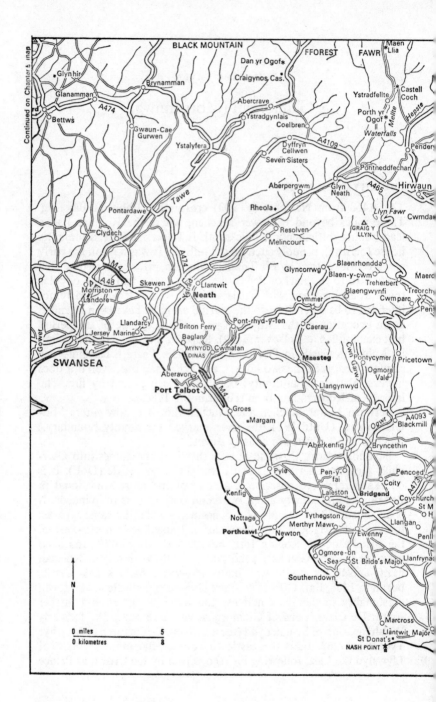

Continued on Chapter 5 map

BLACK MOUNTAIN

FFOREST

FAWR

Maen
Lia

Glynhir

Dan yr Ogof

Craigynos Cas.

Brynamman

Ystradfellte

Castell
Coch

Glanamman

Abercrave

A474

Coelbren

Porth yr
Ogof
Waterfalls

Bettws

Ystradgynlais

Mellte

Hepste

Gwaun-Cae
Gurwen

Dyffryn
Cellwen

A4109

Penderyn

Ystalyfera

Seven Sisters

Pontneddfechan

A465

Hirwaun

Aberpergwm

Glyn
Neath

A465

Pontardawe

Tawe

Rheola

Llyn Fawr

Cwmda

Clydach

Resolven

GRAIG Y
LLYN

Melincourt

Blaenrhondda

Maerd

A474

Glyncorrwg

Blaen-y-cwm

Treherbert

M4

Skewen

Llantwit

Cymmer

Blaengwynfi

Treorchy

A48

Blaengwynfi

Cwmparc

Morriston

Neath

Peni

Landore

Caerau

Llandarcy

Briton Ferry

Pont-rhyd-y-fen

Jersey Marine

Baglan

Gower

MYNYDD
DINAS

Cwmafan

Maesteg

Cwn
Garw

Pontycymer

Pricetown

SWANSEA

Aberavon

Llangynwyd

Ogmore
Vale

Port Talbot

M4

Ogwr

A4093

Groes

Margam

Blackmill

Aberkenfig

Bryncethin

Pyle

Pen-y-
fai

Pencoed

Kenfig

Coity

A473

Laleston

Bridgend

Coychurch

St M

Nottage

Tythegston

Llangan

O H

Porthcawl

Merthyr Mawr

A48

Ewenny

Penll

Newton

Ogmore-on
-Sea

St Bride's Major

Llanfryna

Southerndown

Marcross

Llantwit Major

St Donat's

NASH POINT

N

0 miles   5
0 kilometres   8

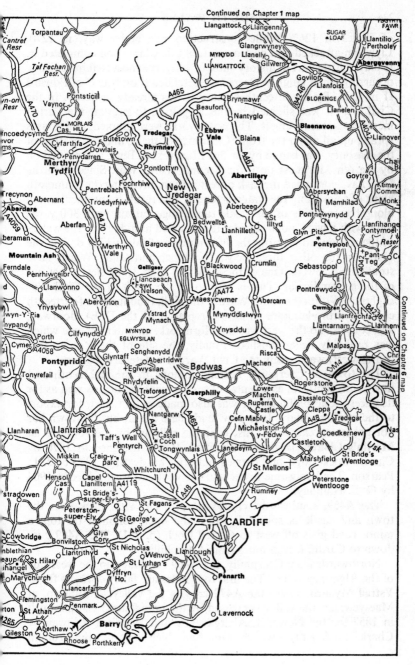

Continued on Chapter 6 map

of Wales in 1267. While construction was under way, in 1270, Llywelyn attacked and destroyed it, but de Clare soon completed it. It played little part in history subsequently, the most striking episode occurring when Hugh le Despenser defended it on behalf of Edward II in 1326. By the fifteenth century it was already in decay. In the Civil War it was slighted by the Royalists, to prevent the Parliamentarians from using it. The waterworks were drained, and houses sprang up all along the front. Clearance of these, and restoration of the masonry, was begun by the 3rd Marquess of Bute, and carried on by the 4th Marquess until the Second World War. Since 1949 the DoE have continued the task of restoration, involving the mammoth work of reinstating the water-defences. The result is spectacular. All along the east side of the castle ran a huge curtain wall, 300 yards long, with a wide moat outside. It also acted as a dam for the waters of the stream, so forming the fifteen acres of lake which defend the castle on the other three sides. The Inner and Outer Wards have stout round towers. One of these, 80 feet high, leans eleven feet out of the perpendicular. This is said to be the result of the Civil War slighting. Within the Inner Ward is the Hall, rebuilt in the fourteenth century, with elaborate windows (replaced by the DoE), doorway, and corbels. To the west was the Hornwork, an outer defence which was probably never finished. Finally, the site of the Roman fort (north-west) was used in the Civil War for a defensive battery.

The town of Caerphilly became famous in the eighteenth and nineteenth centuries as a centre of textile manufacture, as well as for its cheese. Caerphilly cheese was also made in Somerset, for export to the mining valleys. It is now made here again, but the town has not got much character. Just over the railway, by the A469, is St Martin's Church, large and dignified. It was designed in 1870 by Charles Buckeridge, and carried out after his death in 1873 by J. L. Pearson. The handsome tower and the west end were added c. 1904 by G. E. Halliday.

The A469, southwards, climbs steeply. The view back over the town and castle is splendid. From the open common on top, a minor road goes off west to Castell Coch (p. 251). The A469 goes down to Cardiff (seven miles from Caerphilly).

Northwards from Caerphilly, the A469 continues up the west side of the Rhymney valley. The first four miles are fairly open, as far as Ystrad Mynach, where the A472 crosses the valley. A mile up, at Maesycwmer, the valley is crossed by the grand stone viaduct built in 1857 for the Newport, Abergavenny and Hereford Railway by Charles Liddell. (This was the same line which went over the Crumlin

Viaduct – p. 220.) Below the viaduct, on the south side, is an un-expected survival, an eighteenth-century cornmill (later enlarged). For the next few miles, the valley is thickly populated by mining communities. At **Bargoed**, between road and river the Power Station had seven wooden cooling-towers, built between 1912 and 1920 – tapering, rectangular structures, with cross-braced iron frames (now ruinous).

The next town, round a bend in the valley, is **New Tredegar**. Here the winding-house at East Pit, Elliot Colliery (which closed in 1967) is to be preserved by the DoE. Built in 1891, of stone, it is a typical example. Two miles further on is **Pontlottyn**. Beside the road is St Tyfaelog's Church, built in 1863–7 by Charles Buckeridge, one of several commissions in the area given to him by the Rev. Gilbert Harries (see p. 316), who moved to Gelligaer in 1862. It has both a font and a sunken baptistery: Harries was determined that no one should be kept from the Established Church by scruples about total immersion.

Immediately beyond is **Rhymney** itself. Rather insignificant-looking to a stranger, it was nevertheless once known for its iron-works, and later for its collieries, and is still widely known for its brewery. This was founded in 1839 by Andrew Buchan, a local farm-labourer who diverted the river in 1825 to enable two ironworks to combine, and later became manager of the iron company's shop. Originally the brewery supplied the ironworkers, but now its beer is sold over a wide area. The ironworks were under different owners at different times. It was Crawshay Bailey (p. 218) who built the tramway down to Bassaleg. The most remarkable works were built for the Second Marquess of Bute. The designs were shown at the Royal Academy in 1827 and 1828. The three blast furnaces, and their cast houses, were in the Egyptian style, based on the ruins of Dendera. The designer was John Macculloch, MD, FRS, a man of versatile talent, best known as a geologist. Nothing is left of them now. The Rhymney Iron Co. paid for **St David's Church**, built in 1839–43 by Philip Hardwick. It is a solid and handsome classical building, with a tower, round-headed windows, a pedimented east end, and galleries inside.

From the church, the B4257 cuts across the valley: just before it reaches the A465, on the right, is **Butetown**, an interesting example of an early model village. There are three parallel terraces, built of stone, two storeys, but the central blocks a storey higher. The end and centre blocks project slightly. The terraces were built c. 1802–4, and are said to have been designed by R. Johnson, the manager of

the ironworks. They were left isolated by the movement of the works
from the head of the valley to further down.

Back at Pontlottyn, a minor road climbs up on to the mountain
through **Fochrhiw** to the amazing road which follows the moorland
ridge (reaching a height of 1408 feet) for five miles down to **Gelligaer**.
It follows the line of the Roman road from Y Gaer (Brecon) to
Cardiff. On this road stood the fort of Gelligaer, whose remains are
clearly visible in the field beside the road up to the former Rectory,
a few hundred yards south-east from where the mountain road meets
the B4254. The fort was excavated c. 1900–10, but covered up again.
To the north-west are traces of a larger, Flavian camp. The smaller
one was built in stone c. 103–11, and was occupied until late in that
century. It was not large (407 × 395 feet), but the remains were well
preserved. Attached on the south-east was a walled annexe, containing a bathhouse – the finest discovered in Wales, apart from that
at Caerleon. The old Rectory was given a striking extension in 1863
by Charles Buckeridge.

West of Gelligaer, the B4254 goes through wooded country down
to Nelson, passing **Llancaeach Fawr**, a tall sixteenth-century house
(open on written application). The B4255 leads down to the A472:
a minor road opposite leads straight up on to Mynydd Eglwysilan.
The views back northwards are marvellous. The road comes steeply
down into **Senghenydd**, an extremely characteristic mining community, with its horrible church by Bruce Vaughan (1897), its chapels,
including the fine Capel Salem (1899), and its clubs, among them the
'Ukrainian Social Club of Kiev'. Senghenydd was the scene, in 1913,
of the worst colliery disaster ever to occur in Britain. After an ex-
plosion 1950 feet below the surface, fire raged in the pit for days.
439 men died.

Next to Senghenydd is Abertridwr, from which a road climbs west
up to the church of **Eglwysilan**, right up on the ridge with (as so
often) a pub beside it. The view is of fields and moorland, with
industry barely visible except in the form of pylons and ropeways.
Both the pub and the rough stone lychgate are whitewashed. The
church has some eighteenth-century windows, and a chancel of
1873 by Buckeridge. In the porch, a slate tablet commemorates Rev.
William Edwards (1719–89), who was buried in the churchyard. It
shows his most famous work – the bridge at Pontypridd. Edwards
was born in the parish. In 1745 he became pastor of the Independent
chapel at Groes-Wen (near the present chapel). He held the office
until he died, but combined it with the profession of architect. He
built a mill, houses, and barns in the district, and an iron forge at

Cardiff. In 1746 he contracted to build the Pontypridd bridge (p. 253), and afterwards built many others (e.g. Dolauhirion, p. 147). Three of his sons, Thomas, David, and Edward, also became bridge-builders.

From Groes-Wen it is two miles into Caerphilly (p. 223).

NEWPORT TO CARDIFF BY THE A48

The A48 passes round the edge of Tredegar Park (p. 206). A mile beyond the M4 roundabout, on the right, is Cleppa Park, site of the home of Ifor ap Llywelyn, given the name 'Ifor Hael' (Ifor the Generous) by the poet Dafydd ap Gwilym (p. 72), whose chief patron he was. Two miles further is **Castleton**, whose splendid multi-coloured Baptist Chapel (1857, by R. G. Thomas) always catches the eye. From Castleton a road leads north to Michaelston-y-Fedw. A mile west of there, along the B4288 and then across the river Rhymney by a seventeenth-century stone bridge, is **Cefn Mably**. Now a hospital, this was once one of the greatest houses in Glamorgan, the home of the Kemeys family, later the Kemeys-Tyntes. The grounds are very Victorian, with specimen trees and terraces. The house stands (as the name implies) high up on a ridge. It is long and rambling, and archi-tecturally confused. At the west end is the Chapel, medieval in origin but rebuilt in the nineteenth century, and next comes a block with mullioned windows (? seventeenth century). The rest looks uniform, but is not: the left-hand section incorporates fragments of Tudor windows, but was done up with sash-windows, a big coved cornice, and a roof with dormers, at the same time as the right-hand section was built (early eighteenth century).

The Gwent/South Glamorgan boundary is now just beyond Castleton (until 1974 it was the Rhymney river). Over the boundary, a mile from Castleton, the new Cardiff bypass goes off right by way of Llanedeyrn. The old A48 goes through **St Mellons**. The church is well placed up on a hillock, with views over the estuary. It has a very irregular plan, but is quite fine (mostly Perpendicular), and remarkably unrestored-looking; surprising, since it seems to have had two restorations. The first, by Sir Gilbert Scott in 1859, was paid for by the celebrated historian and architectural pundit E. A. Freeman, who lived at Llanrumney Hall near by, and he no doubt ensured that all the medieval work was respected. The second restoration, in 1869, was by Scott's former pupil, Charles Buckeridge. Near the church is a Convalescent Hospital, occupying a vast, asymmetrical house, extremely Gothic and complete with a tower decorated chequerboard fashion in brick and stone. It was built *c.* 1890 by Col. Bruce Vaughan, and, although crude, is a good deal better than most of his churches. After passing through the suburb of Rumney, the A48 enters Cardiff via Roath (p. 242).

NEWPORT TO CARDIFF BY THE B4239

This is a longer, but quieter and more enjoyable route, passing through the Moors of the 'Wentlooge Level'. Wentlooge is the Welsh Gwynllwg, the land of which Gwynllyw (p. 204) was lord. These Moors are similar to those of Caldicot Level, on the other side of Newport (see p. 201). The reens are bridged by well-made little arches of brick or stone. In them grows the remarkably tall Reed Sweet Grass, sometimes reaching a height of six feet. The B4239 leaves the A48 just after it crosses the Ebbw river, and follows the east side of Tredegar Park (p. 206). The first village is **St Bride's Wentlooge**. A road left is signposted 'Beach', but outside the great sea-wall stretches black mud, and the view is dominated by Nash Power Station. The big, grand church is up a lane. The large grassy churchyard is empty of graves. This was because of the dampness of the ground, which is also causing subsidence. The Perpendicular tower (of Somerset type) is richly buttressed and has an ornate parapet with statues in niches. It is built of white stone, with bands of red. A tablet in the rough south porch commemorates 'the great flud, 20 Januarie in the morning, 1606' (as at Goldcliff, p. 203). The atmosphere inside is one of neglect and decay.

Half a mile beyond St Bride's, a road leads north to **Coedkernew** (one and a half miles). 'Cernyw' is the Welsh name for Cornwall. The small church stands in a circular churchyard surrounded by trees, with only a farmhouse near by. Built in 1854 by W. and G. Habershon, it is a bit too fussy. A mile south-west is **Marshfield**, by contrast a greatly overgrown village. Its church, however, is down a quiet lane, by a farm. It has a plain west tower, and a long nave. It was expensively, and surprisingly successfully, restored in 1906–8 by E. M. Bruce Vaughan. The atmosphere (in contrast to St Bride's) is one of wealthy patronage and zealous care. The best medieval feature is the thirteenth-century chancel arch. There is lavish Edwardian woodwork and glass and sculpture by W. Goscombe John. On the road to Castleton (p. 229) is the polychromatic school (now disused), one of the best of the many in the area designed by Prichard and Seddon (*c.* 1860).

From Marshfield, a road leads back over the railway to the B4239.

The next village westwards is **Peterstone Wentlooge**, a dull village, whose church much resembles St Bride's. The path which runs past the church is one of the best ways down to the coast, protected and hidden by the long embankment here called Peterstone Great Wharf. Figures silhouetted as they walk along it seem to belong to another world. On top there is a vast feeling of space and the long shoreline behind it is a separate place, closer to Somerset than Wales.

Three miles on the new housing at **Rumney** (p. 230) is fast swallowing up the moor. Astonishing quantities of waste paper abandoned by the roadside and gangs of enterprising boys escaping to the marsh mark its sudden end.

CARDIFF – CAERDYDD

Cardiff is an unjustly maligned city. Most people think of it as a huge industrial town, its dockland slums made famous in the film *Tiger Bay*, its emotional centre at Cardiff Arms Park, but it has more to offer the visitor than most people would expect.

Its origins go back to Roman times: a fort may have been established in the late first century AD, possibly south of the much bigger fort built *c*. 300. The later fort was used as the site of the Norman castle built by Robert Fitzhamon, Earl of Gloucester, after he had conquered Glamorgan *c*. 1090. Fitzhamon established a borough south of his castle, one of the earliest towns planted by the Normans in Wales. It had a regular plan, with two main streets – one running east and west just south of the castle, the other running north and south (High Street and St Mary Street). The castle protected it on the north, and the river Taff on the west. Walls were built on east and south by the fourteenth century, with six gates. These fortifications were mostly demolished *c*. 1800. The chief parish church was St Mary's, and stood west of St Mary Street: it was destroyed by floods in the seventeenth century. St John's Church survives, and there were also Dominican and Franciscan friaries.

The town did not develop between the late Middle Ages and the end of the eighteenth century, and may even have declined. It was a market town and small port, probably very similar to present-day Chepstow or Conwy. However, the opening of the ironworks up the valleys suddenly increased the importance of the port, since the Taff valley was the chief means of communication between them and the sea. The road from Merthyr to Cardiff was improved in 1767. The Glamorganshire Canal, largely financed by the ironmasters Crawshay, Homfray, and Guest, was opened in 1794. However, it was not one of the new industrialists who was chiefly responsible for developing Cardiff's potential, but a Scottish peer, the 2nd Marquess of Bute. His grandfather, the 1st Marquess, had married (in 1766) Charlotte Windsor, heiress to the Windsor estates. These included the estates in Glamorgan (including much of Cardiff) which had been accumulated by the Herberts, Earls of Pembroke, after William Herbert had been granted the lordship of Glamorgan in 1551. Lord Bute built the first proper dock (the Bute West Dock), opened in 1839. The Taff Vale Railway, built by Brunel (who had been consulted as early as 1833) was opened from Merthyr to Cardiff in 1841. It was the first railway of any size in Wales. Branch railways followed, and the main line from Chepstow to Swansea (also by Brunel) was opened in 1850. It was connected with Gloucester and the GWR line to London in 1851. The export of coal developed from the middle of the century, further docks being opened in 1857 (Bute East), 1874, 1887 and 1903. In 1913 the peak figure of over 10 million tons of coal was exported from Cardiff. The population rise was phenomenal: 1870 in 1801; 39,500 in 1871; 82,800 in 1881; 164,000 in 1901. Now it is 260,000. One result of this rapid development was that no building dating from before 1800 survived in the town centre, except the castle and St John's Church.

The **Castle** is the obvious place to start exploring the city. The Roman fort built *c.* 300 was surrounded with strong stone walls, from which semi-octagonal bastions projected. The two gates, on north and south, had single arches flanked by towers. It was built to protect the district from attacks from the sea – the new menace in response to which the stone walls at Caerwent were erected (see p. 198), and also the walled camp at Holyhead (Caer Gybi – see *North Wales*, p. 213). The site of the west wall and parts of the north and south walls were later used for the walls of the medieval castle. The east wall, and the rest of the north and south walls, were rebuilt, in conjectural form, in the late nineteenth and early twentieth centuries for the 3rd and 4th Marquesses of Bute. The break between Roman and later masonry is clearly marked. The Normans put up a large motte in the north-west corner of the Roman fort. In the twelfth century, a polygonal stone shell-keep was put on top of this, and in the late thirteenth century the gatehouse tower of the keep was rebuilt, and the central wall running southwards from the keep to the Black Tower (on the site of the Roman south gate) was built, by Earl Gilbert de Clare (who also built Caerphilly). Domestic buildings were put up along the west wall of the castle in the fifteenth and sixteenth centuries. In 1774 the 1st Marquess of Bute started to clear

the ruins, under the direction of Capability Brown, and to rebuild
the residential wing, under Henry Holland. Work was abandoned on
his death in 1794, and only completed c. 1817 by Sir Robert Smirke.

In 1865 the 3rd Marquess of Bute, then aged 18, commissioned a
scheme for remodelling the castle from William Burges. The combination of patron, architect, and scheme was a marvellously fortunate one, and the results it produced still stagger every visitor to
Cardiff. Bute was only six months old when his father died. When he
came of age in 1868 his annual income was around £300,000. He was
completely unlike his father, for he was unbusiness-like, scholarly,
passionately devoted to the Middle Ages, a convert to Roman
Catholicism (in 1868) who also dabbled in spiritualism. In his
mixture of introversion and mania for building on the grand scale,
he can be compared to William Beckford and Ludwig II. His architect, William Burges, was the son of a dock engineer whose firm,
Walker, Burges, and Cooper, took over the completion of Bute East
Dock c. 1855. The two probably met through John M'Connochie,
who had worked for Walker, Burges and Cooper, and stayed on in
Cardiff as Chief Engineer to the Bute Docks. Burges was the perfect
man to put Bute's dreams into effect, for he combined a scholarly
knowledge of medieval architecture with a fantastic imagination.

Work began on the castle in 1868, and was carried on by Burges
until his death in 1881. After that it was completed by his assistants.
In 1948 the 5th Marquess gave the castle and its grounds to the
Corporation of Cardiff, who use it for municipal functions. It is
open regularly, and guided tours, with guides of varying degrees of
competence (it has been known for guides never to mention the
name of Burges), are *de rigueur*. It is a good idea to begin by going
into the park west of the castle to look at the exterior, with its
amazing skyline. The buildings are basically medieval, but they have
been heightened and elaborated. For example, the octagonal
Beauchamp Tower (built by Richard de Beauchamp, Earl of
Warwick, c. 1430), has been given a tall lantern of lead and timber,
and the square towers have been given fanciful tops. Most amazing
of all is the clock-tower, 150 feet high – the first part to be built. It
has an elaborate pyramidal roof, and is decorated with coloured
statues representing the planets. The interiors beggar description,
with their painted walls, their rich carving, tiled floors, stained glass,
inlay of exotic woods and polished metals, all illustrating complex
iconographical schemes, or erudite styles. There is the Summer
Smoking Room, at the top of the clock-tower, with its astronomical
decorations, the bathroom with its ancient Roman marble bath, inset

with metal fishes, the Arab Room, with stalactite ceiling covered in gold leaf, the Banqueting Hall, the Chaucer Room, the Chapel, on the spot where the 2nd Marquess died, the Dining-Room with its Moorish ceiling, the Library with its carved bookcases, the spiral staircase with a crocodile waiting to gobble up a baby, and so on.

Parts of the south and west walls were done up with medieval defensive works, a foretaste of what was to be done at Castell Coch (p. 251). North of the castle are the stables, in the same style, but less satisfactory (1869–75). In front of the castle, at the south-west corner runs the 'Animal Wall', a low stone wall whose coping incorporates vigorous sculptures of animals. In the grounds west of the castle, the 3rd Marquess excavated the medieval Dominican priory (Blackfriars): he had low walls built to mark out the various buildings, and paved the whole area of the church with a rich pavement of tiles copied (by Godwin of Lugwardine) from medieval ones found on the site (the originals are in the National Museum). It is typical of him that he also had a former Prior (fourteenth century) exhumed from his grave at Llangadwaladr in Anglesey, and buried him here beneath a tomb with a Latin inscription. The castle grounds form part of Bute Park, which stretches up the east bank of the Taff for the best part of a mile, matched by the even bigger Sophia Gardens and Pontcanna Park on the west bank.

CENTRAL CARDIFF

Just across Castle Street from Bute Park in Westgate Street is **Jackson Hall**, built in 1879 by George Robinson, as a Racquets Court. It is a delightful brick building of great quality, with a deep-eaved roof in Swiss style. Between this and the river is Cardiff Arms Park, the Mecca of Rugby enthusiasts. This whole piece of land, west of St Mary Street, was cut off by a great eastwards bend in the river until 1849–53, when a new straight course was made for it. The reclaimed area was developed as 'Temperance Town'. Castle Street has some good buildings, among them the entrance to **Castle Arcade** (1882–7). Cardiff has an especially splendid collection of pedestrian shopping arcades, all except this one on the east side of High Street and St Mary Street. This is a fine example – three storeys high, with an iron and glass roof. It curves round into **High Street**. High Street and its continuation **St Mary Street** contain a varied collection of buildings, which in scale and style are a microcosm of the city's development. They (and the rest of the city) are admirably described in John Hilling's book *Cardiff and the Valleys*. Note especially the arcades – High Street Arcade (T. Waring and J. P. Jones, 1885–1902), and, further down, Morgan Arcade (Edwin Seward, 1896), and Royal Arcade, the earliest of all (Peter Price, 1858) – and also the vast Market Hall (William Harpur, 1886–91), with shops on two levels, and full of life. At the bottom of St Mary Street is John Evan Thomas's statue (1853) of the 2nd Marquess of Bute, 'the maker of modern Cardiff'. It is appropriate that it should stand here, at the approach to the docks.

From High Street, Church Street runs east to **St John's**, the only surviving medieval church in Cardiff. Its chief glory is the tower, added in 1473, with a gloriously elaborate pinnacled parapet. It is said to have been designed by John Hart, who also did the crown of St Stephen's, Bristol. The rest of the church is partly thirteenth century, mostly mid fifteenth, but greatly rebuilt and extended in 1852–3, and again in 1887–91 (by Kempson and Fowler), when the outer aisles were added. The high altar reredos was carved by W. Goscombe John. The gorgeous reredos in the south aisle (a memorial to Kitchener) is by Sir Ninian Comper, who also did the east window glass. There are two good windows in the baptistery: the north one is by Morris and Co., 1869, richly coloured, and the west one (Christ blessing the children) is of 1890, designed by J. P. Seddon and made by Belham and Co.

From the church, Working Street leads up to Duke Street, the eastward continuation of Castle Street. It is itself continued by Queen Street, in which much the most exciting building is **Queen's Chambers**, a large and ornate exercise in Venetian Gothic. It was designed c. 1870 by C. E. Bernard, who had presumably been bowled over by Ruskin. From Queen Street, Charles Street runs south. In it is a **Congregational Chapel** of 1855 by R. G. Thomas. It has quite an ordinary Gothic front, but this is faced in a kind of crazy paving of different coloured stones – 'brought from all parts of the world, and of every variety of geological epoch' – or so *The Builder* claimed. Parallel to Charles Street runs the wide new Churchill Way, in which stands **Capel Pembroke Terrace**, an unusually solid and sophisticated chapel built in 1877 by Henry C. Harris, and clearly influenced by Burges. Back in Queen Street, a little further on, **Windsor Place** runs north. It was laid out, together with St Andrew's Crescent (an ellipse) and St Andrew's Place, in the 1860s and '70s, with three-storey brick terraces, all remarkably old-fashioned, but handsome and more coherent than any other nineteenth-century development in the centre. Unfortunately, Windsor Place and St Andrew's Crescent are now separated by the big new road, part of

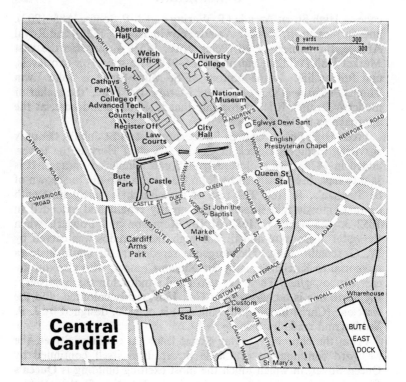

Central Cardiff

the gyratory system. In Windsor Place is the most exciting of all the chapels in Cardiff – not, alas, by a Welshman. It is the **English Presbyterian Chapel**, and was designed by the Scot, F. T. Pilkington (best-known for the Barclay Church in Edinburgh). The fancifully Gothic exterior looks weird, with its bulging sides, but the interior provides the practical explanation – the bulges accommodate curving galleries, intended to seat the maximum number within reasonable distance of the pulpit. The floor slopes, as in a theatre. The chapel was built in 1866, and extended to the west in 1893.

Striking as the plan of this chapel is, it would have been rivalled for originality by the plan of the church built in the centre of St Andrew's Crescent, had that project not run into so many difficulties. Even in its present form it is a fascinating building. Originally dedicated to St Andrew, it is now called **Eglwys Dewi Sant**. Begun in 1860. the church was designed by Prichard and Seddon. It has a wide nave, with narrow aisles intended only as passages. The idea was to seat a large congregation with unimpeded view of the chancel – the Tractarian ideal. This seems to have been the first use of 'passage aisles': the device was taken up a few years later by Street at All Saints', Clifton, and then became increasingly common. The church was to have had a central tower and spire. However, when the church had been built up as far as the clerestory (which is framed within the main pier arches), money ran out. Col. A. Roos, architect to the Bute Trustees, was called in to complete the church within the original cost-limit, which explains why the chancel is the plainest, not the richest, part. In 1884–6 transepts and vestries were added by William Butterfield (one would never guess), also choirstalls and a tiled floor.

St Andrew's Place leads through (west) to Park Place. Turn left for **Park House**, built by William Burges in 1871–4 for John M'Connochie, Lord Bute's Engineer (see p. 233). It is an excellent piece of design, compact but rich, very French in feeling. There is a three-bay loggia along the front. The house foreshadows Burges's own Tower House in Kensington, built soon afterwards. Park House looks over the gardens in front of Cathays Park, populated by a tribe of statues of the eminent.

Cathays Park is the site of the **Civic Centre**, where the astonishing assemblage of bright Portland stone buildings provides a remarkable survey of British architecture of the past 75 years. The land (previously a private park) was sold to the city by Lord Bute in 1898 and was laid out (by the Borough Engineer, W. Harpur) as a rectangle with gardens in the centre, and tree-lined avenues, on the most spacious lines. The first buildings put up were the City Hall and Assize Courts, the two buildings nearest the castle. A competition was held in 1897, and the winners were the young H. V. Lanchester and E. A. Rickards. Lanchester was the planner and technician, Rickards the designer. Rickards was a brilliant architect, passionately keen on Baroque, and a flamboyant personality, much admired by his close friend Arnold Bennett. These characteristics came through loud and clear in this splendid pair of buildings, completely practical, and yet bubbling over with zest and movement. The **City Hall** was completed in 1904. It has a huge dome over the entrance pavilion, surmounted by a magnificent dragon in lead (by H. C. Fehr), and a tall tower which breaks out into all manner of jollities at the top. The exterior is adorned with plentiful sculpture, and the opulent interiors are rich in plasterwork, panelling, bronze light-fittings, and marble columns. The **Assize Courts**, whose main front, surmounted

by twin cupolas, faces east, were completed in 1906. Next to the
City Hall (completing the south side of the rectangle) is the **National
Museum of Wales**. Here the competition (held in 1910) was won by
the firm of A. Dunbar Smith and Cecil Brewer. They clearly wanted
to produce something which would harmonize with its neighbour,
without attempting to rival it. A tendency towards greater simplicity
and severity was in any case characteristic of both the architects
and the age. The result is – not surprisingly – a good deal less
exciting, but then for a museum excitement should no doubt be
left to the exhibits. Again there is a large dome over the entrance, and
lots of sculpture. The first part of the Museum was opened in 1927,
the east wing in 1932, and the west wing (by T. Alwyn Lloyd and
Gordon) in 1967. The Museum itself is first-rate: it is difficult to
know what to single out, but the paintings include the famous
collection of French Impressionist and post-Impressionist paintings
made by Miss Gwendoline and Miss Margaret Davies of Gregynog
(see *North Wales*, p. 292), as well as Welsh views by Richard Wilson
and others, and there is an excellent industrial section, complete with
a full-scale reproduction of part of a coal-mine.

Immediately north of the Museum is the **University College of
South Wales**. The College was the second in the University, after
Aberystwyth, and opened in 1883 in the old Infirmary on Newport
Road. The new building, begun in 1903 and partially completed in
1909, was designed by W. D. Caröe, and is in a highly ornate form
of Mannerist classicism. North of the original building is a large
conglomeration of more recent buildings (Percy Thomas Partnership), which have been allowed to go too high for visual comfort.
In the central gardens stands the **Welsh National War Memorial**,
erected in 1928. It consists of a circular colonnade, with three
porticoes breaking forward from it. In the centre is a bronze figure
of St Michael. The designer was – surprisingly – Sir Ninian Comper,
usually thought of as a Gothic architect, but in fact deeply appre-
ciative of classical styles. On the west side of the Park, the next
building north from the Assize Courts is the large new **Police Headquarters**, by John Dryburgh (the City Architect). Then comes the
University Registry, built in 1901–3 by Wills and Anderson, small
by comparison with its neighbours, but holding its own handsomely.
The Registry is the administrative centre of the University of Wales,
and is here rather than at Aberystwyth because Cardiff Corporation
offered the site and money to build it. Beyond is the main part of
County Hall. The competition in 1907 was won by Vincent Harris.
Harris was a very much better architect than he was usually given

credit for, and this is one of his masterpieces. The front is recessed behind a screen of giant coupled Corinthian columns. On either side are great sculptural groups (Navigation and Mining) by Albert Hodge. The Council Chamber is most impressive. The rear elevation of County Hall is as fine as the facade, although much plainer. Beautifully proportioned, its chief feature is a balcony running the length of the piano nobile and supported on huge brackets. Next after County Hall comes the **University of Wales Institute of Science and Technology** (formerly the Technical College), the earliest of the several buildings in Cathays Park by Percy Thomas. Opened in 1916, it is heavy and dull, with an attached Doric portico as centre-piece. Percy Thomas also designed its neighbour, the **Temple of Peace and Health**. This is even duller, classicism reduced to rect-angular blockiness. The building was paid for by Lord Davies of Llandinam (see *North Wales*, p. 301), and opened in 1938, by a mother bereaved in the First World War. The irony of the date only makes more painful the added irony that the style of the building is reminiscent of nothing so much as German Fascism. It was intended to house a Book of Remembrance, and to commemorate the ideals of the League of Nations. The last building on the west side of the Park is also part of the Institute, built by Sir Percy Thomas's firm. The north end of the Park is occupied by the Welsh Office, designed by P. K. Hanton and opened in 1938, appropriately solemn if un-inspiring.

In Corbett Road, which runs along the top of the Park, are two more university buildings, Aberdare Hall, a decent effort in Pont Street Dutch by H. Wills (1893), and the Music School, built in 1971 by Alex Gordon and Partners. It has a blank brick facade, ingeniously modelled, and with a large sculpture by Barbara Hep-worth in front.

CARDIFF – SUBURBS

This tour begins with Butetown, immediately south of the centre, and then works round anti-clockwise.

From the bottom of St Mary Street (p. 235), Customhouse Street runs east: on its corner with East Canal Wharf stands the old **Custom House**, a clumsy Italianate building of 1845. In front of it ran the Glamorganshire Canal (see p. 231), now almost entirely filled in. From Customhouse Street, **Bute Street** runs south through **Butetown**, which developed alongside the docks from about 1840. It consisted mostly of terraces of two-storey houses, with cement-rendered

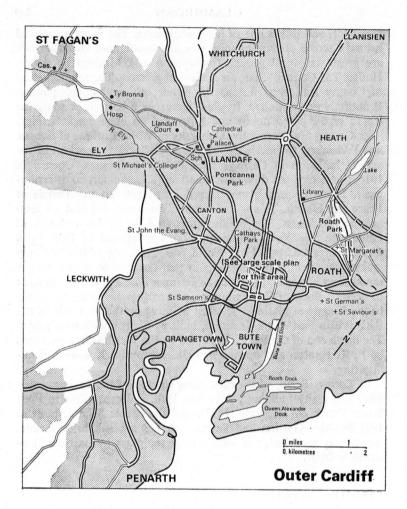

Outer Cardiff

fronts, and occasional squares with grander terraces around them. Later the houses deteriorated and the area became famous for its polyglot population. Now, however, the slums of 'Tiger Bay' have been mostly swept away, together with the brothels, the pickpockets, the opium dens, the gambling-houses and the Chinese laundries; and big blocks of Council flats have taken their place. Near the top of Bute Street is **St Mary's Church**, begun in 1841. Wordsworth wrote

Cardiff Castle from the east.

Caerphilly Castle from the air.

Cardiff City Hall, by H.V. Lanchester and E.A. Rickards, built in 1897-1904.

a sonnet to encourage subscriptions, in which he begged the builders
to

> Let the new Church be worthy of its aim
> That in its beauty Cardiff may rejoice.

'Beauty' is certainly not the word one would apply to the huge neo-
Norman monster put up by Thomas Foster and Son of Bristol,
although it is undeniably impressive. It has twin towers on its grand
'west front', but the whole thing is a sham as the entrance is actually
from the compass west, and the flat main front has within it a
windowless apse. The basilican interior is vast and bare, with an
awful flat roof. Originally it had galleries and a three-decker pulpit
in the apse, but after Fr Arthur Jones, a disciple of Pusey, had been
given the living by the 3rd Marquess of Bute, the church was remodelled (with financial help from Bute) to suit High Church ideas.
The apse was decorated with paintings and statues by J. D. Sedding,
c. 1880, and the reredos was painted by N. H. J. Westlake (the frame
almost certainly by J. F. Bentley). Near St Mary's are a Greek
Orthodox Church and a small mosque. Further down the road are
Bute Street Station, simple classical of 1841, and the new Custom
House by Henry Tanner (1898). Down here there was a second com-
mercial centre, rivalling that further north, and developed on an
ambitious scale in the late nineteenth and early twentieth centuries.
It is now very run down, but some grand buildings survive in a wide
variety of styles. The best is the neo-Grecian National Westminster
Bank (F. C. Palmer and W. F. C. Holden, 1924). Just west of it is
Mount Stuart Square (named after the Bute seat on the Isle of Bute).
In the centre is the vast Coal Exchange, built in 1883–6 by James,
Seward and Thomas in their usual overdone style. The Coal and
Shipping Hall inside is more exciting, reconstructed in 1911 by
Edwin Seward with lots of elaborate woodwork. Around the Square
are tall commercial buildings. Capel Bethel (1858) is now a night
club.

Bute West Dock, which ran parallel to Bute Street (on the east)
has now been filled in. On the very tip of the land which separated
it from Bute East Dock stands the exuberant **Pierhead Building**, built
as the offices of the Bute Docks Company in 1896. The architect was
William Frame, Burges's former assistant. Constructed of fiery red
terracotta, late Gothic in style, its romantic outline builds up to a
tall clock-tower. Near by stands the delightful white-painted Nor-
wegian Seamen's Church, with a broach spire and apse, entirely clad
in corrugated iron. Roath Dock is due east from here, and also the

s.w.   Q

biggest dock of all – Queen Alexandra, opened in 1907. Today the
dock traffic consists largely of the importing of fruit and the exporting of cars from the Midlands.

From the top of Bute Street, Tyndall Street runs east. At the head
of Bute East Dock stands the finest of Cardiff warehouses, built in
1861 by the Engineer, W. S. Clarke. It has a severe cubic exterior in
brick. Half of the ground floor is an open loggia, with a double row
of stout iron columns. The internal structure is also of iron.

From here, the suburb of **Roath** lies north-east. The part between
the railway and Newport Road consists of a grid of humble terraced
streets, with names either astronomical or mineralogical. Between
Star Street and Sun Street (behind the Royal Infirmary) is **St German's
Church**, nothing short of a masterpiece. It was designed by G. F.
Bodley and Thomas Garner, and built in 1882–4. Although tall and
dignified, the exterior is comparatively uninteresting: the excitement
is reserved for the interior, which is light and lofty. The nave windows
are set deep between internal buttresses. Goodhart-Rendel called it
'a sort of greyhound church, strong, lithe, and thin'. The east window
consists of a beautiful triplet of lights, the tracery of the centre light
forming a cross. The glass was designed by Bodley and made by
Burlison and Grylls (1900). The rood is also by Bodley (designed for
a church in London), as are the pulpit and font, but the reredos is
by Cecil Hare, Bodley's later (and greatly inferior) partner.

Less than half a mile east of St German's, there is another church
by Bodley and Garner – **St Saviour's**, in Splott Road. Built in 1887–8,
it is in striking contrast to St German's, for this church is low, spreading, and dark. Much the best of the fittings is the simple organ-case.

Splott is a lively, down-to-earth part of the town, very different
from the select suburban part of Roath around the parish church,
St Margaret's, which stands at the junction of Albany Road and
Waterloo Road (just north of the Newport Road traffic lights). A
new church was begun, on the site of the old parish church, in 1867,
designed by A. Roos. However, as soon as the 3rd Marquess of Bute
came of age, the next year, he got rid of Roos and called in John
Prichard to build a church on Roos's foundations. The exterior is
plain to the point of dullness, especially as the intended octagonal
crossing tower and spire were never built (a low square tower was
added in 1918). But the interior is an astonishing display of uninhibited polychromy. The materials include several different kinds of
stone (from various parts of South Wales, and even further afield).
Penarth alabaster for the chancel, and patterns of red (Bute), white
(Tymawr), and blue (Staffs.) bricks. The reredos is by J. N. Comper.

The church was opened in 1870, but in 1882 Lord Bute had a large, vaulted mortuary chapel added on the north-east, to which the remains of some of his ancestors were moved. They were put beneath monstrous granite blocks, which have been well compared to a herd of elephants with the baby bringing up the rear. From beside the church Roath Park, a very attractive linear park, follows the Roath Brook through Victorian suburbia for two miles. At the top end there is a large lake.

From St Margaret's, follow Albany Street. Roath Park Presbyterian Chapel (Habershon and Fawckner, 1897) has a tall spire. Then Crwys Road, in which is the quirky little Capel Heol y Crwys (J. H. Phillips, 1899), and Whitchurch Road, where, on the corner by the cemetery, the Carnegie Library (Speir and Beavan, 1906) is a charming piece of Arts and Crafts Gothic. From the junction at the top, the A470 goes north-west towards Merthyr Tydfil. North of the road, just over a mile from the junction, is **Rhiwbina Garden Village**. Projected in 1912 by a co-operative group, this was intended to be 'the first real garden suburb in Wales for both the middle class and the lower class'. The plan for the eighteen acres was made by Raymond Unwin (of Letchworth). The architectural scheme was by A. H. Mottram: the houses were to be of stone and rough-cast, with grey or green slate roofs. Red brick and tiles were forbidden. Unfortunately, only a small part of the village was built before the war, and it was not continued in the same spirit afterwards. However, the part completed, around Lon-y-dail (near Rhiwbina Halt) is very attractive. Thirty-four houses in Lon-y-dail, Y Groes, and Lon Isa were designed by Mottram. Houses in Pen-y-dre – some reached by little bridges across a stream, and sheltered by mature trees – were designed by Eric Francis, under the name of H. A. Tipping (see p. 195). More houses were designed by T. Alwyn Lloyd. The parish church of **Whitchurch**, south of the A470, was rebuilt in 1883–5 by John Prichard with a handsome tower, of local type. North-west of Whitchurch was the site of the famous Melingriffith Tinplate Works, which used water from the Taff, and operated from the late eighteenth century until 1957. In the early nineteenth century, the proprietors became involved in a dispute with the Glamorganshire Canal Co., for the Company was neglecting a clause in its Act which ordered it to ensure that it did not interfere with the supply of water to the works. In the end the Canal Company paid the works £700 to build a pump, to return the river water to the canal after they had used it. Remains of the pump survive, including an undershot waterwheel.

Back at the junction at the top of Whitchurch Road, the new by-pass joins St Athan's Road, which leads south-west across the river. The road gives a wonderful view of **Llandaff Cathedral**, down by the river at the foot of a steep slope, among tall trees. By the roundabout at the top of the hill is the Cathedral School, which occupies the former Llandaff Court, a big, plain three-storey house built *c.* 1750 for Admiral Thomas Mathew. It is said that he never occupied it, saying that having lived all his life in a three-decker he had no intention of dying in one. The architect may have been John Wood (see p. 245). In about 1850 the house became the Bishop's Palace, and an apsidal chapel was added in 1869 by Ewan Christian. On the left is St Michael's Theological College. This incorporates Prichard's own house, built *c.* 1880 – the parts on the north, with the cylindrical turret, and at the back. Opposite is the Probate Registry (1857–63), also by Prichard, although Seddon may have had a hand in it. It is one of his best buildings, and shows his masterly use of materials in the contrast of smooth ashlar with finely-split rough stone. High Street leads (right) towards the cathedral. At the end is the massive ruined gatehouse, with twin polygonal towers, which is the most impressive surviving part of the Bishop's Castle, built *c.* 1280–1330. It faces up the delightful Green. It is remarkable how, although completely swallowed up in modern Cardiff, Llandaff manages to preserve the air of a quiet country village. It used once to be an entirely separate entity. On the Green are a medieval preaching cross (with a new head), and the ruins of a thirteenth-century belfry. On the north side are two big Gothic houses, built as the Deanery and Canonry in 1861 by Ewan Christian. The ex-Deanery is now Llys Esgob, the Bishop's Palace. The cathedral is reached through a handsome stone lychgate.

The first church on the site is said to have been founded by St Teilo in the sixth century, and was very small. The only pre-Norman survival is a tenth-century cross now in the south presbytery aisle. The first Norman Bishop, Urban, began the building of the cathedral *c.* 1120. The aisleless nave and presbytery were narrower than they are now, but transepts reached out to the present aisle width. The presbytery terminated in an apse. The only Norman work left now is the arch east of the presbytery (which formerly led into the apse), and the west and south doors, presumably rebuilt. In about 1170 a new nave was begun, starting from the west. The whole building was carried through at the same width as far as the presbytery aisles, until the last part, the narrower, vaulted Lady Chapel, was built *c.* 1280. The west front had twin towers. The subsequent history of the cathedral can only be briefly summarized here. Minor alterations and additions were made in the fourteenth and fifteenth centuries, and one major alteration – the rebuilding of the north-west tower in 1485, by Jasper Tudor, uncle of Henry VII. After the Reformation decay soon set in, until in 1691 choral services were abandoned. The roofs collapsed, in 1720 storms damaged the north-west tower, and three years later the south-west tower fell.

In 1734 a curious scheme of reconstruction was begun by John Wood the Elder of Bath. This resulted in the repair of the Lady Chapel, and a classicization of the presbytery and all except the four westernmost bays of the nave. The result was an absurd mixture on the exterior, with the classical nave clerestory rising above aisles in which several windows had actually been replaced in Gothic (until it was found to be too expensive). The Jasper Tower was given new battlements: otherwise the old west end was in ruins. The interior was more successful. The altar stood beneath a pedimented baldacchino, and a fine bold cornice ran round below the plaster-vaulted ceiling. Above the altar was a Venetian window.

In 1840 the first moves were made to do away with Wood's work and restore the whole cathedral. In that year T. H. Wyatt was called in to replace Wood's ceiling and secure the old walls, and he started fitting out the Lady Chapel in 1841. In 1843 he was appointed Honorary Cathedral Architect, but at about the same time the east window of the Lady Chapel was restored by the young John Prichard, son of one of the priest-vicars, and it was he who restored the rest of the chapel c. 1846–8. In 1847 he was appointed Diocesan Architect, and eventually, about ten years later, Wyatt resigned. Prichard had taken on J. P. Seddon as partner in 1852: on his way to Southerndown (see p. 279), Seddon called to see the cathedral, and met Prichard. Apart from being a brilliant designer, Seddon was acquainted, through his painter brother Thomas, with the Pre-Raphaelites, and this was to produce fruitful results. The restoration, finally completed in 1869, was a tremendous success. The greatest respect was paid to the medieval work, but when Prichard thought he could justifiably strike out on his own, he did so. His decision to rebuild the south-west tower, not as a copy of the Jasper Tower, or a recreation of the thirteenth-century original, but as a magnificently tall spire, created a fierce controversy, but in the end the antiquarians were beaten. It would be a mistake to think that everyone approved of the restoration of the cathedral. The diocese was the poorest in Britain, and yet in the nineteenth century its population had increased more than that of any other. The Church was miserably poor both in buildings and manpower, and neither the land-owning aristocracy nor the new industrialists were of much assistance. There was a sharp division of opinion between the clerics such as William Bruce Knight, a land-owning aristocrat, who became Chancellor of Llandaff in 1817, and in 1843 the first Dean since Norman times, and who was one of the leading spirits behind the restoration, and John Griffith, Vicar of Aberdare 1847–59, and of Merthyr Tydfil 1859–85, who felt that the vast sums poured into beautifying the cathedral would be better spent on the evangelical needs of the industrial areas. In 1941 the cathedral was hit by a land-mine, which gutted the nave, and wrecked the rest of the building. In 1949 the work of repair was begun, under the direction of George Pace of York. It was finished in 1960, although additions have been made subsequently.

The west front of the cathedral is flanked on the left by the Jasper Tower, its ornate crown of Somerset type, reinstated by Prichard, and on the right by Prichard's steeple. The sheer simplicity of the tower contrasts with the richness of the pinnacles and octagonal spire. It is a pity that the crockets have now been shaved off. The interior is dominated by huge concrete parabolic arches, supporting an organ-case also made of concrete (the least suitable material imaginable). Attached to it is a slender aluminium figure of Christ by Sir Jacob Epstein, while little shelves further back support statues of angels and saints which were originally parts of Prichard's choir stalls, and of the 1899 organ-case. The whole thing is far too assertive. The new roof is flat.

In a chapel in the north-west corner is the reredos painted by D. G. Rossetti for the high altar. The paintings cost Rossetti immense trouble, dragging on from 1856 until 1864. Originally they were set within elaborate Decorated Gothic arches of stone. The new blue and gold Dutch Renaissance frame is entirely inappropriate. At present there is no reredos behind the high altar, so that an unbroken vista into the Lady Chapel exists – a serious mistake. The fittings designed for the cathedral by Prichard and Seddon, with the help of their Pre-Raphaelite friends, were unrivalled in Britain, and it is tragic that so many were destroyed in the War, while others were not re-used, or else were incorporated into idiosyncratic and unsympathetic new work. It is fortunate that the organ-case was taken off to Usk in 1899 and survives there (see p. 186). The Bishop's Throne (in the design of which H. H. Armstead, a first-rate sculptor, was involved) also survives more or less intact, and bits of the choir stalls have been rehashed. Only fragments remain of the beautifully

carved stone sedilia (most of the carving was by Messrs Edward
Clarke of Llandaff), Prichard's designs for which incorporated
details by Rossetti (for example, pelicans studied at London Zoo).
Some superb ironwork survives on the presbytery door. Much of the
original glass was by Morris and Co.: some delicately beautiful
windows survive in the south aisle, but most has gone. Prichard
himself is buried, with his father, just south of the last bay east of the
south aisle, near the projecting Chapter House of *c.* 1250, which he
had enlivened by making its upper storey turn octagonal and crowning it with a steep roof. The numerous tombs include that of St
Teilo himself (in the presbytery), several to members of the influential Mathew family (the finest being the elaborate alabaster altar
tomb in the nave to Sir William, d. 1528, and his wife, with effigies
and weepers), and one by Goscombe John to Dean Vaughan,
formerly Headmaster of Harrow (in the north choir aisle).

From Llandaff, the City Centre can be reached by way of Cardiff
Road and Cathedral Road, which leads down to the bridge by the
castle, or (on foot) through the parks. In Cardiff Road is **Howell's
School**, a girls' school founded, like its sister at Denbigh (*North
Wales*, p. 99), in 1860 by the Drapers' Company, with money left
by Thomas Howell (d. 1540). The grim Gothic buildings were designed, as at Denbigh, by Herbert Williams, on the basis of designs
prepared (extraordinary as it may seem) by Decimus Burton.
Cathedral Road is lined on both sides with big stone Gothic villas,
of no great individual merit, apart from some at the south clearly
influenced by Burges's Park House, but impressive as a whole.

To explore western Cardiff further, take Fairwater Road west from
Llandaff. Off it is **Llandaff Court**, an elaborately Gothic house built
for James Insole, the shipowner, in 1873 by E. J. Robinson, and
enlarged in 1875 by James, Seward and Thomas. It is a rather
bungling attempt to rival the castle. Further west, in St Fagan's
Road, is Glan-Ely Hospital, which incorporates (on the north side
of the road), **Ty Bronna**, a house built by C. F. A. Voysey in
1903. Very much in the famous 'Voysey style', it is elegantly
simple. The white roughcast, the battered buttresses, the mullioned
windows of stone, are all typical. Beyond the Hospital is open
country, wooded and hilly, with fields falling away to the river Ely
on the left, and then the village of **St Fagan's**, mostly unspoilt and
rural. It is four miles from the centre of Cardiff, reached most
directly via Cowbridge Road (A48), then right up Western Avenue,
and (second left) along St Fagan's Road. Beside the crossroads is
the castle. The house and grounds contain **The Welsh Folk Museum**,

one of the best in Europe. It is open throughout the year, and is particularly enjoyable on a bright winter day. Those arriving by bus will find themselves by the gate to the castle in the village; those coming by car, at the big car park by the new museum at the lower end of the 100-acre park. This may affect the sequence of your visit which naturally falls into three parts: the museum, the re-erected buildings in the park, and the house. There is a restaurant in the museum and a snack bar in the castle.

St Fagans has only been in existence as the Welsh Folk Museum since 1946, but its collections and the scholarship on which they are based have been accruing and maturing for far longer. Much of this huge wealth of folk culture would probably have sunk without trace in the surge of twentieth-century progress had it not been initially for Dr Iorwerth Peate, who was St Fagan's moving spirit. Many of the artefacts shown have the added interest of being pre-agricultural revolution, since aspects of that change did not reach parts of Wales until the 1914–18 war. The collections on display are impressive; the reserve collections are an Aladdin's cave of treasure: fire-engines and farm wagons, fishing nets, furbelows, furniture . . .

The new museum building (Percy Thomas and Partners) has a big gallery of material culture; an agricultural gallery showing fascinating farm implements; and a department of oral tradition and dialects. But if time is short, make straight for the re-erected buildings. These have come from all parts of Wales (the district of origin is given here in brackets) and, at the time they were moved, could hardly have survived otherwise. The delight is that they are so beautifully shown. The mature trees of the estate tie together what could look a motley collection. The grass between is grazed by sheep, not primly mown. The enclosures round the buildings have appropriate fencing (stone-wall, quickthorn hedge or bank) and there are vegetables in the gardens. Inside, the first thing that strikes one is the smell of the peat or wood fires, which gives an illusion that the houses are awaiting their occupants after a very thorough spring clean. The furnishings are of the right date, hence the sparseness of some.

Kennixton Farmhouse (Gower), the pink-washed building with the thatched roof, is the first house you come to from the museum. It dates from 1630 (the east end), and was enlarged and improved over the next hundred years. Mortar floors were typical of Glamorgan. The thatch rests on woven mats instead of rafters. Thatch was common throughout Wales until the slate boom of the early nineteenth century; its use continued in many parts until the twentieth. Houses like Kennixton would be lime and colour-washed every spring both for looks and weather-proofness. Opposite an eighteenth-century **Cornmill** (Cardigan) is in process of re-erection.

Working clockwise (where possible), **Hendre'r Ywydd Uchaf** (Denbighshire, late fifteenth century) the black and white long house at the edge of the wood, is constructed on four crucks and divided on a typical long house plan with the upper part for people and the lower for stock. The iron gate across the drive beside the house is one designed by Telford for the Holyhead Road.

The **Toll-house** (near Aberystwyth) dates from 1771 but its roof was raised later. The list of tolls is posted on the outside wall by the gate.

Llainfadyn (Caernarvonshire, 1762), the small whitewashed slate-roofed cottage near by, has walls of boulders, some huge. A *tyle* or slate platform keeps the furniture clear of the earth floor.

The round **Cockpit**, from the yard of the Hawk and Buckle Inn, Denbigh, was in existence in 1726 when the silver tankard, now in the museum, was one of its trophies. Its fittings have been reconstructed.

The **Rhayader Tannery** (mainly eighteenth century), the big stone building in the south-west corner, was the last oak bark tannery to work in Wales. The late-eighteenth-century **Smithy** (Montgomeryshire) is on the way up to **Cilewent** (Radnorshire), a two-storeyed long house dating from the sixteenth century. People and stock are separated by the paved feeding passage. The dwelling (*pen uchaf*, upper end) has two rooms up and down, and the lower end (*pen isaf*) consists of cow-house and stable with a hay-loft over.

Abernodwydd (Montgomeryshire) is a black and white farmhouse, sixteenth–seventeenth century. Even at this date the windows are unglazed, and have instead sliding shutters.

Capel Pen-rhiw (Vale of Teifi) is opposite the museum. Maybe originally a barn, it became a Unitarian Chapel in 1777. The gallery is early nineteenth century, and the box pews look that date or earlier. The stone seats set against the bank outside were used during preaching festivals.

Just beyond the gypsy caravan turn left and follow the path through the tunnel, then left again for the **Stryt Lydan Barn** (Flintshire). This timber-framed building has a loading bay for wagons in the middle. The south end is built on crucks, *c.* 1550; the north is post and truss *c.* 1600. The numbering on some of the timbers was for its original construction. The wattle infill of the frame gave excellent ventilation. Farm implements are now stored here.

The **Esgair Moel Woollen Factory** (Breconshire) to the north, is an eighteenth-century mill with nineteenth-century machinery, still working by water-power. Across the old swimming pool are full-scale models of a Chepstow **Net and boathouse** with a display of fishing equipment.

The Gardens. If you have the energy, it is well worth approaching the castle from the main entrance (instead of slipping in from the side), through eighteenth-century iron gates up the walk of pleached limes, and through the arch in the thirteenth-century curtain-wall. These attractive formal gardens were laid out in 1865–6 (except for that immediately north of the house which was created in 1945). Beyond is a mulberry grove and to the east rose gardens, a vinery and flower-house. To the west, terraces drop down to the fish ponds – a particularly successful Victorian design. Neither the architect responsible for the restoration of the house nor the garden designer is known.

St Fagans was originally a Norman lordship, but the present **Castle** is a good-looking gabled house built *c*. 1560–80 by Dr John Gibbon within the curtain-wall of the medieval castle. It has an E plan with a central porch leading into a screen passage to the hall, with service rooms to the left, and a long gallery on the first floor. It was thoroughly restored in the 1850s by the Windsor family (Earls of Plymouth), who owned it from 1730 until they presented it to the museum. They also made various additions, including the present dining-room, renewed the chimney stacks, and built a new staircase. The house is whitewashed in accordance with local tradition.

The museum's aim is to furnish the house mainly with seventeenth-century objects, and a very handsome collection is growing, but there is also good stuff of other periods, including the 1800–10 library from Coed Coch in Denbighshire and the complete dining-room from Glantorvaen House, Pontypool (all the furniture is of the 1860s from Trapnell's of Bristol).

The medieval **Parish Church**, across the road from the castle, is attractive and well set. It was excellently restored in 1859–60 by G. E. Street. Inside there are finely-carved fourteenth-century sedilia, and fittings by Street include the pulpit, font cover, seating, and tower screen. There are monuments to the Plymouth family. Up the lane by the church is the former Rectory, an amazingly big and ornate Gothic house built in 1858–9 by Prichard and Seddon.

On 8 May 1648 the biggest battle fought in Wales in the Civil War took place at St Fagan's, an overwhelming victory for the Cromwellians who took 3000 Royalist prisoners.

On the way back into Cardiff, there are two churches south of

Cowbridge Road which deserve mention. One is **St John's, Canton** (in St John's Crescent), which had almost as complicated a building history as St Andrew's. It was designed by Prichard and Seddon and built between 1853 and 1902. The other church is **St Samson's**, in Pentre Gardens (off Penarth Road); of no conceivable interest in itself but housing fittings from J. D. Sedding's St Dyfrig's, built 1889–1907, and tragically demolished in 1969. The most notable of them is the great reredos by Henry Wilson, a gesso relief of the Adoration of the Magi.

CARDIFF TO MERTHYR TYDFIL, AND BACK BY ABERDARE (THE TAFF AND CYNON VALLEYS)

The Taff valley, running up from Cardiff to Merthyr, has been a vital means of communication ever since the uplands began to be exploited. It is joined at Pontypridd by the Rhondda, and at Aber-cynon by the Cynon, as well as by numerous lesser valleys. Just beyond Cardiff, at **Tongwynlais**, the valley narrows dramatically between steep wooded hills. Through the gorge ran at one time two roads, two railways, and the canal. Now the most conspicuous claimant is the huge new road, which has obliterated yet more of the dramatic Glamorganshire Canal (see p. 231), of which few traces now remain (a pity, as it had no less than 49 locks in its 24½ miles, rising 543 feet).

The gorge was guarded by **Castell Coch** (DoE), whose romantic outline rises above trees on the south-east side of the defile. Its name means 'red castle', and derived from the colour of the stone from which it was originally built, by Earl Gilbert de Clare, *c.* 1260–1300. All that remained was a pile of overgrown ruins when, in 1871, the 3rd Marquess of Bute decided to carry out a complete reconstruction, using William Burges as his architect, as at Cardiff Castle (p. 233). The result is in many ways even more enchanting than there, for Castell Coch is a complete and thorough-going medieval fantasy, rivalling Viollet-le-Duc's Pierrefonds, or Ludwig II's Neuschwanstein. Work began in 1875, and was carried on after Burges's death in 1881 by his assistants William Frame and J. S. Chapple. It went on until the 1890s.

The castle is set among woods carpeted with wild garlic. The exterior is a wonderful exercise in solid geometry, the sheer round towers rising from battered bases, and capped with conical tiled roofs. The drawbridge and portcullis work. The courtyard is sur-rounded by a proliferation of wooden galleries, stairs, sloping roofs, and chimneys. The rooms, which are furnished in appropriate style, include a Banqueting Hall, in which a large statue of the mythical St Lucius adorns the tall hood over the fireplace, the lofty octagonal Drawing-Room, where the Three Fates sit over the fireplace, and the vaulted roof, above the gallery, is bright with birds and butterflies, and the Lady's Bedroom, at the top of the Keep, complete with castellated wash-stand and vast and elaborate bed. The castle was intended for occasional occupation in the summer, but was little used: in any case Lord Bute had so many houses he could hardly have spent much time in any of them. He did, however, plant vineyards in the neighbourhood, and sold the surplus wine in good years.

Beyond the gorge is **Taff's Well**: the well waters are similar to those of Bath, but not so hot. A mile further on is **Nantgarw**, dominated by the immense post-war coking plant, with its own collieries. The name of the place is widely known because of the porcelain factory set up in 1813 by William Billingsley and Samuel Walker, and renowned for the fine quality of its beautifully-painted wares. In 1814 the factory was bought up by Lewis Weston Dillwyn of Swansea (see p. 294), but Billingsley and Walker seem to have returned to Nantgarw after a couple of years and continued production for a short time. Beyond is the **Treforest** Industrial Estate, begun in the 1930s to provide work for the huge number of unemployed in the valleys.

One and a half miles further on, at **Rhydyfelin**, is the old Treforest Tinplate Works. From the weir on the river a watercourse supplied the works. To reach the works (which now belong to P. Leiner and Sons, who convert Pakistani bones into gelatine – ask permission), cross the river (A473), and then turn left. (They are at 087/880.) They were founded between 1820 and 1830 by William Crawshay II, and run by his son Francis (for the Crawshays, see p. 259). The chief remains consist of three very long, narrow buildings roofed with light wrought iron trusses: from south to north they were for rolling, tinning, and finishing off (assorting, polishing, etc.). The Taff water was carried down the west side of the works in a watercourse, with sluice-gates at intervals, which fed waterwheels. On the retaining wall of the watercourse behind the shed is the inscription: PERSEVERANCE – W.C. 1836 – WHO IS NOT A FOOL?? – IF THIS RAISE ANGER IN THE READER'S THOUGHT THE PAIN OF ANGER PUNISHES THE FAULT. The works did not succeed, and this may have been intended as an exhortation to greater effort.

Beyond Rhydyfelin, at **Glyntaff** (where the A4058 crosses the river into Pontypridd), St Mary's Church stands high on the hill, a dreadful Norman thing of 1838–9 by T. H. Wyatt, useful as a landmark to help find the Round Houses, in Craig-yr-Helfa Road, 300 yards north of the church. Turn off the huge new bypass, across incongruous-seeming cattle grids, and go round the back of the church. Perched up on the hillside, these were also built in 1838–9: two three-storey towers, with triangular-headed windows and funny octagonal roofs, flank an iron gate. This gate was intended to lead to an eight-storey tower, containing a Druidical museum and palace (with *camera obscura* thrown in). The site was chosen because of the proximity of the Rocking Stone (Y Maen Chwyf), believed to be Druidical by the man who built the towers, the extraordinary William Price. It was here he came to perform his rites, and chant his 'Song of the Primitive Bard to the Moon'. Unfortunately he had not troubled to ensure first that he owned the site, and his appeal for funds met with limited success, so the project lapsed.

Price (1800–93) was the son of an Anglican clergyman, and a qualified doctor. His views on medicine – as on everything – were highly unorthodox. He thought that doctors should be paid, not when their patients were ill, but when they were well, as it would then be in their interest to keep them healthy. He had no time for conventional religion, saying 'Man is greater than God, for man created God in his own image'. He himself worshipped nature. He did not believe in marriage, which he thought a form of bondage, chiefly devised to protect property, and preferred the idea of free unions. He lived with at least two women, who bore him several children – the last born when he was ninety. He was involved with the Chartists, and had to flee to France after the march on Newport in 1839 (see p. 204). He spent the latter part of his life at Llantrisant, where his notorious cremations took place (see p. 265). The Rocking Stone itself is on Pontypridd Common, further along the same road. It no longer rocks.

Across the river from Glyntaff is **Pontypridd**, at the junction of the Taff and Rhondda rivers. It is the metropolis for the Rhondda townships, and a manufacturing town in its own right – the Brown Lenox Works, specializing in chains and anchors, was established in 1816. Best known to many today as the birthplace of Tom Jones, 'the singing hod-carrier from Pontypridd', three times voted 'the World's Sexiest Man', the town has plenty of character although sadly redevelopment has destroyed much of it. It seems appropriate to start with the famous **Bridge**, even though it is not true that the town (strictly Pont-y-tŷ-pridd) is called after the present structure.

Follow the one-way system northwards, and it will be seen, rudely jostled by the crude new bridge of 1857, but still leaping across the Taff with its elegant single arch spanning 140 feet. It was the masterpiece of William Edwards (see p. 228). He was one of the heroes of Samuel Smiles's *The Pursuit of Knowledge under Difficulties*. His difficulties here consisted chiefly in the collapse of his first three structures (starting in 1746). For the fourth, in 1756, he lightened the weight by piercing three holes in each side. Originally, as old views show, the bridge stood almost alone in a picturesque setting. However beautiful it may have been, the steepness of the bridge made it impractical, and the near-by ford continued to be used. In Gelliwastad Road are the pretty little Town Hall, built in 1904 by Henry T. Hare, and St Catherine's Church, built in 1866–9 by John Norton. The centre of the town is full of life. The late Victorian railway station is impressive, with its long, curving platforms. Pontypridd was the home of Evan James and his son James James, author and composer respectively (in 1856) of the Welsh national anthem, *Hen Wlad fy Nhadau* (Land of my Fathers). Evan had a woollen factory, and James was a publican.

Back on the A470, a mile north of Pontypridd is **Cilfynydd**, aptly named ('the elbow of the mountain'). The same chapel choir here had as members (at different times) Sir Geraint Evans and Stuart Burrows, both now of international repute. Beyond there is moorland, but tips crown the hills on the right. Across the valley left is **Abercynon**, a characteristic mining town with terraced houses, chapels, and workmen's institute. Here the A4059 runs up to Aberdare (p. 262). As well as being the junction of the Glamorganshire and Aberdare Canals, Abercynon was the point where the Penydarren Tramroad joined the Glamorganshire Canal. It was opened in 1802 to relieve overcrowding on the upper part of the canal (due to the many locks). It was chiefly famous as the route of the historic journey made in 1804 by the Cornish engineer Richard Trevithick, when he drove his 'high pressure tram engine', drawing a load of ten tons of bar iron, the ten miles from Penydarren to Abercynon at an average speed of 5 m.p.h., thereby winning a wager of 1000 gns. for Samuel Homfray against Richard Crawshay. This was the first time that a steam engine drew a load on rails. Parts of the tramroad can still be traced, down in the valley near Quaker's Yard, where the river makes a great loop. Just before the loop, the A472 goes east to Nelson (p. 228). On the loop itself, the Taff is joined by the Bargod near **Treharris**, which has an unremarkable church of 1895–6 by J. L. Pearson.

Quaker's Yard, where the river goes north again, takes its name from a Quaker burial ground. Of the two viaducts which crossed the river, one of 1841 on Brunel's Taff Vale Railway, the other belonging to the old South Wales Railway, only the former remains. Half a mile upstream there is a fine old stone bridge, a pre-industrial relic (visible from the road.) The next township is **Merthyr Vale.** Across the valley, reached by the B4285, is **Aberfan,** the scene of the appalling disaster in October 1966 when a coaltip moved, burying a school and killing 114 children. The most spectacular visible result, both in Aberfan and throughout the Welsh valleys, is the sudden appearance of empty green spaces where tips recently stood. Here, and in other communities too, you will see reconditioned terrace housing, the result of an excellent scheme whereby grants are available if the houses can be given a thirty-year life. Most houses in the valleys are privately owned, so individual householders can benefit from the scheme.

The B4285 recrosses the Taff at **Troedyrhiw,** where the church of 1851 by John Prichard was partly paid for by Anthony Hill, owner of the Plymouth Ironworks. These were one of the four great ironworks of Merthyr Tydfil. The site of the Dyffryn Works, a subsidiary of Plymouth, right of the A470, half a mile beyond Troedyrhiw, has been obliterated by land reclamation.

The roundabout marks the beginning of **Merthyr Tydfil.** The name (*martyrium*, or place of martyrdom, of Tudful) is said to refer to Tudful, a daughter of Brychan Brycheiniog, put to death here by the Saxons. This might serve as an allegory for the later history of Merthyr – exploitation of the local people by English industrialists. Iron furnaces were established in the district as early as the sixteenth century (e.g. at Dyffryn, see above), but on a small scale. It was in the mid eighteenth century that large-scale industrialization began. In 1759 the Dowlais Iron Co. was formed, with John Guest of Broseley, Salop, as manager. More important still, in 1765 Anthony Bacon, of London, leased 4000 acres in the Taff valley, and set up the Cyfarthfa works. The land included some of the best coal in South Wales, and rich beds of iron-ore, with plentiful limestone and water near at hand. Bacon also established the Plymouth works, and another at Hirwaun (p. 261). The Penydarren works were set up in 1784 by Francis Homfray (of Stourton, Staffs.), an associate of Bacon, for his three sons. After Bacon's death in 1786, his sons sold the Plymouth works to their manager, Richard Hill, and the Cyfarthfa works to Richard Crawshay, a Yorkshireman. So the four great works and four great dynasties of ironmasters of Merthyr were set up – Dowlais (Guest),

Penydarren (Homfray), Plymouth (Hill), and Cyfarthfa (Crawshay).
The ironmaking industry was greatly boosted by the American and
French Wars. By 1801 Merthyr was the largest town in Wales, with
a population of 7700. In 1831 Merthyr's population was larger than
those of Newport, Swansea and Cardiff put together. In 1861, with
50,000, it was still the largest town in Wales, but from then on, with
the decline in the iron industry, lost the lead. Both Dowlais and
Cyfarthfa went over to steel production, but, unlike the Ebbw Vale
works (p. 221), did not prosper. The Depression hit Merthyr really
hard. By 1932 62% of the working population were unemployed or
working part-time. The population (84,000 in 1913) fell dramatically.
In 1939, Political and Economic Planning recommended that the
town should be abandoned, and its people rehoused elsewhere – its
minerals were spent, 'nor does it seem reasonable to ask the tax-
payers of the rest of Britain indefinitely to pay hundreds of thousands
a year in order to give large numbers of people the doubtful pleasure
and benefit of continuing to live at subsistence level in one of the
least habitable districts of England and Wales'. The War improved
the situation temporarily, and after it Government action brought
new industries, which have given the town a boost.

Merthyr's political history reflects its industrial history. Riots
occurred in 1802, 1816 and 1831. It was in 1831 that 'Dic Penderyn'
was hanged, at the age of 23, on the charge (probably false) of having
wounded a soldier. Chartism flourished. In 1868 Henry Richard, the
'Apostle of Peace' (from Tregaron – see p. 72), was elected Liberal
MP for Merthyr. In 1900 the seat was won for Labour by Keir
Hardie, and it has remained a Labour stronghold ever since. More
recently it has been claimed to be a citadel of the 'Taffia'. Unfortunately, the bitter legacy of Merthyr's past militates against the
preservation of anything which might serve to recall it, whether good
buildings or relics of industrial archaeology. Over the last ten or
fifteen years, a vast amount has gone. More is currently threatened,
including the Triangle, which lies just north of the roundabout at
Pentrebach (where the A4060 leaves the A470). Near here stood the
Plymouth Ironworks, named after the Earl of Plymouth, from whom
the land was leased. In the early nineteenth century, the Triangle and
Long Row, consisting of five terraces of two-storey houses, were
built to house the workers. Plain but attractive, it is said that the
residents considered themselves something special.

Just over a mile beyond Pentrebach there is another roundabout.
By it stands a glorious cast-iron fountain canopy. The fountain itself
has been removed. Made in Glasgow *c.* 1890 (by W. Macfarlane &

Llandaff Cathedral from the south-east (from a photograph taken in 1930).

At Eglwysilan, church and pub stand together on the hill-top high above the mining valleys.

The bridge built by William Edwards at Pontypridd in 1756, shown in a watercolour by Michael Angelo Rooker (1795).

Co.), it was 'Erected by Sir William T. Lewis and W. T. Rees of Aberdare, and presented to their native town in commemoration of Robert and Lucy Thomas of Waunwyllt in the parish, the pioneers in 1828 of the South Wales steam coal trade'. Robert had, in that year, opened a seam at Abercannaid to produce coal for household use (as opposed to smelting), and his widow carried on after his death, even sending her coal to London. The circular canopy is of rich pierced ironwork, and is surmounted by a rhetorical statue. Near by stands St Tydfil's Church. On the site of the medieval church, it was rebuilt in 1829, but completely transformed in 1895 by J. L. Pearson. The interior is impressively moving, in a very simple Romanesque of French type.

From the roundabout, High Street runs up north. Most of the town centre has been destroyed for redevelopment. Behind the nasty red Town Hall runs Tram Road Side, the route of the Penydarren tramway. Just beyond the Town Hall, an alley left of the street leads to Zoar Congregational Chapel, of 1842, which has a grandiose recessed portico of the 'primitive order'. The splendid interior, with its varnished woodwork, galleries on iron columns, and elegant Regency detailing, holds 900. The origins of Merthyr nonconformity go back to the mid seventeenth century, when secret meetings were held on the surrounding hills.

Castle Street leads from opposite the Town Hall down to the river, which until 1966 was crossed here by a remarkable cast-iron bridge built in 1800 by Watkin George, 'the mechanical genius of Cyfarthfa'. It has been removed, on the grounds that it would be out of keeping with the new housing that has replaced the notorious 'China', whose crowded courts were huddled along the east bank of the river, and it is now mouldering away in Cyfarthfa Park. A quarter of a mile south-west of here, near the College of Further Education, stands a tall stone engine house, pierced with round-headed arches in dressed limestone. This distinctive style (together with iron-framed roofs) was characteristic of all the Crawshay buildings. It formed part of the Ynysfach Ironworks, a subsidiary of Cyfarthfa. Near it are remains of four blast furnaces, one with an iron plate inscribed W.C. (William Crawshay) 1836.

High Street runs north into Penydarren Road: on the left is the park where stood **Penydarren House**, home of the Homfray family, whose great ironworks were below the other side of the road. In the park, a large Roman fort, founded in AD 74, was excavated between 1902 and 1904, when most of it was removed to make a football pitch. On the right of the main road is the Trevithick Memorial, incorporating stone sleepers and iron rails from the tramroad.

The road climbs on up to **Dowlais**. The formation of the Dowlais Iron Co. in 1759, with John Guest as manager, has already been mentioned. It was only when John's grandson, Josiah John Guest, took over control in 1807 that Dowlais began to overtake the other Merthyr works, but by 1840 it had even beaten Cyfarthfa, with eighteen furnaces to Cyfarthfa's twelve. The Dowlais speciality was rails – e.g. for the Stockton and Darlington Railway (1821), and even for Russia. By 1840 Guest was sole proprietor of what was then the largest works in the world, employing getting on for 10,000. He was Liberal MP for the new constituency of Merthyr from 1832 until his death in 1852. In 1833, at the age of 48, he married the 21-year-old Lady Charlotte Bertie, daughter of the 9th Earl of Lindsay. She was a remarkable woman: as well as producing ten children, she helped with the business, took a warm (if patronizing) interest in the work-people, and translated the *Mabinogion* (published 1838–49). Her husband was created a Baronet in 1838. After his death she married Charles Schreiber, and made her famous collections of porcelain and enamels (later given to the Victoria and Albert), and of fans and playing-cards (in the British Museum). Her correspondence has been published.

The main Dowlais works occupied the large derelict area south of High Street. Parts of blast furnaces, brickworks etc. survive. Near the road stands the big Blast Engine House, in red and yellow brick, with a rusty cast-iron porch: it was built in the late nineteenth century as part of the doomed campaign to keep the works viable. Immediately north of it, right by the road, stood, until recently, Dowlais House, which was the home of the Guests. In 1846 Sir John and his wife bought Canford Manor in Dorset, but much of their time was spent in this plain and modest house, right on top of the works. It was, however, surrounded by a fair-sized park until the 1850s.

North of the road, the steep, narrow streets of little terrace houses, with the occasional chapel or pub (one is called the 'Vulcan and Friendship') are run down. The great Works Stables, grandly built in stone in 1820, survive, but only just. Their upper storey housed Dowlais's first school. They overlook the site of the Market (demolished 1971). Guest was a good deal more generous than most of the ironmasters. He gave £3000 towards St John's Church (near the Stables), built in 1827, but tediously rebuilt by E. A. Johnson in 1873–93. Further up High Street is the former Guest Memorial Reading Room and Library (now the Guest, Keen and Nettlefold recreational centre), built in 1863, and designed by Sir Charles Barry. Lady Charlotte hoped that the workers would pay for it, to show their respect, but in the end had to bear the cost herself. Near it stood, until 1973, the great Gothic schools, also designed by Barry, and given by Lady Charlotte, at a cost of £8000. Further north are the Ivor works (now GKN), named after Guest's son (later Lord Wimborne), and set up in 1839.

High Street leads up to Dowlais Top, where it joins the A465 (Heads of the Valleys Road). Back in Merthyr, the A470 runs north-west up the Taff valley. The whole floor of the valley was once occupied by the great **Cyfarthfa** ironworks. These were set up in 1765 by Anthony Bacon (see p. 255), and sold after his death to Richard Crawshay. Until overtaken by Dowlais, they were the greatest in the world, and their dramatic silhouette, lit by the flare of the furnaces, had a strong appeal for artists such as Turner and Ibbetson. Little is left of the works. The earlier Crawshays, at any rate, were not unpopular with their men: as Gwyn Williams puts it, in the excellent symposium *Merthyr Politics* (1966), 'whatever their faults, after all, the Crawshays were never gentlemen'. They looked down over the works from a vast stone castle, like tyrants from a citadel. **Cyfarthfa Castle**, by Robert Lugar, stands in a large park, overlooking a lake, which had a practical purpose in supplying the works. The house was built in 1824–5 by William Crawshay II, at a cost of £30,000 – in defiance of his father's wishes. It produces a fine effect from a distance, with its rough-textured walls and picturesque massing, but is unconvincing at close quarters. It was sold in 1909 to Merthyr Corporation: most is used as a school, but the state rooms house an interesting museum and art gallery. Opposite the castle gates is the early-nineteenth-century Pandy Farm Clock Tower, also castellated (open on written application).

Across the valley is Christ Church, Georgetown, built in 1857 (James S. Benest of Norwich). It is sometimes said that it was paid for by Robert Crawshay, but the truth is that he gave a measly £50. Beyond Cyfarthfa is **Cefncoedycymer**, where the Brecon and Merthyr Railway crossed the valley by means of the lofty, curving stone viaduct, built in 1866 by H. Conybeare and A. Sutherland. Here the A470 crosses the Heads of the Valleys Road near the so-called 'Swiss Church' with its quirky spire (mid-Victorian). A little further east the A465 crosses the Taf Fechan on a splendid concrete bridge of 1964 (Rendel, Palmer and Tritton, engineers), reminiscent of the great Swiss bridges of Maillart.

The A470 goes up past the Taf Fawr reservoirs and over the side of the Brecon Beacons to Brecon (see p. 45). Just the other side of the A465, a minor road goes off north-east through housing estates towards Faenor (or **Vaynor**). After a mile, the road winds under, then over the railway, and climbs up to a most extraordinary house, called **Hy Brasail**, which looks like a stray from Italy. It has a four-storey tower, a wing with an open arcaded ground floor, and a big monkey puzzle. The church of Faenor lies off the road, above the wooded valley. The peace and beauty of the country round here are in striking contrast with Merthyr, only a mile away. The nasty church was built in 1868. In the churchyard Robert Crawshay (d. 1879) is buried, beneath a great stone slab, into which is set, in iron letters, the inscription GOD FORGIVE ME. As Crawshay was a remarkably unpleasant character, who bullied his family as much as he tyrannized over his workers, it was generally considered to be an appropriate prayer.

The road beyond Faenor goes on through Pontsticill and past the **Taf Fechan Reservoir**, with its conifers and entertaining straining-tower, and marvellous views up to the Beacons, before climbing over the shoulder of the Beacons at Torpantau (p. 43). The return to Merthyr can be made by going back past Hy Brasail, over the railway, and then turning left down in the valley. The road crosses the river at an idyllic spot, whose picturesqueness is heightened by the splendid stone Pontsarn railway viaduct, built (like the one at Cefn-coedycymer) in 1866 by Conybeare and Sutherland. The road climbs beneath a hill which has been extensively quarried for limestone. On the top is **Morlais Castle**. It was built by Earl Gilbert de Clare, but led to a dispute with de Bohun, Earl of Hereford, who complained in 1289 that it had been built on his land. A local war resulted. De Clare no doubt counted on the support of Edward I, who was his father-in-law, but the astute king used the squabble as an opportunity severely to curtail the power of the marcher lords. The site, at over 1200 feet, is magnificent. Parts of the defences consist of great ditches cut out of the limestone. The ruins have not been excavated, although considerable remains of walls and towers survive. They include one strikingly beautiful fragment, a twelve-sided crypt with its vaulted roof supported on a central pillar. It is less than a mile from here back to the A465.

The A4102 leads up from the centre of Merthyr to join the Heads of the Valleys Road as it climbs up on to bare moorland, reaching a height of 1178 feet at the site of the Dynevor Arms. Here the B4276 leads straight down into Aberdare, while the A465 goes down towards Hirwaun.

It was at **Hirwaun**, situated in the broad upper part of the Cynon valley, that coke was first used in South Wales to fire a blast furnace, instead of charcoal. This was in 1757, at a furnace set up by John Maybery (from Worcestershire). The ironworks here belonged from 1819 to the Crawshays. In the great riots of 1831, the men of Hirwaun soaked their flag in calf's blood – the first time the red flag was used as the banner of revolt in Britain.

From Hirwaun, the A4059 leads down the valley to **Aberdare**. Aberdare feels very different from Merthyr, as the valley is more open, and the industry is mostly scattered round the outskirts, so that the centre feels more like a market town. It developed as an ironmaking town a little later than Merthyr. The Aberdare Canal, which joins the Glamorganshire at Abercynon, was authorized in 1793, but only opened in 1812. The Aberdare Railway, joining the Taff Vale at Abercynon, opened in 1846. But the town's greatest period of expansion came with the coal-boom in the mid nineteenth century. The district produced the finest steam coal in the world – over 2,000,000 tons of it every year by 1869. The population doubled every ten years from 1831 to 1861, and by 1871 it was three-quarters the size of Merthyr.

Where the Hirwaun road enters Aberdare, at Trecynon, a road goes off right to **Cwmdare**. The head of the Dare valley has recently been reclaimed from the effects of coal-mining and laid out as a country park. A little further along Hirwaun Road is Aberdare Park: down Meirion Street, opposite, is what is probably the most interesting feature to survive from the town's ironmaking past. It is an attractively simple iron bridge, built in 1811 to carry over the river Cynon the tramroad which linked the ironworks with the canal.

In the centre of Aberdare, the old church of St John stands in a pleasant churchyard by the main road. Basically twelfth century, it has been much renewed. Just beyond, up to the right, is the plain but handsome Capel Siloa, rebuilt in 1855, in whose vestry hall Henry Richard's election campaign was planned in 1868. Near by, on a low hill, stands St Elvan's Church, built in 1852–3 by A. Moseley, a poor Decorated effort with a lofty spire. In Victoria Square, below the church, a statue of 'Caradog' – Griffith Rhys Jones (1834–97) – by Goscombe John, shows him with baton raised, as if about to conduct his famous South Wales Choral Union, *Y Côr Mawr*, of 456 voices, which won the choral competitions at the Crystal Palace in 1872 and 1873.

North-east of Aberdare, on the hillside, is **Abernant**, where there was an ironworks. Its proprietors put up in the 1850s a small housing estate which formed a remarkable case of social stratification, with the lowest terrace called Agents' Row, and higher terraces, of smaller houses, called Engineers' Row, Foremans' Row, and Colliers' Row. From Aberdare, the A4059 follows the west side of the valley through Aberaman (with the colliery town of Cwmaman up the narrow valley to the west), while the B4275 follows the east side through Cwmbach. Between the two roads is a huge patent fuel works.

Three miles down is **Mountain Ash**, a typical mining town, famous for its choir and band. Many of the emigrants to Patagonia (see *North Wales*, p. 225) came from here, and it was hard hit in the Depression. Deep Duffryn Colliery (started in 1850) is still working, but the famous Nixon's Navigation (begun in the early 1860s) closed in 1968.

The A4059 goes down to Abercynon by way of the wooded east side of the valley, but it is well worth following the B4275 down the west side instead, as it passes through typical mining communities such as Penrhiwceibr, with rows of terraced houses, chapels and several vast Workingmen's Institutes. At Abercynon the Taff valley and A470 are rejoined.

RHONDDA

The two Rhondda valleys – Rhondda Fawr and Rhondda Fach – are the most famous in South Wales. This is due, not just to the excellence and profusion of the coal they produced, but to the character and spirit of the diverse people who flocked to them in such numbers in the great coal boom of the second half of the nineteenth century and the first decade of the twentieth. Before the mid nineteenth century, the valleys were almost deserted: as late as 1848 a traveller wrote of Rhondda Fawr, 'the people of this solitudinous and happy valley are a pastoral race, almost entirely dependent on their flocks and herds for support . . . The air is aromatic with wild flowers, and mountain plants – a sabbath stillness reigns'.

Soon collieries were opening up and down the valleys, and the characteristic linear townships were springing up – linear, because the narrowness of the valleys forced them to develop lengthwise. The townships, known as 'villages', run into one another, and the stranger finds it hard to distinguish one from another, but the inhabitants are fiercely proud of their separateness. The long lines of terrace houses usually run parallel to the contours, but are varied by some set on a slope, the ridge lines of their roofs snaking up and down hill without a break, and others at right angles to the contours, the variety producing intriguing visual patterns. The two-storey houses are built of undressed grey, brown, or black stone, and the trim is of brick or of dressed stone, brightly painted, each house in a different colour – individuality has to be expressed somehow. Eighty-six per cent of the houses are owned by their occupiers. Of the in-numerable chapels, proudly built with the congregation's subscrip-tions, many are now derelict, converted, or for sale. There always were comparatively few churches, but many are now demolished. Nearly all consisted of nave and chancel with bellcote, and were large and dull. There are plenty of pubs, and occasional giant Working-men's Institutes, four or five storeys high. There are surprising numbers of Conservative Clubs and monkey-puzzles.

Not a single colliery is still working in either Rhondda valley, apart from Maerdy in Rhondda Fach. All the others have been dis-mantled, so the valleys have inevitably lost much of their special character. The sites of the collieries, in mid-valley, are now marked by great blank spaces – sometimes occupied by new factories, sometimes derelict, sometimes reclaimed as grass 'play areas'. Less easy to dispose of are the great tips piled up the hillsides, although the Aberfan disaster has hastened efforts in this direction.

Pontypridd is the 'gateway to Rhondda'. The A4058 leads up the valley, past a surviving colliery, to Porth, where the two valleys separate. As there is also a valley running south-west, containing the township of Cymer, the convergence of four valleys, each built up, produces a remarkable effect of town spreading in all directions. The A4058 follows Rhondda Fawr. Two miles from Porth, the A4119 comes up from Tonyrefail (p. 266), through Penygraig, from where there is a splendid view ahead up the valley before the road comes down the hill into **Tonypandy**. The name recalls the great miners' strike of 1910, when Churchill, as Home Secretary, ordered the troops in to deal with 'riots' here.

At Llwyn-y-pia the valley bends to the west, and then runs straight for six miles up to its head. Beyond Ystrad is **Pentre**, which has far the grandest church in Rhondda. Built 1888–91, it was paid for by Griffith Llewellyn of Baglan Hall, a prominent local landowner. Like Penyfai (p. 282), it was designed by Kempson and Fowler, in thirteenth-century style.

The next township is Treorchy, famous for its male voice choir. From here the A4061 runs south-west up above Cwmparc, where the miners' tradition of breeding fine whippets survives, and climbs, by spectacular hairpins, over to the Ogmore Valley (p. 266). These inter-valley roads are fine feats of engineering, and always give amazing views (in the right weather). Two miles beyond Treorchy is **Treherbert**, where the Bute family owned land. Further on is **Blaenrhondda**, where collieries stood right at the head of the valley, below the towering sandstone cliffs of Pen Pych. West of Pen Pych, above Blaen-y-cwm, are the waterfalls of Berw Nant-yr-Ychain.

Back at Treherbert, the A4061 climbs round a big hairpin and then goes along above the upper part of the valley to reach a height of 1581 feet. The views back are stunning. The mountain-top is wild moorland. A mile north-west of the summit is **Graig y Llyn** (1969 feet), the highest mountain in Glamorgan. Below its steep, north-facing cliffs are two lakes, Llyn Fach and Llyn Fawr. The road comes down (enjoying huge views over Breconshire) by zigzags, passing close to **Llyn Fawr**, now a reservoir among conifers. When it was drained, to make the reservoir, a remarkable collection of prehistoric metalwork was found, including bronze axes, a bronze cauldron, and a wrought-iron sickle (now in the National Museum), also hewn timbers which may possibly have belonged to a lake settlement. A mile below the lake is a colliery which is still operating.

The A4061 comes down to join the Heads of the Valleys Road (A465) a mile west of Hirwaun (p. 261). Follow the A4059 down into Aberdare (p. 261), and then, in the town centre, take the B4277, which climbs very steeply straight up the mountainside, out of the town, and then zig zags up on to the top. The views over Aberdare are splendid. After a couple of miles of moorland and forestry, all over 1200 feet, the view over the Rhondda Fach suddenly opens out – and, of course, hills beyond and beyond. The head of the valley is black with mine spoil. The road comes down into **Maerdy** – locally known as 'Little Moscow' – whose tiny church is utterly dwarfed by the colossal Workmen's Institute. The townships of Ferndale, Tylorstown, Pontygwaith, Wattstown, and Ynyshir lead back to Porth (p. 263).

The return to the Taff valley can be excitingly varied by taking the minor road which goes up east from **Ferndale**, and then climbs steeply south-east up the side of the valley onto the hill-top. It enters the vast St Gwynno Forest, and, two and a half miles from Ferndale, reaches **Llanwonno**, where church and pub keep each other company at a height of 1100 feet. This ancient parish church of a huge area was rebuilt by Halliday in 1893–4. The return can be made either straight down to Pontypridd, or by way of the mining valley of Ynysybwl.

CARDIFF TO THE WESTERN VALLEYS

The A4119 goes out from Cardiff through Llandaff. Three miles beyond Llandaff a minor road goes north to **Pentyrch**, a hilly village, whose characterful church, rebuilt in 1853–7 by John Prichard, has an elaborate octagonal bell-turret. Half a mile south-west of Pentyrch (also accessible by the next turning right along the A4119) is **Craig-y-parc**, a delightful house of 1913–18 by C. E. Mallows, one of the best domestic architects of his time (now a Spastics Society School).

A little further on, **Capel Llanilltern** stands beside the main road. Nicely situated among trees, this little chapel was built in 1862 for the Windsor family, as a chapel of ease to St Fagan's, by G. E. Street. It is an excellent example of his work, and has a richly-fitted interior. It is four miles from here to **Llantrisant**, a remarkably striking place, as it is a real hill-town, with church and castle right at the top, and the town tumbling down the hillside. The hills to west and east of the church are fortunately still bare. Much new development has taken place recently, particularly since the Royal Mint moved here from London in the 1960s. As so much of it, being on the slope of the hill, is very visible, it is a pity that its quality is poor. The windswept church looks out over the whole Vale of Glamorgan. It has a squat sixteenth-century west tower, and the rest was much restored in 1873 by John Prichard. His restoration is commemorated by the glass in the east window, by Burne-Jones and Morris – a beautiful Crucifixion. It commemorates his ancestors, the Prichards of Collenna. The south chancel windows are excellent Clayton and Bell.

East of the church is a grassy open space, in front of the castle. All that remains is the ruined Tower of the Raven, completely covered in ivy, and the tree-lined ramparts which now surround a neat vegetable garden. Nearby is the small, plain Guildhall, built in 1773 by Lord Mountstuart. The town was a medieval borough, receiving its charter in 1346. But in spite of a certain amount of early industrialization it remained a quiet market town. Its winding, narrow streets are a paradise for connoisseurs of townscape.

The hill west of the town, known as Caerlan Fields, was where Dr William Price (see p. 253) attempted in 1884 to cremate the body of his illegitimate son Iesu Grist, who had died aged five months. A furious crowd almost burnt Price instead, but the police rescued him. Two months later, his second attempt at the cremation succeeded, as a result of which he was prosecuted, but acquitted. He himself was cremated, on his death in 1893, at the same place, in front of a huge audience. It was the first public cremation in Britain.

From Llantrisant, the A473 goes north-east to Pontypridd, and west towards Bridgend. Half a mile west, the A4119 runs north up the Ely valley, which soon narrows, the Coedely colliery heralding the approach of Tonyrefail, a workaday little town. From here the A4119 leads over to Rhondda Fawr (p. 263), while the A4093 goes due west. One and a half miles from Tonyrefail, the A4164 runs up north to **Gilfach Goch**, a completely enclosed valley town. The road runs around the edge in a loop, with the terraced houses and chapels along it. The mines were in the middle, but a massive reclamation scheme has removed all trace of them, and instead there is now a huge area of grass. Thousands of trees are being planted, some donated by the publishers of Richard Llewellyn's famous novel *How Green Was My Valley*. Gilfach Goch was the setting for the book. It is an extraordinary transformation. The houses appear to have lost their *raison d'être*: some, at the top, are even falling derelict. Will the valley end up by being bare once again? Llewellyn has published a sequel to his novel called *Green, Green My Valley Now*.

Further on, the A4093 becomes quite countrified, and the deep wooded Ogwr (Ogmore) Fach valley opens out on the left. The road comes down to join the A4061 at **Blackmill**, where the Ogwr Fach joins the Ogwr Fawr. Half a mile up the valley, an inter-valley road (A4093) goes over west to Cwm Garw which has lots of character – a strong sense of enclosure from its narrowness and the fact that it is a cul-de-sac. A colliery still operates at Ffaldau. The valley is built up right to the head, but beyond the last terrace the hills beckon the walker.

By comparison, **Ogmore Vale**, back over the hill, is much less satisfying. Here again a colliery is still working, at Pricetown. The inter-valley road which links Ogmore Vale with both Rhondda and the Afan valley, constructed between the Wars, is one of the most spectacular in South Wales. At the head of the Vale it climbs beneath towering cliffs by means of a great diagonal hairpin. From the mountain-top, the A4061 goes down to Treorchy, doing another big zigzag beneath the curved cliffs at the head of Cwmparc, while the A4107 climbs still higher to the west on to the narrow mountain-shoulder, reaching a height of over 1700 feet.

Over the top, a picnic area overlooks the Afan valley, appropriately provided by the Forestry Commission, since such vast areas of hill-top in this district have been afforested. The road comes down into the little town of **Blaengwynfi**, and follows the winding valley round to **Cymmer**, passing some oak woodland which provides a refreshing change from the conifers. Cymmer is an extraordinarily up and down and criss-cross place, with its road bridges and railway viaducts, and houses right up the hill to the south. North from here runs the short Corrwg valley, with **Glyncorrwg** at its head, a neat and regular little mining-town which is the wettest place in Glamorgan.

Beyond Cymmer, the narrow Afan valley winds between wooded slopes. Three miles down, at Afan Argoed, the Forestry Commission has set up a Countryside Centre. At **Pont-rhyd-y-fen** the splendid great stone aqueduct (Bont Fawr) was built in 1827 by John Reynolds to supply water for the blast furnaces of his copper-works. The B4287 follows the Pelenna valley north-west over the hills to Neath (p. 287). Below Pont-rhyd-y-fen, the Afan valley opens out, and there, grandly rising from the valley floor, is a tall and slender spire of unusual outline. This is the new church, All Saints', built at **Cwmafan** in 1855 by Prichard and Seddon. It has a very tall nave, lit by a west window of original design, a choir lit by circular windows (with the spire above it), and a lofty sanctuary lit by lancets. The church faces down an old tramway, and near by is an old stone bridge of three arches, collapsing into the river. The neat little town is spread out on the flat valley floor between steeply-rounded hills. Although there were also collieries, it was chiefly a metal-making town, and a huge flue, 1200 feet long, led up to a chimney on the summit of Foel (1218 feet), the hill north of the town, in order to carry copper-smelting fumes well away.

From Cwmafan, both the A4107 and the B4286 lead down, on opposite sides of the river, to Port Talbot (p. 286), in just over a mile. From the A4107, the B4282 leads east over the hills to **Maesteg**, where it meets the A4063, coming over from Cymmer (above) through the mining valley of Caerau. Maesteg, a sizeable town, was once the site of ironworks, but later developed as the centre of the colliery district of the Llynfi valley. A mile down the A4063 from the town, a minor road goes off right and up to the hill-village of **Llangynwyd**. The place is chiefly famous because of the pathetic tale of the 'Maid of Cefn Ydfa'. The story goes that Ann Thomas, born in 1704, was heiress to Cefn Ydfa. A poet-plasterer called Wil Hopcyn worked on the house and they fell in love. Ann's mother wanted her to marry a rich young lawyer, so she was locked up in a cellar, while Wil wrote the famous song, *Bugeilio'r Gwenith Gwyn* (Watching the Wheat). Some versions even have Ann writing letters in blood to Wil – either her own, or taken from the cat's ear. Ann married the lawyer, and Wil went off to Bristol. Ann produced a daughter, who died, and within two years was herself on the point of death. Mother and husband begged Wil (who had returned opportunely) to comfort her, but she died in his arms.

Alas, the tragic tale is almost complete fiction. Ann Thomas existed, and married the lawyer Anthony Maddocks, and did die two years later. So did Wil Hopcyn exist. But there is no evidence that he was in love with her, and it is not certain that he even wrote the song in question. It is a pity that such a beautiful composition – whose contents do not even correspond with the supposed situation – should have become overlaid with so much mawkish sentiment.

Here is the first verse (in Mrs Pendril Llewelyn's translation):

> A simple youthful swain am I,
>   Who loves at fancy's pleasure;
> I fondly watch the blooming wheat,
>   And other reaps the treasure:
> Oh! wherefore still despise my suit,
>   Why pining keep thy lover?
> For some new charm, thou matchless fair,
>   I day by day discover.

Five miles below Maesteg, the Llynfi valley meets the Ogwr at Aberkenfig. From here it is two miles south to Bridgend (p. 282), while the A4065 runs east, crossing the Garw (p. 266) just at its confluence with the Ogwr, and then crossing the Ogwr to meet the A4061 (p. 266) at Bryncethin. At the junction, the B4280 runs east across Hirwaun Common to join the A473 at Pencoed (p. 270). Three miles east along this road is **Llanharan**. Like many villages in this part of the country, it was a quiet place until the mines were opened at the end of the last century, but then expanded enormously. It has a nice little church of 1858 by Prichard and Seddon, with a square bellcote. Just beyond the village, Llanharan House is set proudly up above the road in a big park. It is a handsome stone building, early eighteenth century, to which pedimented wings were added later. Two miles beyond Llanharan is Llantrisant (p. 265).

THE VALE OF GLAMORGAN

The vale does not feel like a vale in the usual sense. Except on clear days, when you can see across the Channel to Exmoor, and up to the Brecon Beacons, there is no sense of being enclosed by higher land. It is rich, rolling land, much sought after for housing and air-fields, as well as for farming, on which its prosperity has traditionally depended. The villages are much more like English 'nucleated' villages than in most parts of Wales. Castles and manor houses are frequent. Churches are so numerous that many get no mention, while chapels form a comparatively inconspicuous feature of the scene. English, or hybrid, place-names and family names are common.

The late Cardiff Rural District Council is to be congratulated on confining new housing, both private and council, to the villages (many of which have been declared Conservation Areas), and insisting on white, thus giving some cohesion. Similarly those responsible for the roads have done something rare in Britain – improved a few, and left tight lanes between big thorn hedges. The A48, the main road west, is a roaring barrier through the Vale, not easy to cross.

NORTH OF THE A48

Leaving Cardiff either by way of St Fagan's (p. 247), or by Fairwater Road, it is surprising how quickly one is in deeply rural country. Two miles out of the city is **St Bride's-super-Ely**, whose church, hidden away among trees, has a saddle-back tower and a Norman door and (recut) chancel arch. The lovely seventeenth-century Madonna over the altar was brought from Italy in 1969, to replace a medieval figure destroyed at the Reformation. It is worth going down the lane south to **St George's**, not so much to see the scanty remains of the medieval castle (incorporated in a later house), or the cruciform church, with its odd central tower of 1886, as to experience the level crossing, on the main line west from Cardiff. Before opening the gates, the keeper has to telephone to see if a train is coming.

Just over a mile south-west of St Bride's is **Peterston-super-Ely**, whose church has a big buttressed fifteenth-century tower. A little beyond it, a pretty timber bridge leads across the river Ely into **Glyn Cory** (also called Wyndham Park), a model village established by the Cory family in 1910. It was intended for Cardiff commuters. The estate plan was made by Thomas Adams, in consultation with T. H. Mawson. The only part of architectural interest is the terrace in Pwll-i-Min Crescent, said to have been designed by M. H. Baillie Scott. It is remarkable for its date (1908), since the style can only be described as 'modernistic'.

Opposite Glyn Cory, a road leads due north, under the railway. Turn left at the next crossroads, across the Ely valley, then right, then left, and ahead is **Hensol Castle**, now a Mental Hospital. This fascinating building would repay further study. An older building is said to have been enlarged *c.* 1735 by Lord Chancellor Talbot, who had married the heiress. His son added to the house, which later passed to the Lords Dynevor, and then to Benjamin Hall, the industrialist and father of Lord Llanover (see p. 184), and eventually to Rowland Fothergill, the Aberdare ironmaster. In about 1848 he called in Wyatt and Brandon to enlarge the castle with a profusion of elaborately turreted castellation. The main front is theirs, while the plainer side elevation, with pointed windows, is clearly eighteenth century.

A mile north of Hensol is **Miskin** (Meisgyn), a pleasant village, set above a wooded valley, but growing fast. From here the B4264 runs west to join the B4270 (from Llantrisant to Cowbridge). Three miles down this road is **Ystradowen**, which has a delightful little church of 1861 by Prichard and Seddon. Two miles south is Cowbridge (p. 280). The town is bypassed on the north by the A48. Two miles north-west **Penllyn Castle** stands up above the road on the top of a ridge. It consists of an eighteenth-century house, with some Victorian additions, but a medieval tower with herringbone masonry survives at the back. The gardens are sometimes open: the 'wild' parts are particularly delightful. The old parish church of Penllyn is Llanfrynach, on the other side of the A48 (see p. 280). One and a half miles north-west of Penllyn, reached by a maze of lanes, is **Llangan**, a quiet little village well worth a visit for the sake of the two crosses in its churchyard. One is a well-preserved fifteenth-century cross: at the head of the shaft is the Crucifixion, with a Pietà on the reverse, and above is a hexagon with six saints in niches. The other cross, under a little roof at the west end of the church, dates from the ninth century. It is a big, low wheel-cross, bearing a crude representation of the Crucifixion with two figures, one holding a spear.

A mile due north of Llangan, as the crow flies (a good deal further for non-crows) is **St Mary Hill**, in nicely pastoral country, where the much-restored church stands right on top of the hill. It too has a fifteenth-century churchyard cross, but much less well preserved than Llangan. Due west of here, on the A473, is **Coychurch**, whose late-thirteenth-century church is so grand that it is known as the 'Cathedral of the Vale'. Unfortunately the central tower collapsed in 1877, destroying the south transept: both were rebuilt in rather harsh masonry. The lofty nave arcades are especially fine, and the fifteenth-century roof is ornamented with figures of angels (some of them excellent Victorian work).

Just beyond Coychurch, turn right on the B4181, and, when it goes left under the railway, keep straight on to **Coity**. To explore the castle (DoE), go first to the Key Keeper's Residence – a perky house with coloured glass in the porch, on the way to the church (i.e. the far side from the castle entrance). The circular inner ward and keep are late Norman, built by the Turberville family. In the thirteenth century the high round tower was added to protect the wall by cross fire, and the east gatehouse was built. The big outer ward was added in the fourteenth century and this may have helped in the long siege the castle withstood against Glendower's troops. The Tudors domesticated it further, their chief mark being the tall chimney.

About this time Sir Edward Stradling (see p. 278) arranged the marriage of the sole heiress, Barbara Gamage, to Sir Philip Sidney's brother Robert. Three volumes of letters between the pair survive. The wedding took place speedily in St Donat's church for fear the queen might intervene (she was not pleased). Barbara spent much of her life at Penshurst and the Sidneys held Coity until the eighteenth century.

St Mary's Church is a big aisleless cruciform fourteenth-century building with a low tower over the vaulted crossing. Inside it is light and spare with the chancel washed blue like a dairy. The east window is a beautiful and unusual early work of the Morris firm, installed in 1863. The borders and pattern-work were designed by Philip Webb, and the figures by Peter Paul Marshall. Marshall was a sanitary engineer by profession, but this is a lovely piece of work. The small fourteenth-century effigies on either side of the altar commemorate Turbervilles. There are other interesting memorials but by far the most enjoyable is a tablet on the east wall of the south transept, difficult to see on account of the safe there. It is to Joan William, wife of David Howell, who died in 1710 aged 84. It reads:

R
AWAKe DVLL MORTALS SEE Y DVBIOVS STAY
FRAIL IS OVR MAKE & LIFE SOON POSTS AWAY
MYRIADS OF CHANCeS TAKe AWAY OUR BREATH
AND MULTIFACIOUVS WAYS THERe ARe TO DeATH
BeNEATH ONe LIeS eSTEeMD FOR LIFe AND AGe
                                        STAGe
BY THVNDeR FORC,D TO QUITT THIS WORLDLY
TReMeNDOVS DeATH SO SUDDENLY TO Be
                                            Y
FROM LIFe,S SHORT SCeNE MOVeD TO eTERNIT

It is a mile from Coity to the A4061, and a mile south on that road into Bridgend (p. 282).

PENARTH AND BARRY

Penarth Road goes out from Cardiff across the reclaimed marshland between the Taff and Ely rivers. Soon after it crosses the Ely, a lane goes up right to join the A4055 near the church of **Llandough**. The present building is a rather nasty thing, with an attenuated saddleback tower, built in 1866 by Fripp of Bristol. It is dedicated to St Dochdwy, who founded a monastery here in the sixth century. Llandough, Llancarfan (p. 275), and Llantwit Major (p. 276) were the three most important Celtic religious houses in Glamorgan.

Penarth was a little village in the middle of the last century, with a population of under a hundred. Then, in 1859, docks (now closed) were built at the mouth of the Ely, to take pressure off the overcrowded Cardiff docks. Terraced housing was built immediately behind for the workers. Soon after came the development of the place, under the aegis of the Windsor family, the principal landowners, as a select residential suburb of Cardiff and as a genteel seaside resort. Up on the headland is St Augustine's Church. The tiny old church was replaced in 1865–6, at the expense of Lady Windsor, with one of William Butterfield's finest churches. It cost £10,000. The tough exterior is in grey Radyr stone. Its tall saddleback tower is in striking contrast with the humble one it replaced. The interior is an extraordinary exercise in geometrical polychromy. The characteristic fittings include a splendid reredos. The view is magnificent, over the whole of Cardiff, with Castell Coch clearly visible in the Taff gorge. In the churchyard is buried Joseph Parry (1841–1903). Born at Merthyr, he was a pit-boy at nine, and an ironworker at twelve, but became first Professor of Music at University College, Aberystwyth. His numerous compositions include the Welsh opera *Blodwen* and the famous hymn-tune *Aberystwyth*.

From the church, Albert Road leads into the town centre. In Windsor Road is the Windsor Arcade (1898), similar to those of Cardiff. Windsor Terrace and Beach Road lead down to the esplanade, formed in the 1880s by Lord Windsor. The pier has a pavilion with a slightly Moorish character. Above the Esplanade are terraced gardens, and higher up stand the large and elaborate mansions of the coal-owners and shipping magnates, in wooded grounds. The atmosphere of this part of Penarth remains strongly and evocatively Victorian.

Opposite the Station, in Plymouth Road, is the **Turner House Art Gallery** (Seward and Thomas, 1888), built by James Pyke Thompson to house his collection, and now a branch of the National Museum. Across the railway, Victoria Street leads to Victoria Square, where next to the dull All Saints' Church stands the **Parish Hall**, by J. Coates Carter (who also designed the church), built in 1906. With its rough stonework, its circular turret with a conical roof, its recessed doorway under a broad semicircular hood, it could almost be by H. H. Richardson. Carter also designed several houses in Penarth, the most interesting being Red House, further down Victoria Road. It was built for himself and his Swiss wife, and has a slightly Swiss air, especially on the garden side.

Two miles south of Penarth, reached by a lane off the B4267, is **Lavernock**, whose little church (rebuilt in 1852) stands near Lavernock Point. A plaque commemorates the fact that the first message ever transmitted by means of wireless telegraphy across water was sent between Flat Holm, the island three and a half miles offshore, and here, in 1897, by Guglielmo Marconi and G. S. Kemp (of Cardiff). The cliffs around this part of the coast are of great geological interest: towards Penarth is an old alabaster quarry.

From Lavernock, it is three miles to **Barry**, which is reached more directly from Cardiff by the A4055 (through Dinas Powis). Barry is one of the most astonishing examples of mushroom growth in Britain. In 1881 the population was 500; in 1891 it was 12,665. It is not too much of an over-simplification to say that this was the result of one man's quarrel. The man was David Davies of Llandinam (see *North Wales*, p. 301), and his quarrel was with the Marquess of Bute and his agents, over their refusal to improve both communications down the Taff valley and dock facilities at Cardiff, as Davies and his fellow Rhondda coal-owners wanted. Davies decided to build his own docks at Barry, and succeeded, despite fierce opposition. The first was begun in 1884, and completed in 1889 (engineers John Wolfe Barry, Thomas Forster Brown, and Henry Mark Brunel). It cost over £2 million, and was at the time the largest in the world. Already in 1889 over one million tons of coal and coke were exported, in 1894 nearly five million, and in 1913 (by which time further docks had been added) over eleven million – more than from anywhere else in the world.

Curiously enough, the development of Barry Island, immediately west of the docks, as a holiday resort, went on simultaneously with the development of the docks. Needless to say, with the decline in the coal trade, the docks have lost custom, and bananas are now its

staple fare. Not surprisingly, Barry has little to offer to the archi-
tecturally-minded tourist. Its situation on the side of the hill, and its
fairly spacious layout, are advantages, but the overwhelming impression is of endless quantities of red pressed brick. In front of the
grandiose Port Building (A. E. Bell, 1898) stands Alfred Gilbert's
statue of David Davies, a duplicate of the one at Llandinam.

Beside the main road (A4055) where it comes down close to the
docks, in the west part of the town, is a railway yard which contains
what must be the biggest graveyard of steam engines in Britain. The
rows of rusting black monsters are a poignant sight. Perhaps 'graveyard' is not quite the word, as this is where the enthusiasts who reopen
lines come to choose their locomotives.

BETWEEN A48 AND THE COAST, WEST OF A4050

A4050 (the Barry road) and A4226 (near the coast) are the only
direct roads. The country between is meshed with lanes and only
negotiable with an O.S. map.

St Nicholas is the first village on the main road; great care has
been taken over its postwar council housing. Turn left in the village
for **Tinkinswood Burial Chamber** (2500–1900 BC). The path to it
leaves the road on the right about half a mile on. It has the funnel-
shaped entrance and kerb round the barrow of herringbone drystone
walling typical of the Severn-Cotswold long barrows, but it is chiefly
memorable for its low but gigantic capstone (40 tons).

Dyffryn House, one mile on, built in 1893, has large gardens,
originally laid out by T. H. Mawson (open to the public). Bear left at
the next corner and in the field on your right is **St Lythan's Burial
Chamber**, another long barrow, but here the barrow has been dug
away, leaving the cromlech splendidly isolated.

St Lythan's Church, further down the road, is reached through a
garden. A simple late medieval building restored by J. P. Seddon;
its south chapel is connected by two low, primitive arches supported by a huge pillar. By contrast there are several elegant but
diminutive wall tablets about the church. It is nicely lit by oil lamps
and the font is Norman.

This road brings you back to the A4050, the main Barry road,
where you turn right. South of the village at **Wenvoe Castle** (now a
golf club), only Henry Holland's fine stable courtyard (c. 1780)
survives.

Short of Barry, bear right on the A4226, which runs west a mile
or so inland from the Bristol Channel. Opposite Rhoose Airport

(civil), look out for signs to **Lower Porthkerry**. The first leads down under the big stone viaduct of the Vale of Glamorgan Railway (1894–8, designed by Sir James W. Szlumper), to a hidden flat-floored green valley on the shingly edge of the sea. It belongs to Barry and is now a miniature golf course. Alternatively take the turning from the main road which leads to the church (its bold tower can be seen from the corner), in an attractive spot with some cottages at the end of the lane. It is basically thirteenth century, with a plain screen *c*. 1500, and an unusual 1629 memorial in low relief on the north wall.

Beyond the church a path leads down through the woods close to the viaduct, to the valley. A pleasant grey house looks out over the low wooded cliffs towards Somerset, and beyond (west) are the remains of a promontory fort, the Bulwarks, built in the Iron Age, but reoccupied (possibly as a farmstead) in Roman times. Inland from Porthkerry, a mile the other side of the B4265, is **Penmark**, where, near the church, the much overgrown ruins of a medieval castle stand above a wooded valley.

Llancarfan, one mile north of Penmark, is an attractive village in a steep hollow with a stream running through it. The church, probably on the site of a sixth-century *clas*, is late thirteenth century, double-naved and light, with a grand early-sixteenth-century window in the north wall of the chancel; the arcade has simply carved capitals, while the reredos is a most intricate piece of perpendicular carving – once the canopy of choir stalls.

Back on A4226 the view ahead is dominated by the huge power station and cement works at **Aberthaw**, once a little port (the lime used by Smeaton for Eddystone Lighthouse came from here). The power station emits regular grunts like a methodical dinosaur, somewhat disconcerting to visitors to **Gileston**. (Turn left at the power station sign opposite St Athan RAF station.) Here you are suddenly in remote lanes again. The church, tucked in beside Gileston Manor, a charming stone house whose Georgian facade overlooks the Bristol Channel, is chiefly fifteenth century. It has a big south porch, with a remarkable timber door carved with armorial bearings of that date. Inside there is a good Giles monument, of 1724.

Flemingston Court (not open), one and a half miles north of B4265, beyond St Athan, is now a farmhouse. It was once fortified and has a fine Jacobean hall. Iolo Morganwg is buried in the churchyard beside the house.

Two miles west of St Athan, the B4265 passes through Boverton, where the gaunt ruins of the Manor House stand above the road.

Just beyond is **Llantwit Major**, or Llanilltud Fawr, a pleasant little town with a resounding ecclesiastical history. Its narrow streets wind up and down the hill, with the so-called Town Hall (it was never a borough) in the middle. The building is largely sixteenth century. Further down is **St Illtud's Church**. Here St Illtud founded a famous school in about AD 500. The site, in a sheltered valley near the sea but not visible from it, is similar to that of other Celtic religious settlements such as Bangor, Llanbadarn Fawr, and St Davids. The school came to an end with the arrival of the Normans, but the church remained collegiate until the Reformation. It is an amazing building, of enormous length, consisting of four linked sections: the chancel and nave (with aisles and west tower), which formed the collegiate church; the 'western', or parochial, church; and, at the extreme west, the Galilee Chapel, now in ruins. It was restored in 1888–1905 by G. E. Halliday. The eastern church has a large and elaborate fourteenth-century reredos (much restored), which goes from wall to wall. In the south aisle is a thirteenth-century niche, richly carved with a Jesse tree. There are wall-paintings dating from the thirteenth–fifteenth centuries. The western church has a splendid timber roof, and contains a fine collection of Celtic crosses and medieval tombs. The crosses include the Illtud cross-shaft, seven feet high, and decorated in knotwork; the wheel-cross of Houelt (ninth century); and the pillar of Samson (also ninth century). The ruin south of the churchyard was the house of a chantry priest.

The monastery is said to have stood above the church, to the west. The medieval gatehouse and dovecot here probably belonged to a monastic grange. The town contains a number of old houses, including the Old Swan Inn, and – finest of all – **Great House** (Ty Mawr), a big gabled house of stone, north of the town near the junction of the B4270 and B4265 (open on written application).

From Llantwit Major a minor road leads directly to **St Donat's Castle** (now Atlantic College), on the coast two miles west. It is open on Sunday afternoons in July and August and on August Bank Holiday. The earliest features of the present castle date from 1300, when its de Hawey heiress married Peter de Stradling. He had come from Switzerland in the train of Otto de Grandison, whom Edward I had made Justiciary and Keeper of North Wales, thus, with James of St George, Master of the King's Works, making at least three Swiss to have important influence in Wales at that time. The last male heir of this outstanding family died over four hundred years later in 1738. The castle then passed to cousins. In 1862 it was bought and partly restored by Dr Nicholl-Carne, and in 1901 by Morgan

Williams of Aberpergwm (p. 290), who employed first Thomas Garner, and then, after his death in 1906, G. F. Bodley. Williams was followed in 1925 by Randolph Hearst, the American newspaper millionaire, an avid collector, particularly of medieval items. Thanks to the finances of *Good Housekeeping* and other popular journals, he imported an astonishing medley of the Middle Ages, including actual buildings. His architect was Sir Charles Allom who had re-decorated parts of Buckingham Palace.

The castle is built to a concentric plan with an inner bailey protected by a dry moat and strong outer and inner curtain walls, most of which is early fourteenth century.

Once in the courtyard the atmosphere changes dramatically. You are now in the heart of a peaceful Tudor manor house. The terracotta roundels are part of the set at Hampton Court given by the Pope to Wolsey, representing Roman Emperors and their wives. To your left, on the south side of the courtyard, is the great hall of 1450–1500, reached by the Stradling entrance, a Tudor door with a pretty oriel window above. The other buildings round the courtyard are early sixteenth century, except that immediately to the right of the gate-house. This is contemporary with the hall, but the little oriel and bell turret are nineteenth-century embellishments. The great hall has its original fine chimneypiece and Tudor ceiling.

From here on historical confusion reigns, and the wonder is that it all fits together so comfortably. Morgan Williams had already raised the roof of the west wing when Hearst gutted it for new and grander schemes. The first floor was one long room for his collections (now the college library). Below he created a large dining-room and an ante-room. The chimneypiece in the ante-room came from the Prior's lodging at Bradenstoke Priory (Wiltshire). Its splendid ceiling, like that in the grand dining-hall ahead, is said to have come from Boston Parish Church. The fifteenth-century stone screen came from a Devon church and the fireplace perhaps from France.

The Bradenstoke Hall, behind the Great Hall, was erected in 1937 in place of Morgan Williams's library (its panelling may have gone to St Simeon, California). Its roof (*c.* 1320) came from Bradenstoke Priory; the windows from the Prior's lodgings.

Hearst remodelled the apartments to the north of the courtyard. The eighteenth-century panelling in this part came from the north wing; the 'plaster' ceiling is in fact of copper. They were for use by himself on his rare visits and by Margaret Davies, the film star, who virtually ran St Donat's. The constant stream of visitors included film stars and politicians from Europe and America. Lloyd George was present at an eisteddfod here. There were a hundred bells on the bellboard and telephones in every room including the summer houses.

The south-facing terraced gardens step down the valley towards the sea sheltered on each side by wooded slopes. The Queen's Beasts in the 'Tudor' garden were put there by Morgan Williams; the rose garden below was praised by the Elizabethan poet Thomas Leyshon; Hearst's swimming pool is on the site of the jousting ground; and the range of ruined stables were those of the royalist cavalry during the Civil War. There are walks along the low cliffs but one is warned that they are liable to fall.

The **Parish Church** is tucked down in the valley to the west of the castle. The ruins here are the remains of the parsonage and other houses demolished by Morgan Williams, who had bought St Donat's because both collieries and people were too close to Aberpergwm. It is a modest little building whose glory is the splendid tombs in the Stradling Chapel, particularly the fine early-seventeenth-century monument to Edward Stradling and his wife. There is also a remarkable series of paintings on wood, commissioned by Sir Edward in 1590, depicting himself and other members of the family, and a big altar tomb commemorating the last Sir Thomas.

From Marcross, one mile west of St Donat's, a road, tolled for the last part, runs down a little valley to the cliff at **Nash Point**. Fearful wrecks have occurred here, hence the two lighthouses (the earlier, 1832, by J. Nelson) and there are remains of a promontory fort, but it is the cliffs themselves which are really extraordinary. The limestone is so neatly stratified that they look like a man-made wall, and at low tide you can see them stepping out to sea ('wave-cut platforms').

Back on B4265, you can continue west for St Bride's Major (below), but agriculturally-minded antiquarians may first wish to see one of the so-called 'pigsties' of which a few survive in Glamorgan and Monmouthshire. It is beside the farmhouse called Downs (951/701), at which permission should be asked. It is not beautiful, roughly circular, about seven feet across, with a stone corbelled roof like the beehive huts in Ireland, and with a low doorway. There is another at Heol-y-march near Welsh St Donat's.

The church at **St Bride's Major** contains medieval tombs of the Boteler (Butler) family, including one with recumbent effigies beneath an ogival canopy, and later monuments to the Wyndhams. Both families lived at **Dunraven Castle**, one and a half miles due south, spectacularly sited in a sloping park right on the precipitous coast. It was demolished after the War. The B4524 leads from St

Bride's round the coast. The cliffs of Dunraven Bay recall those of Gower.

At **Southerndown**, just where the road goes left, is the Welsh Sunshine Home for Blind Babies, built as the Dunraven Arms Hotel in 1852–3. It was one of the first buildings designed by John Pollard Seddon: he was given the commission by an uncle. Rather clumsy, it has been altered (e.g. by the addition of the verandah and the wing on the left), but it is interesting as a very early example of tough High Victorian Gothic.

The road goes on through Ogmore-by-Sea, and then turns northeast to follow the Ogmore estuary, overlooking Merthyr Mawr Warren and the caravan rash of Porthcawl. Beside the road is **Ogmore Castle** (DoE), a stronghold of the Norman de Londres family, with a mighty twelfth-century keep, as well as later work. It is beautifully situated overlooking stepping stones: they lead across the Ewenny River (which joins the Ogmore a short distance below) to a path leading to Merthyr Mawr (p. 282).

A mile further on, the B4524 meets the B4265, which comes straight from St Bride's through a narrow valley, at **Ewenny**. The Priory (DoE) is reached by a lane which keeps close to the river. It is a delightful place, quiet and rural, a mixture of medieval church and fortification wall, great house and farmyard. The church was founded *c.* 1120 (probably on the site of an earlier one) by William de Londres, of Ogmore Castle. The Benedictine Priory was founded in 1141 by his son Maurice, as a daughter house of Gloucester Abbey. Building went on till about 1300. After the Dissolution, the nave of the church remained, as before, the parish church, while the rest of it, and the monastic buildings, were granted to Sir Edward Carne. The last of the Carnes died in 1700, and the property went to the Turbervilles.

The great precinct walls, with their towers and gateways, were built in the twelfth–thirteenth centuries to surround the Priory and church. They were not so much for defence as for prestige: the vulnerable east side was unfortified. The earliest part of the church is the nave, built by William de Londres. It, and its north arcade, were heightened later in the twelfth century, at the time when the chancel, crossing, transepts and tower were added. The nave was originally longer: the west wall is nineteenth century. The present aisle and porch are sixteenth century (rebuilt 1895). The font is of *c.* 1200. In the crossing arch is a thirteenth-century screen wall.

But it is the eastern part which is the glory of Ewenny, of marvellous grandeur and dignity. (Turner made a superb watercolour of it –

now in the National Museum.) The chancel is barrel-vaulted, and
the masses of plain masonry are beautifully set off by bands of
decorative carving. There is a fourteenth-century wooden screen,
with sixteenth-century linenfold panels. The north transept, and
south transept chapels, are now ruinous. In the south transept is an
interesting collection of monuments, including some pre-Norman
ones. The tomb-slab of the founder, Maurice de Londres (*c.* 1200)
is particularly lovely, with a richly-carved border and floriated cross.
The conventual buildings have disappeared, except for a few fragments incorporated in the house of the Carnes and Turbervilles
which occupies their site.

From Ewenny, it is a mile into Bridgend (p. 282). The B4524 goes
back east onto the A48. A long straight stretch follows the line of a
Roman road towards Cowbridge. Just after it passes Penllyn Castle
(p. 270), and just before the Cowbridge bypass goes off left, a lane
leads down right to **Llanfrynach Church** (980/746). Here two coffin
stiles can be seen. One is in the north boundary of the churchyard,
and another in the hedge a little nearer the main road. Each 'stile'
is really a pair of stiles with a low wall between, on which the coffin
could rest while the bearers changed over. It also allowed them to
negotiate the stile without tipping the coffin.

Cowbridge, the 'Capital of the Vale', is a pleasant little market
town, which has regained its quiet since the building of the bypass.
Yet its physical character, as well as its former prosperity, were owed
chiefly to the fact that the main east–west road ran through it. The
town was probably first built in 1091 by Robert Sancwinton (St
Quintin), and received its charter in 1254. Towards the west end
stands the recently restored Old Hall: a Queen Anne wing at the
back has been gutted, but its facade still stands. Down Church Street
is the large and grand Parish Church, which has a low octagonal
tower. Beside it is the celebrated Grammar School, founded in the
seventeenth century by Sir John Stradling of St Donat's, and rebuilt,
in a picturesque and irregular Tudor style, in 1848–50, by Jesus
College, Oxford, who were the school's patrons. The architect was
the young John Prichard. Next to the school, the medieval south
gate of the town survives, together with a stretch of the walls. They
can be seen from the fields outside. In the High Street, near the
site of the east gate, stands the handsome Town Hall, built in
1823–30 to designs by the Rev. John Montgomery Traherne.
He was a local landowner, and the leading local antiquarian of his
time. It has been considerably added to.

The castle of the Sancwintons was at **Llanblethian**, south-west of

the town, of which it is now almost a suburb (reached by way of
Church Street). It is a rich valley village with some very attractive
houses and a canalized stream. The large medieval church stands
high on the hill above; it has a fine Somerset-type Perpendicular
tower, elegantly pinnacled. The ruins of the castle stand to the west.
It is known as 'St Quintin's Castle', although the remains date from
the fourteenth century. The big gatehouse is impressive.

Llanmihangel, a couple of miles south, consists of Llanmihangel
Place (not open), now a farm, and the church. The attractive rambling towered house, partly castellated, has a grand seventeenth-
century room, panelled and plastered. The saddleback tower of the
church juts out of the wooded dell beside the pool just below.

Marychurch, one and a half miles east, crowns an expanded hill-
top hamlet. The church is a neat job by Prichard and Seddon, 1862,
with a medieval west tower. Much more interesting is their
Llandough Church School (now church hall) out in the country on the
road between the two villages. The proportion of window to wall
and plain roof is particularly well handled. Llandough Church,
restored by Buckeridge in 1869, stands in the castle enclosure behind
a high wall, remote from the press of new houses. The castle has
long been converted to a pleasant bow-windowed house; its old
gatehouse survives behind it.

Old Beaupre Castle (Booper) (009/720) must be one of the most
impressive and unexpected ruins in Wales. It is in the care of the
DoE, and happily it is not over-accessible. Leave your car by the
bridge on the Cowbridge–Marychurch road and take the path
through the fields near the river (in winter the castle can be seen
from the road). Beaupre is not a castle but a medieval manor house,
largely rebuilt round a courtyard in the sixteenth century by Richard
Basset. His grand gatehouse of 1586 marked the completion of this
part of the work. Not content, he built an even grander porch inside
the courtyard in 1600, reminiscent of that at Kirby. Its three storeys
are graced by the three orders, the Basset arms, and a long inscription.
The porch has delightful graffiti of ships scratched on the inside
wall (near the first-floor opening which is for a spy-hole); one is of
an early-seventeenth-century vessel. The hall directly inside the
porch and the wing to the left date from the medieval house.

A mile north-east of Old Beaupre is **St Hilary**. The Rev. J. M.
Traherne (see p. 280) had been intending to restore the church
himself, but, after he died in 1860, his wife called in Sir Gilbert
Scott to do the job as a memorial to her husband. The church was
reopened in 1862 after one of Scott's characteristically splendid

restorations. He added a new porch and new roofs, carved pews and pulpit, Clayton and Bell glass, and a stone and marble reredos.

From St Hilary it is two miles east to **Llantrithyd,** a pretty hamlet, where passion fruit ripen out-of-doors. The dullish church stands in a flowery churchyard. Inside, a stunning early-seventeenth-century Basset (see Beaupre) and Mansell tomb crowds out the chancel: a big wall tablet and altar tomb with life-size figures and seven weepers. There is a sanctus bell above the chancel arch and good Aubrey memorials in the nave. A member of this family had also married a Basset heiress and they lived at Llantrithyd Place, the ruined house adjoining the churchyard; its roof is said to have gone by 1836.

From Llantrithyd, it is a mile back onto the A48, near Bonvilston, which is eight miles from Cardiff.

BRIDGEND TO NEATH

Bridgend is a disappointing town, greatly overgrown, with a huge industrial estate on the east, and its centre being redeveloped. It is divided into two parts by the river Ogmore – Oldcastle, or Nolton, on the east, and Newcastle on the west. The name Oldcastle is comparatively modern, and there is no evidence that there was a castle on this side of the river. This is where the town centre is, but the parish church, of St Mary, Nolton, is some way to the south, between the main road and the river. It was built in 1885–7 by John Prichard, but the fine spire was added after his death, in 1897. There is a magnificently ornate War Memorial reredos by J. Coates Carter.

The old stone bridge over the river still stands, next to the new one. Up the hill the other side is **Newcastle** itself (DoE), built in the late twelfth century. Much the finest feature is the segmental-headed gateway, elaborately decorated with attached columns, carved capitals and lines of billet ornament. Near it is the restored parish church. A mile north of the town along the same road (A4063), a minor road leads west to **Pen-y-fai,** where the large and elaborate church, crowned by a central tower and lavishly furnished, was consecrated in 1903. Designed by Kempson and Fowler, it is more or less a paraphrase of the far superior church at Baglan (p. 287). The reason for this is that it was paid for by another branch of the Llewellyn family, whose home was Court Colman. The church stands by the gates of this mid-Victorian mansion (well seen from the railway).

Two miles south-west of Bridgend is **Merthyr Mawr,** reached by any of three turnings off the A48. It is a delightful little estate village by the wooded banks of the Ogmore. The big house, seen across its park, is a handsome Regency villa, built *c*. 1803 by Sir John Nicholl, a judge, and strong opponent of Reform. Most of the little cottages in the village are thatched, and originally had the peculiarity of outside staircases. The pretty church (1849–51), surrounded by trees, is by John Prichard, apparently in association with Benjamin Ferrey. The lane beyond leads down to the vast sand warrens stretching between the Ogmore estuary and Porthcawl. In them many prehistoric finds have been made. On the edge stand the ruins of Candleston Castle, a fifteenth-century fortified manor house. Its former lands lie beneath the sand. North of Merthyr Mawr mansion, the Ogmore is crossed by a four-arched medieval bridge.

The A473 (from Bridgend) joins the A48 just beyond **Laleston**, whose old church has a fine tower. A nice myth derives the name from Lalys, a Saracen architect captured in the Crusades, said to have built the church: other works attributed include Margam Abbey, Neath Abbey, and Caerphilly Castle! The A48 goes up over Stormy Down, whose name really derives from the Norman Sturmi family but suits the bleak hill well. Before it, a mile beyond Laleston, the A4106 goes left to Porthcawl, by way of Tythegston.

Two miles beyond the A48 roundabout is **Newton**, a pleasant old village now rather swamped by Porthcawl. The church lies off the main road, to the left, by the large village green. It has a stout saddle-back tower, and a most unusual stone pulpit, of the fifteenth century, crudely carved with a flagellation scene. On the other side of the green is St John's Well, reached down steps within a stone structure. When the tide is in, a quarter of a mile away, the well is almost empty, but when the tide goes out the well fills. A Latin poem on the subject (and a translation) are inscribed on a slab: the author was the prolific poet Sir John Stradling of St Donat's (1563–1637).

From Newton a road runs due south along the sea-front to Newton Point, with splendid views over to Ogmore-by-Sea: between this road and **Porthcawl** stretches an immense caravan park, divided up into rectangular plots. It is like a bad dream. The A4106 comes close to Sandy Bay, whose huge funfair is called CONEY BEACH. The harbour on the point beyond is the most attractive part of Porthcawl. It has a long quay with a lighthouse on the end, and is now full of pleasure-boats. On it a stretch of iron rails has been recently uncovered. This was part of the Dyffryn Llynfi and Porthcawl Railway, authorized in 1825 to carry iron and coal down from the Maesteg valley to the harbour. The dock was built in 1866, but never flourished. North-west from the town a road runs out over the rocky moorland of Locks Common to **The Rest** (1874–8), designed as a convalescent home for miners, by John Prichard, at his most bloody-minded. The gables have widely-projecting eaves. Rest Bay, down below, has a popular beach.

The B4283 leads due north from Porthcawl past Nottage Court, a sixteenth-century house. Opposite it, a minor road goes off left, and after two miles reaches **Kenfig**, a small village near Kenfig Pool, the biggest natural lake in the county. Between here and the sea stretches a vast area of sand dunes. Beneath the sand lie the remains of the medieval walled town of Kenfig. The borough was founded in the twelfth century beside the substantial Norman castle, whose ruins (partly excavated) stand near the railway line. By the sixteenth century the advancing sands had already led to the place's abandonment, and now nothing is visible of the town. However, it still had a portreeve, recorder, and aldermen until 1886. The road joins the A48 at **Pyle**, a surprisingly large place which owes its growth to the development of the collieries around Kenfig Hill to the east.

Two miles beyond Pyle, a large, well-wooded park appears on the right, between the road and the hills, and a vast Gothic house can be glimpsed among the trees. This is **Margam Castle**. Margam Abbey, founded in 1147, on the site of a Celtic monastery, was one of the greatest Cistercian monasteries in Wales. At the Dissolution, it was bought by Sir Rice Mansel, of Penrice (p. 301) and Oxwich. The daughter of the 1st Lord Mansel married John Ivory Talbot of Lacock Abbey, and their son, Thomas Mansel Talbot (1747–1813) inherited Margam and Penrice. His son was Christopher Rice Mansel Talbot, who was Liberal MP for Glamorgan from 1830 until 1890, becoming 'Father of the House of Commons' in 1874. The castle was built for him in 1830–5. (The old Mansel house had been demolished in 1780.) It was designed by the versatile Thomas Hopper (whose work in Wales includes Penrhyn Castle – see *North Wales*, p. 136).

It is one of his masterpieces – richly Tudor, in warm red stone, with a great octagonal tower, splendidly pinnacled, rising from the centre. Unoccupied since the War, it is now derelict and its future is uncertain, although the estate has recently been bought by the local authorities for use as a Country Park. This will enable the public to visit the grounds, with their magnificent specimen trees, and also the other buildings. These include a summer house with a delightful seventeenth-century facade, the famous and immense Orangery, built in 1787 by Anthony Keck, and said to be the largest

Orangery in the world, and also the surviving ruins of the Abbey, dating from *c.* 1200. The finest of these is the dodecagonal Chapter House: unfortunately the central column supporting the vaulting collapsed in 1799. Some beautiful doorways and other fragments survive.

The church was 262 feet long – longer than Tintern or Neath. Its Norman nave still stands, in use as the parish church, and is reached by a lane right from the main road. The plain and severe arcades, and the richer west doorway and three windows above, survive, but the rest is the result of a most remarkable rebuilding, carried out by Thomas Mansel Talbot in 1805–10. The west and east ends are flanked by tall square piers, with curious projecting tops, decorated with arcading. Their Italian look is said to be owed to Talbot's travels in Italy. The aisles have plaster vaulting, but the nave roof dates from a later refurbishing in 1872–3. This was done under the supervision of Theodore Talbot, only son of C. R. M. Talbot. He was responsible for the strongly Tractarian atmosphere, complete with seven brass sanctuary lamps. He had a remarkable life. Born in 1839, he went to Christ Church, became a Colonel in the Volunteers, and farmed. Then in 1869 he happened to hear Father Stanton, the celebrated curate of St Alban's, Holborn, preaching. The result was that he went to work in the slum parish of St Alban's, and took a prominent part in the Ritualist crisis of 1875. Then he went back to Wales, where he was a Master of Hounds, and suffered a hunting accident. Another hunting accident the next year finished him off, at the age of 37. In the north aisle there is a marble effigy of him, by H. H. Armstead, beneath an elaborate Gothic canopy (erected in 1881).

In the south aisle is the splendid group of sixteenth–seventeenth-century Mansel tombs, including three table tombs of alabaster with recumbent effigies, and kneeling children along the sides, and two wall-monuments. On a nearby pier is a brass to the huntsman Evan Rice, put up by Thomas Mansel in 1702: the inscription is worth reading. The three west windows are filled with Morris glass of 1873 – figures of the Virgin and Child and SS. Barnabas (or Bernard) and David, designed by Burne-Jones, against delicate quarries.

North of the church is the charming little **School House**, now a Museum (DoE), which contains one of the finest collections of inscribed and sculptured stones in Wales, some from Margam itself, others from the surrounding district. They include a Roman milestone, later used as a Christian memorial; the sixth-century Pumpeius stone, inscribed in Latin and Ogam; the Cross of Einion (ninth century); the Wheel Cross of Cynfelyn (*c.* 900), the finest of all, with its elaborate all-over decoration (it used to stand in the village street); several grave-slabs of abbots, among them one of an abbot of Rievaulx in Yorkshire, who probably died on a visitation; and numerous others. Up above, on the hill, stand the gaunt ruins of the fifteenth-century Capel Mair.

Near the church, and towards the main road, are a number of pretty estate cottages. Back on the A48 at **Groes**, near to the round-about where the Port Talbot bypass goes off right, is Beulah Calvin-istic Methodist Chapel (1838), a curious octagonal building of stone, Italianate in style.

Left of the road, beyond the railway, are the gigantic Abbey works of the British Steel Corporation, which cost £100 m. (consultant architect Sir Percy Thomas). These have contributed substantially to the growth of **Port Talbot**, now a town of more than fifty thousand inhabitants. It takes its name from the Talbots of Margam: C. R. M. Talbot was responsible for the Acts of 1834 and 1836 for the improvement of the harbour of the old town of Aberavon, as a port for the export of metals and coal from the Afan valley. For a town of its size it is singularly lacking in any real urban feel-ing, and is a drab place, its drabness intensified when it is covered by a thick pall of pinkish fumes, blighting the trees and fouling the laundry, and reminiscent of the worst horrors of nineteenth-century industrialization (compare Ebbw Vale, p. 221).

There are two churches in Port Talbot worth seeing. The first, **St Theodore's**, is beside the old A48. It was built in 1895–7 by Emily Talbot of Margam, in memory of her brother Theodore (see p. 285). Designed by J. L. Pearson, it is big and noble, in his usual Early English style. Just beyond St Theodore's, the A4107, coming down the south side of the Afan valley (p. 267), joins the A48. Nearly a mile further on, the B4286, coming down the north side, also joins it, and just across the railway from here is **St Mary's**, the parish church of **Aberavon**. The borough of Aberavon was granted its charter in 1158. The medieval church was replaced in the eighteenth century, and again in 1856–9, by Prichard and Seddon (north aisle added 1898). The elaborate reredos of 1890 was carved by H. H. Armstead. In the churchyard is buried 'Dic Penderyn' (see p. 256), who was born in Aberavon. The sandy beach down by the sea has a Lido called 'Miami Beach'.

The main road goes beneath the steep wooded slopes of Mynydd Dinas: beyond, a broad valley opens out, now filled with suburbia above which rises the elegant pinnacled spire of St Catherine's

Church, **Baglan**. This is probably the masterpiece of John Prichard, built at the end of his life, and consecrated in 1882. It was paid for by Prichard's cousin, Griffith Llewellyn of Baglan Hall (demolished), whose family were agents to the Margam estates, as well as owning land in Rhondda and elsewhere. (Griffith also built the church at Pentre – see p. 263 – and his cousin William built Pen-y-fai – see p. 282.)

Everything in the church is rich, colourful and well done. Inside, pink alabaster (from Penarth) contrasts with different shades of grey stone. The floors are of mosaic. The striking reredos, of incised marble, is by H. H. Armstead. North of the chancel is the Cosmatesque tomb of the founder (d. 1888). The glass is by the Morris firm, and dates from 1880. The Crucifixion in the east window, and St Cecilia in the south transept, were designed by Burne-Jones, and all the other windows have pretty flowered quarries. In his recent book on Morris glass, A. C. Sewter says that the St Cecilia window 'has some of the most beautiful colour and the most accomplished silver-stain work ever produced in English glass'.

On the hill behind are the ruins of the old church, burnt out and roofless, in a vandalized churchyard. It is said that in the seventeenth century the graves here were being dug into coal. The church was founded by Baglan, a disciple of St Illtyd, who came here from Llantwit Major (p. 276) in the sixth century. He was told to found his church where he found a tree bearing three kinds of fruit. Here he found a tree with a crow nesting in its branches, bees swarming in its trunk, and a sow and her piglets rooting below.

Just beyond Baglan, the Port Talbot bypass rejoins the old road. A mile further on is **Briton Ferry**, where, instead of the old ferry, a modern bridge now leads over the estuary of the river Neath towards Swansea. Giraldus Cambrensis commented on the dangerous quicksands here. Later it became important as the terminus of the Neath Canal, authorized in 1790 (the same year as the Glamorganshire – p. 231), and as a port. Docks were built in 1861. Industry – especially tinplate – tended to concentrate in this direction rather than at Neath itself. Apart from the wooded hillside above it is difficult now to appreciate why the place should have appealed so much to late-eighteenth- and early-nineteenth-century artists such as Turner.

From Briton Ferry it is two miles (completely built up) to **Neath** (Castellnedd), now a busy industrial and commercial town, but with a long history, whose surviving remains are not at all prominent. It was the Roman *Nidum*, and a Norman castle may have existed near the site of the Roman fort on the west side of the river. The existing castle (late thirteenth century) stands on the site of one established by Robert Fitzhamon in 1111. A town grew up around it, and was given a charter in 1280 by Gilbert de Clare. The great abbey was founded in 1129. The industrialization of the area began with copper smelting in the late sixteenth century, and this was energetically developed at the end of the seventeenth century by Sir Humphrey Mackworth. In 1698 he acquired large interests in the Cardiganshire silver and lead mines, and Neath, with its copious supplies of water, wood and coal, and its situation on a navigable estuary, was well placed for the processing of the Cardiganshire minerals and copper from Cornwall. Later, ironworking also became important, and other industries have followed. The arrival of the railway in 1850 was a stimulus to growth. Another significant factor was that, until the new bridge at Briton Ferry was built in 1954, the main Cardiff-Swansea road went through the town.

The chief landmark is undoubtedly **St David's Church**, built in 1864–6. Designed by John Norton, it has an extraordinary south-east tower, capped by a fanciful pyramidal spire with elaborate pinnacles around it, and a polychromatic interior. Near the old Parish Church of St Thomas, further north (off New Street), is the **Mechanics' Institution** of 1847, outgibbsing Gibbs with its proliferation of quoins. A plaque records that it was designed by Alfred Russell Wallace, then a surveyor in Neath, but who later collaborated with Charles Darwin in the first publication of the theory of evolution. Behind St Thomas's, in an area recently cleared of dereliction, stand the scanty ruins of the **Castle**, with a pair of drum towers flanking the gateway. In the town centre the only other buildings of note are the Gwyn Hall, an exceedingly gloomy Gothic pile, of 1887, also by John Norton, the characterful late-Victorian Railway Station, and the bustling Market, c. 1900, with an iron and glass roof.

Across the bridge, the main road to Swansea runs right over the site of the Roman fort, of Flavian origin, but rebuilt in stone c. AD 120. The remains of the south-east and south-west gates, excavated in 1949–50, have been left exposed. Half a mile beyond, a road leads left under the railway to the ruins of the **Abbey** (DoE), until comparatively recently begrimed and built around by the industries which hemmed it in, but now happily surrounded by immaculate lawns. The monastery was founded in 1125, as a daughter house of Savigny, and became Cistercian in 1147. The buildings were erected in the late thirteenth–fourteenth centuries, and included a church 215 feet long. Of the large quantity of splendid heraldic floor-tiles with which it was paved, many are in museums, but some remain *in situ*. In the mid seventeenth century the abbot's lodging was converted into a house by Sir Philip Hoby. Near the abbey stand the ruins of two blast-furnaces. These belonged to the Neath Abbey Ironworks, founded in 1792 by Cornish Quakers. They specialized in making engines, two of which survive at Glyn Pits, Pontypool (see p. 220). In the early nineteenth century the works were run by Joseph Tregelles Price, founder of the Peace Society. He refused to make cannons or shot, and went to London to intercede with Lord Melbourne for Dic Penderyn (see p. 256).

Further on, the Swansea road goes through Skewen, site of the enormous BP refinery of **Llandarcy** (beside the new A48). D'Arcy was not a Celtic saint who established a settlement here: he was the Anglo-Iranian oil concessionaire. The vast assemblage of circular tanks and complex ironmongery can give real aesthetic pleasure in sympathetic light.

THE VALE OF NEATH

From the town centre, the B4434 runs due north up the valley. Half a mile out, it passes the church of **Llantwit** (Llanilltud), rebuilt in 1859, except for the old tower, and picturesquely situated beside the canal, with the river beyond. Seventeenth-century tablets are built into the south wall in patterns: some have nice inscriptions. Opposite the church, a lane leads up the hill past the cemetery. After a mile, it passes close to Ivy Tower, a ruinous eighteenth-century 'belvedere, shooting box and banqueting hall', as Barbara Jones puts it in *Follies and Grottoes*. It has battlements and pointed windows. The road carries on up onto the bare hill-top, with enormous views over the Neath Valley and the estuary. A mile beyond Ivy Tower, the road passes through an exceptionally large Roman marching-camp, covering 62 acres.

The B4434 follows the south side of the Vale of Neath, a place of pilgrimage for all lovers of the picturesque in the eighteenth and early nineteenth centuries. Since then the development of industry – in particular, of collieries and metalworking establishments – has spoilt much of it. Enormous areas have more recently been planted with conifers, but some deciduous woodlands survive. Five miles beyond Neath is **Melincourt**, whose celebrated waterfall (80 feet high) can be reached by a path following the stream. At Resolven the road crosses the valley to join the A465, which runs along the north side. A mile further up are the colossal works of the British

Aluminium Company. Hidden behind it is **Rheola**, now used as its Residential Training Centre. A small existing house was bought in 1800 by John Edwards, a mysterious London lawyer who appears to have been a cousin of John Nash, although sometimes referred to as his uncle, or nephew. Edwards (who was nineteen years younger than Nash) was closely involved in some of his building speculations, and even shared the grandiose mansion which he built for himself in Regent Street. He also got Nash to enlarge Rheola, in 1815, but in a very modest way. In 1828 he sent the king what was said to be the largest pineapple ever grown in the kingdom, from his hothouse here. To gain a legacy he added the name Vaughan to his own. In 1833 he died. When Nash died two years later, he left the bulk of his estate to his 'cousin's' son, named after himself, Nash Vaughan Edwards Vaughan. The part of the house added by Nash seems to be the north-east wing, plain and with a canted bay. The rest looks mid-Victorian. Behind is a pretty dairy with a cupola.

Two miles further on, at **Aberpergwm**, there is a thriving anthracite colliery. Just beyond, on the left, a drive leads between gatepiers to the odd little church, mostly nineteenth century, with a funny squat bellcote. The drive goes on, past a new housing estate, to Aberpergwm House, a dismal sight. The big stone Tudor mansion is derelict and boarded up. It is pretty unpleasant in any case: although partly old, it now looks mostly nineteenth century, nasty in texture and poor in proportions. Yet from the sixteenth until the twentieth century it was the home of the Williams family, one of the most important in Glamorgan. They began the exploitation of the local coal, which finally drove them out. In 1901 Morgan Williams bought St Donat's Castle (p. 276), and since the War the family have settled at Llanharan (p. 268).

A mile beyond Aberpergwm is Glyn Neath, now torn apart by the construction of the new A465, which goes up the south side of the valley from here to Hirwaun (p. 261). From near the bridge, the B4242 goes on up by the river to **Pontneddfechan**, a quiet little village beneath steep hills. It was the terminus of the Neath Canal. The bridge over the river Neath (which forms the boundary with Breconshire) is the starting-place for the wonderful walk up to the Pyrddin waterfalls. It is a good one and a half miles each way, and the path is not all as level as the first stretch, but it is thoroughly worthwhile. The path follows the Neath for a mile. Steep cliffs overhang the wooded river. Where the Pyrddin comes down to join the Neath, it is crossed by an iron bridge. One path goes right up the Neath, but ours goes left beside the Pyrddin. Not far beyond is the first fall,

Ysgwd Gwladys: the river cascades over one end of a sharp sandstone ledge, within a great natural amphitheatre of cliffs. Above, it flows over a rock pavement. The path beyond here is less good, and not for the infirm, but it is well worth pressing on to see the second fall, **Ysgwd Einion Gam**. Within an even grander amphitheatre of towering cliffs, the river falls in broken spray, from a huge height, into a rocky pool, out of which it gurgles through a little curved spout over a low shelf. The sublime and the picturesque are combined.

From Pontneddfechan, one minor road zigzags up the hill towards Ystradfellte (p. 46), while another follows the river Mellte westwards, crossing it half a mile beyond the village. From here, the river can be followed up to its famous falls (see p. 46). Over the bridge, a road leads left up to **Craig y Ddinas**, a spectacular great limestone cliff, rising sheer for 200 feet.

FROM THE VALE OF NEATH TO SWANSEA

Back at Glyn Neath, the A4109 climbs up the north side of the valley, and then heads north-west towards the bleak uplands between the heads of the Pyrddin and Dulais valleys. The anthracite collieries up here are the highest of a series running down the Dulais valley towards the south-west. The A4109 follows this valley back down to Neath, through the colliery town of **Seven Sisters**. The origin of the name is that the first mine here was going to be called Isabella after one of the seven daughters of the owner, David Bevan, but his son said that preference should not be shown to any of them, and so it was called after them all.

However, rather than follow the Dulais valley, take the turning right from **Dyffryn Cellwen** towards Coelbren. Half a mile down, just west of a crossroads, the ramparts and gates of a Roman fort are clearly visible. Subtly sited, like so many forts, on a low plateau with an unexpected command over the surrounding territory, it was founded in the Flavian period and occupied until c. 150. Looking from the fort, the Roman road to Brecon Gaer can be seen, beyond the valley, running up north-east. To see this well-preserved stretch of road (marked on the map as **Sarn Helen**), carry on along the Coelbren road (into Breconshire), passing under the old Neath and Brecon Railway, then turn right over the railway for a little over a mile. The Roman road goes over moorland which is now used by the Glyn Neath Gliding Club. Its stony core is exposed, and the ditches are visible.

The famous Henrhyd Waterfall at **Coelbren** (National Trust) is accessible either by a steep path down the valley-side starting just outside the east end of the village, or – more comfortably, if less dramatically – from the car park a short distance north of the bridge. The river Llech falls over a cliff (in which a thin coal seam is exposed), unbroken for 90 feet, into the lovely wooded valley.

Beyond Coelbren, the road drops down to **Abercrave** in the Tawe valley (for the upper part of which see p. 49). At the junction of the Twrch and Tawe, just in Glamorgan, is **Ystalyfera**, important in the nineteenth century for its ironworks and tinplate works, and later for its collieries. The Swansea Canal crossed the Twrch by means of its longest aqueduct, dramatically set over a high weir, and still surviving although the canal is dry at this point. In the narrow valley below the town, the old road runs up along the north side through Godre'r-graig, while the new A4067 runs along the valley floor, obliterating the canal. Further down, however, it comes into view, right of the road. It was opened in 1796–8, and ran up to Abercrave.

The next town is **Pontardawe**, situated at the crossroads of the A4067 and the A474, which comes over from the Amman valley (see p. 153) by way of the colliery town of Gwaun-Cae-Gurwen, and then, after crossing the Swansea valley, climbs over to Neath. Pontardawe was another steel and tinplate town. Its chief landmark is St Peter's Church, an elaborate exercise in Decorated Gothic, built in 1860 by J. H. Baylis of Swansea.

The valley gradually opens out, then widens at **Clydach**. Near the junction with the B4291 stands a statue of Ludwig Mond, co-founder of what is now ICI, in tall hat and beard. He was responsible for the big nickel works which dominate the village. Nearby is St John's Church, plain Early English (1847, William Whittington), in a vast and closely-packed graveyard. Large numbers of the men buried here died young as a result of the toxic effects of working in Mond's enterprise. A splendid mountain road comes south from Ammanford to Clydach.

Two miles below Clydach is **Morriston**, where the new A48, from Cardiff to Llanelli, crosses the valley. The town takes its name from Sir John Morris, whose father, a Shropshire man, had, from 1717 onwards, set up copper-works, brass-wire mills, and collieries in the district. It is not certain whether it was the father or the son who built the extraordinary edifice known as 'Morris Castle' whose gaunt stone ruins can still be seen up on the hill above the town. This 'castellated mansion of collegiate appearance' (W. Davies, *General View of the Agriculture of S. Wales*, 1814) was intended to house forty families of workpeople, with a shoemaker and a tailor to serve them. It must have been one of the earliest large blocks of flats in South Britain.

Between 1790 and 1796 the 'model village' of Morriston itself was built, according to tradition to the design of William Edwards, the bridge-builder (see p. 228). The plan was a straightforward grid, with the church in the middle of a central square where two roads crossed. Nothing survives except the lay-out. The present church is a handsomely sober one of 1862 by R. K. Penson. It is completely overshadowed by the splendid great Capel Tabernacl near by, the so-called 'Cathedral of Welsh Nonconformity'. It was built in 1870 by John Humphreys of Morriston. The lofty front is ornamented with tall round arches and a slender spire, but the interior is surprisingly cosy, richly but elegantly decorated. With its curving galleries, it can seat over 1800 people. It is the home of the famous Morriston Orpheus Choir.

Morriston is now a suburb of Swansea, and marks the top of the notorious Lower Swansea Valley, once one of the most appalling areas of dereliction in Britain. A major multi-disciplinary study of it, by members of University College, Swansea, was launched in 1961, and its report was published in 1967 (as *The Lower Swansea Valley Project*). A little has been done towards implementing its proposals. The best way of appreciating the problem is to enter Swansea by train from the east. One of the first people to travel on Brunel's new broad-gauge line from Gloucester in 1850 was the ecclesiologist J. M. Neale, and he described the experience in a letter: 'The night entrance into Swansea is awfully beautiful. I can imagine no scene on earth more nearly resembling Hell. I have seen the Birmingham and Newcastle works by night, but they are not to be compared for ghastly effect to the green flames of copper furnaces.' A hundred years later, the accumulated effects of industry were a good deal less susceptible of romanticization. The derelict remains of old works have interest for the industrial archaeologist. But even today industry can blight the area, notably the Swansea Vale Smelting Works opened at Llansamlet (east of Morriston) by Rio Tinto Zinc in 1960, which after causing severe pollution in the vicinity were closed in 1972.

A mile south of Morriston, the railway crosses the road at **Landore**, long a centre of metalworking – first copper, and then steel. A verse of 1890 again associated the area with hell –

> It came to pass in days of yore
> The Devil chanced upon Landore.

Quoth he, 'By all this fume and stink
I can't be far from home I think.'

SWANSEA – ABERTAWE

The Welsh name, Abertawe, refers to the town's situation at the mouth of the Tawe, but the English name is, as often, more revealing historically: it is said to come from two Old Norse words, Swein (a man's name) and Ey (island). The town's origin is said to go back to the Viking raids of the ninth century. Its real importance began when the Norman Henry de Newburgh chose it as the capital of his new Lordship of Gower, and built a castle (probably south of the present one). A small port and market town grew up, receiving its first charter as a borough c. 1165.

By the Tudor Act of Union the Lordship of Gower was merged with the Lordship of Morgannwg to form the new county of Glamorgan. But the town's prosperity continued to increase, owing largely to its importance as a coal port, even as early as the sixteenth century. It was an early home of Puritanism, and by 1660 was the chief centre of Puritan worship in South Wales. In 1722 Defoe described Swansea as a 'very considerable town for trade'. By the early eighteenth century industry was making an impact on the Lower Swansea Valley (e.g. Morriston, p. 292), and by the early nineteenth century it was one of the leading metallurgical districts in Britain. The copper ore came from Cornwall, Ireland, and Parys Mountain in Anglesey (see North Wales, p. 206). By 1798 Swansea Canal was built, linking the whole Tawe valley with the port. In 1804 the Oystermouth Rail Way or Tram Road Act was passed: opened in 1807, this horse-drawn railway (later known as the Mumbles Railway) was intended chiefly to carry limestone from the Mumbles quarries to the Swansea Canal, and also coal from the Clyne valley, but it carried passengers too, and so was in fact the first passenger railway in the world. It closed in 1960. In 1850 the South Wales Railway, from Gloucester to Swansea, opened (see p. 232), to be followed by others. The population increased rapidly: in 1800 it was 6000, in 1831, 15,000, in 1871, 63,000.

There were attempts to avoid the industrialization of the town, and boost it as a fashionable watering-place – the 'Welsh Weymouth'. More genteel industries included the famous Cambrian Pottery, run by the Dillwyns from 1802 until 1850, and connected with the pottery at Nantgarw (p. 252). But it was the copper and tinplate industries that were most important. Among the leaders of industry, the outstanding family were the Vivians. John Vivian came from Cornwall at the end of the eighteenth century. In 1810 his sons John Henry and Richard Hussey founded the famous Hafod Works. John Henry's son, Henry Hussey Vivian (1821–94), later became 1st Lord Swansea. He was an outstanding metallurgist, and was partly responsible, after the South Wales coal strike of 1875, for introducing the famous 'sliding' wage-scale. At the end of the century steel-making became important. Some of the experiments by which the Siemens brothers perfected the open-hearth method were carried out at Landore.

Swansea's intellectual life bore fruit in the first newspaper in Wales, *The Cambrian* (1804), and the first all-Welsh weekly journal, *Seren Gomer* (1814–15), and also in the foundation in 1835 of the distinguished Swansea Philosophical and Literary Society, known since 1838 as the Royal Institution of South Wales. The former Swansea Technical College became the University College of Swansea in 1919, and has since expanded enormously.

Swansea has always remained far more distinctively Welsh than Cardiff. Swansea people are inclined to be scathing about their neighbours in the capital – a cosmopolitan lot, with no real tradition, not much interest in their own local history, mostly unable even to speak Welsh. They are not slow to point out that it was only in the last century that Cardiff became more important than Swansea.

The town is situated between two completely different types of scenery, reflecting its schizophrenic character. On the east are the horrifying dereliction of the Lower Swansea Valley, the docks, and the refineries, while on the west, stretching round in a grand curve to the Mumbles, is Swansea Bay, which W. S. Landor preferred to the Bay of Naples, and beyond it the delectable land of Gower. The town itself contains similar contrasts, between the drab and dirty old dock area, and the pleasant suburbs to the west. As for the centre, considering its importance, as the second largest town in Wales (population over 170,000), it has remarkably little of the feel of a great city. Some find this appealing, but it is undeniable that the centre is a sad mess. The tremendous destruction that took place in the War provided an opportunity for bold planning which has produced nothing better than the inanity of Kingsway and St Mary's Square.

The approach by the railway has already been described. The approach from the east, by the A483 (from Briton Ferry), is little more prepossessing. The bare hills soon give way to industry at

Jersey Marine, once intended to be a watering-place. A curious octagonal brick tower stands right of the road. On the slopes of Kilvey Hill are the industrial suburbs of Port Tennant and Kilvey, while left of the road are the newer docks, which are built on the site of the old tidal dock of Port Tennant. The docks still handle a considerable quantity of goods, and in recent years the passenger facilities have been improved to accommodate the Swansea–Cork car ferry.

Just across the river, the vast bulk of the former **Weavers' Provender Mill** comes into view. It was the first multi-storey reinforced concrete building in Britain, and it is sad that it has been derelict for some years. The French pioneer of reinforced concrete, François Hennebique, sent over one of his engineers, Louis-Gustave Mouchel, in 1895, to supervise its erection, using materials also shipped from France. At the roundabout, Somerset Place goes off left: in it is the handsome former **Town Hall**, built by Thomas Collingwood in 1825–9, and remodelled by Thomas Taylor in 1850–2. Further on is the much grander home of the **Royal Institution of South Wales**, a stately Ionic pile, with a portico, built in 1838–41, by Frederick Long of Liverpool. It houses an interesting museum of local history. Behind it, in an old dock warehouse, is the new **Maritime Museum**. **Castle Wind Street** leads up north from the roundabout, much the best commercial street remaining, with some good banks and offices. In it, on the right, the grubby ruins of the **Castle** are being restored by the DoE. It was rebuilt *c.* 1340 by Bishop Gower: the elegant arcaded parapet on the south side is like that at his Palace at St Davids (p. 112). Beyond, High Street leads up to the Station and on to the Neath and Carmarthen Roads.

In Alexandra Road, opposite the Station, is the **Glynn Vivian Art Gallery**, which has a fine collection of Swansea pottery and porcelain. South of here is the new centre of Swansea, about which the less said the better. Princess Way leads to St Mary's Square, which even has a large post-War block in half-timbering. **St Mary's Church**, large and desperately dull, is the old parish church of Swansea. Rebuilt in 1896–9 by Sir Arthur Blomfield (except for the Herbert Chapel), it was burnt out in 1941, and rebuilt in 1954–9, by Leslie T. Moore and Sir Percy Thomas. Near it is the over-restored Cross Keys, which incorporates fragments of the fourteenth-century Hospital of St David.

Alexandra Road continues into **Mansel Street**, lined with stuccoed terraces, which become more elegant in Walter Road. St James's Church (T. Nicholson, 1867) has a nice leafy crescent behind it. On the steep hillside north of these roads, terraced housing gives way to more spacious suburbs. Right on the top of the hill, above the cliffs, is the celebrated **Town Hill** estate, laid out just before the First World War by Sir Raymond Unwin.

Walter Road leads to Sketty Road, and so to Sketty, where, up at the top end of Singleton Park, stands **St Paul's Church**, much the finest in Swansea. It was built and endowed by John Henry Vivian (of Singleton Abbey), and his son Henry Hussey in 1849–52. Their architect was Henry Woodyer. The broach spire is clad in oak shingles. The church was sensitively enlarged in 1908 and 1929.

Across the road is a School of 1853, with timber loggia and flèche, also by Woodyer.

Singleton Park, with its attractive trees and shrubs, is now public, as well as housing several institutions. The chief of these is the **University College of Swansea**. Its buildings, mostly by Sir Percy Thomas and Son, are of very varying merit, and, to avoid spoiling the park, tightly jumbled on top of one another. The administrative headquarters is Singleton Abbey. J. H. Vivian bought an octagonal villa of 1783 (by William Jernegan), called Marino, and had it converted into a lavishly Tudor fantasy, *c*. 1823–31. His architect was P. F. Robinson. It has subsequently been enlarged and altered.

South of the Park is Mumbles Road, or the Esplanade, with the line of the old Mumbles Railway between it and the beach. Back towards the town is Victoria Park, in which stands the Patti Pavilion, formerly the Winter Garden of Adelina Patti's Craig-y-nos Castle (see p. 48). Further on is the immense Portland stone **Guildhall**, opened in 1934. It is an outstanding specimen of the stripped-down Neoclassicism of which Hitler's architect Albert Speer was such a master. The interiors include some lavishly gilded neo-Grecian pomposity. The concert hall is called the Brangwyn Hall, after the series of huge murals painted by Sir Frank Brangwyn between 1924 and 1931 for the Royal Gallery of the House of Lords, as part of the Peers' War Memorial. They were rejected as too gaudy. Brangwyn was bitterly disappointed, but was delighted when they were presented to Swansea (his parents were Welsh – his father was an unsuccessful church architect who settled in Bruges). He said 'The only thing that would give me joy is to know that in years to come a few people will stand in front of my murals at Swansea and say "Hullo! there's a fellow who loved colour and nature!"' The original idea was to depict war scenes, but Brangwyn decided instead to show what the men were fighting for – the spirit of the various countries of the British Empire. They succeed in giving warm richness and rioting

colour to the great bare space of the hall, which was specially designed for them. They are nothing short of a stunning achievement,
a brilliant combination of superb pattern-making and assured
draughtsmanship. In the corridors around the Hall are hung a
splendid series of studies and drawings for the murals.

Mumbles Road leads round the sweeping curve of Swansea Bay.
Near the further end, **Oystermouth Castle** stands on a grassy bump
above the road. Probably founded by William de Londres of Ogmore (p. 279), it was burnt by the Welsh in 1287, and rebuilt after
that. The ruins are picturesquely irregular. The poor old church,
further south, rebuilt by R. K. Penson in 1859–60, has had a whacking
great new nave and chancel slammed up against its north side. This
was done by L. W. Barnard, *c.* 1890, to accommodate the holiday-
makers, retired people and commuters who were causing this whole
promontory to become more and more built up around that time.

This process was, of course, stimulated by the Mumbles Railway,
which was extended right to the end of the rocky **Mumbles Head** in
1898. The railway company also built the pier at their terminus.
Beyond are two islands, with the lighthouse, erected in 1793, on the
further one (reached by a causeway). The origin of the name Mumbles
is uncertain.

GOWER

Gower juts out westward from Swansea's doorstep. The peninsula is
only eighteen miles by five, but despite its small size and the immediate proximity of town and industry Gower remains a world on
its own, more West Country than Welsh to the outsider. This is
partly the result of geology (little coal), geography (easy trading
across to Devon), and settlement (the Danes came and the Normans
stayed).

Gower is justly renowned for its superb cliff scenery, particularly
in the south: carboniferous limestone prevails south of a diagonal
line from Whitford Point to Mumbles, wooded dingles run down to
the sea and wild flowers abound. Old Red Sandstone outcrops,
notably on Rhosili Down to the west, but right down the middle it
makes a high moorland divide. In the north, Burry Inlet gives a
totally different but compellingly beautiful landscape of salt marsh,
mud and dunes.

The peninsula, particularly to the east, has its share of post-war
houses, being especially attractive for retirement and weekending,
but its beaches, many of which must be walked to, are remarkably

free of development although naturally popular in summer. Walking is the only way properly to appreciate Gower, especially in summer when the roads are packed. A couple of days spent following the cliffs along the south coast make a rewarding experience.

From **Mumbles** (p. 298), the A4067 leads west to end at the popular **Caswell Bay**, recently threatened by the spread of the development which sprawls behind it. A minor road leads north to **Bishopston** (it can also be reached by the B4436 from Black Pill on Swansea Bay). It has lots of new houses but the **Church** is now mercifully bypassed. It has an attractive leafy setting near a retired watersplash. Low west tower. Inside, the massive out-of-plumb walls give character to the unostentatious restoration; detail is dullish but the general form good. A path by the watersplash leads down to **Pwlldu Bay** (National Trust), two and a half miles. Marvellously flowery in spring but heavy with foliage by mid-summer. The old Beaufort Hotel and two cottages stand by the shore. The bay can also be reached from the Knap to the east where there is a small car park on the cliffs. Fine cliffs continue west, a great gift to the National Trust under Enterprise Neptune. The famous Mitchin Hole and Bacon Hole caves, accessible only at low tide, are in this stretch.

Pennard is the hamlet with the toy-like church on the sharp bend of B4436. A medieval building with a boat-shaped nave ceiling, restored west gallery, seventeenth-century pulpit (from Shiplake, Oxfordshire) and seventeenth-century font cover, and good memorials.

B4436 joins A4118 a mile north of the church, a very busy narrow road which serves the south coast of Gower. For **Pennard Burrows** you can park by Shepherd's Shop, and follow the unsigned path opposite the concrete fencing posts. For **Pennard Castle** bear left keeping up hill and over the edge of the golf-course. The early-fourteenth-century castle is a commanding ruin on the edge of the burrows; its gatehouse and curtain walls survive on the landward side but to the south they are down and give a fine view of the sea and the valley where ponies graze the saltings in the loops of the river, and herons flap across. The remains of a church survive in the burrows near by.

The path on down the valley leads to **Three Cliff Bay**; good bathing clear of the river (dangerous near its mouth). Great Tor protects the bay from the west. Park in **Penmaen** in front of the council houses near the whitewashed Post Office. Follow the path through the field gate. The headland is decked with yellow roses and surrounded by splendid views including the great sweep of Oxwich Bay. A good but

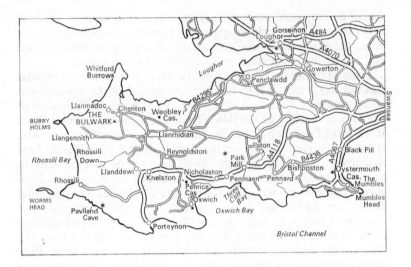

not spectacular burial chamber is hidden in a hollow in the brackeny burrows about two hundred yards from the end of the track. The commanding white hotel-like building inland was built as a workhouse.

For stormy days there are good inland walks too. For **Ilston Cwm**, park near the Gower Inn east of Park Mill. The first part of this lovely winter or early spring walk has been rather municipalized by the approaches to the Myles memorial. In 1649 John Myles established the first Baptist church in Wales up this Cwm. Its ruins survive although their atmosphere has been transformed by the fencing and memorial unveiled by Lloyd George in 1928.

The path meanders up the closely wooded valley to **Ilston** (also accessible by moorland road across Fairwood Common to the north). St Illtud's Church has a huge low tower and is built by the stream close under the hill, with a big yew tree. **Parc Cwm** or **Parc le Breos** (537/899), best approached from Park Mill, is a particularly good example of a chambered tomb (3000–1900 BC) of the Severn-Cotswold type which are noted for the very carefully built drystone walling which forms a kerb round the barrow. The tomb has a remote park-like setting in a hidden valley, submerged in forestry. An old lime-kiln survives in the woodland and, in June 1973, strange stone altars were being erected on the edge of the glade (perhaps merely work-tops for camp cooks?).

Nicholaston Church, hard by the main road, is a complete period piece (down to the copper baptismal bucket) of 1892–4, by G. E. Halliday. No expense has been spared on this little building, particularly on the elaborate carving (by Clarke of Llandaff), and it comes off. On the pulpit are statues of Keble, Liddon, and Pusey.

A mile west is the romantic ruined entrance lodge of **Penrice Castle** (open on written application). The bulky ruins of the thirteenth-century castle stand above and separate from the house built in 1773 by Anthony Keck, who later designed the Orangery at Margam (p. 284), for Thomas Mansel Talbot, who also demolished the old house there. The nineteenth-century additions have recently been demolished leaving an all but symmetrical building with a central bow-fronted saloon looking down over Oxwich Bay. The unusual small square brick building topped by an octagonal lantern beside the main road to the west is a grain store.

Oxwich Bay has good sands, backed by reed-beds, caravans and car parks. **Oxwich** has whitewash and thatch and a church well worth visiting. It stands in woodland on the very edge of the cliff on the right arm of the bay. The big tower looms out of a green gloom of sycamore and you enter the little church through the west door under it. The diminutive chancel has a lovely fourteenth-century tomb to the Delaware family and a ceiling painted at the expense of Dame Lilian Baylis of Old Vic fame. The two slabs now in the porch are thirteenth and fourteenth century and bear the names of former rectors. The oil lamps are notable.

Oxwich Castle (DoE) is a vast fortified house on a fine site above the woodland to the south of the village. It includes a six-storeyed tower and a wing with huge flat arches, and a dovecot. It was built *c.* 1540 by Sir Rice Mansel (who bought the lands of Margam Abbey from the Crown) and his arms survive above the gateway. Good views of Penrice Castle.

Due west, **Porteynon** is now for holiday rather than fishing. The walk along the magnificent cliffs from here to Worm's Head is highly recommended. Round Porteynon Point is Culver Hole, an enigmatic walled-up fissure in the limestone cliffs. It is said by some to have been a dovecot (from French *couvoir*, a hatchery?). Further west is the famous **Paviland Cave**. In 1823 the skeleton of the Red Lady of Paviland together with remains of elephant and mammoth and flint tools were discovered here. This palaeolithic burial turned out to be that of a man, ceremonially buried and stained with red ochre. The cave is cut off at high tide.

The last bay west is **Mewslade Bay**, with towering cliffs, happily inaccessible by car. Beyond is **Worm's Head**, the south-west tip of

Gower, thrusting out into the sea for all the world like some palaeolithic creature from Paviland magnified to gigantic proportions. The
Head is accessible for a few hours on either side of low tide.

The grand sweep of **Rhosili Bay** runs north to Burry Holm, a
three-mile stretch of low-tide sand and a great place for summer
shells and winter beachcombing, for Viking landings, wrecks, and
ghosts. The small church at Rhosili has a good Norman doorway
and a monument to Petty Officer Evans who perished with Captain
Scott's party on their return from the Pole.

Rhosili Down (National Trust) above is the highest land in Gower:
superb views and even a taste of the Atlantic when a westerly gale is
thundering on to the beach below. Early tombs include two dolmens
known as the Sweyn (swine) Houses. At the other end of Rhosili
Down is Llangennith, but to reach it by road you have to go back on
to the A4118, and turn left at Knelston via **Llanddewi**, whose church
up on the hill is well worth a detour. The side approach by the grass
farmyard is in character with this most attractive primitive building,
restored in 1876, with a low saddleback tower. Nice iron gate and
shell path. Bright and polished within; a planked floor; clear east
window; barley-sugar communion rails and a painted altar table
with Gothic arcading; and a huge flower-pot font.

Carry on northwards up the winding lane and bear left. **Llangennith** is loosely grouped around a sloping green from which the
church composes well. It has a very plain square tower, saddlebacked and battlemented. The lychgates were carved by Mr W. H.
Melling, ship's carpenter on a Trinity House boat, while he was at
sea. (He is now retired and lives opposite.) They depict scenes from
the nearly miraculous life of St Cennydd. Being illegitimate and born
deformed his parents (from the court of King Arthur) put him in a
wicker basket which they cast into the sea. This minicoracle came
ashore on Worm's Head where, with the help of seabirds and angels,
the boy grew up. The church is built on the site of his monastery.
The stone incised with an interlacing pattern now set in the west wall
of the nave (inside) is traditionally from his tomb.

Burry Holms, the small high-tide island to the west, has Iron Age
fortifications and St Cennydd is believed to have lived here as a
hermit. It is backed by Llangennith Burrows and the point forms the
north arm of the vast west-facing sweep of Rhosili Bay (*q.v.*). Back
along the road from Llangennith, a lane leads north to **Cheriton,**
which has a West Country feel. The mid-thirteenth-century church
stands opposite a vine-clad cottage in a sheltered dingle. It has a
sturdy low central tower with a gabled roof behind its battlements.

Early English carving includes decorated capitals and a sculpted head reset oddly above the chancel arch.

Llanmadoc is the next and last village to the north of the peninsula. The church (J. Prichard, 1860) has an enthusiastic little stepped-gabled saddlebacked tower. Llanmadoc Hill, topped by Bronze Age cairns and defended by a big Iron Age fort, the Bulwark, is well worth the twenty-minute walk up for its splendid views. The ascent from the village gives a grand panorama north and west (take the lane near the Post Office and leave the car at the rough track).

Whitford Burrows (National Trust), jutting into the treacherous estuary at your feet, is a national nature reserve: wild dunes and all that goes with them. Seaweed for laver bread is gathered here. Its preparation is a slow job but the bread can be bought, ready to cook, in markets as distant as Fishguard (roll in plenty of oatmeal, fry and eat with bacon).

Beside the road which runs east from Cheriton is **Weobley Castle** (DoE), a very attractive thirteenth–fourteenth-century fortified manor house – thus described as early as 1410. The buildings are grouped around a courtyard, entered through a gatehouse. To the left are a hall and solar over kitchen and cellar, and ahead a generous guest-chamber. A square tower guards the landward side, and beyond it was the chapel.

From Llanrhidian, an attractive minor road runs below the B4295 along the edge of the marsh. Here ponies abound, and you may meet the cockle gatherers unloading their sacks into vans for the factory at **Penclawdd**. The estuary has the marvellous melancholy of empty saltings, but the Dickensian-seeming cockle-women here dispel gloom. These cheerful ladies (TV naturals), complete with shovels, sieves, and maybe a handbag which would not be out of place in Oxford Street, can be seen about the village driving their flat two-wheeled carts, or as tiny figures silhouetted against the sky on the distant mud. They have recently been limited to four hundred-weights per day instead of three. They would like to wage violent war upon the oystercatchers, claiming that the birds steal their harvest, but conservationists are far from convinced by their argument. Ironically, the cockle factory on the shore in Penclawdd, easily identified by the huge heaps of cockleshells around it, bears the name BIRDS SEA FOODS. The shells are sold for hard surfacing in these parts and for digging into gardens.

GOWER TO PONTARDDULAIS

From Penclawdd, the B4295 goes east to **Gowerton**, where there was a steelworks, and from where the B4296 crosses the Llan valley to meet the A4070. A mile back towards Swansea, just north of this road, are two Roman practice-camps, connected with the Roman settlement of *Leucarum*, a name which closely resembles that of Loughor (Casllwchwr), two miles west, where the A4070 meets the A484 just before it goes over the Loughor estuary and into Carmarthenshire (three miles from Llanelli – p. 154). Guarding the crossing is **Loughor Castle** (DoE), whose scanty ruins stand on a Norman motte. Recent excavations have shown that the castle occupies the south-east corner of a Roman fort, established *c.* AD 75, and rebuilt in stone *c.* 110.

The A484 leads back through Gorseinon, a sizeable industrial town, to the Penllergaer roundabout, where it meets the A48, which comes up from Morriston (p. 292), and here heads north, across the Lliw valley, to **Pontarddulais**. This friendly little town (formerly a centre of the tinplate industry) is situated at the junction of the Dulais and Loughor rivers. It has a celebrated male voice choir. The Loughor is the county boundary, and over the other side the A4138 goes south-west to Llanelli, while the A48 goes north-west to Carmarthen (p. 158). Pontarddulais has a new church, replacing the old parish church of **Llandeilo Talybont**. This was abandoned as being too inaccessible, since it is situated on a peninsula at the confluence of the Loughor and Gwili rivers, only half a mile from the town as the crow flies, but much further by road. To find it, take the B4296, south from the A48, take the first turning right beyond the railway, then follow the track back under the railway. The whitewashed church is beautifully set in a wooded churchyard, surrounded by a whitewashed wall, among the marshy river-meadows. It has suffered sadly, but fortunately the Friends of Friendless Churches are befriending it. It dates from the thirteenth century, and the chancel arch and arches to the aisle are extremely crude. The medieval roofs, however, are splendid. Some old windows survive, but there are also big Gothic ones put in in 1810, when the church was fitted out with box pews and a two-decker pulpit. Since then it has remained untouched, except by vandals.

Glossary

❧

1. ELEMENTS USED IN WELSH
PLACE-NAMES

2. SOME OTHER USEFUL WORDS
AND PHRASES

3. PRONUNCIATION

1. Elements used in Welsh Place-Names

❧

It is well worth familiarizing oneself with these, for Welsh place-names are usually descriptive, and reflect an acute perception of a place's physical character.

One essential point that must be taken into account is that many initial consonants in Welsh are mutated when used in compounds. To give a few examples: **Llan + Mair** (Mary) becomes **Llanfair**; **Llan + Pedr** (Peter) becomes **Llanbedr**; **Llan + Sant + Braid** (Saint Brigid) becomes **Llansanffraid**; similarly **moel**, but **y foel**; **ban**, but **y fan**.

The following table of mutated consonants, and the glossary of elements in Welsh place-names, and notes on pronunciation, are taken from *Rhestr o Enwau Lleoedd: A Gazetteer of Welsh Place-Names*, edited by Elwyn Davies, and published by the University of Wales Press (3rd edition, 1967), with whose permission they are here reprinted.

	Radical	p	t	c	b	d	g	m	ll	rh
	Soft	b	d	g	f	dd	—	f	l	r
Mutation	Nasal	mh	nh	ngh	m	n	ng	No change		
	Spirant	ph	th	ch	No change			No change		

aber estuary, confluence
afon river
allt hill, hillside, slope, wood
ar on, upon, over, by
arth *see* **garth**

bach (*adj.*) small, little, lesser
bach (*noun*), *pl.* **bachau** nook, corner, bend
ban, *pl.* **bannau** peak, crest, bare hill, beacon

banc bank, hill, slope

bangor consecrated land or monastery within a wattled fence

bedwen, *pl.* bedw birch

bedd, *pl.* beddau grave

betws chapel of ease

blaen, *pl.* blaenau head, end, source of river, upland

bod abode, dwelling

bont *see* pont

braich ridge, spur, arm

bro region, vale, lowland

bron hill-breast, hillside

bryn, *pl.* bryniau hill

bwlch pass, gap

bychan little, small, lesser

cadair, cader seat, stronghold

cae, *pl.* caeau field, enclosure

caer, *pl.* caerau fort, stronghold

canol middle

capel chapel, meeting house

carn, *pl.* carnau cairn, rock, mountain

carnedd, *pl.* carneddau, carneddi cairn, barrow, tumulus, mountain

carreg, *pl.* cerrig stone, rock

cas (as in Cas-bach) castle

castell castle, stronghold

cefn ridge

celli grove, copse

cemais river bends

cerrig *see* carreg

ceunant ravine, gorge, brook

cil, *pl.* ciliau corner, retreat, nook

cilfach cove, creek, corner, nook

clawdd dyke, hedge, ditch

clogwyn precipice, crag

clun meadow, moor, brake, thicket

cnwc hillock, knoll

coch red

coed trees, wood, forest

cors bog

craig, *pl.* creigiau rock

crib crest, summit, arête

croes cross, crossroads

croesffordd, croeslon crossroads

crug, *pl.* crugiau knoll, tump

cwm valley, combe

cwrt court, yard

cymer, *pl.* cymerau confluence

dan under, below

dâr, *pl.* deri oak

darren *see* tarren

dau, *f.* dwy two

derwen, *pl.* derw oak

diffwys precipice, desolate place

din hill fortress

dinas hill fortress

diserth hermitage

dôl, *pl.* dolau, dolydd meadow, water meadow

domen *see* tomen

dre *see* tre

drum *see* trum

drws gap, narrow pass

du, *f.* ddu black, dark

dwfr, dŵr water

dwy *see* dau

dyffryn valley

eglwys church

eithin furze, gorse

erw acre

esgair ridge

fach, fechan *see* bach, bychan

faenor *see* maenor

fan *see* ban

faerdref *see* maerdref

fawr *see* mawr

felin *see* melin

foel *see* moel

fron *see* bron

ffin boundary

fforch bifurcation, fork

ffordd way, road

ffos ditch, trench

ffridd *pl.* **ffriddoedd** rough grazing enclosed from mountain, sheepwalk, wood

ffrwd, *pl.* **ffrydiau** stream, torrent

ffynnon, *pl.* **ffynhonnau** spring, well

gaer *see* **caer**

gallt hill, slope, wood

garn *see* **carn**

garnedd *see* **carnedd**

ganol *see* **canol**

garreg *see* **carreg**

garth hill, height; enclosure

garw rough, coarse

gelli *see* **celli**

gefail smithy

gilfach *see* **cilfach**

glan river-bank, bank, hillock

glas green, blue

glas, glais (as in Dulas, Dulais) brook, stream

glyn deep valley, glen

goch *see* **coch**

goetre woodland dwelling or farm

gors *see* **cors**

graig *see* **craig**

grib *see* **crib**

groes *see* **croes**

gwaun moor, mountain pasture

gwern place where alders grow, swamp

gwyn, *f.* **gwen** white

gwyrdd green

hafod, hafoty summer-dwelling, shieling

haidd barley

haul the sun

helygen *pl.* **helyg** willow

hen old

hendre(f) winter dwelling, permanent home, *lit.* old home

heol, hewl road

hir long

is below, under

isaf lower, lowest

isel low

las *see* **glas**

lwyd *see* **llwyd**

llain, *pl.* **lleiniau** narrow strip of land

llan church, enclosure

llannerch clearing, glade

llawr flat valley bottom

llech slab, slate, stone, rock

llechwedd hillside

llety small house, shelter

llethr slope

lluest hut, cottage, shieling

llwch, *pl.* **llychau** lake

llwyd grey, brown

llwyn grove, bush

llyn lake

llys court, hall

maen, *pl.* **meini** stone

maenol, maenor residence of district chief

maerdre(f) hamlet attached to chief's court, lord's demesne

maes, *pl.* **meysydd** field, plain

mawr great, big

meini *see* **maen**

melin mill

melindre(f) mill village

melyn yellow

merthyr burial place, church

mign, *pl.* **mignedd** bog, quagmire

moel bare hill, bald

morfa marsh, sea fen

mur, *pl.* **muriau** wall

mwyn ore, mine

mynachlog monastery

mynydd mountain, moorland

nant, *pl.* **nentydd, nannau** brook

newydd new

odyn kiln
onnen, *pl.* **onn, ynn** ash tree

pandy fulling mill
pant hollow, valley
parc park, field
pen head, top, end
penrhyn promontory
pentre(f) village, homestead
pistyll spout, waterfall
plas hall, mansion
pont bridge
porth gateway, harbour
pwll pit, pool

rhaeadr waterfall
rhiw hill, slope
rhos, *pl.* **rhosydd** moorland
rhyd ford

sain, san, sant, saint saint
sarn, *pl.* **sarnau** causeway
sych dry

tafarn, *pl.* **tafarnau** tavern
tair *see* **tri**
tal end
tan end, below
tarren, *pl.* **tarenni** rocky height, precipice
teg fair
tir land, territory

tomen mound
ton grassland, lea
traeth strand, beach, shore
trallwng wet bottom land
traws cross, transverse; direction, district
tre(f) homestead, hamlet, town
tri, *f.* **tair** three
troed foot
tros over
trum ridge
trwyn point, cape (*lit.* nose)
twyn hillock, knoll
tŷ, *pl.* **tai** house
tyddyn, ty'n small farm, holding

uchaf upper, higher, highest
uchel high
uwch above, over

waun *see* **gwaun**
wen *see* **gwyn**
wern *see* **gwern**

y, yr, 'r (*definite article*) the
ych ox
yn in
ynys island, holm, water meadow
ysbyty hospital, hospice
ystrad valley floor, strath
ystum bend (in river)

2. Some other Useful Words and Phrases

✿

Names of old (pre-1974) counties

Brycheiniog (Sir Frycheiniog)	: Breconshire
Caerfyrddin (Sir Gaerfyrddin)	: Carmarthenshire
Caernarfon (Sir Gaernarfon)	: Caernarfonshire
Dinbych (Sir Ddinbych)	: Denbighshire
Fflint (Sir Fflint)	: Flintshire
Maesyfed (Sir Faesyfed)	: Radnorshire
Meirionnydd (Sir Feirionnydd)	: Merioneth
Môn (Sir Fôn)	: Anglesey
Morgannwg (Sir Forgannwg)	: Glamorgan
Mynwy (Sir Fynwy)	: Monmouthshire
Penfro (Sir Benfro)	: Pembrokeshire
Trefaldwyn (Sir Drefaldwyn)	: Montgomeryshire

Some saints' names
Braid: Brigid (as in **Llansanffraid**)
Dafydd/Dewi: David (as in **Llanddewi**)
Mair/Mari: Mary (as in **Llanfair**)
Mihangel: Michael (as in **Llanfihangel**)
Pedr: Peter (as in **Llanbedr**)
Siôn/Ioan: John

Terms used in Chapel inscriptions

Annibynol: Independent	Adeiladwyd: built
Cynulleidfaol: Congregational	Ailadeiladwyd: rebuilt
Bedyddwyr: Baptists	Helaethwyd: enlarged
Methodistaidd: Methodist	Adnewyddwyd: renewed

Some other words and sayings

Abaty: abbey
Bore da: good morning
Chwarel: quarry
Croeso: welcome
Cyfleusterau: conveniences
Cymraeg (yr iaith Gymraeg): the Welsh language
Cymreig: Welsh
Cymru: Wales
Cymru am byth: Wales for ever
Cymru rydd: free Wales
Cymry: the people of Wales
Diolch yn fawr: thank you very much
Duw: God
Dynion: men
Y Ddraig Goch: red dragon
Fferm: farm
Heb Dduw, heb ddim: without God, without anything
Hen Wlad fy Nhadau: Land of my Fathers
Hiraeth: longing, nostalgia (German *Heimweh*)
Hwyl: ecstatic fervour
Llwybr Cyhoeddus: public footpath
Merched: women
Ogof: cave
Plwyf: parish
Nos da: goodnight
Sant: saint
Sir: shire
Tân: fire
Ysgol: school

3. Pronunciation

❧

Welsh is not as hard to pronounce as it seems at first sight. In fact, its pronunciation is almost entirely phonetic.

CONSONANTS
Each has only one sound.
b, d, h, l, m, n, p, t as in English
c   always hard, as in **cat**
ch   as in Scottish **loch**
dd   the same sound as **th** in **this**
f   as English **v**
ff   as English **f**
g   always hard, as in **gate**
ll   almost impossible to represent exactly, but something like **hl**
r   trilled as in **merry**
s   hard as in **essay**

DIPHTHONGS
ng   usually as in **long**, but sometimes as in **longer**, e.g. **bangor**
ph   as in **phone**
rh   a trilled **r** followed by the aspirate
th   as in **thin**

VOWELS
In Welsh these are **a, e, i, o, u, w, y**, and they have two values, short and long.
Long **a**   as English **ah**
Short **a**   a pure flat sound as in French **à la**
Long **e**   a pure sound similar to **a** in **face, gate** in Northern pronunciation
Short **e**   as in **pen**
Long **i**   as in **machine**
Short **i**   as in **pin**

Long **o**   as in **gore**
Short **o**   as in **not**
Short **u**   in North Wales, not unlike the French **u**, but not rounded;
   in South Wales it approximates to long and short **i** as above
Long **w**   the **oo** sound in **pool**
Short **w**   the **oo** sound in **good**
y   long and short, has two sounds, the 'clear' sound which is
   similar to the Welsh **i**, and the 'obscure' sound which, when
   long, is like **u** in **further**, and when short is like **u** in **gun**.
In general vowels are short when followed by two or more consonants or by c, ng, m, p, t, and long when followed by b, ch, d,
f, ff, g, s, th.

STRESS

As a rule the stress is on the penultimate syllable. In some place-
names it is thrown forward on to the last syllable, e.g. Caerdýdd,
Pontyprídd, Llanrwst.

Who's Who and What's What

❧

This section includes only characters and subjects which cannot be easily located in any particular part of Wales.

Act of Union, 1536. Brought Wales under English law and gave Welshmen the same rights as the English. It abolished the powers of the Lords Marcher.

Archaeological dating. Through the recent process known as Carbon 14 dating a revised chronology has been worked out by archaeologists. Readers may find considerable discrepancy between this and that used in older books and on signs on some ancient monuments.

Neolithic	beginning	3500 BC
Late Neolithic (Beaker people)	,,	2500/2400 BC
Bronze Age	,,	1900/1800 BC
Iron Age	,,	600/500 BC

Arthur: the early sixth-century soldier king who was more than legendary but about whom no facts emerge. A heroic figure who lived after the departure of the Romans and led the Britons against the Saxons. King Arthur is associated with Caerleon (on the Usk) as well as Cornwall. During the twelfth century a legend emerged that he would return and liberate his fellow countrymen. In 1485, the year of Henry VII's accession, Malory's *Morte D'Arthur* was printed by Caxton's press. Henry named his eldest son Arthur, who, had he lived, would have succeeded instead of Henry VIII.

Baldwin, Archbishop, conducted his famous recruiting campaign in Wales for the 3rd Crusade in 1188 (see also Giraldus Cambrensis). Over 3000 Welshmen took the Cross, but Henry II delayed the expedition and, by the time Richard I was ready, the Welsh were too occupied in fighting at home to join. Baldwin died in camp at Acre.

Bards. See also Eisteddfod. Bards played an important role in the courts of the princes and continued to attach themselves to the households of the gentry right up to the seventeenth century; some of their descriptions of houses and demesnes survive. The quality and intricacy of structure of their poetry is greatly prized, but a minor by-product, the keeping of law and order in the community through their use of satire, was also of great value.

'Bevan, Madam' (Bridget Bevan), 1698–1779, was the chief patron and adviser of Griffith Jones, founder of the Welsh Circulating Schools, which she organized after his death. She was a Vaughan of Derllys Court, Carmarthenshire, and her father was organizer of the SPCK schools in the county. She married Arthur Bevan, a barrister in Laugharne.

Buckeridge, Charles, 1832/3–73. A pupil of Sir Gilbert Scott, he practised in Oxford. A keen High Churchman, he was primarily an ecclesiastical architect. He designed Holy Trinity Convent, Oxford (1865–8, now St Antony's College) for Mother Marian Hughes, a disciple of Pusey, as well as Llanthony Abbey, for Father Ignatius. He did much work in Breconshire and Glamorgan, through the Rev. Gilbert C. F. Harries, Rector of Llandyfaelog Fach and Rural Dean of Breconshire, and after 1862 Rector of Gelligaer.

Cambrian Archaeological Association. Founded 1846. The first President was Sir Stephen Glynne, and the Vice-Presidents were W. W. E. Wynne and Sir Samuel Rush Meyrick. The first volume of its celebrated journal, *Archaeologia Cambrensis*, was published the same year. In 1847 it held its first Annual Meeting, at Aberystwyth, and these have continued ever since. They are held in a different area each year, and combine scholarly investigation with friendly merriment.

Caractacus (d. AD 54). The last leader of the Ordovices. He put up a long fight against the Romans and, on his defeat in AD 51, was taken to Rome and exhibited in triumph by Claudius. This was the end of any organized resistance to Rome in Wales.

Caröe, William Douglas, (1857–1938). Of Danish origin. For nine years J. L. Pearson's chief assistant. A London architect, prolific and inventive, and a sensitive and skilful restorer of old buildings, he did much of his best work in Wales. His practice is carried on by his son Alban D. R. Caroe and his grandson Martin Caroe.

Celtic. Strictly a branch of the Indo-Germanic group of languages (not a race). These include Breton, Cornish, Gaelic, Irish, Manx and Welsh. However the term is widely used to describe the settlers who came to Wales from Central Europe during the Iron Age. They are always described as tall and fair (as distinct from the earlier Iberian settlers who are small and dark) and form the aristocracy of the *Mabinogion*.

Charles, Thomas (1755–1814), the great evangelical reformer, was, at the end of his life, chief leader of the Calvinistic Methodists and was directly responsible for the formation of their separate church although he had done his utmost for many years to prevent the schism between it and the Anglicans. The final break came in 1811 when he ordained six of his leading lay preachers so that they might administer the Sacrament.

Church in Wales. The Anglican Church in Wales was disestablished in 1921. It has a governing body of bishops, clergy and laity. The archbishop is elected by an electoral college, so may be a bishop of any diocese.

Clas. A monastery of the Celtic church consisting of a body of hereditary canons, often headed by a layman (marriage was allowed). *Clasau* were outposts of scholarship and some held important schools. The Normans did their utmost to Romanize the Celtic church and the *clas* was suppressed or replaced by cathedral chapters or collegiate churches.

Council for the Protection of Rural Wales (Cymdeithas Diogelu Harddwch Cymru). Founded in 1928 'to secure the protection and improvement of rural scenery and amenities in the Welsh country-side'. This active but level-headed society does splendid work, not only in protesting against harmful developments, but also in more positive ways.

The Court of the Council of Wales and the Marches was established by Edward IV 'to restrain the wild Welchmanne'. In 1534 it became a regular court sitting at Ludlow Castle. It brought a measure of peace to the borders, often by ruthless hangings.

Crucks take the place of roof trusses in some old buildings. A pair of arched timbers spring from floor level instead of resting on the top of the wall. A surprising number survive in Wales, chiefly in houses and barns.

Cunedda Wledig (fl. 450?). A Brythonic (British) prince from Scotland (the shores of the Forth). He drove the Goidels (Irish) from NW Wales thus laying the foundations of Gwynedd at the time when the last legions had left Britain. Most Welsh rulers have claimed descent from one of his eight sons.

Cybi, Saint. Mid sixth-century. Quarrelsome and aristocratic. Born in Cornwall, with a prince as great-grandfather and a saint as uncle. Went to Monmouthshire (Llangibby-on-Usk) then via St Davids to Arran for four years. Settled in Anglesey where Holy Island is called Ynys Gybi and Holyhead Caergybi after him. He is reputed to have said 'There is no misfortune like wickedness.'

David, Saint, d. 601 (1 March), the patron saint of Wales. Tradition- ally the grandson of Ceredig, king of the region centred on Cardigan, and son of Sant and Non, a nun. He may have been a descendant of Cunedda which would add political strength to the tradition of his refutation of the Pelagian heresy (Pelagius was Irish). After spending some time as a pupil of Paulinus, David went on several preaching journeys before founding his monastery in West Pembrokeshire (now St Davids). The earliest life was written by Rhygyfarch c. 1090. He was canonized in 1120.

Double-naved churches. Churches consisting of two naves of equal size. Often called 'double-aisled', but this can cause confusion with churches like St John's, Cardiff, which have two aisles on each side of the nave. Numerous explanations have been offered for this phenomenon. The simplest is that it was the easiest way of sub- stantially enlarging a church, as it involves least alteration to the existing structure. Those who find this dull may prefer, e.g., to see it as a reflection of the fifteenth-century popularity of the cult of the Virgin, requiring a second altar of equal prominence with the high altar. These churches are particularly common in the Vale of Clwyd.

Eisteddfod (meeting). A public meeting at which contests in literature and music are held, chiefly poetry and singing, both of which were of such importance in the courts of the princes. Today's ceremony of the chairing of the bard is an echo of the regard in which the medieval court poets were held (modern bardic chairs are quite often to be seen in churches or chapels, having been presented after the owner's death).

The first recorded eisteddfod is claimed by Cardigan, 1176. One of the most famous was that at Caerwys (1568) held by order of Queen Elizabeth I to test the claims of vagrants calling themselves poets and harpists who were sponging on the hospitality of the great houses.

The romantic movement of the eighteenth century saw a great revival of interest in Welsh music and literature among the gentry who promoted eisteddfodau. In London societies were formed for the study of Welsh literature. Iolo Morganwg, a young stonemason turned antiquarian, of great imagination, invented in 1792 the ceremony of the Gorsedd, which many of his contemporaries believed he had discovered in old manuscripts. The 'Gorsedd of the Bards of the Isle of Britain' is the union of all the enrolled bards. It was grafted on to the eisteddfod, and today it is responsible for administering the National Eisteddfod. The Gorsedd ceremony takes place in a stone circle, which explains why modern ones are to be found all over Wales.

Today numerous local eisteddfodau are held in towns and villages throughout Welsh-speaking Wales (Cardiganshire is particularly prolific). The National Eisteddfod moves to a different town each year, alternating north and south. The International Eisteddfod is held annually in Llangollen.

Most eisteddfodau are held entirely in Welsh and are in effect celebrations of the Welsh language.

Fenton, Richard (1746–1821), topographical writer, antiquary and barrister. Born at St Davids where he was educated at the Cathedral School. Entered the Middle Temple. Lived and died in Fishguard.

Flower Sunday. Palm Sunday is so called in many parts of Wales because of the custom of dressing the graves. Quiet churchyards and grey cemeteries blaze yellow with daffodils. It is like a dress rehearsal for the Last Trump, or a rite of spring.

Gavelkind (partible succession). The Welsh system of inheritance by which a kingdom or property was divided equally among the children, instead of that of primogeniture, was a principal cause of lack of unity among the Welsh.

Giraldus Cambrensis (1146–1223), topographical writer and priest, was the youngest son of William de Barri, of Manorbier Castle, where he was born, and a grandson of Nest. He was a student at the University of Paris where he later lectured (very successfully, he records). Giraldus was a passionate Welshman, despite or because of his Norman blood, and it was probably this, combined with his intelligence and vigour, that caused his nominations to the See of St Davids to be repeatedly turned down by the Pope through the intervention of the Crown. He travelled three times to Rome to plead his cause. This remained his life's ambition and he would accept no other bishopric. He later campaigned to free St Davids from the archbishopric of Canterbury (achieved in 1921). He is best known for the accounts of his travels and particularly for the journey he made through Wales with Archbishop Baldwin on his recruiting campaign for the 3rd Crusade. *Itinerarium Kambriae* has been translated into English.

Goodhart-Rendel, Harry Stuart (1887–1959). Grandson of Lord Rendel, related to the Gladstones of Hawarden. He was a versatile architect and a brilliant architectural writer. His card-index of Victorian churches (copies at the National Monuments Record and at the RIBA) is the prime source for architects and dates, and often contains penetrating and witty comments on churches he had visited.

Harris, Howell (1714–73). Religious reformer and Methodist leader.

Haycocks, The. Edward Haycock Sr. (1791–1870) was a pupil of Sir Jeffry Wyatville. He practised in Shrewsbury. He built numerous feeble Gothic churches, and a few splendid Greek Revival houses, notably Clytha Park, Monmouthshire, and Millichope Park, Shropshire (1835). His son, Edward (1830–82), also practised in Shrewsbury, chiefly as a church architect.

The Historic Buildings Council for Wales was set up in 1953 to advise on the allocation of government grants for the restoration of historic buildings. As well as houses these include a great variety of structures, many of which are given a new use and, therefore, a new lease of life: mills, follies, farm buildings . . . The Council, which receives no publicity, deserves the gratitude of anyone who enjoys this book.

Howell the Good (Hywel Dda), grandson of Rhodri Mawr, reigned 910–50 and eventually ruled most of Wales. He greatly admired

King Alfred of Wessex (d. 899) and was on friendly terms with his successors. A great man whose outstanding achievement was the codification of the laws of Wales. Their practical and compassionate nature, for instance in their attitude to women's rights (it is surprising that Women's Lib. have not quoted them freely) and to those of illegitimate children, was quite different to those of the Roman Church. Bastards were received into the father's family after oaths had been sworn on the altar of the Celtic church:

> And thus he is to be received: the chief of the kindred is to take the hands of the child between his own hands, and give him a kiss; for a kiss is a sign of affinity; and then to place the right hand of the child in the hand of the oldest of the other men, who is also to give him a kiss; and so from hand to hand and unto the last man . . . (*The Myvyrian Archaiology of Wales* 2nd ed. 1870.)

Illtud, Saint, d. 505 (6 November), fought for his cousin King Arthur and was one of the three knights in charge of the Holy Grail. Left his wife to become a solitary and later founded the famous school and monastery of Llanilltud Fawr (Llantwit Major). Also said to have founded the monastery on Caldey Island. A famous teacher who also introduced an improved method of ploughing.

Iolo Morganwg (Williams, Edward, 1747–1826), poet, antiquary, inventor and stonemason. See also Eisteddfod.

James of St George (d. *c.* 1309). Master of the King's Works in Wales. Came to work for Edward I from the court of his cousin Count Philip of Savoy for whom he built numerous castles. In spring 1278 he was bound for Wales 'to ordain the works of the castles there' (Flint, Rhuddlan, Builth and Aberystwyth). After the revolt of 1282, the plan for the North Wales chain of castles was conceived. He was responsible for Caernarfon, Conwy, Harlech and Beaumaris. These are undoubtedly among the finest medieval castles in Europe. In 1290–3 he was Constable of Harlech and from 1298 worked in Scotland.

Jesus College, Oxford, was founded in 1571 by Queen Elizabeth I on the initiative of Dr Hugh Price, Chancellor of St Davids, who provided the money for the first buildings. The College has always had a very close association with Wales, and nearly all of its endowments have been provided by Welshmen.

Jones, Griffith (1683–1761), was the creator of the imaginative and influential Welsh Circulating Schools (See p. 162).

Kilvert, Robert Francis (1840–79) is renowned for his diaries (1870–9) which give a fascinating and endearing close-up of the country and life around Clyro in the Wye valley where he was curate (1865–72), and of St Harmon, Radnorshire, where he was rector (1876–7).

The Landmark Trust was started in 1965 by John and Christian Smith with the object of protecting small buildings or sites of special value and where possible finding new uses for them so that they can be enjoyed (usually as holiday accommodation). In Wales these include cottages, a nineteenth-century fort, a tower in Caernarfon town wall, and an eighteenth-century folly. The address is Shottesbrooke, Maidenhead, Berks.

Leet. A channel taken off a stream, usually to operate a waterwheel.

Llywelyn the Great (Llywelyn ap Iorwerth) (1173–1240) was indeed a great leader. His father died about the time of his birth so he probably was brought up in Powys, his mother's home, safe from his father's half-brothers to whom he was a potential menace. He took to arms at a tender age and seems to have quickly proved this point. By 1199 he ruled the whole of Gwynedd and was clearly an able statesman as well as a successful soldier. At first he was on terms with King John, marrying his natural daughter Joan in 1205, but the royal armies took some of his territory in 1211. He then took advantage of the unrest leading up to Magna Carta, taking the key castles of Carmarthen and Cardigan from the king and becoming the acknowledged leader of all the Welsh princes. However, he never called himself Prince of Wales, realizing the jealousy this title would cause. He was a signatory of Magna Carta in which three clauses dealt specifically with Wales, the most important being the confirmation that disputes within Wales were to be settled by Welsh law.

In 1218 he paid homage to Henry III, the new boy-king, and his authority was not disputed seriously again. Thus Wales enjoyed a rare spell of peace.

Llywelyn the Last (Llywelyn ap Gruffydd) (d. 1282), grandson of Llywelyn the Great, seems to have veered between statesmanship and intransigence. This eventually broke the precarious unity of the

Welsh princes, which he had to some extent re-established. As a prince of Gwynedd he first reunited North Wales, annexed much of mid-Wales and raided the south. He supported Simon de Montfort against Henry III and became engaged to his daughter Eleanor (the English prevented their marriage until 1278). Llywelyn was recognized as Prince of Wales after the Treaty of Montgomery (1267) provided he paid homage to Henry III. He later refused to attend the coronation of Edward I and the treaty was broken on both sides. War broke out in 1276. Neither Powys nor South Wales were on Llywelyn's side; his brother Dafydd was in Edward's army as were many Welsh soldiers from the Marches. Edward's coup was to burn the crops in Anglesey, the granary that fed Llywelyn's army in Snowdonia. By the Treaty of Conwy, 1277, Llywelyn was deprived of all lands except Gwynedd. War broke out again in 1282 and Llywelyn was killed by chance near Builth. Edward I rapidly built his grand chain of castles to control the north.

Llywelyn's life was full of contradictions: he strongly supported the monastic orders but was excommunicated by the Archbishop of Canterbury. His adoption of the style Prince of Wales caused much jealousy in his lifetime but its passing was deeply lamented by ballad writers after his death: it was the embodiment of the idea of a united Wales.

Long house. A long building in which stock was housed in the lower end and the family in the upper, with an interconnecting door. Once common in Britain, a few survive in Wales and Scotland.

Mabinogion, The. A strange and wonderful collection of heroic tales, passed down by word of mouth from the Dark Ages. The earliest surviving manuscripts are the *White Book of Rhydderch* (c. 1300–25), now in the National Library, Aberystwyth and the *Red Book of Hergest* (c. 1375–1425), now in Jesus College, Oxford. They rank with Chaucer's tales in their importance to European medieval literature. The eleven tales include the earliest Arthurian tale in Welsh (*Culhwch and Olwen*). The collection was given its name (a misnomer) by Lady Charlotte Guest as a title to her translation (1838–49). An English version (by Gwyn Jones and Thomas Jones) is available in Dent's *Everyman's Library*.

Marcher Lordships, granted by the Norman kings to reward their earls and control the country, covered a large area of Wales, much of it remote from the Welsh border but accessible from the sea; it was mostly rich lowland. The earls could exploit the land and people as they saw fit and were not answerable to any judiciary. They had power over life or death within their territories. Throughout the Middle Ages there were thus three factions in Wales, not two: the Crown, the Welsh princes and the Marcher Lords.

Nesfield, William Eden (1835–88). Nephew of Anthony Salvin, and son of a well-known landscape gardener. Pupil of Burn and Salvin. In the 1860s he was, with Norman Shaw (with whom he worked), a pioneer of the Domestic Revival. His Welsh country houses include Kinmel, Bodrhyddan, Gloddaeth, and Gwernyfed. Drink tended to get the better of him.

Nest, the 'Helen of Wales' (fl. 1120), daughter of Rhys ap Tewdwr, is renowned for her compelling charm and numerous offspring, one of whom was a son of Henry I. The king arranged that she should marry Gerald of Windsor who held the earldom of Pembroke. Giraldus Cambrensis (*q.v.*) was her grandson.

Offa's Dyke. King Offa of Mercia (757–96) constructed the dyke as a boundary between his kingdom and the Welsh from Prestatyn in the north to the Bristol Channel. Where possible its line follows natural boundaries – rivers and hills. There are eighty miles of earthworks. A long-distance footpath has been opened along the Dyke; see *Offa's Dyke Path* by Frank Noble (a Shell book) for details. It is particularly spectacular in the uplands of Radnorshire but there are many lovely stretches in both England and Wales.

Ordovices. The Brythonic Celtic settlers who controlled North Wales *c.* 200 BC to AD 50. They built many border forts. See also Caractacus.

Owain Gwynedd (1137–70) was described by Giraldus Cambrensis as 'a man of distinguished wisdom and moderation'. His aim was further to strengthen Gwynedd and extend its supremacy by resisting the Marcher Lords and making treaties with the South Wales princes, notably the Lord Rhys. When the English throne was weak he achieved great success, but Henry II (1154–89) attacked both North and South Wales and Owain and Rhys wisely paid homage. However, Becket's quarrel with Henry II encouraged them to rebel. The king's great army, sent to subdue the united princes in North-East Wales, was defeated (1165) by a combination of wild weather, inhospitable hill country and a Welsh army who knew how to exploit both. Affairs elsewhere occupied Henry II and for many years Wales knew comparative peace.

Owen Glendower (Owain Glyn Dŵr) (*c.* 1354–1416), born a country squire in the Upper Dee valley, was descended from the princes of Powys through his father and Deheubarth through his mother. Married Margaret, daughter of Richard Hanmer, an Anglo-Welsh judge (*North Wales*, p. 76). His education included a spell in the Inns of Court, and he later served in the English army on Scottish campaigns. In his late forties, a quarrel with his neighbour, Reginald, Lord Grey of Ruthin, seems to have precipitated his attack on Ruthin (1400) which was followed by fourteen years' guerrilla warfare against the English in much of which he was very successful, taking castles and laying waste the country. His aims were Welsh independence, a Church independent of Canterbury, and the establishment of a Welsh university. He wanted to replace Henry IV by a Yorkist. The Mortimer family, to whom he was allied by the marriage of his daughter Catherine, had claims to the crown through kinship with Richard II. In 1404 he established himself in West Wales by taking Aberystwyth and Harlech. He made a treaty with France and the Scots supported him.

Tantalizingly little is known of Glendower. He can have borne little resemblance to Shakespeare's character. The time was ripe for his rising and in calling himself Prince of Wales he allied to himself popular support restless under foreign rule. Eventually in 1414 he disappeared and is believed to have died in the house of his daughter, Anne Scudamore, near Hereford. Henry V sent him a special message of pardon before his death. Whether he received it is not known.

Padarn, Saint, late fifth century (15 April). Born in Brittany and said to have sailed for Wales as a young man and to have studied at the college of St Illtud. Founded the monastery of Llanbadarn Fawr (near Aberystwyth). A great preacher. Rhygyfarch in his life of St David says that Padarn accompanied St David and St Teilo to Jerusalem.

Penillion is the free improvization by a voice or voices on an air which is played over and over again by an instrument, usually the harp. There is a marked contrast between the strict metre observed by the instrument and the freer vocal line. This traditional form is very popular today.

Pennant, Thomas (1726–98). Topographical writer, antiquary and zoologist, lived at Downing, Flintshire. See bibliography.

Pensons, The. Thomas Penson the elder (d. 1824), was a Wrexham mason, auctioneer, and architect. He was County Surveyor of Flint until he was dismissed after Overton Bridge collapsed, in 1814. His son **Thomas** (1791–1859) was a pupil of Thomas Harrison of Chester. He practised in Wrexham and Oswestry, and was County Surveyor of Denbighshire and Montgomeryshire. A versatile stylist, he was a practical man, interested in new materials like terracotta and iron. He married the daughter of Richard Kirk, a Wrexham ironmaster. His elder son, **Richard Kyrke Penson** (1816–86), trained in London, practised in Ferryside, Carmarthenshire, also in Swansea and (later) in Oswestry. He was County Surveyor of Carmarthenshire and Cardiganshire, and succeeded his father as Surveyor of Montgomeryshire. He was a sober and accomplished Gothicist, and his numerous ecclesiastical works nearly always have a touch of refinement. He retired in 1864, and went to live in Ludlow. His younger brother **Thomas Mainwaring Penson** (1818–64) practised in Chester, where he initiated the half-timber revival. He built all the stations etc. on the Chester and Shrewsbury Railway, *c*. 1848, and was County Surveyor of Flint.

Powys. The modern county has similar boundaries to the ancient kingdom of East Wales of which Shrewsbury was once the capital. The princes of Powys were often hostile to those of Gwynedd and were allies of Henry III and Edward I in their fight against the Llywelyns. The Powys lands were restored after Edward I's conquest.

Prichard, John (1817–86), son of Rev. Richard Prichard, priest-vicar of Llandaff. Pupil of T. L. Walker, who had been chief assistant to A. C. Pugin (the elder). Partnership with J. P. Seddon (1852–63). They were Llandaff Diocesan Architects: Prichard took the Glamorgan jobs, and Seddon those in Monmouthshire. Their greatest work was the restoration of Llandaff Cathedral.

Rebecca Riots, 1843–4. These riots, though best known in connection with the attacks on the turnpikes, came as the culmination of many grievances caused by economic depression and took place throughout South Wales. The rioters were principally farmers and small-holders. Eventually a Royal Commission was appointed to look into their grievances. See *Genesis XXIV*[60] and Efailwen for the origin of the name.

Rhodri Mawr ('the Great') (d. 877), succeeded as king of Gwynedd *c.* 844 and extended his rule over the whole of North Wales and much of the South. He was thus the first to unite Wales and became the ideal of the medieval princes; those of both North and South could claim descent from him. The terrible menace of the continuing Viking raids (beginning 850) against which he effectively led the Welsh, may have been the reason for their rare unity. His reign overlapped with that of King Alfred (871–99). On Rhodri's death Wales was divided between his six sons, one of whom paid allegiance to Alfred, who was the acknowledged protector against the Vikings. Later demands of homage from the Welsh princes by the English throne sprang from this precedent.

Rhys ap Thomas, Sir (1449–1525), head of the Dynevor family and chief Welsh supporter of Henry VII. When Henry Tudor landed in Pembrokeshire in 1485, Rhys rallied the men of South Wales and marched to join him on the Long Mountain, near Welshpool, and thence to Bosworth where tradition has it that it was he who slew Richard III. At all events Rhys was knighted on the battlefield and was rewarded by becoming virtual ruler of South Wales. He was granted numerous castles and took a mortgage on Carew, Pembrokeshire. His tomb is in St Peter's Church, Carmarthen, having been moved there on the dissolution of Greyfriars monastery.

The Lord Rhys (Rhys ap Gruffydd) (1132–97), one of Wales's great medieval rulers, was four when his father died and at thirteen was fighting alongside his elder brothers against the Normans in the South-West. He succeeded as ruler of Deheubarth in 1155 and united the Welsh against the Lords Marcher in the East as well as West. He achieved peace and paid the traditional homage to Henry II, remaining consistently loyal. On Owain Gwynedd's death (1170) paramount power in Wales shifted to the South for the rest of Rhys's life. He built Dynevor (his capital) and Cardigan castles (at Cardigan he held the first-recorded Eisteddfod). On Henry's death, Richard I was indifferent to his special position *vis à vis* the throne and Rhys spent his last years fighting the Normans again. His old age was marred by quarrels with and between his eight sons. Henry VII was descended from his only daughter who married Ednyfed Fychan. According to tradition, he is buried in St Davids Cathedral.

Roman occupation of Wales. *c.* AD 47–400. The Romans exploited Wales's mineral wealth, and built roads so that the country could be controlled from a network of military stations, notably *Deva* (Chester), just outside to the North-East; *Segontium* (Caernarfon), *Isca Silurum* (Caerleon, Monmouthshire) and *Moridunum* (Carmarthen). These four bases, one in each corner, were joined by main roads. During the Roman period Wales probably enjoyed a longer peace than at any time until the accession of Henry VII.

Rowland, Daniel (1713–90). Great evangelical preacher and Methodist leader (See p. 68).

Scotts, The. Sir George Gilbert Scott (1811–78) restored three cathedrals in Wales (St Davids, St Asaph, and Bangor), and many churches. He also built new churches (e.g. at Rhyl), and one of his best houses (Hafodunos). He had two architect sons. The elder, also **George Gilbert** (1839–97), was a fine architect, an associate of Bodley and Garner, but became insane. The younger son, **John Oldrid Scott** (1842–1913) carried on his father's practice. **Sir Giles Gilbert Scott** (1880–1960), the architect of Liverpool Cathedral, was the son of George Gilbert Scott Jr.

Seddon, John Pollard (1827–1906). Son of a Regency furniture designer, and brother of Thomas Seddon, a Pre-Raphaelite painter. Partner of John Prichard 1852–63, he had a London office from 1857. A friend of Street, Burges, Rossetti etc. (he designed and owned the bungalow at Birchington in which Rossetti died). From 1885 until 1904 he was in partnership with **John Coates Carter**, a highly original architect. Seddon was an extraordinarily inventive, somewhat quirky designer, as interested in the design of woodwork, ironwork, tiles, stained glass, etc., as in buildings themselves.

Surnames. Surnames did not come into existence in Wales until comparatively recently. The old system of naming was for the son to use his father's name – so Llywelyn ap Gruffydd (*ab* or *ap* means 'son of'). The *ap* was often omitted: e.g. James Thomas's son would be John James. This practice continued until within living memory in some remote areas. Pride in pedigree, coupled with the need to know your ancestry for legal purposes, meant that most people could extend the series over numerous generations, when precision was required. When surnames did come to be used (largely as a result of pressure from English judges), they were based on the Christian names. Three possibilities existed: either the name was kept intact, e.g. John, Harry, Howell (Hywel); or the genetival – *s* was added, e.g. Jones, Harris, Howells; or the *ap* was elided, e.g. Parry (ap Harry), Powell (ap Howell), Price (ap Rhys). The result of this was inevitably too few surnames to go round. In country areas individuals could be distinguished by the names of their farms, e.g. John (Jones) Hafod, and John (Jones) Bryngwyn. Or they might be distinguished by their occupations, e.g. Jones the Milk, Evans the Coal. Alternatively, nicknames might be used. In industrial communities, neither of the first two methods would work: large numbers of people did identical jobs, and addresses were not handy (e.g. John Jones 46 Victoria Terrace). So nicknames were normal. Some were highly picturesque, e.g. Sam Half a Mo, Dic Bol Haearn (Dic Iron Stomach), Dan Bach Drifa i (Little Dan I'll drive), Twm Cwrcyn Carcus (Tom the Careful Tom Cat). A good story concerns David Jones, who went to work in the pit. The overman said that there were already seven David Joneses there, so he would have to have a nickname. The lad said he didn't mind, as long as it was something substantial. From then on, he was known as Dai Substantial. The tradition continues: a dealer in polythene bags is known as Disposable Des.

Thirlwall, Connop (1797–1875) had considerable impact on the Anglican church, particularly in West Wales, during his thirty-four years' bishopric at St Davids, which See he was given by Melbourne after he had been forced to resign his university appointments on account of his liberal views. He was responsible for much new building in the diocese and it was during his bishopric that the restoration of the cathedral under Scott began. He continued to take part in national affairs. He learnt Welsh and insisted on preaching in it, often, it is said, to the mystification of his Welsh congregations. His tomb, in Westminster Abbey, is by Edward Davis of Carmarthen.

Tudor. Henry VII, the first of the Tudor dynasty, was descended from the Tudor family of Plas Penmynydd in Anglesey. His claim to the throne was through his mother Margaret Beaufort, great-granddaughter of John of Gaunt. She married Edmund, Earl of Richmond, and was already widowed, aged fifteen, when Henry was born. The Tudor accession brought much-needed peace to the country and made a great difference to the prosperity of Wales, as the numerous parish churches enriched and enlarged at this time, and many notable houses dating from this period, show.

The Unit System is a name given to describe two or more houses occupied by members of a family and built close together. Each is a complete unit in itself and is of roughly equal status, but they share the same yard or open space. It is found in various parts of Wales.

Welsh, old English, *welisc*, from the Anglo-Saxon name for the Briton, *wealh*, a foreigner.

Welsh Black Cattle. A very ancient and gentle breed. 'Britain does not afford a more useful animal', wrote William Youatt, the renowned English authority in 1838, adding that they were 'very fair milkers with a propensity to fatten'. The drovers took thousands to the English markets.

Welsh Cob. Once pulled nearly every London milk van (whence 'vanner') and were widely popular with farmers and tradesmen because of their equable temperament, strength and sound feet. 'Few or none can equal them for the road; none stand our turnpikes like them . . .' (George Culley, *Observation on Livestock*, 1794). Having become nearly extinct the cob is enjoying a great comeback through the popularity of riding and trekking.

Welsh Corgi. This breed was first brought to the notice of the Kennel Club by Captain Jack Howell, who had long noted the intelligence of 'the little yellow cattle dogs' in Pembrokeshire. Immediately after registration, he presented Princess Elizabeth with her first corgi; the breed never looked back. Cardies (from Cardiganshire) are similar but darker and of heavier build.

Welsh Hound. Pure Welsh hounds are now rare; many have been crossed with English foxhounds. They were bred from hounds imported by French monks at Margam Abbey and have some pointer and Scottish deerhound in them. They are small, mostly white and rough-coated with heads like setters and long ears set low. Some say they think for themselves too much when they should be hunting with the pack.

Welsh Mountain Sheep. Small, active, hardy animals who will prosper where few other breeds can. Long prized for sweet small joints and soft wool. Black Welsh Mountain were bred by enthusiasts in the last century, particularly those who had all black stock on their home farms, e.g. Llanover. Some flocks survive.

Welsh National Opera, founded in 1946, started with an amateur choir giving a fortnight's season. Now a full professional company based in Cardiff but touring regularly in the UK (and also performing in Europe). Enthusiasts should look out for local advertisements.

Williams, William, Pant-y-celyn (1717–91). Great Methodist leader, hymn-writer and author (See p. 150).

Withers, R. J. (1823–94), a competent and imaginative London architect with a large church practice, notably in South and West Wales, 'where he imparted to many a barnlike structure some semblance of life and feeling' (*Building News* obituary.) His most unusual and vigorous work is probably Cardigan Market Hall.

Wyatt family, The. This vast tribe, of Staffordshire origin, included an extraordinary number of members of the architectural and related professions. **William Wyatt** (1701–72) was steward to Lord Uxbridge (see Plas Newydd, Anglesey). His younger brother, **Benjamin Wyatt** of Weeford (1709–72) had no less than five architect sons. The second, **Samuel** (1737–1807), worked for Lord Penrhyn, through his younger brother **Benjamin** (1744–1818), who was Lord Penrhyn's agent. In this capacity Benjamin designed new buildings as well as developing the slate quarries. Some buildings on the estate were designed by his own fourth son, **Lewis William** (1777–1853). The elder Benjamin's fifth son, **James** (1746–1813) was the most famous of all. He had a big London-based practice, both as a neo-classicist (supplanting Adam in fashion) and as a Gothicist (in which style his most famous work was Fonthill Abbey). His work in Wales includes examples of both styles – classical at Wynnstay, Erddig, etc., Gothic at Plas Newydd, Eglwys Newydd (Hafod), etc. **Jeffry Wyatt** (1766–1840), later **Sir Jeffry Wyatville**, was the son of the elder Benjamin's third architect son, Joseph. As architect to George IV, he transformed Windsor Castle. In Wales he built Golden Grove, Carmarthenshire, and the Nant-y-Belan Tower at Wynnstay. **Thomas Henry Wyatt** (1807–80) came of another branch of the family, descended from the William Wyatt mentioned above. An amazingly prolific architect, he was competent but had little aesthetic talent. His uncle, **Arthur Wyatt** (1775–1833), was agent to the Duke of Beaufort, and brought him much work in Monmouthshire. Thomas Henry also did a lot around Flintshire, as architect to the Earl of Denbigh. His younger brother was **Sir Matthew Digby Wyatt** (1820–77), buried at Usk. Arthur Wyatt's son **Osmund** (1811–94) was also agent to the Duke of Beaufort.

Bibliography

❧

GENERAL
This list includes only the better known and readily accessible titles – there are many obscurer works of charm and interest, particularly describing tours in the eighteenth and nineteenth centuries.

Bell, Idris: *Welsh Poetry.*

Borrow, George: *Wild Wales.*

Carter, Harold: *The Towns of Wales.*

Condry, William: *Exploring Wales.*

Davies, Elwyn (ed.): *A Gazetteer of Welsh Place Names.*

Dictionary of Welsh Biography (to 1940).

Evans, Emrys: *The University of Wales: A Historical Sketch.*

Famous Welshmen. University of Wales Press (paperback).

Fenton, Richard: *Tours in Wales 1804–13.*

Fitzgibbon, Theodora: *A Taste of Wales in Food and Pictures.*

Frazer, D.: *Wales in History, I, to 1066, The Invaders.*

Frazer, D.: *Wales in History, II, 1066–1485, The Defenders.*

Giraldus Cambrensis: *Itinerary of Wales*, 1188.

Griffith, Wyn: *The Welsh.*

Howe, Melvyn G. and Thomas, Peter: *Welsh Land Forms and Scenery.*

Howe, Melvyn G.: *Wales from the Air.*

Jenkins, J. Geraint: *The Welsh Woollen Industry.*

Lewis, Samuel: *Topographical Dictionary of Wales 1833.*

Lewis, W. J.: *A History of Lead-Mining in Wales.*

Lloyd, D. M. and E. M.: *A Book of Wales* (Collins National Anthology Series).

Lloyd, J. E.: *History of Wales.*

The Mabinogion, tr. Gwyn Jones and Thomas Jones (Everyman's Library).

Nash-Williams, V. E., rev. Jarrett, M.: *The Roman Frontier in Wales.*

Noble, Frank: *The Shell Book of Offa's Dyke.*

Owen, Trefor: *Welsh Folk Customs.*

Peate, Iorwerth C.: *The Welsh House.*

The Penguin Book of Welsh Verse, trans. Anthony Conran.

Pennant, Thomas: *A Tour in Wales.*

Poucher, W. A.: *The Welsh Peaks.*

Rees, D. Morgan: *Mills, Mines and Furnaces: Industrial Archaeology in Wales.*

Rees, D. Morgan: *Industrial Archaeology of Wales.*
Rees, Wm.: *Historical Atlas of Wales.*
Roderick, A. J. (ed.): *Wales through the Ages.*
Smith, Peter: *Houses of the Welsh Countryside.*
Steegman, John: *A Survey of Portraits in Welsh Houses.*
Taylor, A. J.: *The King's Works in Wales 1277–1330.*
Trueman, A. E.: *Geology and Scenery in England and Wales.*
Williams, Bryn R.: *The Welsh Colony in Patagonia.*
Williams, David: *A History of Modern Wales.*
Wright, Christopher: *A Guide to Offa's Dyke Path.*

SOUTH WALES: GENERAL

Davies, Margaret (ed.): *Brecon Beacons National Park Guide.*
Hadfield, Charles: *The Canals of South Wales and the Border.*
Hilling, John B.: *Wales, South and West.*
Kilvert, Rev. Francis; edited by William Plomer: *Kilvert's Diary* (3 vols. – also abridged in 1 vol.).
Morris, J. H., and Williams, J. L.: *The South Wales Coal Industry.*
Parry-Jones, D.: *Welsh Country Parson.*
Rees, Vyvyan: *Shell Guide to South-West Wales* (Pembrokeshire and Carmarthenshire).
Vaughan, H. M.: *South Wales Squires.*
Watson, Katherine: *South Wales* (Regional Archaeology Series).
The Royal Commission on Historical Monuments in Wales and Monmouthshire: Inventories of Ancient Monuments
    Carmarthenshire 1917
    Pembrokeshire   1925.

BRECONSHIRE

Jones, Theophilus; enlarged by Sir Joseph Bailey: *A History of the County of Brecknock.*
Verey, David: *Shell Guide to Mid Wales* (Brecon, Radnor and Montgomery).

CARDIGANSHIRE

Inglis-Jones, Elisabeth: *Peacocks in Paradise.*
Lewis, W. J.: *An Illustrated History of Cardiganshire.*
Meyrick, Samuel Rush: *The History and Antiquities of the County of Cardigan.*
Parry-Jones, D.: *Welsh Country Upbringing*
                  Welsh Country Characters
                  My Own Folk.
Rees, Vyvyan: *Shell Guide to Mid-Western Wales* (Cardiganshire and Merioneth).

CARMARTHENSHIRE
Cule, John: *Wreath on the Crown* (on the Fasting Girl).
Lloyd, Sir J. E.: *A History of Carmarthenshire.*
Pryce Jones, A. J.: *The Story of Carmarthenshire.*

GLAMORGAN
Addis, J. P.: *The Crawshay Dynasty.*
Edwards, A. Trystan: *Merthyr, Rhondda and the Valleys* (Regional Books).
Evans, C. J. O.: *Glamorgan: Its History and Topography.*
Guest, Lady Charlotte; edited by the Earl of Bessborough: *Extracts from her Journal 1833–52; 1853–91.*
Hilling, John B.: *Cardiff and the Valleys.*
Hunter-Blair, Abbot Sir David, Bt.: *John Patrick, Third Marquess of Bute,* 1921.
Kelly, L. V. (ed.): *Llantwit Major: A History and Guide.*
Nicholas, Islwyn ap: *A Welsh Heretic: Dr William Price, Llantrisant.*
Rees, J. R. (ed.): *The Cardiff Region: A Survey* (British Association).
Rees, William: *Cardiff: A History of the City.*
Taylor, Margaret Stewart: *The Crawshays of Cyfarthfa Castle.*
Thomas, Ivor: *Top Sawyer* (biography of David Davies).
Victorian Society 7th Conference Report: *Victorian South Wales – Architecture, Industry, and Society.*
Williams, Glanmor (ed.): *Merthyr Politics: The Making of a Working-Class Tradition.*
Williams, Stewart (ed.): *Glamorgan Historian* (annual volumes since 1964).

MONMOUTHSHIRE
Boon, George C.: *Isca: The Roman Legionary Fortress at Caerleon.*
Bradney, J. A.: *A History of Monmouthshire.*
Calder-Marshall, Arthur: *The Enthusiast* (Fr Ignatius).
Crossley, Fred, and Ridgway, Maurice: *Screens, Lofts and Stalls in Monmouthshire.*
Evans, C. J. O.: *Monmouthshire: Its History and Topography.*
Fox, Sir Cyril, and Lord Raglan: *Monmouthshire Houses* (3 vols.).
Waters, Ivor: *The Unfortunate Valentine Morris.*
       The Town of Chepstow.

PEMBROKESHIRE
Barrett, John H.: *The Pembrokeshire Coast Path.*
Fenton, Richard: *A Historical Tour through Pembrokeshire* 1811.
Howells, Roscoe: *The Sounds Between.*
John, Brian: *Pembrokeshire.*
Jones, W. B., and Freeman, E. A.: *The History and Antiquities of St Davids* 1856.
Laws, Edward: *Little England beyond Wales* 1888.

Miles, Dillwyn (ed.): *Pembrokeshire Coast National Park Guide.*
Owen, George: *The Description of Pembrokeshire* 1603.
Roberts, E. and T.: *The Islands of Pembrokeshire* (*Pembrokeshire Handbooks*).
Williams, James: *Give me Yesterday.*

Index

❦

S.W.   Y

Pace, G. G. 208, 246
Padarn, St 57, *325*
Palmer, Samuel 192
Pant-teg 212
Pantycelyn Farm 150
Pant-y-Goitre 183
Parc Cwm 300
Parc Howard 155
Parc le Breos 300
Parkington, J. L. 87
Park Mill 300
Parrog 99
Parry, James 46; Joseph 272
Parry-Jones, D. 69n., 82, 85
Partrishow *37*, 168
Patrick, St 103, 109
Patrisio (*see* Partrishow)
Patti, Adelina 48-9, 297
Paviland Cave 301
Paxton, Sir William 138, 158; Paxton's
  Tower 138, 157, *158*
Peacock, T. L. 51
Pearson, J. L. 35, 37, 39, 40, 170, 212,
  217, 226, 254, 257, 286
Peate, Dr Iorwerth 248
Pelenna R. 267
Pembrey 155
Pembroke 89, 93, 119, 122, 125, *128-32*,
  189; Dock 122, 124, 125, 127, *128*, 132;
  Power Station 123, 128; River 128, 129
Pembroke, Earls of 117, 223 (*see also*
  Herbert family); Jasper 131, 138
Pembrokeshire 81, 93-142
Penally 136
Penarth *272-3*, 287
Penberi 97, 102
Pencader 85-6
Pencelli Castle 43
Pen Cerrig Calch 38
Penclawdd 303
Pencoed Castle *200*, 268
Penderyn 46; Dic 286, 289
Pendinas 58, *61*
Pendinaslochdyn 77
Pendine Sands 162
Penglais 60
Penhow 199
Penllyn Castle 270
Penmaen 299
Penmark 275
Pennant, Thomas 326
Pennard 299
Penoyre 35
Penpont 46-7
Pen Pumlumon Arwystli 57
Pen Pych 264
Penrhiwceibr 262
Penrhyncoch 54
Penrice 284, *301*
Penry, John 34
Penson family 326; R. K. 66, 132, 152,
  155, 156, 157, 161, 293, 298, *326*
Pentre, Glam. 263; Pem. 88
Pentrebach 256
Pentre'r felin 35

Pentre Gwenlais 153
Pentre Ifan *98*, 140
Pentyrch 265
Pen-y-bont 65
Pen-y-Clawdd 165
Pen-y-Crug 35
Penydarren 221, 255-6; House 257;
  Tramroad 254, 257
Pen y Ddinas 148
Pen-y-Fai 263, *282*, 287
Penyfan 44
Pen y Gader Fawr 26
Penygarn 216-17
Penygraig 263
Penyrwrlodd 25
Peris R. 66
Perrot, Sir John 122, 162
Peterston-super-Ely 269
Peterstone Wentlooge 231
Peterwell 75
Philip, Lewis 195
Philipps, James 91; Sir John 163
Phillipps, Sir Thomas 76
Phillips, Griffith 157; J. H. 243; Thomas
  204
Picton Castle *119-20*, 121, 163; family of
  Poyston Hall 119; General, of Colby
  Lodge 160
Piercefield 191-2
Pilkington, F. T. 236
Pirie-Gordon family 38
Plas Gogerddan *54*, 55
Plas Gynmel 99
Plas Llangoedmor 81
Plas-y-Wern 76
Plymouth Ironworks 255, 256
Pocock, W. F. 62
Pontalltycafan 86
Pontardawe 153, *292*
Pontarddulais 304
Pontarllechau 49
Pontaryscir 36
Ponterwyd 54, 56
Pontlottyn 227
Pontneddfechan 290
Pontnewydd 215
Pontnewynydd 215, *217*
Pontrhydfendigaid 71
Pontrhyd-y-fen 267
Pont-rhydygroes 63, 64, 65, 71
Pontrilas 164
Pontsarn 260
Pontsticill 260
Pontygwaith 264
Pontymoile Bridge 215
Pontypool 41, 184, 204, 208, 212, 214,
  215-17, 219, 220, 250; Park 216
Pontypridd 228-9, 251, *253-4*, 263, 264
Popton Point 132
Porteynon 301
Porth 263, 264
Porthcawl 283-4
Porthclais 112, *114*
Porth Mawr 38
Porth Stinian *114*, 115